WILLIAM JAMES AND C.G. JUNG

Doorways to the Self

Other Works by the Author

(2009) *William Everson: The Shaman's Call.* New York, NY: Eloquent Books.
(2010) *Walt Whitman: Shamanism, Spiritual Democracy, and the World Soul.* Durham, NC: Eloquent Books.
(2014) *Spiritual Democracy: The Wisdom of Early American Visionaries for the Journey Forward.* Foreword by John Beebe. Berkeley, CA: North Atlantic Books (Sacred Activism Series).
(2016) *William Everson: The Shaman's Call. Expanded Edition.* New York, NY: Eloquent Books.
(2018) *Emily Dickinson: A Medicine Woman for Our Times.* Cheyenne, WY: Fisher King Press.

WILLIAM JAMES AND C.G. JUNG

Doorways to the Self

STEVEN HERRMANN

ANALYTICAL PSYCHOLOGY PRESS
Oberlin, Ohio, United States

Copyright © 2020 by ANALYTICAL PSYCHOLOGY PRESS
Text copyright © 2020 by Steven Herrmann
All rights reserved. No part of this publication may be reproduced, distributed, or transmitted in any form or by any means, including photocopying, recording, or other electronic or mechanical methods, without the prior written permission of the publisher, except in the case of brief quotations embodied in critical reviews and certain other noncommercial uses permitted by copyright law. For permission requests, write to the publisher.

Published in 2020
Printed in the United States of America

ANALYTICAL PSYCHOLOGY PRESS
280 Elm Street, Oberlin, OH 44074-1504, United States
https://analyticalpsychologypress.com
Book Design: Elijah Satoru Wood and Dyane Sherwood
Typesetting: Elijah Satoru Wood and Dyane Sherwood

INDIVIDUAL AND GROUP ORDERS, US AND INTERNATIONAL:
https://analyticalpsychologypress.com/store
Group discounts are available (10 or more copies)

US DISTRIBUTOR: ITASCA BOOKS (orders@itascabooks.com) manages distribution to libraries, retail stores, and book dealers. Telephone orders: +1 800 901 3480, ext. 118 (9-5 Central US Time). FAX: +1 952 920 0541

William James and C. G. Jung: Doorways to the Self / Steven Herrmann
ISBN-13: 978-1-7346582-7-9

To
JOHN BEEBE
with gratitude for his support and friendship

Contents

Hummingbird Song — x
Portraits of C. G. Jung and William James — xii
Preface — xv

Part I

The Untold Story of an Encounter

1. Prologue: Jung in America — 5
2. The Clark Conference: Hall, Freud, James, and Jung — 11
3. The Significance of the Father — 15
4. Psychic Conflicts in a Child — 23
5. *Liber Novus* — 29
6. A Violent God — 41
7. Fields of Consciousness — 71
8. Erickson and Jung on James — 83
9. James's Experience of the San Francisco Earthquake: The Opening of a Door — 87
10. Movement Toward a Psychological Attitude — 103
11. James on Instinct, Emotion, and the Significance of Life — 113
12. Doorways to the Self — 119
13. The Call to Vocation — 133
14. The Meaning of the Cross — 145
15. The Child Archetype and the God Behind the Door — 149

PART II

SPIRITUAL DEMOCRACY AND THE FIGHT WITH THE SHADOW

16	C. G. Jung's Vision of Spiritual Democracy	163
17	Jung's Vision of Spiritual Democracy in *The Red Book* and in *Psychological Types*	167
18	*Atmavictu*: "The Breath of Life"	176
19	The Fight with the Shadow	181
20	Eight Principles of Spiritual Democracy	189
21	Transnationality	193
22	Swami Vivekananda, William James, and Samadhi	197
23	India's Mission: To Promote World Spirituality	203
24	A Few References for the Term Spiritual Democracy	205
25	C. G. Jung's Views on Yoga	209

PART III

RADICAL EMPIRICISM AND THE DREAM OF PHILEMON

26	The Radical Empirical Psychology of William James: An Overview of the Problem	221
27	Psychology as an Empirical Science	233
28	*The Varieties of Religious Experience*	245
29	*Pragmatism*	251
30	A Pluralistic Universe	261
31	C. G. Jung's Psychology of the Self	265
32	Kundalini Yoga and Analytical Psychology	283
33	The Influence of William James	291
34	The Supreme Meaning as the Bridge to What Is to Come	307

35	The Religious Function of Spiritual Democracy	323
36	Self and Cosmos in Jung's Writing	329
37	Vocational Dreams and Synchronicity	337
38	The Transpsyche	351
39	Synchronicity and the Psychology of Groups	355

PART IV

THE FUTURE OF ANALYTICAL PSYCHOLOGY

40	Psychology as a Natural Science	361
41	The Psychological Rediscovery of Ecstasy	369
42	Empirical Evidence for the Supraconscious	375
43	James's Hypothesis of the Transmission of Consciousness	387
44	Reflections: Non-ordinary Experience, the Spiritualization of Matter, and Synchronicity	393

Permissions	406
Acknowledgments	407
Appendix: Journaling Method	409
Bibliography	411
Index	421
About the Author	440

PLEASE NOTE: For consistency across editions, references to *The Collected Works of C. G. Jung* are cited in the standard form of volume and paragraph number. For example, CW 16, ¶451. Multiple paragraphs are indicated by double paragraph symbols: CW 16, ¶¶451-457.

Hummingbird Song

In every dream is a song.
So today I sing a hummingbird song;
Such was the visitation of the spirit
In the dim light of early morning.

I had cut a bunch of fresh salvia
With lush purple flowers from our garden
And placed them in a vase in the center
Of our living room in the hills of Oakland.

I left the French Doors wide open
And was resting on the couch,
When I heard an excited female voice say:
"Steven, a hummingbird has flown into the house
And is fluttering over the salvia plants!"

When I looked at the vase
The hummingbird was inspecting the purple flowers
And winged with amazing speed to settle lightly
On my right hand. And then she
Looked at me with piercing eyes

I awoke thinking of my garden
and my book on Emily Dickinson
Was it Emily? Or, was I dreaming
of a hummingbird thanks-giving
That came my way from beyond?
Was the spirit of the hummingbird
thanking me for the purple blossoms
Of salvias I planted in February and March?

The female dream-voice
That called to me
May have been my wife,
Or Anima, Or Soul.

The hummingbird also flew through
the open French doors of the house!
Were these doors subliminal doorways
To the unitary reality?

The hummingbird landed on
My right hand - the one
That holds the Montblanc pen,
The writer's hand, hand of the poet.

Was my dream visitation a call
from the Hummingbird-spirit
To wake up, to compose a poem,
To sing a hummingbird song?

I hover above the salvia and sip its purple-infused
nectar with my tongue, a thirsty tongue, poet's tongue.
I drink and I soar with inexpressible delight.
I am wild and awake with hummingbird consciousness,
        Hummingbird being, hummingbird bliss!

Carl Gustav Jung (26 July 1875 – 6 June 1961)
Photograph Circa 1902-1903. (Photographer unknown)

William James (11 January 1842 – 26 August 1910)
Photograph Circa 1907 by Alice M. Boughton
(National Portrait Gallery, The Smithsonian, Washington, D.C.)

Preface

The subject of Jung in America has not been written about at any great length by a single author, and I am not, by vocation, called to write such a grand historical work. But the task does await a bigger mind than mine in the future, and hopefully, the world will not have to wait too long for that fulfillment. The phrase "Jung in America," which I use in the first chapter, does not mean Jung's physical presence in America, nor the many talks he gave while he was here during his seven trips to the United States. I'll take a brief look at a few of his talks, such as his first child case, one of three presentations he gave at Clark University in 1909. I'll also take a look at a few passages from his Terry Lectures, given at Yale University in 1937. This seventh visit was the last time Jung stepped foot on our shores prior to his leave-taking for India in the fall of that same year. Jung's psychology of the Self[1] and its relationship to the American mind is what I'll be looking at, how it relates to the present and future, and I'll show how James's work helped to shape Jung's theories of the collective unconscious, instinct and emotion, psychic energy, archetypes, individuation, psychological types, and synchronicity while he was at his writing desk in Switzerland. Jung in America is also James's psychology in Jung's mind and how it helped to shape his thinking about the Self.

James had something to say about Samadhi; he had something to say about Hatha Yoga; he had something to say about mysticism, about the moral equivalent of war; he had a lot to say about American education, about the future of democracy, which he said is still on its trial; he had much to say about the Absolute; about monism, about his alternative to monism, his own dispensation of radical empiricism. He had much to say about pragmatism and panpsychism. Like Jung, James cautioned against identifying with the Self.[2] He introduced a *field* notion into modern psychology, and possibly influenced the principle of *complementarity*, which was introduced to modern physics by Niels Bohr.³ James wrote about depression, multiple personality, suicide, what makes life worth living, what makes a life significant, and the *meaning* of truth. He wrote about cosmic consciousness, the energies of men and women, and transpersonal happiness. He had a great deal to say about parapsychology, psychic phenomena, crystal-gazing, hypnosis, trance states, automatic writing, and clairvoyance. James was a painter before he became a natural scientist, and he was the third president of our American Psychological Association.

So little has been written previously on Jung and James, even though there is a very important connection here. In the pages ahead, I'll show how much Jung derived from James and from his time in America, a subject that has been largely overlooked by the European Jungian movement. There is a rising respect and interest in James in academia, and there is a need, therefore, to put a whole new angle on him from a fresh perspective. Jung, moreover, has been mostly excluded from academia, and this book might be a "backdoor" entrance for his work to enter more into the mainstream of psychology and education and college classrooms! I've chosen to use a "short chapter" approach to make their ideas more accessible and engaging. For all of these reasons and more I'm compelled and excited to publish this work today.

Coincidentally, James attended school in Switzerland when he was a boy, and he visited his colleague and friend Theodore Flournoy in Geneva on many occasions; he traveled on a trip to Zürich, moreover, while he was suffering from symptoms of angina in the summer of 1910, shortly before he died at age sixty-eight. James spent more time in Switzerland than Jung spent in America, yet their paths did cross on two occasions in 1909. Their concepts of the unconscious (Jung) and subconscious (James) are strikingly similar.

As I see it, Jung's hypothesis of the Self and the nuclear concept of vocation is the alpha and omega of his psychology of individuation. It's probable the concept of the Self incubated for several years after his first arrival to the States, and it eventually caught fire in Switzerland, after his three chance meetings with James. Jung's scholarly work on the subject of the Self encompassed a much broader international vista. But James's works are nevertheless nourishment for a global audience.

In order to read this book, according to the way in which I've structured it, a kind of circumambulatory thinking, feeling, sensing, and intuiting is encouraged of the reader—a "letting go" of any of these four functions of consciousness and an opening to what James called "the streams of consciousness" in 1890. It has to be clarified at the outset that James was far more influenced by French and British schools of psychology than by the German school that attempted to study the unconscious systematically through laboratory experiments. His use of the term *subconscious* came from his reading and personal relationships with such leading figures as Pierre Janet in France and F. W. H. Myers in England. Jung, on the other hand, made liberal use of Hartmann's and Freud's term *unconscious* throughout most of his writing while speaking about the human psyche. This subtle distinction between their theoretical premises makes for a complementarity between their two systems, on Swiss and American soil. My study of radical empiricism and analytical psychology, when compared, yields similar results. It is my personal belief that Jung carried home with him, after his first visit to the States, a living image of the "American Self," an image that stayed with him until his final days while he recollected fondly on James and his genius.

For James, the study of consciousness is a study of the subconscious Self, whereas for Jung the study of consciousness is a study of the unconscious through dream work, fantasy-thinking (1911–1912), active imagination (1915–1928), and visions (1930–1940) in a relational field between the ego and the Self. Such subtle distinctions are, I think, significant, when it comes to my cross-cultural comparisons; these two great intellectually endowed personalities formed theoretical constructs with an integrative transnational perspective. Both developed a Self-concept that is compatible with contemporary ideas about consciousness, personality development, neuroscience, cognition, destiny, vocation, instincts, emotions, temperament types, and spiritual experiences; yet they differed on the questions of consciousness and meaning in the Cosmos, on the individual's place in society and Nature.

As a Jungian analyst who has been studying Jung for the past forty-four years, I've been conditioned by my reading and education in analytical psychology to use the term *unconscious* while speaking with patients, students, or while writing about Jung. When it comes to the authoring of this book, however, I've made a conscious choice to allow myself to employ Jamesian terms, as a complement to Jung's. James's four interconnected Selves can help me clarify Jung's ideas in a simpler way. I cannot side with

Jung about the term *unconscious* over *subconscious*, if I am to represent James properly and move toward an *integrative theory of the Self* that will hopefully satisfy the needs of transpersonal researchers and theorists for a clarification of what Jung actually meant by the term *collective psyche*. Therefore, I will use the term *Self,* with a capital *S,* as James originally conceived it in 1890, as well as speak about his revisions of the concept of the Self between 1902 and 1910. James's thoughts about the Self underwent a complete metamorphosis over a period of two decades, although in the end he confirmed what he'd hypothesized at inception. Interestingly, Jung's concept of Self, from approximately 1912 to 1952, also underwent major transformations across a much broader period of time.

Jung outlived James by about twenty years. One wonders where James's quaternary concept might have led him if he had managed to live to eighty-seven, like Jung did. As I'll argue in my book, they ended up in a similar place with regard to the Self, its limited and illimitable extent. James and Jung both started their careers as natural scientists, researchers in parapsychology, occult phenomena, mediums, psychopathic personalities; both were professors of psychology, writers, empiricists, and they each opened themselves up to metaphysical considerations, such as the possible survival of consciousness after death. Each went far beyond their previous Self-conceptions during midlife and following a sacrifice of their heroism to incarnate the Divine in a more transnational way. Jung was the first psychologist in history to include a concept of the Shadow (personal and transpersonal shadow) in his hypothesis of the Self, which, without doubt, was an act of supreme individual genius. Good and evil were to him as close as identical twins. James, in his own way, made strides in this direction with his own inclusion of evil in his inventory of the Self. But Jung went understandably further in this regard, in part because he lived through two horrific World Wars; also, because he read and reread the Book of Job, which he wrote about passionately in his controversial *Answer to Job*. James too was highly influenced by the Book of Job, and it led to a similar revolution in his thinking about the Self, which includes, in his psychology, seraph and snake. All of these issues I cover in this book.

The concept of the Self is an ancient Hindu idea that can be traced to the end of the Vedas, *The Upanishads,* which both James and Jung read. But the idea of the American Self, which James was writing out of, evolved organically from Puritan origins. According to Sacvan Bercovitch, the Puritans laid special emphasis on the concept of *vocation,* the inward calling to redemption, and summons to a social duty was believed to be imposed upon us by God for the sake of the common good.⁴ One of the primary promoters of the notion of the American Self was John Winthrop, another was Cotton Mather. The problem with this early Puritan notion, however, is that it lacked a psychological concept of the shadow, which got tragically projected on to indigenous Americans, who were viewed as "snakes" in their path. The Puritans regarded "the country as theirs and its natives as an obstacle to *their* destiny as Americans."⁵ Another major influence on the notion of an American Self was Jonathan Edwards, who believed America was a "forerunner of what is approaching in spiritual things, when the world shall be supplied with spiritual treasures from America."⁶

Yet the real "Myth of America," the one for which we are destined, if we are to fulfill Walt Whitman's dream of democracy,⁷ only began to emerge in the 1830s and 1840s, when Ralph Waldo Emerson began to speak about the grand "feeling, which the geography of America inevitably inspires," and of a Selfhood distinguishing America's own "natural theology" from Europe's (mainly Christian) religion or that of any other nation.⁸ It was Whitman who answered the call for an American masterpiece that would specify what that myth actually was. He did this in *Leaves of Grass,* which he called a "language experiment," a phrase that Sonu Shamdasani has recently used to describe Jung's process of composing his *Red Book*.⁹ Henry David Thoreau made his own subjective contribution to this notion in *Walden,* as did Herman Melville in *Moby-Dick,* and Emily Dickinson in her poetry. All of these works of art, literature, and poetry were written roughly between 1840 and the Civil War. In them the concept was gradually taking shape, simmering in the American Mind.

Whereas in Europe Schelling had claimed that "each truly creative individual must create his mythology for himself," an idea Jung would later take up as his own endeavor as a Swiss citizen of Europe, Emerson had already given birth to his own version of a modern myth for the United States by creating an extended oeuvre through the vehicle of his many talks and essays.¹⁰ In fact, it was in an essay called "The Poet" that the American myth achieved its first real clarification, a calling Whitman would take up as his own unique destiny and give answer to for the United States. "Where are the American writers," Emerson had asked, who could give rejoinder to the "great questions affecting our spiritual nature"? When would our nation "realize the spiritual religion of the future"? Where was the great "genius" who could carry the myth of the American Self to apotheosis in the States? Emerson's personal answer to such big questions came in another important essay called "The American Scholar," where, as Bercovitch conjectures, the scholar became Emerson's prediction for the fulfillment of that myth.[11] Who that scholar would be as a psychologist and philosopher had yet to be seen.

By the time he stepped foot on American soil, Jung was already aware of a working Self-concept that had been slowly evolving as a *nuclear image* in the American mind. In other words, there was a relationship that had already been building in Jung between the evolution of his thinking and the ideas of James, because by 1902 he had read James's *Principles of Psychology*. James had fulfilled Emerson's calling for an American scholar in the fields of natural science, philosophy, parapsychology, and psychology, and he would give answer to the great conundrums affecting our spiritual nature and the spirituality of future generations of Americans in his masterwork *The Varieties of Religious Experience* in 1902. There, James's Self-concept expanded to the breaking point, where it opened a doorway between the empirical limits he set on himself in 1890 and the new standpoint at which he now arrived—open to metaphysical realities and the numinous, beyond the known world of our immediately perceivable empirical experiences. Even here, however, he only opened the doorway wide enough so others could peer in through it in brief glimpses; but his own expansive experiences of transpersonal reality and personal myth were still largely hidden. By 1909, however, when they first met, James had opened a doorway to the Self from a much wider vista, to include a pantheistic vision that embraced matter, force, energy, nature, physics, evolutionary biology, questions of life after death, immortality, a theory of the brain as a "transmissive organ," an Earth-Soul, and the study of consciousness of the infinite Cosmos. This late panpsychic or *cosmic vision* is sure to have imprinted itself on the mind of C. G. Jung, who carried it away in his impressions of America.

One of the three lectures Jung gave in America in 1909 was a case study of a four-year-old girl. Later he would write a paper on the child archetype in 1940, where the child was viewed as one of the primary symbols for the Self. He would continue to write about the child archetype and children's dreams until 1961, three weeks before his death. The subject of child and adolescent psychology is where Jung got much of his personal insights into the nature of the Self, from the infra-rational end of instinct and emotion, to the ultraviolet end of compassion, being, and bliss.

Insofar as James was a carrier of a destiny to conceive a concept of the Self in the United States and the mythologem of the divine child was *alive* in him from birth onward, it has to be acknowledged that the Self-notion he was destined to give voice to, in his pragmatism, was part and parcel of the national need; for the archetype of the Self had been evoked personally in his infancy and childhood by the very man who was a living embodiment of the American Scholar, namely Emerson himself. Emerson was not only good friends with James's father, Henry James Sr., a post-Swedenborgian, but Emerson had a special room in their house where he often stayed and where he could close the door to his room, sleep and dream at night about the future of America. In the room nearby lay the carrier of the American dream of a prospective "analytic" psychology, the child prodigy, William James. The psychic influences in the household must have been particularly transmissive to such a sensitive, brilliant mind as James's. James received a *blessing* from this former Unitarian who would become his master. For James, the concept of the American Self extended beyond poetry and literature to include a science of the *subconscious* dimensions of the Self as well as a *supraconscious* dimension that I refer to as a *higher Self*, a term Jung used in his *Dream Seminars* and in *Aion*, where it is said to extend, in his structural diagrams, from the empirical to the metaphysical Self, from snake-brain to Anthropos as an image of wholeness in the Aquarian Age.

James was the first to teach the new scientific psychology in the United States in 1875, which happens to correspond exactly with the year of Jung's birth. He was the first American to write a world-famous textbook: *The Principles of Psychology*. In his chapter "The Functions of the Brain," James first discussed whether "the cortex was the sole organ of consciousness in man."[12] This is a question that would preoccupy him until the time of his death. James also spoke in this book about a unique "feeling tone" of each "passing thought."[13] Like Jung who would later conjecture that affects or emotions are the chief source of consciousness, James said in *The Principles*, "Feelings are the germ and starting point of cognition, thoughts the developed tree."[14] The accent James placed on *feelings* has much to do with his own particular temperament type, which was introverted thinking, with extroverted feeling as his inferior function. This might say something significant about the American Self and James's preference for the French experiential laboratory over the German experimental workshop. James's feeling and intuition were clearly extroverted. I'll have more to say about typology later. But James clearly recognized, in print by 1902, that some of the most "intense imagery is associated with states of religious awareness" and that "certain kinds of numinous images had transforming power" to alter human consciousness.[15]

It has to be noted, furthermore, that James was not an analyst like Jung, and he did not see patients. James was primarily a professor, researcher, neuroscientist, physiologist, scholar on mysticism and world religions, and he taught on such diverse subjects as parapsychology, psychopathology, multiple personality, dissociation, philosophy, education, and metaphysics; he was an evolutionist who was drawn to the study of chemical changes in the brain, hypnotism, trauma, trance states, transpersonal happiness, Vedanta, Hatha Yoga, pranayama, Buddhist meditation, and automatic writing. James's psychology is a psychology of consciousness, reason, meaning of truth, instinct, emotion, motivation, will, cognition, the sick soul, healthy-mindedness, and the subconscious and supraconscious Self. Neuropsychology is where he started at Harvard Medical School. His thinking about the brain and consciousness is why he is still widely read today.

Whether the Self is a conscious or unconscious entity in the human psyche is one of the main questions that I will explore in the pages ahead. James and Jung each had something significant to say about this very question. Everything depends on human consciousness. Our very subsistence and the survival of our planet, and the life of many living species, depend on individuals assuming moral responsibility for our own individuation, something Jung and James believed in and lived out, each in their own singular ways.

NOTES

1. The term Self is capitalized throughout my book because this is the way the term was originally used in the first book Jung read by William James, Principles of Psychology.
2. In James's initial 1890 hypothesis of a comprehensive set of principles for modern psychology, he said that the Self consists of four basic constituents: the (1) Material or Body Self, (2) Social Self, (3) Spiritual Self, and (4) Metaphysical Self, or Transcendental Thinker. These four Selves were said to subsume the totality of the Empirical Self. In the chapters ahead, James's formula will be employed generously as a way to make intelligible his psychology of the Self and also help to clarify and simplify some of the most fundamental premises of Jung's analytical psychology.
3. Von Franz, Projection and Re-Collection in Jungian Psychology, 64.
4. Bercovitch, The Puritan Origins of the American Self, 6.
5. Bercovitch, 141.
6. Bercovitch, 156.
7. I will discuss how Whitman's notion of religious democracy applies to modern psychology in Chapter 16, "C. G. Jung's Vision of Spiritual Democracy." To give my readers a simple understanding to any question that may have arisen regarding what I meant by "Whitman's dream of democracy," it will be helpful to keep in mind that Whitman predicted in 1871 that America had entered a stage of development in the evolution of our national consciousness that he termed "religious democracy," a phrase I've changed to read Spiritual Democracy in a variety of writings about him and his work that are listed in my Bibliography at the end of the book. What is Spiritual Democracy? In brief, Whitman conjectured there are three strata of American Democracy: (1) the economic, (2) the political, and (3) the Spiritual. As we celebrated the Walt Whitman Bicentennial across our nation last year, on May 31, 2019, it will be obvious to anyone who looks closely at his vision from an historical vista, it is an ideal that has not yet been born in history. Nevertheless, it has been emerging gradually over the course of the past century and one half through the work of sentient individuals who have managed to make the God-image conscious in themselves through their lives, relationships, and vocations. It certainly happened in Walt Whitman; it happened in William James; and it also happened in C. G. Jung, who visited our shores and said during his seventh visit here that the world was then, in 1937 even, on the verge of a profound spiritual transformation. Writing

this endnote a year after I delivered my Bicentennial talk on Whitman's myth at our National Cathedral, thanks to the warm welcome I received from my good friend in Washington D.C., Neil Richardson, it is my personal belief that the time has now come for such wide-ranging metamorphoses to begin to really happen in our democracies world-wide. What it will take, as Whitman, James, and Jung all showed through the power and conviction of their vocations, the force of their characters, and their endless compassion for the sufferings of humanity, are the efforts of singular individuals who are attempting to make the unconscious conscious for themselves and society. I have great hope in Whitman's vision for the present and future. It is a vision I think America needs today and I believe the works of James and Jung can help us usher it in.

8. Bercovitch, 158–159.
9. Bercovitch, 162; Shamdasani and Beebe, "Jung Becomes Jung."
10. Bercovitch, 165.
11. Bercovitch, 168.
12. Taylor, William James on Consciousness Beyond the Margin, 12, 13.
13. Taylor, 35.
14. Taylor, 35.
15. Taylor, 143.

PART I

*The Untold Story
of an Encounter*

Chapter 1

Prologue - Jung in America

In 1909 C. G. Jung was invited along with Sigmund Freud, Ernest Jones, and the Hungarian psychoanalyst Sandor Ferenczi to deliver a lecture on the association experiment and a clinical case at Clark University, in Worcester, Massachusetts. It was there that the four psychoanalysts met the American psychologist William James. Freud, Ferenczi, and Jung met up in Bremen, Germany, on August 20. The first three companions traveled together on the steamer *George Washington,* on a decisive journey that would last for seven weeks, a trip that would have fateful consequences for the future direction of psychoanalysis.

Jung's reputation had preceded him, since several of his articles describing his laboratory experiments at the Burghölzli had been published in American journals. Jung recounts in *Memories, Dreams, Reflections* of the much-discussed incident of Freud's fainting fit in Bremen, which was apparently provoked by Jung's interest in peat bog corpses in certain districts of Northern Germany, bodies of prehistoric people who had either drowned in the marshes or were buried in the bogs. Jung says this interest got on Freud's nerves when they were dining together and Freud suddenly fainted. Afterward, Freud said he was convinced that all of Jung's chatter about corpses meant he maintained death-wishes toward him.[1]

Freud and Jung were together every day, and they attempted to analyze each other's dreams. Jung regarded Freud at this time as an older, more mature, and experienced personality, and he felt somewhat like a son in Freud's presence. But he tells us further that something happened, which proved to be a severe blow to their whole relationship. Freud had a dream that Jung attempted to interpret, as best he could. Freud would not supply some additional details from his private life to aid Jung with his interpretation. When Jung pressed the issue, Freud allegedly said, "But I cannot risk my authority!" At this point, Jung says, Freud lost his authority in his eyes altogether. The sentence about Freud's authority "burned itself into my memory; and in it the end of our relationship was already foreshadowed. Freud was placing personal authority above truth."²

Jung says Freud was able to interpret his dreams only incompletely or not at all. These were all dreams with collective contents, he reports, dreams containing a great deal of symbolic material. One dream in particular was extremely important to Jung, for it led him, for the first time, to his concept of the collective unconscious and it formed a kind of prelude to his book *Wandlüngen und Symbole der Libido*.³

Jung's big dream took place in a two-storied house. It was Jung's house. He found himself in a *salon* on the upper story. After looking around, Jung's dream-ego proceeded down some stairs to a *ground floor*, which dated from the fifteenth or sixteenth century CE. The furniture was medieval. Exploring it further Jung says, "I came upon a heavy door and opened it." *Jung passed through the door*. Then he discovered a stone stairway that led down to a cellar. Descending again, he found himself in a *vaulted room* that looked exceedingly ancient. The room dated from Roman times. The floor was made of stone slabs. Jung found a ring on one of the slabs. When he pulled it, the stone lifted, and again, he saw a stairway of narrow stone steps leading downward into the depths. Jung passed through this second *doorway*. He descended the lower steps and entered a *low cave* that had been cut into the rock. On the floor were some broken pottery shards and some scattered bones amid the dust, like the remains of a primitive culture. Jung then discovered two very old and half disintegrated human skulls in the subsoil of the dusty cave, and then, he says, he awoke.⁴

The dream provided him with a pictorial representation of the unconscious in four structural layers, or strata:

1. The upper story of the house was the salon of the conscious ego personality, and the upper layer of what he called the personal unconscious;
2. The lower story of the house consisted of a first layer of the collective unconscious, represented by the ground floor, dating from the fifteenth or sixteenth century, and a heavy door that Jung opened;
3. The second strata of the collective psyche was represented by the vaulted room dating from Roman times and a stone-slab doorway into the depths below; and
4. The lowest strata of the collective unconscious was represented by the cave, broken pottery, and two human skulls, dating from primitive times.

So there were really two doorways through which Jung passed in his dream:

1. Between the second the third layer and
2. Between the third and fourth layers.

This dream gave Jung his first map of the human personality. I've divided segments of Jung's dream into four strata, in numerical outline:

1. The upper story of the house representing the personal unconscious and the conscious personality, dream-ego, or self, in the salon
2. The lower story of the house, the first layer of the collective unconscious dating to approximately 1400–1500 CE and extending to the ground floor, where Jung discovered the first doorway
3. The third layer of the collective unconscious extending back to Roman times with a stone slab with a ring, which Jung's dream-ego pulled and opened so he could pass through a hidden, narrow second doorway
4. To a deeper and more primitive layer of the transpersonal unconscious

After Jung awoke from the dream it was plain to him (retrospectively) that the house represented a kind of structural image or map of the human psyche. Beyond the two doorways was the cave, where Jung discovered the remains of a primitive culture, the world of archaic man hidden deep within himself—a world he said that can scarcely be reached or illuminated by consciousness:

> It obviously pointed to the foundations of cultural history—a history of successive layers of consciousness. My dream thus constituted a kind of structural diagram of the human psyche; it postulated something of an altogether impersonal nature underlying that psyche... It was my first inkling of a collective a priori beneath the personal psyche. This I first took to be the traces of earlier modes of functioning. Later, with increasing experience, and on the basis of more reliable knowledge, I recognized them as forms of instinct, that is, as archetypes.[5]

In Jung's dream we can see his calling to found a new psychology, foreshadowed in images. For a period of time, Jung believed he had a calling to become an archeologist. Hence, his interest in peat bog corpses and the two skulls in the cave. Then, for a short time he fancied himself to be a philologist. In the midst of his vocational indecision, he had a dream about a giant radiolarian, or protozoa, shimmering in a pool in the woods with opalescent hues, which helped him decide overwhelmingly in favor of science.⁶

Jung's father was religious, like William James's father. But Jung's father (unlike James's) did not mirror his vocational interests in religious matters in childhood or in adolescence, by which I mean Jung's original thinking. This lack of mirroring in the religious domain led Jung to become, like James, somewhat rebellious toward authority figures when his ideas were challenged. One of the authorities Jung rebelled against was Freud, beginning with the 1909 conflict over dream interpretation on the ship heading to America.

Jung was searching in 1909 for an outer figure in the world who could mirror his twin interests in natural science and religion. By viewing neurotic symptoms as a symbolic defense against the inner voice, moreover, Jung was led to the conclusion that *destiny* contains a prospective solution to emotional disturbances stemming from early childhood. This prospective view derived from Flournoy's work and Jung's dissertation, modeled on Flournoy. By making neurotic defenses conscious through analytical techniques, Jung found that prospective dreams of wholeness could emerge and that contained within such dreams is a destiny, a vocation to live by:

> Generally the psychic conditions that have caused the disturbance have to be made conscious with considerable effort. But the contents that then come to light are wholly in accord with the inner voice and point to a predestined vocation, which, if accepted and assimilated by the conscious mind, conduces to the development of the personality.⁷

In 1908, prior to meeting James, Jung had written a paper called "The Significance of the Father in the Destiny of the Individual," where he took up the topic of vocation in an original and insightful way. I'll discuss this paper in Chapter 3.

NOTES

1. Jung, *Memories, Dreams, Reflections,* 156. Hereafter references to *Memories, Dreams, Reflections* will be referred to as *MDR*.
2. Jung, *MDR*, 158.
3. Jung, *MDR*, 158.
4. Jung, *MDR*, 158–159.
5. Jung, *MDR*, 161.
6. Jung, *MDR*, 85.
7. Jung, "The Development of Personality," CW 17, ¶316.

Chapter 2

THE CLARK CONFERENCE: HALL, FREUD, JAMES, AND JUNG

Some important books have been written on the subject of Jung's first trip to America, where he spent two memorable evenings with American psychologist William James. Perhaps the most interesting was published in 1992 by Saul Rosenzweig: *Freud, Jung, and Hall the King-Maker: The Historic Expedition to America* (1909) with Stanley Hall as Host and William James as Guest. The author confirms for us that Jung talked privately with James on the evenings of September 9 and September 10. In this Chapter, I will provide a few facts about the Clark Conference and introduce some of its key figures and their ideas.

Hall, who had invited Freud and Jung to come to America to lecture at the twentieth anniversary celebration of Clark University, had been interested in the problem of sexuality for many years prior to Freud's and Jung's visit in 1909. In his autobiography, for instance, Hall noted that the Freudian approach "came to me to seem almost like a new dispensation in the domain of psychology, so that from 1909, when Freud visited us, it [sex] and its wider implications became a central interest to me."[1] Five years before the twentieth anniversary sessions, Hall had written a two-volume work called Adolescence, where he devoted an entire chapter to "Adolescent Love."[2] Moreover, Hall had criticized James for failing to recognize the paramount role of sexuality in religious experiences of youth and pointedly rejected James's "dicta concerning sex."[3] Thus, unlike Jung, James appears to have downplayed the importance of sexuality in human development or overlooked it as a variable in his psychology of the Self. As we will see, he certainly made room for it in his postulate of a Material, or Body Self, but he scarcely mentioned it in his works. Did this lacuna play a part in the direction of psychology in America in modernity towards a more psychoanalytic direction in our teaching and training institutions?

The reason I ask this question here is because it may be pertinent to the role that psychoanalysis has played in shaping the course of modern psychology, and how the invaluable contribution of James and Jung has been underrepresented.

Hall was a former student of James and the first to receive his PhD in psychology under James's watch at Harvard. Moreover, Rozenzweig's book reveals rather transparently the way in which the movement of modern psychology was tending under Hall's direction: toward a Freudian slant on the issue of sex. Did Hall leave spirituality out of his equation? Hall was not antireligious by any means, for he'd already established the American Journal of Religious Psychology and Education by May 1904 and was a well-related colleague of James. Nevertheless, the tendency to reduce religion to sexual events in childhood or adolescence was Hall's forte, and his personal equation, as Jung might have said, was not an empirical fact in every case.

The Clark Conference was without precedence in the history of modern psychology. Many competing theories were presented there. As James's student, Hall had become the first president of Clark University on April 5, 1888. He was very interested, moreover, in the study of children. In 1893, for instance, the National Association for the Study of Childhood was formed and Hall had published a paper for its inauguration entitled "Child Study: The Basis of Exact Education." In the following year, 1894, James became the third president of the American Psychological Association (APA) and was instrumental in supporting Hall's career as a mentor. In 1909, furthermore, Theodore Roosevelt called the first White House Conference on the welfare of children. So the study of the child was much in the air by the time the three European psychoanalysts landed on our shores, as James and Hall had already been debating their very different views. To be sure, Hall and Freud were both fixed on proving their theories of the sexual origins of most mental disorders. To exaggerate its place in all psychopathology is clearly one-sided. To overlook it, on the other hand, was tantamount to shutting a doorway to the Self that is undeniably relevant to any careful study of psychology's field. It needs to be remembered that James was much older than Freud and Jung when they met. Jung was only thirty-four years old, and he was clearly the youngest psychoanalytic presenter at the gathering.[4] James was close to death and his interests in the Self had taken him well over a decade into a vertical dimension that included the furthest reaches of spiritual experience. As Freud recalled of James in his autobiography:

> I shall never forget one little scene that occurred as we were on a walk together. He stopped suddenly, handed me a bag he was carrying and asked me to walk on, saying that he would catch up with me as soon as he had got through an attack of angina pectoris which was just coming on. He died of that disease a year later; and I have always wished that I might be as fearless as he was in the face of approaching death.⁵

James was clearly interested in the body, as we will see in my review of his 1909 essay "The Energies of Men," but by this time he was focusing on the body's spiritualization and its highest stages of conscious Self-realization. I think this kind of spirituality is something he did not see in Freud's work. Instead, he may have felt there was too much focus on sexuality and not enough on the Spiritual Self. Perhaps this is one of the reasons that James said about Freud: "he made on me personally the impression of a man obsessed with fixed ideas."⁶ By the time of the conference, Jung was not entirely convinced either that all cases of serious pathology had a causal origin in sexual disturbances. Jung was expected by the organizers to lecture on child psychology at Clark University. Ingeniously and intuitively and as a complement to Freud's case of Little Hans, therefore, Jung (whether wisely or unwisely) decided to present the case of his first daughter, Little Anna. Anna was the four-year old child who was actually Agatha Jung, Jung's first-born child. Her birth date was December 26, 1904. Ever-careful of not wanting to create a rift with Freud, Jung did not attempt to disprove Freud's views of the importance of childhood sexuality in the genesis of neuroses or emotional disturbances in his case presentations. He did take advantage of the event, nevertheless, by courageously extending Freud's hypothesis, inserting into his study that he'd discerned in infantile sexuality: "the seeds of higher spiritual functions."⁷ This rejoinder to Freud was not meant to cause any "split" but, rather, to broaden the field of psychoanalysis in such an integral way that it would appeal not only to Freud and Hall but also to William James.

Another issue I will raise in closing this Chapter is whether, by the time Jung met James in 1909, Jung was beginning to see how Freud's theory on sexuality had closed a door to an inclusion of spirituality that James was championing in his appreciation for religious experiences. Did Jung in holding the opposites on the importance of sex and the religious function, matter and spirit, make better use of James's writings as a springboard for a much broader empirical view of the psyche and articulate a more complete view of what constitutes Self-realization across the course of an entire lifetime? Of course, as a Jungian analyst, I have my own particular bias on the issue of sex and spirituality. Dreams provide us with a clue as to how there need be no division between psychology and religion, the Material Self and the Spiritual Self. This very issue that James valiantly fought for, even though he overlooked the sexual problem of his times, is what Jung would later discuss in his 1937 lectures at Yale University, where, as we shall see, he did not neglect to give a modest nod to the sagacious old man, William James, who, I believe meant too much to him at a time when he was still searching for a solid ground to stand on.

A final interesting event worth mentioning here is that during the post-conference events at Clark University, Freud, Ferenczi, and Jung were all invited for a five-day sojourn to the Putnam Camp in Keene Valley, located in the heart of the Adirondack Mountains in New York. James had once co-owned this camp with James Jackson Putnam (1846–1918) and Henry Pickering Bowditch (1840–1911). James was not with the group at the camp,[8] however, it is where he had his famous panpsychic experience on Mount Marcy a decade earlier, which I'll discuss later.

NOTES

1. Rosenzweig, *Freud, Jung, and Hall the King-Maker*, 105.
2. Rosenzweig, 106.
3. Rosenzweig, 106.
4. Rosenzweig, 280, footnote 23.
5. Rosenzweig, 171.
6. James cited in Kerr, *A Most Dangerous Method*, 245.
7. Kerr, 154.
8. Rosenzweig, 16.

Chapter 3

THE SIGNIFICANCE OF THE FATHER

To understand the nature and dynamics of the James-Jung relationship and its significance for today, we need to grasp the power of the personal and transpersonal father complex Jung was grappling with prior to his trip to America. "From my eleventh year," Jung wrote, "I have been launched upon a single enterprise which is my 'main business.' My life has been permeated and held together by one idea and one goal: namely, to penetrate the secret of the personality. Everything can be explained from this central point, and all my works relate to this one theme."[1] James would play a modest role in helping Jung remember that secret. In his 1909 paper (originally written in 1908) "The Significance of the Father in the Destiny of the Individual," Jung attempted to penetrate into the depths of his secret. In the 1926 "Forward to the Second Edition" of the paper, Jung noted that when he was writing about the mother complex in *Wandlüngen und Symbole der Libido* (revised in 1952 and translated as *Symbols of Transformation*), it became clear to him what the deeper causes of the neuroses are that go beyond the horizontal complexes of the "family romance." As early as 1909, Jung saw that it is not only the father, but the mother, too, who plays an *equivalent* deciding role in the shaping of a child's fate.[2] So the title of Jung's paper might sound somewhat misleading. Behind the horizontal dimension of the parental complexes in the personal unconscious are what Jung later called the *mother and the father archetypes,* and these two archetypes sink their deepest roots into the subsoil of the collective psyche, while extending into the higher realms of the *Spiritual Self* (a term coined in 1890 by James), which grounds the individual in a more-than-personal-destiny.[3] These powerful twin *dynamisms,* mother and father archetypes, operate out of an instinctive and spiritual foundation, transcendent of any causal determining factors, or personal complexes, that may influence a child's fate.

Jung began this paper with a quote from the third-century BCE Stoic philosopher, Cleanthes: "The Fates lead the willing, / but drag the unwilling." He then reminded readers that for Freud, the *emotional* relationship of the child to his or her parents, particularly the father, is of decisive significance in regard to the content of any later neurosis. The paternal relationship is the infantile channel, Jung said, along which the libido flows back into pockets whenever it encounters obstacles in later years, thus reactivating the long-forgotten psychic contents of childhood.[4] It is ever so in life, Jung continued, when we draw back from too great an obstacle, some severe disappointment, or risk of some too far-reaching decision. The energy stored up for a solution to the conscious task flows back to the old riverbeds, and the obstacle systems of the past are filled up again.[5] The obstacle systems of the past are the parental complexes, and they may include aunts and uncles, stepparents, or grandparents. These horizontal relationships form the parental complexes; and they may, like all complexes, become filled with toxic emotions evoked by developmental traumas. Yet, Jung was painfully aware near the end of his life that *all theories that place an emphasis upon psychic traumata* "[presuppose] a knowledge of the traumatically affected psyche which no human being possesses," since there had been no "comparative anatomy" of the human psyche.[6] Still today, we lack sufficient scientific knowledge to formulate a comprehensive theory of the cumulative effects of personal and transgenerational trauma on the traumatized psyche as a whole, although important strides are being taken to fill in the gaps. In the "Father" paper, Jung was speaking about failures of adaptation with regard to trauma, when libido gets dammed up in the parental complexes and they become filled with toxic emotions and fixed ideas that may stunt personality development. In the opening paragraph, Jung stressed, moreover, that in the face of a difficult task, the neurotic can regress to *more* than one causal "chain—the relationship to father and mother."[7] Yet even "if we normal people examine our lives," Jung continued, then we might "perceive how a mighty hand guides us without fail to our destiny, and not always is this hand a kindly one."[8]

The mighty hand of destiny is the hand behind the door; a hand like that is vertical in nature and comes down, so to speak, from above. In a footnote to this passage, Jung cited Arthur Schopenhauer's essay "On Apparent Design in the Fate of the Individual" as one of the key sources

3 - The Significance of the Father

for his text. Jung's reading of Kant, Schopenhauer, and Nietzsche was beginning to help him break away from the horizontal hand of Freud here, prior to his chance meeting with James. What he was attempting to articulate was a theory of a vertical influence, an *archetype of destiny* and its influence on the development of an individual for good or for ill. Behind the mother and father complexes and their helpful, or hindering, influence is a *mightier hand, a destiny-principle,* that emanates from the Self, from above and below. Jung reminds us that it was Freud who had the naïve opinion that all "divine" figures have their roots in the *father-imago*. He questioned Freud in a table-turning way by suggesting that the parental imago is possessed of an *extraordinary* power that can so influence the psychic life of a child that we might be led to ask ourselves whether we may attribute such *magical power* to an ordinary human being at all. Jung's answer was that we simply cannot reduce all the God-images of culture to the imago of the father. Jung didn't deny that the father-imago is a source for the emanation of divine figures, but he took issue with Freud on another point, namely that what we "possess" comes from the *ancestors*. Although Jung did not insert references to gender here, he did say that we are no different from the animals: we bring with us at our birth, systems of adaptation that are organized and ready to function in a specifically human way, and we owe such instinctive endowments to millions of years of human evolution.[9] This congenital and preexistent instinctual system, or pattern of behavior, Jung called the *archetype* in 1919, a transpersonal factor, charged with a dynamism and numinosity that we simply cannot attribute to an individual human being. The emotional power or driving force of the archetype is not controlled by us; on the contrary, we are at its mercy to an unsuspecting degree. There are many who *resist its influence and compulsion,* Jung added, but equally many who *identify with the archetype,* and because everyone is in some way "possessed" by his or her "specifically human preformation," we are all held fast and fascinated by it.[10]

Jung then went on at length to describe the case of a rather delicate-looking eight-year-old boy who was brought to him by his mother on account of his enuresis. Characteristically, Jung took the boy aside and asked him if he had any dreams. Jung arrived at some important insights, given that he was not a child analyst and the field of child analysis would not emerge for another sixteen years. After his interesting "case" discussion,

Jung wrote:

> The child is guided by the power of the parents as by a higher destiny... The parental influence, dating from the early infantile period, is repressed and sinks into the unconscious, but is not eliminated; by invisible threads it directs the apparently individual workings of the maturing mind. Like everything that has fallen into the unconscious, the infantile situation still sends up dim, premonitory feelings, feelings of being secretly guided by otherworldly influences.[11]

The higher destiny is what Jung was seeking during his quest to rediscover his individual secret, the secret of his personality. This passage, written in 1909, is pivotal to understanding the changes that were taking place in Jung's conscious and unconscious self, in his thinking and feeling about the nature of the sexual libido, at this time. The word *premonitory* comes from the Latin root *premonēre,* which means to "forewarn." I will suggest, therefore, that this passage might have been an intuitive forewarning of the invincible guiding power of the child in Jung that had been guiding him since the age of three to eleven by a higher destiny. The parental influence, dating from Jung's early infantile period, had been repressed and sank into the unconscious, but it was not eliminated; by invisible threads it directed the apparently individual workings of his maturing mind. Like everything that had fallen into the unconscious, the infantile situation still sent up dim premonitory feelings, *feelings of being secretly guided by otherworldly influences.* These collective or transpersonal influences, emanating from the power of the personal parents as by a *higher destiny,* would take Jung far beyond the limiting horizons of Freud's horizontal theories of sexuality into the psychology of the second half of his life, which he called *transformation* or *individuation.* "What is it, in the end," Jung wrote in his 1932 paper, "The Development of the Personality" "that induces a man to go his own way and to rise out of unconscious identity with the mass as out of a swathing mist?"

> True personality is always a vocation and puts its trust in it as in God, despite its being, as the ordinary man would say, only a personal feeling. But vocation acts like a God from which there is no escape. The fact that many a man who goes his own way ends in ruin means nothing to one who has a

vocation. He *must* obey his own law, as if it were a daemon whispering to him of new and wonderful paths. Anyone with a vocation hears the voice of the inner man: he is *called* ...The neurosis is thus a defense against the objective, inner activity of the psyche, or an attempt, somewhat dearly paid for, to escape from the inner voice and hence from the vocation . . . Behind the neurotic perversion is concealed his vocation, his destiny: the growth of personality, the full-realization of the life-will that is inborn with the individual.[12]

In the 1948 edition of the "Father" paper, Jung added:

Normally, these feelings are not referred back to the father, but to a positive or negative deity.... In other words, behind the father stands the archetype of the father, and in this pre-existent archetype lies the secret of the father's power, just as the power which forces the bird to migrate is not produced by the bird itself but derives from its ancestors.[13]

We can sense Schopenhauer's, Nietzsche's, and Goethe's influence in some of Jung's statements here.[14] Yet, as we'll see, the paper was published the same year he met James, whose radical empiricism would help him postulate his ideas beyond where they had been able to go before. Not that James was a father-figure for Jung. *James was probably more of a grandfather-figure than a father-figure to Jung,* being over three decades his senior. But the poet in Jung is speaking eloquently here, the mythopoetic language-maker, who would make his first mark in America with a lengthy analysis of the fantasies of an American woman, Miss Miller. What gives the father complex its particular power in the life of an individual is the *father archetype, the transpersonal typos, the earth Father and spiritual Father* that stands behind the personal parents. This transpersonal archetype is not a horizontal factor in the personal unconscious, but a vertical power of the collective unconscious that extends from the instinctive foundation and sexuality in a man or woman to the uppermost regions of human consciousness at the crown of the head. Part of the task of analysis is to strip the parental complexes of their centrality and to realize the higher calling from the *transpersonal father, the mighty hand of destiny* at work behind the infantile father fantasies of the patient. By stripping the father complex of its illusory power, the analyst may, by working within the father transference, help a patient break the spell of developmental blocks that are causing his or her neurosis.

In sum, in the emotional *dynamism* of the preexistent archetype of the father lies the secret of the personal father's power, and it's significant that in the edited version of the paper Jung used an image of verticality, a *higher destiny,* to speak of the emotive power of this archetype, as when he equates it with the power that forces a bird to migrate (such as, for instance, using a familiar symbol from Vedanta, the flight of a wild gander). This vertical power to guide the individual as by a *hand of God* to a personal and transpersonal destiny is not produced by the bird, Jung said, but derives from its ancestors, and this is also true in Jung's view of the life of man and woman. The ancestral psyche shapes us to an unsuspecting degree.

NOTES

1. Jung, *MDR,* 206.
2. Jung, "The Significance of the Father in the Destiny of the Individual," CW 4, 301–302.
3. I will be using the term *Spiritual Self* in my study on Jung and James to connote a third level of the Self that subsumes a Body Self and Social Self at a higher level of organization, according to James's 1890 theory in Volume I of *The Principles of Psychology*. A fourth level of the Self extends to the metaphysical dimension. I will be referring throughout my text to this fourth strata as the *Higher Self,* or what James termed the *Knower*. My reasons for using Jamesian terms in this book to speak about the Self is because of the clear and unequivocal correspondence I find with Jung's most important theoretical formulation on the subject of *vocation,* or what James called an *acting Self.* In Jung's (1934/1954) essay "The Development of Personality," for instance, he placed great significance on individuation as a task for the second half of life—not for childhood or adolescence, but strictly for the mature adult. The state of *wholeness,* according to Jung, can only be relatively realized. But its central vehicle is a *calling*. To fulfill its summons, Jung says specifically: "A whole lifetime, in all its biological, social, and spiritual aspects, is needed" (CW 17, ¶289). Now, here we can see that *(1) biological, (2) social, and (3) spiritual corresponds in Jung's definition, exactly with*

James's three-tiered hypothesis of hierarchal organization in the Self! This may be a pure coincidence, but Jung had read *The Principles* by the time he wrote his doctoral dissertation in 1902, "On the Psychology and Pathology of So-Called Occult Phenomena," located in Volume 1 of the *Collected Works,* where James is cited. Jung published the work in the same year James published *The Varieties of Religious Experience.* So he was well-aware of James's tripartite model of the Self three decades later, when the above passage was written. What James adds to the Jungian lexicon on the Self (and it is vast indeed) is a simpler understanding of a plurality of Selves in the structure of the personality, or what Jungian analyst Andrew Samuels has called *The Plural Psyche* in a handsome book by that name.

4. Jung, CW 4, ¶693.
5. Jung, CW 4, ¶693.
6. Jung, *Symbols of Transformation,* CW 5, p. xxvi.
7. Jung, CW 4, ¶693.
8. Jung, CW 4, ¶727.
9. Jung, CW 4, ¶728.
10. Jung, CW 4, ¶729.
11. Jung, CW 4, ¶739.
12. Jung, "The Development of Personality," CW 17, ¶300, ¶313.
13. Jung, CW 4, ¶739.
14. As I showed in my Preface, the same kind of spiritual influence by a great literary figure was present in the life and work of William James, namely Emerson. In James's life, the laying on of hands by a "master" of his *destiny* as an American scholar was direct: Emerson blessed the baby William James at his birth and was a close family friend of his father's, a Swedenborgian. Thus, the father archetype that was constellated as an essential variable of his active Self in society was both personal and transpersonal.

Chapter 4

PSYCHIC CONFLICTS IN A CHILD

As we've seen in Chapter 1, Jung's decent into the cave was through a stone doorway leading downward into the archaic psyche. He had this dream shortly before his first two meetings with James. The significance of these two events were not causal, but what Jung would later call a *meaningful acausal chance event,* or *synchronicity.* Now I will return to my story of Jung in America that I briefly introduced in Chapter 2.

After a nine-day voyage on the *George Washington,* the three traveling companions arrived in New York, and from there they traveled together with the fourth friend, Ernest Jones, who they met up with in New York. In Worchester, the four men spoke with the president of Clark University, Stanley Hall, and Harvard professor and father of American psychology, William James. Freud delivered five lectures. Jung delivered three: one dealing with his association experiments; a second with investigations he'd carried out at the Burghölzli hospital where he had worked with his mentor, Eugen Bleuler, and through which he'd become known in the United States; and a third lecture, which was a clinical and theoretical paper called "Psychic Conflicts in a Child."

In his study of the processes of metamorphosis in a four-year-old girl, Jung conceived of her process in this paper, first, in rhythmic sequences — sequences of a natural evolutionary process that occurs through the emergence of what he called *elegiac reveries.* In Jung's essay, he spoke eloquently about the emergence of "reveries, the first stirrings of poetry, moods of an elegiac strain" in a four-year-old girl he called "Anna." Examining the nature of elegiac reveries in children is one of the best ways to study the processes of *metamorphosis* in young children. I've observed, in confirmation of Jung's hypothesis, for instance, that in exceptional cases of metamorphosis a child may sometimes dance and sing with the whole *rhythms* of her body. There's something transpersonal about elegiac reveries, some sonorous quality of speech patterns, localized in the voice, which I've sensed on a few occasions while interacting with such musically attuned children. Typically, in Jungian child psychotherapy, such movements are accompanied by *bittersweet* emotions of sadness or joy.

Jung conjectured that elegiac reveries arise in a child's experience following the withdrawal of libido from outer love-objects. When the libido no longer attaches itself to outer love-objects—when a child feels rejected, left alone, or abandoned—she may withdraw into herself and activate structures of emotion, sound, and *reveries* latent in her unconscious. Her whole body may begin to move in *elegiac* rhythms with a grace and elegance that can be delightful to behold. In Jung's words, elegiac reveries "express the fact that part of the love which formerly belonged, and should belong, to a real object, is now *introverted,* that is, it is turned inwards into the subject and there produces an increased fantasy activity."[1] In *Psychology of the Unconscious,* published in 1912, moreover, Jung traced the beginnings of elegiac reveries to an "earlier epoch" of "displaced rhythmic activity" that "coincides in a general way with the time and development of the mind and speech. I might designate the period from birth until the occupation of the sexual zone," Jung wrote, "as the presexual stage of development. This generally occurs between the third and fifth year, and is comparable to the chrysalis stage in butterflies."[2]

Jung's hypothesis of elegiac reveries and his metaphor of the *chrysalis stage* between the ages of three and five was confirmed in my psychotherapy practice through a symbolic process I had the good fortune to have witnessed in a young five-to-six-year-old girl, whose Spiritual Self morphed into a butterfly, "The Case of Clare."[3] As we know from anthropology, moreover, in aboriginal societies shamans or medicine women or men are typically seen as seers and visionaries of the tribe, holy people, or medicine people; as mediators between the sacred and profane they have ways of *seeing into* the instinctive and spiritual worlds. The *shamanic archetype* has left indelible traces on the collective psyche of humanity, and such imprints of experience may be examined in the transference/countertransference projections of children undergoing analysis. Such projections are living "subliminal vestiges," Jung wrote in his 1916 definition of the concept of the collective unconscious, "archaic functions that exist *a priori* and can be brought back into function at any time through an accumulation of libido. These vestiges are not merely formal but have the dynamic nature of instincts. They represent the primitive and the animal in man."[4]

For Jung, the two skulls in the cave, therefore, had nothing to do with a death-wish toward Freud, but rather, with an *emergent* process that had to do with an activation of a primordial level of his mind that was mythopoetic in nature. The way into this primitive domain was through rhythms or waves in the unconscious that Jung had heard in the *field* in the words of his four-year-old girl subject in his study, a child who happened to have been his little daughter, Agathe.

What I believe Jung revealed in his paper from a psychobiographical point of view is a projection of his child anima, or soul, onto his young daughter, who evoked *elegiac reveries* in him, wave-like patterns, stemming from rhythms in his own childhood. Jung spoke in a letter to his wife, Emma, for instance (sent from Clark University on September 14, 1909), of his time in America as having been dreadfully crowded. "The Americans are Masters at that" he wrote; "they hardly leave one time to catch one's breath." Jung was worn out from all of the fabulous things the four European psychoanalysts had been through together, and being an introvert by nature he longed for some quiet introspective time in the mountains. His head was spinning from the previous evening, moreover, when he'd been awarded, with Freud, an honorary doctorate in Law. Jung had to deliver an impromptu talk for some 300 persons, and his mind was by this time in a whirlwind of extraverted activity that distracted him: "I am looking forward enormously to getting back to the sea again, where the overstimulated psyche can recover in the presence of that infinite peace and spaciousness."[5]

After imbibing with his four companions some fine champagne in celebration of their accomplishments at Clark, Jung wrote again to Emma, on September 22, 1909, from the steamer *Kaiser Wilhelm der Grosse*, on the return trip from America to Bremen, that

> The sea is like music; it has all the dreams of the soul within itself and sounds them over. The beauty and grandeur of the sea consists in our being forced down into the fruitful bottomlands of our own psyches, where we confront and re-create ourselves in the animation of the "mournful wasteland of the sea."[6]

He was recalling the trip of the travel-weary Odysseus on his journey homeward to rejoin with Penelope.

Jung later wrote, a few years after Emma's death, with fond memories to an American woman engaged in writing her doctoral thesis on the Clark University conference:

> I do remember the Clark Conference of 1909... Two personalities I met at the Clark Conference made a profound and lasting impression on me. One was Stanley Hall, the President, and the other was William James whom I met for the first time then... I spent two delightful evenings with William James alone and I was tremendously impressed by the clearness of his mind and the complete absence of intellectual prejudices. Stanley Hall was an equally clearheaded man, but decidedly of an academic brand... I was a young man then. I lectured about association tests and a case of child psychology. I was also interested in parapsychology and my discussions with William James were chiefly about this subject and about the psychology of religious experience.[7]

What stands out to my mind about Jung's first experiences in America are the remarkable synchronicities he encountered along the way: first, his confrontation with Freud in Bremen over his preoccupation with peat bog corpses and Freud's first fainting spell; second, Freud's reluctance to risk his patriarchal authority in relationship to Jung at the expense of his scientific objectivity; third, Jung's "big" dream on the *George Washington* that gave him his theory of the collective unconscious and the two *doorways* he had to pass through to descend to the ground floor where the two skulls lay; fourth, his presentation of a child case (his daughter) at Clark University; and fifth his chance meeting with William James and discussions about the *psychology of religious experience*.

Contrary to Freud's interpretation of a supposed death-wish by Jung, my analysis of the two skulls in the cave is that they may have portended the death of the Freud-Jung relationship. They were emergent symbols of *death* to the father-son relationship that prospectively prepared the way for a *rebirth* of Jung's own authority as the father of his own Zürich school of analytical psychology. That Jung's first case presentation in the United States was the case of a four-year-old girl is significant, moreover, in light of the research questions I'll explore in the last chapter of this book. But the discovery of a fourth and hidden layer of the collective unconscious and chance meeting with James at Clark University provides us with a prelude to the main questions in my book generally, about the structure and dynamics of the human psyche, and whether there is evidence for a *supraconscious* dimension in the collective psyche.

Shortly before his death, in June 1961, Jung completed a lengthy essay composed completely in fluent English called "Symbols and the Interpretation of Dreams," in which he placed an accent on "language" and its importance in the practice of analytical psychology. By "language" Jung meant the *dream language,* or archaic language of fantasy thinking. Dreams can only be understood when we are "able to learn the language of the patient" and "we must pay particular attention to the language of dreams that we consider to be symbolic."[8] The dream language arises from the patient's "original nature," his or her "instincts" and "peculiar thinking."[9] The study of this language," Jung said, "is almost a science in itself."[10] Earlier in this final essay, written several weeks before his passing over, Jung made it clear that in order to interpret dreams properly, we need to cultivate a relationship to "what Freud had called 'archaic remnants'—thought-forms whose presence cannot be explained by anything in the individual's own life, but seem to be aboriginal, innate, and inherited patterns of the human mind."[11] By this Jung meant the inherited mind structure of "archaic man, whose psyche was still similar to that of an animal."[12] Jung went on to define the term *archetype* as "an inherited *tendency* of the human mind to form representations of mythological motifs—representations that vary a great deal without losing their basic pattern."[13] He then added: The best examples of the spontaneous production of archetypal images are presented by individuals, particularly children, who live in a milieu where one can be sufficiently certain that any direct knowledge of tradition is out of the question.[14]

The archaic psyche, according to Jung, is what we were as infants. We *were* that mind but did not *know* it, because our ego consciousness was completely submerged within it. "We got rid of it before understanding it."[15] Thus, a question among analytical-oriented psychologists who are interested in research today is how to constellate the "original mind" again in our analytic dialogues with adult patients. Jung emphasized that "we do not appreciate the far-reaching complexities of the infantile mind that stem from its original identity with the prehistoric psyche. That 'original mind' is just as much present and still functioning in the child as the evolutionary stages are in the embryo."¹⁶ As a Jungian child psychotherapist this correlation that interested Jung at the time he met James is one that holds a great deal of meaning for me and the field of depth psychology as a whole. Before we turn to James, however, I must first say a few words about psychobiography[17] and theoretical speculation.

Notes

1. Jung, "Psychic Conflicts in a Child," CW 17, ¶13.
2. Jung, *Psychology of the Unconscious*, 142.
3. Herrmann, "The Case of Clare."
4. Jung, "The Structure of the Unconscious," CW 7, ¶520.
5. Jung, *MDR*, 368.
6. Jung, *MDR*, 369.
7. Jung, *Letters*, vol. 1, 530–531.
8. Jung, "Symbols and the Interpretation of Dreams," CW 18, ¶518.
9. Jung, CW 18, ¶518.
10. Jung, CW 18, ¶521.
11. Jung, CW 18, ¶521.
12. Jung, CW 18, ¶522.
13. Jung, CW 18, ¶523.
14. Jung, CW 18, ¶531.
15. Jung, CW 18, ¶590.
16. Jung, CW 18, ¶593.
17. I must point out here that I will not be writing an ambitious psychobiography of James and Jung in my two abbreviated sketches of their lives in Chapters 6 and 27. I will use this method, nevertheless, to provide a few basic facts about their developments for the reader to consider.

Chapter 5

Liber Novus

In "Jung Becomes Jung: A Dialogue on *Liber Novus* (*The Red Book*)," Jungian historian Sonu Shamdasani speaks with Jungian analyst John Beebe about a *fear* that exists that there might be something in *Liber Novus* (or any other unpublished materials by Jung for that matter) that could overturn prior understandings of Jung.[1] With the exception of the protocols that went into the making of Jung's semiautobiographical memoir, *Memories, Dreams, Reflections,* Shamdasani mentions Barbara Hannah's memoir as the only one with any lasting value.[2] The dialogue is a fascinating one because it gets at a source of a controversy about the interpretation of a text, whether produced as "speculation" or as "fact," during the writing of a historical psychobiography, such as the one I will be attempting. The discussion is relevant to this book, when I examine Jung's life and works and the life of James.

When speculation attempts to pass itself off as fact, something important may be lost in the narrative, namely an author's *integrity,* which can move a work of interpretation in a subjective direction, in accordance with his or her own style or theory of psychological or literary interpretation. For instance, one might have a preconceived notion, or presumptive "theory of truth," that one is attempting to prove through the writing of a psychobiography. Such a biased explanation can then become one's central theoretical focus. This kind of analysis, says Shamdasani, as long as it is *specified as speculative,* can have a kind of honesty to it because the subjective element of one's personal myth is then identified at the outset, and the reader is thus prepared to read it as such, without any expectation of the writers having discovered some general or universal theory that could be misconstrued as a grand hypothesis. It is true as a subjective work, not as an objectively verifiable statement of the facts as such. Thus, clearly stated as hypothetical, it may be seen, rather, as an expression of one's own personality, work, or personal understanding.[3] As Beebe adds in the dialogue, "Jung is saying we are what we observe. There is no way to observe the psyche except via the psyche."[4] This is the issue I grapple with in this book on Jung and James: the *relativity* of a theory based on data of the psyche I've selected to support my observations.

The problem for Jung, during his reflections in 1912–1913, three to four years after he met James, was the enigma of what particular myth could provide him with a sustaining meaning on the road toward the expansion of his consciousness beyond the hero's battle for liberation from the mother. What he was in quest of after he traveled to America in 1909, and later in 1911, was freedom of his anima, spaciousness, or the treasure of his soul and her jewels of wisdom for the transformation of the collectivity via a discovery of a psychological attitude that could be fruitful for the generality.[5] The subjective factor or Jung's personal myth of meaning is what he was in search of from 1913 onward, during the post-heroic period of his life, following the death of his hero function (*introverted intuition*) and initiation into a more spacious psychological attitude that he later called *psychic objectivity,* or the reality of the psyche, *psyche observing psyche*. This is the *spaciousness* he felt on the *George Washington:* "The sea is like music." This is a rhythmical and dialectical process of *conversing* in elegiac reveries with specific complexes, voices, and archetypes of the collective or transpersonal unconscious. Such a colloquy with the soul began after the sacrifice of the hero and overcoming of his overreaching heroism.[6]

The discussion between Beebe and Shamdasani also revolves around the issue of self-sacrifice of Jesus to become the Christ as being one of the central motifs of *Liber Novus*.[7] Beebe makes a connection between the murder of the hero in "Liber Primus" and the sacrifice of Jung's psychoanalytic persona, so that he could "allow himself to be himself." Shamdasani replies that what had to be left behind during Jung's descent to the underworld was the "spirit of the times," or his egotistical attachment to any preunderstandings in the area of his career interests.[8] Jung had to be alone with himself and free of any external images and theories and techniques of psychoanalysis to discover his own unique gifts with their individual stamp, free from Freud's influence and all other researchers, including Jean Charcot, Pierre Janet, and Eugen Bleuler. In *Liber Novus* a "disidentification" occurs through the sacrifice not only of Jung's psychoanalytic persona, but also of psychoanalytic discourse in the Freudian and Adlerian genres. The problem Jung was faced with was no longer how to adapt himself to the spirit of the times, as he'd done between 1902 and 1912, a ten-year period when the hero in him was rising toward its zenith as a shining star of the psychoanalytic movement, but how adaptation could continue toward the nadir; he thence descended into Hell as a result of his painful self-sacrifice in 1913.[9]

What this seminal dialogue reveals is that it was only through the composing of *Liber Novus* that "Jung became Jung," or, as Beebe says, "returns to the real Jung."[10] The real Jung, Jung as Jung, not the hero, but the man in midlife who bowed his head to the Self, as the author of his destiny, is the true Jung I'm in quest of in this book, just as I'm in search of the real William James. In *Liber Novus* Jung becomes conscious, as Beebe says, of what it means "to speak from psyche to psyche," thereby becoming a "psychological writer" in his own unique language and idiom.[11] Shamdasani calls *Liber Novus* moreover a "language experiment," and he informs us further that the word *psychology* does not appear in the text at all. Instead we find another word. "*Religion* appears, *psychology* doesn't," Shamdasani says. He adds, "I mean, in a sense, it's all psychological."[12]

This may sound like a paradox to the reader, which it is. Because, from a Jungian standpoint, psychology is the broader attitude through which to understand religion as psychological. As you'll see, this attitude was conveyed to Jung from James at Clark in 1909. Jung's aim in *Liber Novus* was transmutation, metamorphosis, change on a large scale. In fact, Jung tried to "transmute" what he'd created in *The Red Book* into *psychology*, or the path of individuation. This path is related, says Beebe, to a Self as the center of our experience. For Jung this Self-experience is the way that is to come. Jung was very interested not only in a language experiment but also with the future direction of modern psychology. *Liber Novus* is a text, says Shamdasani, that is "articulating the way of the future."[13]

What that future is, I believe, is what the world wants to know today. Where is the field of psychology heading? What is its course? Where are we going? What is forthcoming? What's so surprising to me in this insightful study of *Liber Novus* is how few dreams are actually mentioned and yet, astonishingly, how much "Theory making, cosmology making emerge," says Shamdasani, from Jung's "active engagement" with inner images.[14] In other words, Jung does not rely on data from dreams alone (such as his dream of the four-storied house) to formulate a theory of psychology; he generates theories out of his study of his own experimentations with the method he practiced and taught to his pupils, active imagination. Among the different theoretical ideas that emerge in *Liber Novus* is the central problematic, not of psychology, but of Christian theology: "How should one understand the imitation of Christ?" Or "What does it mean to take up one's own cross?" The book attempts to get at the core of the Christian message of crucifixion of the hero by the sacrificer, which is the self/Self. Shamdasani points out further that one of the passages from the *Handwritten Draft of Liber Novus* (1914–1915) reads: "Not one title of Christian law is abrogated, but instead we're adding a new one: accepting the lament of the dead." Among Jung's precursors to his understanding of Christianity is Friedrich Schleiermacher. "But the figure whom Jung said he most identified with, and I think that there is a very powerful argument in this text for that, is Meister Eckhart."[15] Shamdasani clarifies for us that Jung was reading Meister Eckhart from the age of fifteen onward![16]

What Jung is describing in *Liber Novus* is a new "theology of the dead," which cannot be found in Eckhart.[17] It is a preoccupation that arose in him quite naturally in *Septem Sermones ad Mortuos* ("Seven Sermons to the Dead"), where the dead pray that Jung let them in and where, in Sermon VII, the voice says: "Man is a gateway, . . . Small and transitory is man."[18] Later, in 1935, Jung remarked in his *Seminars on Nietzsche's Zarathustra:*

> Meister Eckhart has shown very clearly. The godhead in itself is not blissful, but must be born in the soul of man again and again: only then does it become God. Otherwise, man would be of no importance whatever; he would be the most foolish and imperfect invention God ever made. But just because man is man, a living something living in three dimensions, in a very small space in the here and now, God is forced to go through the narrow doorway, the gate of man, in order to become God. That is the teaching of Master Eckhart and that is also the meaning of the Christian mystery, that God first became man and underwent the most miserable fate in order to become God.[19]

I'll explore this connection with Eckhart, who James also cites, later.

We learn further in the dialogue that Jung's composition—"From the earliest experiences of my life" —leaves off at the age of nineteen. Following his reflections on this period, there is a hiatus. The narrative in the protocols picks up again with the opening of "Liber Primus" and

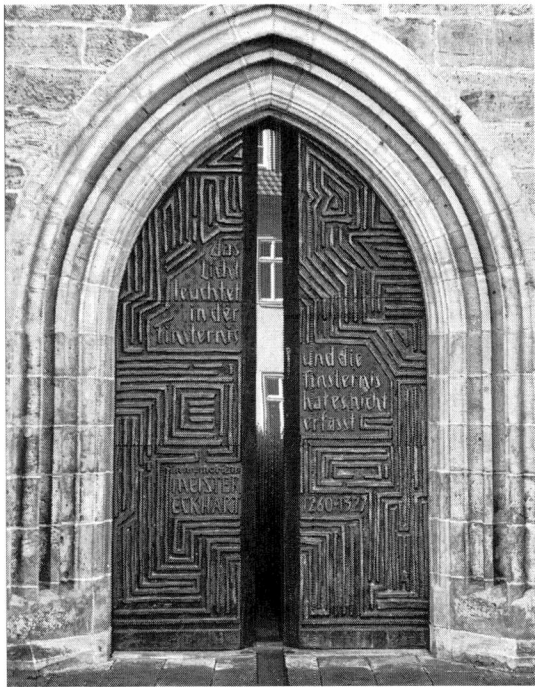

Figure 5.1 Eckhart Portal at the Predigerkirche ("Preacher's Church") in Erfurt, Germany, 2019 (Photograph by the author)

the refinding of his soul. Yet from 1902 to 1913, a period of eleven years, Jung pursued the spirit of the times and adapted himself to the collectivity and his career. He lost the solitude of his soul and his vocation to write about religious ideas through his wanderings in the world. In 1913, Jung says he lost contact with his soul in the year 1902, which corresponds exactly with the publication date of James's masterpiece *The Varieties of Religious Experience*.[20]

In section 3 of the dialogue, Beebe says: "We all have dead we owe something to who weren't able to get somewhere … We have to pick it up and carry it forward." He then asks whether "people resist taking up their duty to the dead?"[21] Do we really owe anything to the dead? As the author of this book, do I have a duty to the dead? What is it I feel I have to pick up and carry forward? Well, I do *know* from my dreams that I have a duty to my dead father, who received his PhD in educational psychology from the Univerity of California, Berkeley in 1968, and my teachers, the Santa

Cruz poet William Everson and San Francisco Jungian analyst Donald Sandner. This I *know*. I feel it strongly as a calling from my unconscious.

What about Jung and James? Certainly, all Jungians owe something to Jung. As an American Jungian, I will go further: as an American, I feel we may all have a debt to pay to James, as Jung did also. For me this tribute to James is undeniable. I feel it in my bones. It's part of my heredity and spiritual make-up as a Californian.

Moving onward, Beebe clarifies that he thinks we all have a *conscience* to the dead, and answering the calling to redeem the dead is a *task* we all need to take up, as a heavy burden we must carry in life.[22] This may sound to some readers as mystical, or superstitious, or magical, but it's not that. It is perhaps partly parapsychological. After all, we need to remember that both Jung and James began their careers as psychologists with studies of mediums. Both were interested in parapsychology. Both were interested in psychics. In *The Red Book* Jung is not interested in repeating the mistakes of his doctoral dissertation, however. The task in *Liber Novus* is Jung's calling to recast his imaginary experiments within a post-mythopoetic language that will be acceptable to a "medical and scientific audience."[23] To accomplish this task Jung could not cast it solely within the language of what he called personality number 1; he also had to cast it in the mythopoetic language of personality number 2, which is to say—*in the language of myth, the language of images, and the language of science, philosophy, alchemy, and religious thought.* It is only by returning to religious thought, however, after a rigorous eleven-year period, when he was preoccupied with the formulation of an academic psychology of schizophrenia, experimental psychology, and an elaborate system of word association testing and heuristic theory of complexes that he *recovered the self/Self he'd left behind* during his heroic rise to fame as a prominent world-renowned Swiss psychiatrist, professor of psychology at the University of Basel, and as chief editor of the *Journal of Psychoanalysis*. There were several personae Jung dissolved, therefore, during his initiatory period in which his new nonheroic identity was incubating.

What excites me about this dialogue is the centrality of Meister Eckhart to Jung's early development during a time of his most heated debates with his father, the theologian Paul Jung, during Jung's late adolescence—and at a time when he was strongly gripped by the Judeo-Christian religious complex. I'd seen Eckhartian notions in *Liber Novus* in 2013, when I began an exchange of letters with the now deceased Jungian analyst and Eckhart aficionado John Dourley. Yet Dourley could not answer my question of when it was Jung first began to read the Dominican. With my recent reading of the dialogue between Beebe and Shamdasani, my intuitions have been pleasantly confirmed, that the influence was indeed quite early in Jung's development. When I read in the dialogue that Jung was fifteen when he first read Eckhart, it confirmed my hunch that the basic attitude Jung found in William James and that so appealed to him when he was rediscovering his soul is a similar one he'd discovered first in adolescence when he studied Eckhart. Eckhart spoke to Jung's nascent psyche in a direct way in which no other theologian could, because he was the same basic psychological type. Later, Jung would be preoccupied with the writing of an important essay on Eckhart, which he published in *Psychological Types*. It is also in this book that Jung made his comprehensive study of William James. In other words, I can now speculate that Jung felt he owed something to Eckhart, just as he did to his mentor in Geneva, Théodore Flournoy, and to William James, namely, a psychology of the unconscious that would speak from the spirit of the depths to the spirit of the times in a new language he called *analytical psychology.*

In a second paper, written for *Quadrant,* "The *Red Book* as a Work of Conscience," Beebe makes it clear, moreover, that the winged figure who appeared in a dream to Jung and identified himself as Philemon and who carried with him *four keys*, was a religious figure from Alexandria who Jung later referred to as his inner guru, or sage-like figure. Beebe calls him "a source of wise introverted thinking for Jung."[24] This is an important psychological realization on Beebe's part, for what it tells us is that what arose concomitantly with Philemon in the dream and the later portraits Jung painted of him, is an attitude Jung had been seeking to develop inside himself ever since he was an adolescent when he had tried his best to understand Eckhart.

Later, at a more mature, nonheroic stage of life, he would refer to it in his essay on the Dominican as the attitude of *psychological relativity*. By this, Jung means Eckhart had somehow managed to break into a *spaciousness* that opened him up to an understanding of what it might mean to live in a postheroic myth, where one can carry a heavy burden of one's own cross of suffering without foisting it off on the historical Jesus, as some superficial Christians do. Moreover *Liber Novus* may have had what Beebe calls "a redemptive effect on Jung's father problem" and what "he owed to his dead father."²⁵ By redemptive Beebe means a redeeming outcome on his father's loss of faith in Christianity, which Jung suffered when he was a boy.²⁶

In sum, what Jung attempted to do in *Liber Novus* was to see whether through a "language experiment" certain theoretical notions could emerge that might pave the way beyond psychoanalysis toward a more universal theory of modern psychology, which might satisfy the scientific spirit of the times in which he was living and in which we are still living today. As Beebe reformulates it, through his own unique understanding of psychological types, and as he recently conveyed to me via a personal communication: "Jung was not an introverted thinking type, he was an introverted intuitive. James, on the other hand, was an introverted thinker, with auxiliary extraverted intuition." The function of extroverted intuition is a function we need to be able to see and outline the possible and even *probable* lines of development for the future of psychology as an "interactive" and an *integrative* field that is apparently inclining toward a more positivistic, Jamesian direction, rather than a strictly and reductively materialistic, behavioral, or experimental one.²⁷ This complementarity of types in James and Jung makes for an interesting comparison of two minds.

My main hypothesis throughout is that it was only in William James that the young Carl Jung, who had lost his soul, could find a strong precursor who had the psychological acumen well enough developed that Jung could recognize in him an older and more evolved peer in the field of psychology, one in whom the religious and psychological attitudes had already set a standard in American and European teaching institutions. The evidence I provide to support my thesis is presented in Chapter 33. Philemon, who would later emerge in a dream to dispense to Jung in the period of *Liber Novus* his own unique mythopoetic contributions, would help Jung formulate, in the language of personality number one, the empirical psychologist, his own undeniable contributions to modern psychology, with his theories of psychological types, archetypes and the collective unconscious, techniques of analysis and dream interpretation, active imagination, alchemical research, and synchronicity, notions that would revolutionize the world and open new areas of scientific research.

The basic attitude Eckhart, Flournoy, James, and Philemon all possessed, moreover, is the attitude of *detachment* from emotional objects.

This is the religious and psychological attitude Jung was after. Thus, in William James Jung may have recognized a man who could think with a kind of introverted thinking that he himself aspired to in his inquiry into the nature of phenomenon. As an adolescent, he'd admired this capacity for introverted intuitive thought in Eckhart. Yet, in James, the psychological relativity he admired in Eckhart was lucidly formulated into an elaborate psychological theory of religious phenomena and a philosophy of pragmatism, even though James could become excitable and infused at times with excess uplifts or down-drags of emotionality. Like Jung, James had his own debt to pay to what he felt he owed to the dead, chiefly to his deceased father, but also to Gustav Theodor Fechner (1801–1887), the father of psychophysics, and to his beloved godfather, Ralph Waldo Emerson (1803–1882). James had his own debts to pay to the dead through his teachings and writing. In *A Pluralistic Universe* James wrote an apology for his own psychological interpretations on Fechner's psychophysics: "I owe to Fechner's shade an apology for presenting him in a manner so unfamiliar to the most essential quality of his genius."[28]

Many of us who came of age reading Jung have read at least a portion of William James's works, or know something about him. It is important to stress, to my Jungian and Jamesian colleagues and readers generally that Jung, although he never read James comprehensively, read at least three of his major texts, and as you shall see, he never tired from telling his seminarians: "Read William James!"

It is only by reading James and getting to know his psychobiography, in-depth, that we may come to understand why he was so *pivotal* to Jung as a mediatory figure toward the arrival at a new psychological attitude that finally subsumed the religious.

What I owe to Jung and James is simply incalculable. I can only hope I've paid a portion of my debt to these two ancestors of modern psychology through my *tasks of conscience* in writing it. I believe any attempt to paint a portrait of Jung in America must begin with James. He was one of the true giants in American psychology, and he was standing on the shoulders of such luminaries as Ralph Waldo Emerson, Walt Whitman, Swami Vivekananda, Gustav Fechner, and many of the same European philosophers and depth-psychologists that Jung read.

Notes

1. Shamdasani and Beebe, "Jung Becomes Jung."
2. Shamdasani and Beebe, 412.
3. Shamdasani and Beebe, 414.
4. Shamdasani and Beebe, 416.
5. Shamdasani and Beebe, 416.
6. Shamdasani and Beebe, 417.
7. Shamdasani and Beebe, 418.
8. Shamdasani and Beebe, 419.
9. Shamdasani and Beebe, 420.
10. Shamdasani and Beebe, 421.
11. Shamdasani and Beebe, 422.
12. "All psychological" suggests to my mind the arrival at a *fifth* attitude that subsumes the four cultural attitudes: 1) religious, 2) philosophical, 3) social, and 4) aesthetic. Joseph L. Henderson calls the fifth the "quintessence."
13. Shamdasani and Beebe, "Jung Becomes Jung," 423.
14. Shamdasani and Beebe, 424.
15. When I read this line of the transcript by Shamdasani, I was excited, for I'd written my thesis on Meister Eckhart at the University of California, Santa Cruz, under the tutelage of the Jungian, post-Dominican poet William Everson in 1981 to 1982. Although I'd seen the centrality of Eckhart to Jung's thought almost forty years earlier, I had no idea when Jung first read the Dominican. In my unpublished "Notes from a Conversation with Sonu Shamdasani, on April 14, 2019," I asked Sonu where he had discovered in Jung's writings that he was reading Meister Eckhart in his teens. I mentioned I'd recently seen this statement in his published conversations with John Beebe. Sonu told me these statements are located in the protocols that were used to write *Memories, Dreams, Reflections*. I told him how exciting this was for me to learn about now, since I would be doing a Jungian dream workshop in Meister Eckhart's church, *die Predigerkirche,* in Erfurt, Germany, in June 2019, with Matthew Fox. We discussed the many Eckhartian themes in Jung's *Red Book*, such as the birth of the god Izdubar in "Incantations," where Jung speaks as a mother who gives birth to the new god. Eckhart said similarly he laid in the maternity bed and gave birth to the Word of God. Sonu agreed about Eckhart's influence in *The Red Book:* "Eckhart is everywhere." I believe Jung's reading of Eckhart came before his heated theological debates with his

father in his late teens. Furthermore, when Jung talks in *Liber Novus* about what he owes to the dead, he is therefore including Eckhart in what he owes to his Christian ancestors, his forebears.

16. Shamdasani and Beebe, 425.
17. Shamdasani and Beebe, 427.
18. Jung, *MDR,* 389.
19. Jung, *Nietzsche's Zarathustra,* 723.
20. Shamdasani and Beebe, "Jung Becomes Jung," 428. My reasons for pointing out this fact about the meaningful chance correspondence is that had Jung made it a point to read James's book deeply at this time, it might have given him some solace from the general loss of soul he was raised in Swiss Protestant Reform society. I don't think Jung was aware until a decade later about what James actually meant by a "science of religion," which is ingrained in the American psyche, and which would later so appeal to Jung, once he came of age during his mid-life passage.
21. Shamdasani and Beebe, 430.
22. Shamdasani and Beebe, 431.
23. Shamdasani and Beebe, 433.
24. Beebe, "The *Red Book* as a Work of Conscience," 52.
25. Beebe, 54.
26. Beebe, 55.
27. Personal communication from John Beebe, January 18, 2019.
28. James, *William James Writings*: *1902–1910,* 711.

Chapter 6

A VIOLENT GOD

Shortly before his death in 1961, Jung spoke about his conception of God in an interview with *Good Housekeeping:* "To this day God is the name by which I designate all things which cross my willful path *violently* and recklessly, all things which upset my subjective views, plans and intentions and change the course of my life for better or worse."[1] How did Jung arrive at this view of God as a *violent* and reckless force lurking beneath the Christian conception of God? Can Jung's definition of God as a violent force in body, psyche, and Cosmos help us understand the violence we are seeing erupting across our world today? There is no idea more pivotal to Jung's psychology of individuation than emotion, combustion, or force as the chief source of human consciousness itself. I believe it true about the nature of the Self, at its most archaic level, and any psychobiography of Jung must begin there. I will begin, therefore, with a hypothesis: *Violence is patterned by a veritable human instinct, an imprint of experience that is millions of years old.* It has an instinctive and a spiritual dimension to it: an impulsive pole at the infra-rational level and a reflective pole at the ultra-violent end. These two dimensions of the impulse, an upper and a lower half, are united through the symbol.

Throughout Jung's *Collected Works,* seminars, and published letters, he makes it clear that instinctive violence of affects and their associated symbol formations can act as machines, or transformers, through which the libido, or psychic energy, may be transmuted into higher forms of spiritual representation in the Self. According to Jung, "A symbol is never an invention. It *happens* to man."[2] Thus, based on over thirty years of clinical work with children, I hypothesize the symbol of violence is what makes the *transitus,* or transition, from an instinctive-energetic dynamism of the aggressive instinct to the spiritual pole of archetypal representations possible in a child. The same can be said, I believe, for the evolution of human culture as a whole. Violence must be symbolized before it can become spiritualized. Without the symbol, the transition is made much more difficult for an individual and society. Preventive psychotherapy, or proper religious education, can offer to the world a remedy of *nonviolence* as a universal medicine. This is the greatest contribution to the world that the religions have offered.

In Jung's childhood, for instance, the problem of violence occupied him at the remarkable age of three. As a little boy, Jung was traumatized by a God of violence and terror in the world and psyche. If you read the opening chapter of *Memories, Dreams, Reflections* carefully, you will see how deeply the boy was wounded by God and how hidden away in Jung's childhood memories was an "objective problem" that he felt it was his "fate" to answer.[3]

For Jung, as we will see, the problem of God's dual nature was symbolized by an enormous dream-phallus, a huge underground phallic deity, seated on a royal king's throne. It had a numinous aura of light shining above its head and an eye staring motionlessly upward, a nimbus of seeing in the unconscious. Such a terrifying symbol was not invented by the boy, it simply happened to him. He trembled afterward when he thought of it. It appears to have arisen in conjunction with a *fear* that had been infused into him by his inner dream-mother, who said to the boy's complete horror about this upright apparition: "That is the man-eater!" Whether the underground phallus of the dream was the "man-eater," or whether the "man-eater" was symbolized by the dream-phallus, the fact remains that God appeared to the boy as a giant phallus that filled him with a secret *dread*. The secret of Jung's personality, then, is that it was shaped first and foremost by *terror* and *affective violence:* potential violence and a very real terror of the phallic man-eater.

Perhaps Jung's sense of vulnerability in his eighty-third year, when he told his story to his secretary, Aniela Jaffé, arose from a painful realization that he had lived with this "secret" for as long as he could remember. The three-year-old boy faced fears of being devoured, or eaten, by God. What event might have evoked such fears in him? One fragment of evidence remains: Jung was frightened by his mother. She is said to have appeared to the little boy as "one of those seers who is at the same time a strange animal, like a priestess in a bear's cave. Archaic and ruthless; ruthless as truth and nature."[4] This, of course, was Jung's perception of her. It was, therefore, his projection of an archaic ruthless archetype of the bear mother in his own psyche, and perhaps he may have also perceptively seen this image activated in her personality too. He was attempting to describe something he experienced as a little boy, a subjective experience of a ruthlessness in his mother's secondary personality, her instinctive and religious character as a seer. This *ruthlessness* of his mother's personality (what Jung called her personality no. 2, not her dream-ego, but an archaic aspect of the Self) typically surfaced at night. He reported that he had frequent anxiety dreams about her. In addition to his fears about his mother's no. 2 personality, Jung's childhood sleep problems (fevers, eczema, and his entire childhood "illness") all appear to have been evoked by a *violent traumatic shock of separation from his mother* who required a lengthy hospitalization prior to the dream.[5] During this separation from his mother, Jung was taken care of by a maid, who apparently saved the boy's life during a moment of severe psychic distress. Jung and the maid were crossing a bridge over the Rhine Falls when he was suddenly gripped by an impulse to slip his leg under the railing of the bridge and plunge violently to his death into the turbulent falls below. He was caught just in the nick of time by the maid as he was getting ready to slip through cracks in the bridge's barrier. Jung attributed this self-destructive impulse to a "suicidal urge" or a "fatal resistance to life in this world."[6] (As I discuss in my sketch of William James in Chapter 28, he suffered from a similar impulse to suicide.) Jung's abandonment trauma and suicidal urge were followed after his dream by obsessive "ruminations" about the "man-eater." Yet Jung did not will these ruminations. They happened to him. They arose from the unconscious, from the Self. The creative forces are beyond ourselves. As Jung said, "You cannot rule them; they create what they choose."[7]

Jung tells us, moreover, that he suffered terribly from "ruminations" about God. He did not choose his obsessive thoughts, but for some unknown reason, they chose him. The religious fantasies selected him to be their instrument, and they centered on the dual figures of Satan and Jesus; the little boy feared that both Jesus and Satan "ate" children and "took" them into a dark hole in the earth. The word *ruminate* comes from the Latin *ruminatus,* which means "to muse upon, contemplate over in one's mind, or to ponder." It comes from the past participle *rumen,* or *rumin,* which means "throat." How did such ruminations begin?

Jung's conscious fears about God as a "man-eater" began with a simple and seemingly harmless prayer his mother had taught him to assuage the vague terrors of night, and all Jung the child could do to slake his thirst for understanding was to repeat it every evening. Listen:

> *Spread out thy wings, Lord Jesus mild,*
> *And take to thee thy chick, thy child,*
> *"If Satan would devour it,*
> *No harm shall over power it,"*
> *So let the angles sing!*[8]

What was frightening the boy? Let's hear what Jung has to say about this:

> The muted roar of the Rhine Falls was always audible, and all around lay a danger zone. People drowned, bodies were swept over rocks. In the cemetery nearby, the sexton would dig a hole—heaps of brown upturned earth. Black, solemn men in long frock coats with unusually tall hats and shiny black boots would bring a black box … I would hear that they had been buried, and that Lord Jesus had taken them to himself.[9]

Jung's frightful ruminations about Satan and Lord Jesus led to his "first conscious trauma."[10] Some of the most difficult memories to reach in analysis are preverbal, extending far back to the earliest experiences of infancy. Such unconscious memories are emotional and somatic in nature, and they can have a far-reaching effect on the formation of post-traumatic symptoms and affect-complexes in very young children. Some emotional memories are too unbearable to endure consciously and, thus, cannot be kept in awareness, so they are either repressed or dissociated as split-off bits, or personality fragments that are subsequently forgotten; they may lead a sequestered life as compartments of affective memory in the unconscious or subconscious mind. These deposits are what Jung calls *affect-complexes,* and their emotional effects may continue to linger in the form of affective *turbulence* just below the threshold of consciousness; their wave-patterns are sometimes violent at their nuclear cores. Reverberations of unconscious affects, depressed moods, and symptoms of anxiety, negative thoughts, frightening sensations, may continue to erupt for many years; and if they are not worked through in analysis, they will have to find another way to become transformed.

Jung's experience of abandonment appears to have been catastrophic for him, as it evoked a suicidal urge toward life—violence directed inward against himself. At an unconscious level, his nascent ego must have been split to pieces by it, and defenses of the Self, protective walls, or fortresses most likely were formed. What such defenses may have been is difficult to discern, but whatever they were, what is beyond any shadow of doubt is that they were *religious strongholds* in nature. Let me say why I think this is so.

Jung reports a horrifying memory from the age of three of a man dressed all in black, coming down from the woods and looming large above the frightened boy "in a strangely broad hat and a long black garment." It was the figure of a Jesuit. This dark figure led the three-year-old boy to run terrified "helter-skelter" into the house to seek shelter in the "darkest corner of the attic." It caused such a "hellish fright to cling" to his limbs that he kept tucked away, hidden in the rafters in the forbidden attic, until the terrifying apparition had safely passed and he could breathe comfortably again. At this impressionable age, the Jesuit and Jesus were both believed to take little "chicks" into the ground, and like the deathly grave scenes he had witnessed and over which priests had presided, Jesus and the Jesuit were believed to have "evil intentions."[11]

Jung tells us he could never remember if his conscious "ruminations" about Lord Jesus preceded his first remembered dream or not, but whatever the case may be: the abandonment trauma appears to have preceded it. Here, we can see in Jung's reconstructions in old age the first evidence for the eruption of Jung's violent affect-complexes in early infancy: *fear*, not anger, was operating in Jung as a projective mechanism around the time of his abandonment, and this *terror complex* needed to find some way to be integrated into consciousness. It is important to note here that child psychotherapy did not emerge as a profession until the mid-1920s, so Jung had to find a way to heal himself by following his intuitions and somatic experiences. His searching alone for ways to initiate himself through the curative powers of his mind, into the realm of the primitive unconscious, was purely instinctual and natural.

In addition to the burial scenes Jung witnessed at the age of three, other traumatic memories haunted the boy and left indelible impressions upon his nascent mind. He tells us that fourteen people drowned and were dragged down the yellow flood-waters of the Rhine to their deaths;

some of the bodies got stuck in the sand, and when the water receded, Jung could not be held back by his mother from viewing the ghostly scene. He "found the body of a middle-aged man, in a black frock coat; apparently he had just come from church."[12]

Thus, church was associated in his mind with death and drowning. Not only Jesuits, but also the Protestant church to which he belonged, took on a distrustful visage in the boy's mind. Viewing violence was not something Jung was averse to, however. Although he was frightened by violence, he was also fascinated by it. He experienced violence as a *fascinosum*. He tells us, for instance, that he watched "a pig being slaughtered" with great interest and to his mother's complete horror.[13] At the age of six, moreover, he gave a boy he disliked a terrible "hiding," and the boy's mother was so distraught she hastened to tell Jung's mother about it, whereupon his mother is said to have made a "great to-do" over his outburst of incipient "violence."[14]

Although the dream of the underground phallus haunted Jung for many years, he tells us that he found a way to lessen his anxiety through different kinds of games, fantasies, and symbolic play during his transition through latency.[15] His childhood "games" had their point of inception in his seventh or eighth year. At seven, Jung says, he began playing alone with "fire," which is not uncommon for boys at that age.[16] He also engaged in forms of violent play that he could not remember, save for the memory of building a tower with bricks, which he says he "rapturously destroyed" with an "earthquake."[17] Between eight and nine, Jung "drew endlessly—battle pictures, sieges, bombardments, battle engagements."[18] Art was central for his *symbolization of violence*. When Jung was not doing his schoolwork, he appears to have been ceaselessly engrossed in such aesthetic activities.

Prior to Jung's adolescence, his resistance to going to school was suddenly supported, moreover, by an event that involved his provocation by a peer, who apparently attacked Jung on his way home from school. Jung was standing at the cathedral square, waiting for a classmate to join him for their walk home, when an aggressive boy apparently gave Jung a forceful shove, knocking him completely off his feet. Jung struck his head so sharply against the curbstone that he almost lost consciousness. From then on, he began having fainting spells. Rather than forcing him to return to school, Jung's parents decided to let him stay home, so he could then dream for hours and pretty much go anywhere he wanted, into the woods or by the water, and draw as much as he liked. At this time, Jung resumed his drawings of "battle pictures and furious scenes of war, of old castles that were being assaulted and burned."[19] He wrote, moreover, that he never became "angry" at the boy who pushed him down because, he realized, some diabolical part of him had set up the whole disgraceful situation so he wouldn't have to go to school, a split in his psyche that suggests dissociation.[20]

Throughout Jung's *Collected Works,* he speaks of individuation as a biological, social, and spiritual development—a development that begins in childhood and is made excruciatingly difficult at midlife because the process of Self-realization involves intense *suffering,* a suffering of the ego equivalent to agony. Jung's psychological understanding of the Self is quite different than what we read about in the New Testament. The Self is not only loving and compassionate and good, but also violent, evil, and bloody. Jung's ultimate symbol for this is the symbol of the crucifixion of Jesus. In his paper "A Psychological Approach to the Trinity," he wrote, "He suffers, so to speak, from the violence done to him by the self."[21]

From where we stand today, in the twenty-first century, following the frightful destruction of the World Trade Center on September 11, 2001, and the still smoldering War on Terror in the Middle East, solving the problem of violence remains a central human concern. Jung's life-long vocation, from the age of eleven onward, was to keep his eyes riveted on this central human problem. Not enough has been written about Jung's views on violence, particularly as it relates to his reflections about God in childhood and the creative ways he found as a boy to *spiritualize violence.*

Jung eventually found a channel through which his affective violence could become transformed into nonviolent action through rigorous feeling-toned religious debates with his father. "What about the omnipotence of God if he has to suffer the existence of a partner in the cosmic game?" Jung asked himself. "That question bothered me already when I was a little boy," he exclaimed. "I gave my father a bad time over this problem. I always used to say: 'If God is omnipotent why doesn't he prevent the devil from doing evil?'"[22]

In Jung's view, it is only through extreme pain that we come to experience the Self and know exactly who we are.[23] Why does violence emerge in young children and adults? Is there an instinct at work in the human psyche upon which the violent impulse is patterned? What role does personal trauma and religion play in constellating violence? These are tough questions to answer. Based on Jung's theory of the Self, the probability is that we each have a potentially *violent Self* inside, a burning, fiery, powerful potential, whether we acknowledge it or not, whether expressed or still, whether in the sunlight of day-consciousness or hidden away in the shadows of our moon-minds. I believe there is a violent Self teeming with possibilities within us all, and this Self of the Cosmos holds the keys to our destiny. Jung's Self-concept far surpasses anything that has been taught in university textbooks about its structure and dynamics, from the psychological to the metaphysical dimensions. The only theory that comes close to being comprehensive enough to encompass its vast extent is the theory of the Self proposed by James.

According to Jung, the reconciliation of the opposites in the Self must take place in full moral consciousness. Although Jung never wrote much about the origins of violence in human beings, he said that what is most important in our *auseinandersetzung* ("having it out") with the unconscious is that we take a moral stand in relation to the opposites. We cannot remain neutral with regard to human cruelty and violence when we experience it; we must judge it accordingly and hope, in our hearts, for a better world to come. Jung took a moral stand against violence with the most powerful weapon ever devised by nature and human: the mind of common kindness toward humanity.

When I examine the origins of the word *violence* I find it comes from the Latin root *vis*, which means "force" plain and simple. Sometimes, in analytic work with children and adults, we are called to take a moral stance toward violence if it exceeds the bounds of social responsibility in a person's cultural attitudes, words, or physical behaviors. Another question to consider, as psychotherapists, school teachers, parents, or spiritual teachers and guides, is not so much the moral question as an ethical one: How can we work together to treat violence when it has become a problem of excess destructiveness, or self-destructiveness, in a person's life or in our nations? This is a question around which my book turns.

A further question for the reader to consider is not so much how we may eradicate violence from our lives, but how we can channel it into higher forms of spiritual activity. For violence is a natural part of the human psyche, and it is, in its essence, ineradicable. To try and surgically remove this force from our lives would be to remove perhaps the most robust part of our energy-source. The main question to ask, therefore, might be this: *how can we help channel the impulse of violence into nonviolent action?* This, I think, is a central question of human life. I do not want to give the reader an impression that Jung was at all interested in prettifying religion by giving it lovely names. On the contrary, what he was most interested in understanding was the nature of evil in humans. That was the chief problem that was on his mind when he went to India in 1937–1938. For Jung being true to himself meant listening, not to what gurus had to say about God, but what the Self had to say in him.

Jung's life was, in a sense, the quintessence of what he had written.[24] The way he thinks and the way he writes form a unitary, Self-realized whole. All of Jung's ideas and works are what he called "myself." A book of Jung's was always a matter of *fate*. When something in Jung was touched and a gradient had been formed, his I, "myself," had to write. He had little choice in the matter. Once a decision was made, Jung had to bow his head to forces in the unconscious that were moving him in a creative direction in order to fulfill his destiny-pattern. In sitting down to write *Memories, Dreams, Reflections,* he realized that there were certain *objective problems* that called for closer examination. These problems were not purely personal. They were problems of fate, which he suffered from, and they each required an individual answer. Fate, in Jung's view, calls each person to provide answers to life's inevitable sufferings, due to the inherent duality between ego and Self. All of the outer aspects of Jung's life were merely, as he said, "accidental." Only what was interior proved in the end to have substance and depth and determining value. Religion was not to be found for him in the Church or in any organized religion. Fate demanded from Jung more than adherence to a creed. It demanded devotion to the inner law of the Self: *the voice of his personal and social destiny*. For Jung the Church was where creeds were organized; it was not the living Word of God, the voice of the Self that can be found only within. The Self, by its very nature, is *religious*. Jung's life-story, his memoir, was the Self-realization of the unconscious, the gradual coming into consciousness of certain transpersonal problems that pressed him to think.

Fate played the pivotal role in Jung's autobiography, so much so that his inner experiences must be read in light of the fateful knowledge he gained in the course of his scientific endeavors across the span of his entire life. When Jung said that all of his ideas and endeavors were "myself" in the Prologue to *Memories, Dreams, Reflections*, he means the fateful combination of the dialogue between personality no. 1 and personality no. 2, a dissociation he had first observed as a child in his mother, the priestess in a bear cave. The "myself" in his narrative is always a reference to the wisdom he gained from personality no. 2, the Self. The fully realized man he became in old age through the arduous tasks of his individuation was a result of the encounter between personalities no. 1 and no. 2. Responsibilities were given to Jung from the Self as unconscious *action-possibilities* that motivated him to speak up for what he knew, to vocalize the truths of his nature.

Jung was given over to his decision to write his autobiography only when he realized that the Self demanded that he submit to his vocation, to tell the story of his subjective myth. Without knowledge of one's personal myth, one cannot properly understand the Self. Jung was not writing an Absolute truth for the Aquarian Age, a new philosophy, or theology for some future creed, nor was he stating any final psychoanalytic theory of the personality as such. He was telling his own tale, his subjective truth as given to him by the Self in the form of a personal confession, which was best revealed through the language of *myth*. Such a story was limited by the subjective factor of Jung's being in the myth when he was writing it. But that is how it is for all of us who strive to tell the truth of our "language experiments" in life. Thus, Jung's readers must decipher the meaning of his myth and determine its significance for their times.

What can Jung's myth tell us about the nature of the human psyche today? How does his myth apply to Jungian analysis? Can Jung's myth help us live a meaningful life? How does his myth correspond to his psychology? Where might we begin to search for such a doorway between James and Jung, if there is one?

First-generation Jungians made many attempts to explain Jung's myth. Such attempts, as I see it, were limited, because they relied heavily on Jung's self-analysis, and they are mostly slanted, therefore, toward a European understanding of the Self. Jung was born into a Swiss family with a long line of Protestant ministers, and his personal struggle to found a psychology was also a cultural struggle for an understanding of God exceeding what the churches, or the philosophy of his day, could offer the West. Jung's psychology was a psychology of the Self. His calling began with his wrestling with organized religion. Nevertheless, his analytical psychology was less influenced by European philosophy than it was by the radical empiricism of James and the psychologies of the East. Jung's concept of the Self was shaped by his reading of Indian thought, particularly Yoga, and Jamesian pragmatism.

The first principle of an objective criterion for understanding Jung's criticisms of Hinduism and Indian Yoga is subjective: Jung's inner experiences must be understood first and foremost as the *prima materia* of his scientific work. We must examine his comments on Yoga in light of his inner experiences to comprehend how his psychology developed from the inner dialogue between his Western ego and the Eastern ideas that shaped the direction of his scientific hypotheses, for it was out of his inner confrontation with the Self that his concept of the collective unconscious emerged from dreams and visions. But the quest to formulate a theory of the Self for modern psychology inevitably led him to America and a representative of the American Mind. "I speak chiefly of inner experiences," Jung explained, "amongst which I include my dreams and visions. These form the *prima materia* of my scientific work. They were the fiery magma out of which the stone that had to be worked was crystallized."[25]

Jung was a stonemason. He carved a number of his inner visions and dream images in stone, among which is the figure Atmavictu, which appears on the front cover of this book. In this stone carving, active imagination takes place through an *auseinandersetzung* with his inner voice, which he says in the narrative is synonymous with the Word of God. Jung carved a number of forms from his inner experiences. Atmavictu is a primary symbol of the Self. I will discuss the figure's relationship to Hinduism next.

Jung spoke at great length about his first remembered dream of individuation from the age of three, the dream of a large underground phallus standing upright on a throne in a chamber in the earth. This dream haunted him for years. Although Jung told the story of the dream from a subjective standpoint, his objectivity at the age of eighty-three revealed a fundamental imperative from the Self to make its meaning known. The confusion between the underground phallus, Lord Jesus, Jesuits, and what his inner dream-mother called the "man-eater" reveals Jung's struggle to comprehend what, in ancient India, was regarded as a representation of the creative urge of Lord Shiva, the divine Lingam; only in Jung's dream the phallus had human flesh, and it seemed to be alive. It shined brightly, moreover, with an aura of numinosity over its head, and its eye stared motionlessly upward, which suggests it is, in fact, a consciousness in the unconscious with a lens of seeing, the open visionary function of perception in human beings, through which *openings* or doorways to the supraconscious may come. Like James, who was an artist, Jung was a visionary. Nowhere in Christianity do we find such an attribution of a royal phallus associated to Christ's character. The best amplification for it appears to be found in Hindu ritual, myth, and archeology. This dream was terrifying for the three-year old boy, not so much because of the naked nature of the symbol itself, but because of the cautionary words of his inner dream-mother: "That is the man-eater!"

We do not expect such dreams to appear in clinical work with young children in an ordinary population. In fact, in my thirty years of clinical practice as a Jungian child psychotherapist, I've never heard anything like it. What Jung's dream reveals is the extraordinary nature of his calling as a religious thinker, born into a family of nine Swiss parsons, including his father—a calling to link an Eastern religious symbol (*Lingam*) with a Western symbol of the Self (*Lord Jesus*). The dream of the phallus pushed Jung to develop a new style of thought that he called *psychological thinking*. This kind of thinking must be distinguished at the start from philosophy, theology, or metaphysics. A Vedantist reader might be inclined to associate the phallus to the *linga* of Shiva. Yet, to Jung's mind, the symbol must be seen as a *living thing* patterned by *instinct* (phallus below) and *spirit* (eye of consciousness and numinosity above), a uniting symbol between East and West, fusing the creative and destructive sides of the Divinity.

For Jung, the dream-phallus was a living symbol for the Self as the author of both good and evil. In other words, in Jung's view the phallus in his dream was not a symbol for Shiva, but the phallus, Lord Jesus, and Shiva were all images of the Self. In analytical psychology, metaphysical thinking is turned upside down. The phallus is not merely spiritual; it is sexual too. Phallic symbols carved in stone have been found everywhere around the world. Their first appearance starts in archeological records with the advent of shamanism. Shivaism is an early form of worship of this collective archetypal symbol.

Jung's inner narrative began, therefore, with a *nuclear image of the Self, a vocational imprint for something transcendent in his nature: the phallus with an Eye of God-Consciousness and an aura over its head was a symbol for the non-dual Self in the person.* Jung's storytelling was merely a myth, a narrative that was given to him by God. He did not say his autobiography was a Revelation for the world's future. Jung was more modest than that. He did not say he was presenting any new Revelation of truth for his times or for ours. He was simply providing readers with *his* understanding of his own truth, his way to the goal of individuation, a path of personality development that may be followed by anyone. This does not mean that Jung identified with the archetype. He always retained a critical distance from images of the Self that were given to him by God. "Like every other being, I am a splinter of the infinite deity."[26] Jung did not say he was Shiva. He did not identify with the Absolute. He saw that there were images of the Self that are inborn in each of us and that it is our life task to integrate these splinters of the Divine into our conscious personalities.

Jung asked himself this question while reflecting on who created his dream: "What kind of superior intelligence was at work?"[27] To be sure, some kind of *superior intelligence* placed a twelve- to fifteen-foot phallus in Jung's dream and seated it on a "golden throne" for the small boy to behold.[28] This superior intelligence is the *instinct for Self-conscious reflection in human beings,* the urge for individuation. In other words, the Self placed it there for the young child to see and reflect upon. The Phallus wanted to become Self-conscious in Jung in both its instinctual and spiritual forms; as an unconscious king in the underworld the image needed Jung to realize its meaning. The superior intelligence that designed the dream was the knowledge of the Self that was beyond the capacity of Jung's ego to understand properly at that time. Jung went on: "Who talked to me then? Who talked of problems far beyond my knowledge? Who brought the Above and Below together, and laid the foundation for everything that was to fill the second half of my life with stormiest passion?"[29]

Bringing Above and Below together into a hypothesis of the Self was one of Jung's central-most concerns during the evolution of his scientific ideas at midlife and beyond. His travels throughout America, Africa, and especially India played pivotal roles in grounding his understanding of the Self as a living symbol uniting instinct and image, body and spirit, violence and nonviolence, good and evil. Jung acknowledges that the problems he was called to take on for humanity, even as a child, far exceeded the knowledge of personality no. 1, the ego consciousness of the Swiss school boy. Some superior personality with a superior knowledge far surpassing personality no. 1 was operating in his thoughts and feelings as a destiny principle. This was the destiny of the Self inside of him. The Self spoke to Jung in a secret language of symbols and words from some superior knowledge that needed to be deciphered. Jung needed a method to circumscribe the image and make it Self-conscious of Itself in him.

The role trauma played in the shaping of Jung's consciousness cannot be denied. From Jung's point of view, *fear of the underground Phallus was at its core the most significant affect that thrust him toward consciousness of his inborn destiny.* The dream and its principal emotions of fear and dread forced Jung to think. The urge to become conscious was in part innate. The fear and terror in the dream was also from his inner dream-mother who told him to look upon It. Thus, Jung's individuation was to some degree evoked by his mother complex; to another degree it was evoked by the phallus and its numinous eye of Self-awareness as a potential in his own evolutionary makeup. What does this dream have to do with Jung's calling to construct a bridge between East and West? The answer to this question can be found in Jung's struggle with the reality of evil and the nature of God or the Self.

Jung was pressured with a moral and ethical problem that was given to him by his family, culture, and ancestry, a calling to make the dark side of God conscious for the twentieth century: "Yes, just look at him," his inner dream-mother said, "That is the man-eater!"[30] The twelve- to fifteen-foot phallus was one-and-a-half to two-feet thick. The little boy at first mistook it for a tree trunk. Jung was terrified upon awakening. The dream awoke him to a consciousness of God's dark side.

The personal, cultural, and collective unconscious all played parts in this terror, because the Christian God-image Jung had been introduced to as a child was one-sided. All he knew of God was that he was a Lord of Love. He had heard nothing about God's dark side, which according to Jung's analysis of Christianity, had been completely split-off. The *injury* in Jung's narrative was not only personal and dominated by the mother or father complexes, but also radiated outward to fears evoked by his six uncles on his mother's side, his father's two brothers and mother and father, all of whom were part of an unconscious *God complex of his Christian culture that was lacking an awareness of the Shadow and Evil.* To Jung, God had a terrible side. God was Good, and God was also Evil. Jung was called to heal the dualism in the Divine for Christianity. Jung's dissociation was also a cultural dissociation.

The injury to Jung's maturing mind was a trauma inflicted not by his parents or culture alone, but by God Himself. The God of Hebrew-Christian culture invoked fear in him and assigned to him a heroic fate. The tragedy in Jung's life is that he had to carry inside of him a "personal secret" that almost no one else could comprehend. We still struggle to understand his myth, to see where his religious ideas are connected with his trips to America and India. This is because Jung did not use the language of conventional religion in his scientific work. Rather, he spoke in the language of empirical psychology.

Jung's first experience of God was horrifying. It frightened him to the bone. It was from this transpersonal experience of a suprapersonal Divinity that his need for secrecy developed. Such secrecy was designed by the Self to protect the integrity of his vocation throughout his lifetime. This design eventually led him to become the great psychological thinker he was destined to be, the analyst of God's unitary nature.

One can talk about complexes all one wants in an effort to explain Jung's sense of psychic injury as a child and his secret, but such attempts only help us understand personality no. 1, the Swiss schoolboy, not his spiritual character as the cocreator, with God, of his destined vocation. His calling came not from his ego but from the penetrating power of personality no. 2: the voice of the living God of creation and destruction that assailed him and threatened him with a sense of complete ego annihilation from within. Jung speaks in his narrative of a sense of *splitting*, moreover, that has to do with the duality of personality no. 1 rather than any clinically definable childhood psychopathology. For instance, before he could even read, he pestered his mother to recite aloud from a richly illustrated children's book, the *Orbis Pictus*. This book contained an account of exotic religions, including that of the Hindus. Jung's inexhaustible interest in this book led him to return frequently to its pictures, which included illustrations of Brahma, Vishnu, and Shiva. "Whenever I did so, I had an obscure feeling of their affinity with my 'original revelation'—which I never spoke of to anyone. It was a secret I must never betray."[31] The experience of inner division in Jung's personality was partially resolved through his precocious intellectual curiosity in the religious myths of the world.

Although he was raised Protestant and was taught to have faith in Jesus as a Lord of Love, he always had a doubting reservation: "What about that thing under the ground?"[32] The secret of the underground God, hidden in the depths of the earth, marked Jung out as a *visionary*, a religious psychologist, even as child, who was carrying the message of a new myth for modern people, one that instructs us to embrace our transcultural and transnational foundation (Above) as well as our biological instincts (Below). Interestingly, what helped the boy make sense of his dream were illustrations he viewed and stories his mother read that included myths of India. This book was all Jung knew about Indian religion at the time. Later he would find the hidden parallels he was looking for as a European.

From birth to death, Jung was a carrier of a message of the *Paraclete,* the Holy Spirit, which makes room for all religions and includes a wide scientific worldview of modern physics and astrophysics in its scope. Within Jung's empirical framework, he later arrived at the hypothesis of the relativity of the God-concept, as it may be experienced transnationally in virtually all religions. He theorized that all metaphysical assertions are patterned on a *God complex,* operating transculturally in all societies. Jung's discovery of the scientific idea for which he would later become world famous, the *theory* of archetypes, arose from the dream he had as a mere three-year old boy, for *the phallus, he would later learn, is an archetype of the Self that is found worldwide.*

At the age of seven, Jung suffered from choking fits and had recurrent fears of suffocation. He interpreted these episodes as being related to conflicts in his parents' marriage, as the "atmosphere in the house was beginning to be unbreathable."[33] Interestingly, the name the unconscious gave to the figure during his passage through midlife (he carved the statue in 1920 at the age of forty-five)—*Atmavictu*—means the "breath of life," the creative impulse.[34] Part of the unbreathable atmosphere in the Jung home was the Christian attitude of his parents and uncles who believed the teachings of the Protestant church and its injunction that God is Love but who knew nothing about God's violent side. Although Jung was fascinated by religious symbolism as early as age four, when he returned to the pictures of the *Orbis Pictus,* the dream of the phallus pursued him through his latency years and pressed him to make its meaning known. At the age of ten he began imaginary play activities, writing little scrolls of paper in a secret language to a little manikin he carved from a ruler and placed secretly in his pencil case.[35]

These play activities formed a prelude to the role Jung would later play in his adulthood as a psychological writer, who took on the dualisms in organized Christianity and the splits in the Persian and Hebrew God-images as well as in transcendentalism. In addition to the little manikin, Jung also placed an oblong blackish stone from the Rheine in the little pencil case. He painted the stone with watercolors, separating it into an upper and lower half, representing Above and Below. This was the little manikin's stone. The play activities were all teleological in nature, in the sense that the enactments of his future scholarship were prospectively foreseen through his efforts to unite the opposites. The symbolic nature of the play contained the *telos* of Jung's future life pattern, a vocation by which his sense of purpose would be made known to him through writing. Writing became the vehicle by which the objective factors he was destined to grapple with for world culture as a psychologist would be made visible, with radical constructs about the nature of God, or psychological God-image, which included thoughts on Buddhism and Yoga.

Through the method of analytical psychology Jung enabled the archetypes of various religious cultures to speak through him with the formative power of truth, wisdom, and conviction. These archetypes were essentially ego-alien to Jung the child, not to be found in his Swiss or European cultural milieu, but located in deposits of the unconscious spanning various religious cultures of the world. He would later visit many of these cultures: Tunis, Egypt, America, New Mexico, Africa, and India.

God began to interest Jung in earnest by the age of eleven. Interestingly, at this time he became ill. A year later, one doctor said he was suffering from epilepsy.[36] For years, modern anthropologists thought shamans were epileptics. Personality no. 2 laughed at the nonsense that his symptoms were merely epileptic fits. Jung's superior intelligence knew better than that. The symptoms had a *religious significance*. He was suffering from a general split in his whole Christian culture. The healer inside Jung knew that the split in his personality was due to a religious problem, and his play activities helped him resolve the duality in himself. Thus, in adolescence, Jung arrived at the resolution of his dual nature, the remedy for the so-called split between the two personalities: "Now I am *myself!*"[37]

With the union of personalities no. 1 and no. 2 Jung came to realize his own inner authority. "I must think," Jung said to himself. Jung let the inner voice, the voice of the Self, have its way with him. *He allowed himself to think the Self's thoughts.* In such an act of voluntary subordination to the voice of the Self, Jung placed himself in the role of being in service to the unitary God. In one of Jung's most disturbing visions, God let a giant defecation fall from the sky and shatter His own church: "I saw before me the cathedral, the blue sky. God sits on his golden throne, high above the world—and from under the throne an enormous turd falls upon the sparkling new roof, shatters it, and breaks the walls of the cathedral asunder."[38]

If the Judeo-Christian deity could destroy his church in such a despicable manner, then this must point, Jung conjectured, to God's displeasure and hatred with what the church had done with Christ's revelation of truth. This vision revealed to Jung's developing mind God's reckless and violent actions on his own life and personal fate: his "original revelation" and the new disturbing thought sought to correct for the one-sidedness of the Christ-image that was without any apparent imperfection. Jung was not anti-Christian nor had he abandoned Christianity altogether. He was fated rather to speak unwanted truths to a theological elite and a mostly Western public who had become overly Christianized by the doctrine of God's essential Goodness. He sought to complement that teaching with a nondual understanding of God that he could not find anywhere in the annals of Western theology. In the Middle Ages he might have been condemned as a heretic. Yet, through a release of violent affects from the ground of the Judeo-Christian religious complex in an age when religious persecution was mostly passé, the phallic God beneath the earth, the creator-destroyer God, incited Jung's anger at the church. Thus, Jung became a post-Christian revolutionary thinker, with a new psychological truth of the Self, as a uniting principle in humans.

Looked at psychologically the experience of the unconscious side of the Christian-God complex led Jung to an experience of divine wrath, which paradoxically opened him to God's *grace*. Jung described this religious experience in detail from his adolescence as an overpowering emotion of *ecstasy* such as he had never experienced before. He asked himself: "Who has the impudence to exhibit a phallus so nakedly, and in a shrine? Who makes me think that God destroys his church in this abominable manner?"[39] He then says remarkably: "These talks with the 'Other' were my profoundest experiences: on the one hand a bloody struggle, on the other supreme ecstasy."[40]

This aspect of religious emotion—*happiness*—is, to my mind, the strongest evidence for the Holy Spirit's operation on Jung's life and spiritual character. It points to an authentic revelation of God in the form of the third person of the Holy Trinity. I must, therefore, linger for a moment on this experience in Jung's adolescence, the emotion of ecstasy, which accompanied his religious experiences. Through an infusion of ideas, affects, and images from the violent and destructive side of God, Jung was led to an authentic experience of the Self: "God was kind and terrible—both at once."[41]

Thus, the spiritual emotions that arose in Jung emerged through an integration in his mind and bodily affects of an image of a creator-destroyer Divinity at the core of the Judeo-Christian God complex, which had somehow been split into a pair of warring opposites between good and evil, love and violence, Christ and Satan, by his Christian culture. The influx of ideas opened his adolescent psyche to an infusion of *bliss,* which he never forgot. It confirmed for him that the Self is essentially nondual, a union of apparently irreconcilable contraries. In discussions with his father at this time, the "fear of God" was mentioned, but this fearful side of the Divinity was "considered antiquated, 'Jewish,' and long since superseded by the Christian message of God's love and goodness."[42] Jung never abandoned the Old Testament's teachings about the importance of the *fear of God*. God, for Jung, was not the loving Divinity alone. God was a paradox of opposites. "God alone was real—an annihilating fire and indescribable grace."[43]

"Why did God befoul his cathedral?" Jung continued to question. "That, for me, was a terrible thought. But then came the understanding that God could be something terrible. I had experienced a dark and terrible secret."[44] Jung let the dark secret side of the Self flow into the Christian side of his nature, and it *healed* him. By dissolving the neurotic defenses of an overly socialized and conventionally good boy, the Self became the author of his nondual destiny, as a bearer of the tension between good and evil and the agent of his healing. When Jung overcame his fear of annihilation by God, he found, to his surprise, that *bliss* came through—grace. Jung understood grace to be the product of God's wanting him to do wrong, to sin against his Christian conscience. For Jung's having endured such torments, he felt he was "either outlawed or elect, accursed or blessed."[45] We can see in this paradoxical encounter that the healing of his neurosis was accompanied by an influx of the Holy Spirit operating upon him, and it came through the doorway of his introverted thinking, his own authentic thoughts from the Self, not from outside. This Spirit was a curative aspect of the Divine and Its transformational capacity to alter his moral and spiritual character.

At this time Jung learned what true obedience was: submission to the fear of God and devotion to the tasks of fulfilling God's will, whatever they might be. It was not obedience to dogma or Christian doctrine that mattered to Jung. It was obedience to the Self that brought him grace. Grace and bliss are not what he heard while listening to his father praying. Rather, he saw weakness and fear in his father's doubtful faith in organized religion. Thus, Jung learned in adolescence that by courageously surrendering to the call of his inner voice, the voice of God, he could solve the split in his Western personality and thereby offer an antidote to dissociation on a global scale when it came time for him to lay down his psychological theory of the Self for modernity. "The play and counterplay between personalities no. 1 and no. 2, which has run through my whole life, has nothing to do with a 'split' or dissociation in the ordinary medical sense," he wrote.[46] In Jung's self-diagnosis, he was suffering from a *cultural neurosis,* from which the whole European West was also suffering. Nations were in search of a *remedy,* although the Western world and modern psychotherapy had not come close to grasping the significance of what this might mean for humans in Jung's day. In Jung's later thoughts, he hypothesized further that nothing mattered except fulfilling the will of God. This kind of submission to God, or the nondual Self, became Jung's remedy for the problem of duality. All of his theories revolved around this one core idea: *the idea of healing the world's split in the notion of the Self via a psychology of vocation.* It formed a *nuclear image of psyche* around which all of Jung's thoughts circumambulated: the remedy for life's sufferings consists of a process of submitting to the psychological guidance of the Self and taking appropriate actions in one's life.

Personality no. 2, the Self, infused Jung with a sense of evil and something sinister. Jung experienced God's thoughts as bolts of lightning: shocking, penetrating, forces of wildness, sent from the terrorizing principle of God—and yet these electrical rhythms also filled him with the blessings of divine grace when he submitted to the guidance of the Self.

Jung's later pattern of heated relationships with theologians were all prefigured in his earlier violent debates with his father during his adolescence. Jung was a solitary for most of his lifetime, an obedient observer of the inner voice. For him all religious statements were seen as subjective confessions of faith. Jung's criticisms of his father's vision of God revealed Jung's defiance and protest, as one who wrestles mightily with God.⁴⁷ "None of you know anything," he said to himself, referring again to the interplay between personality no. 1 and no. 2. I am not suggesting that the two spheres of his character were fully healed during his adolescence, but the splitting ceased in Jung whenever the inner dialogue was allowed to go on as a form of *fantasy-thinking*. God was thinking new thoughts in Jung, the aim of which was to show as a religious psychologist that the Self is as much loving as destructive, as much compassionate as violent, as much good as evil. Such inner grappling with the opposites did not enter the field of Jung's objective relations with theologians until much later, after the split had been repaired, but his attempts to quarrel with Christians about the nature of God began with his father and his nine uncles and continued to evolve as an internal dialogue with God until the end of his life.

The inner unity he once projected onto the Rheine stone, which reveals the unity of the Self as a totality containing Above and Below, shines through all of Jung's theoretical writings. There is nothing psychopathological about Jung's dialogues with God as an adolescent. To a member of an organized religion his conceptions of God might sound rather shocking, which, of course, they are. Yet they are purely natural. It's just that the average form of cognition in churches, synagogues, mosques, and temples have little inkling into the true nature of deep *psychological thinking* about God. Part of the duality in theology is a result of our religious education. We do not have images of Christ as a phallic being, for instance. Nor do we typically think that God *hates* the Church or wants to destroy it by defecation. Such thoughts are simply unheard of, blasphemous, really. Our religion in the West has been prettified with an overly loving portrait of Divinity. Jung's religious imagination was called to change this understanding utterly. It's highly significant, moreover, that he turned to India to amplify the meaning of his first dream. Clearly, he was searching for a religious foundation to help him understand his dream and grasp *why* it had been revealed to him.

We have to develop additional criteria to augment standards of medical diagnoses in order to explain the extraordinary phenomenon of the nondual personality that was constellated in Jung, an individual with a *religious vision* who was called by fate to heal divisions in Christianity, Judaism, and Islam; to heal the splits between Christ and Satan, God and the Devil, Allah and Iblis, Good and Evil. What Jung describes in his narrative is an idea of passing over into a state of mind where one knows one's true Self, personality no. 2, through grace; and by grace, as we've seen, he means ecstasy, happiness, or bliss. The ego's relationship to the Self as the center and circumference of all being has its archaic roots in the history of religions in the archetype of the shaman who can enter such transpersonal emotional states at will. Jung's mental states resemble the nonordinary experiences of mystics, those who are masters of the technique of ecstasy, just as Indian yogis are masters of the technique of bliss.

I suggest we simply cannot use ordinary conventions of psychoanalysis to judge or critique the psychology of an extraordinary personality such as Jung's. We need a new language to follow him here. "The symbolism of my childhood experiences and the violence of the imagery upset me terribly."[48] Yet *the Self spoke to Jung in violent imagery.* It was upsetting for Jung's ego to have to endure God's violent side, but if he hadn't, he might have remained neurotic, he says, and like the rest of us when we are living in fear, it is hard to know who we truly are then. *A religion that preaches sin produces a culture of fear, not joy, ecstasy, or bliss.* Individuation cannot happen in such an atmosphere. The aim of religion is to help individuals rise above fear, so they can begin to live out the true meaning of the "secret" hidden in their destiny pattern. Fear is what pressures people to join or remain in religious organizations, to cling dependently and desperately to institutions. Jung's father was captured by such fears of living an independent life. Jung had to develop a weapon of truth to withstand the tests of God by standing on his own solitary ground at Küsnacht and Bollingen. To truly fear God is to submit to God's ruthlessness and violence, to stand up to the arrows of fate, and become thereby compassionate in one's actions and intentionality, as a bearer of the message of peace. Even when Jung's father raged at him during their intellectual skirmishes about God, Jung remained calm and assured. He simply listened to him rage. But he practiced nonviolence and held his ground.

It would not be an exaggeration to say that Jung was wounded by the fierceness of his religious fantasies and by his father's outbursts. But despite his suffering from the inevitability of fate, as the son of a Swiss parson, Jung's religious experiences of the dark side of God led him to *feel* indescribable relief: "Instead of the expected damnation, grace had come upon me, and with it an unutterable bliss such as I had never known. I wept for happiness and gratitude. The wisdom and goodness of God had been revealed to me now that I yielded to His inexorable command." Jung then went on to say: "In his trial of human courage God refuses to abide by traditions, no matter how sacred. In His omnipotence He will see to it that nothing really evil comes of such tests of courage. If one fulfills the will of God one can be sure of going the right way."[49]

Consciousness of evil helped Jung to transcend and resolve the moral opposites in his conscience and paved the way toward his spiritual vocation through grace. In his narrative Jung puts forth a nondual vision of God as transcendent of good and evil. By allowing God to think evil thoughts through him, he opened himself to God's goodness and righteousness, which was bestowed upon him as the reward for his bravery. His courage was the surest sign of his fearlessness before God's terrifying aspect, and the spiritual reward, the payback, was bliss.

What gave Jung such confidence to express his religious convictions to his father without flinching? Where did his moral and ethical valor come from? Where did he develop the strength of personality to stand up to his fate? In addition to the world of the schoolboy, the "good" and fearful Swiss Parson's son, Jung said:

> ...there existed another realm, like a temple in which anyone who entered was transformed and suddenly overpowered by a vision of the whole cosmos, so that he could only marvel and admire, forgetful of himself. Here lived the "other," who knew God as a hidden, personal, and at the same time suprapersonal secret. Here nothing separated man from God; indeed it was as though the human mind looked down upon Creation simultaneously with God.[50]

This cosmic vision shows that Jung was well aware of the Self as a universal Divinity, where nothing separates the individual from God and the two (the suprapersonal Self and personal "myself") are coequal. Thus, from the protocols we can see how Jung derived his hypothesis of the nondual Self for modern psychology. It came to him first from that personal experience of an emotional quality of bliss in his own religious nature, as a function of God.

During communion, the pinnacle of Jung's religious initiation in adolescence was reached. Jung had expected something significant to happen, but nothing happened at all; there was nothing of the vast *despair* he felt in his own religious experiences, nor the overwhelming *elation* and outpouring of *bliss and grace* he'd experienced, which for him, constituted the true essence of God. For Jung, God was a dispenser of bliss. Through courage to integrate evil inside oneself and one's culture, bliss comes. If one can overcome one's fear of God (the fear of allowing God to think His own good and evil thoughts in us), then we can be sure of God's reward. Communion was empty for Jung. None of it had anything to do with the blissful God. On the other hand, it was quite clear to Jung that the man Jesus did have to do with God.[51]

To anyone who reads the New Testament, with an open and unbiased mind, Jesus was not only Good. This was a misunderstanding of the Church's teachings about Him. Jung clearly saw this. "Why, that is not religion at all," Jung conjectured after his communion. "It is an absence of God; the Church is a place I must not go to. It is not life which is there, but death."[52] Organized religion was, for him, a sham. Jung's sense of union with the Church was "shattered" then, and he suffered the greatest "defeat" of his life. Jung's religion—*by which he means his personal experience of God*—recognized "no human relationship to God, for how could one relate to something so little known as God?"[53] Here Jung parted ways with the theologians who insisted upon a doctrine of the infallibility of God as an anthropomorphic Deity. *For Jung the only true spiritual experience came from the Self as a gift of God's grace,* and that was a reward from the Self and nature. Suddenly it dawned on Jung that neither the Church, nor his family, nor philosophers or theologians, offered any viable explanations about the "dark deeds of God."[54] By dark deeds he meant the actions of God throughout human history, with their awful legacies of bloodshed, cruelty, violence, and war. It seemed obvious to Jung that God's creation had "been infected and thrown into confusion by the devil," and he was not about to adopt the accepted traditional Christian formula that the Devil, or Satan, was solely to blame for this, and that evil was a mere falling away from the goodness of God.[55] Theology left Jung lifeless and cold. Nevertheless, there were Christian mystics who truly spoke to him and a few became his teachers of what Christ truly taught humanity. One, in particular, was Master Eckhart: "Only in Meister Eckhart," Jung wrote, "did I feel the breath of life—not that I understood him."[56] Later, in 1920, Jung would write a brilliant chapter on Eckhart's Sermons in his book *Psychological Types*. Curiously, this is the same year he carved the stone figure that his psyche named Atmavictu, the "breath of life."

To Jung the school boy, the church fathers seemed to use their logic to try and "prove a belief" or "trick" believers into adopting "faith" in Lord Jesus, when actually, religion to him was "a matter of experience."[57] This accent on *experience* is very much in line with the teachings of William James and Indian Yoga as taught by Vivekananda. There was no doubt, in Jung's mind, however, even as a schoolboy, that personality no. 2 had something to do with the creation of dreams, and he found it easy to credit this "Other" inside himself with the "necessary superior intelligence."[58]

Thus, one difference between Jung's psychology of individuation and the path of meditation, Yoga, or prayer is that dreams hold the kernel of one's individual secret, the secret of the personality. Jung's understanding of the Self as a unity came from his first childhood dream. The hidden doorway to the Self was an entrance into the earth into which he descended. Jung's objections to the practice of Yoga for Westerners, as we will see, can be understood within the context of this one central idea: *The dream is a doorway to the Self in its personal and cosmic aspect. Everything should be done to protect the integrity of the access to this pivotal entranceway into the infinite psyche.*[59] One cannot enter into this door to the Self's supreme reality by being good alone; one must find courage to accept good and evil alike and, to some degree, incarnating the opposites takes place through one's inner work and in analysis. Yet prior to his discovery of a method for modern psychology, Jung himself had to suffer it out with his own conscience.

Jung's most "vehement" confrontations with his father took place between his seventeenth and nineteenth years. They were prelude for his future confrontations with the Catholic Dominican theologian, Father Victor White, and the Jewish scholar, Martin Buber. Also, with God Himself in his most controversial book, *Answer to Job*. In his *vehement* (nonviolent, really) encounters with his father, Jung saw that his father, unbeknownst to himself, was tormented and troubled by religious "doubts" concerning matters of his "faith."[60]

Theology alienated Jung from his father. He suffered another "fatal defeat" during such times of alienation. Jung saw clearly enough through their rupture in relationship that his father was hopelessly entrapped by the church and its theological thinking. At that point, Jung understood the deepest meaning of his childhood experience: "God himself had disavowed theology and the church founded upon it."[61] Jung's spiritual calling, his vocation as a psychological thinker, was to open up a channel, to create a vehicle, or construct a lifeboat upon which any person might be transported, with the assistance of analysis, to reach the Self through direct living experience. On the yonder shore, beyond religious belief and beyond organized creeds and schools of theology, the Self could be realized and meaning could be found through devotion to one's works.

Contrary to his father, Jung "could not subscribe to the tendency to move Christ into the foreground and make him the sole decisive figure in the drama of God and man." To Jung, this "absolutely belied Christ's view that the Holy Ghost, who had begotten Him, would take his place among men after his death." For Jung "the Holy Ghost was a manifestation of the inconceivable God."[62] This is the God that disavowed theology and the Church founded on it in Jung. It was the personal God, the Holy Spirit, that spoke through him. Jung had no other choice but to submit to its will. The other option would have been to remain neurotic and split inside. But thankfully, Jung listened to the Self and followed its dictates. To Jung Lord Jesus was "unquestionably a man and therefore a fallible figure, or else a mere mouthpiece of the Holy Ghost."[63] Later, Jung realized, through the technique of active imagination, that the products of the unconscious are *facts of God:* manifestations of the Divine will, coursing throughout the arts, sciences, and literature. God is not Absolute and cut off from humans, in Jung's view, but rather, a *psychological function that exists in everyone, a healing function that is spiritual at its core.*

Such a psychological position enabled Jung to arrive eventually at a conclusion that God in history is relativistic and that all religious dispensations have been an attempt to make the *God-function* conscious in human beings. God is a living power that exists in every individual.

By getting outside God, Jung proclaimed the relativity of the *Self-path* as the new way to walk upon. At the foundation of his myth of meaning and expansion of human consciousness, on the eve of the Aquarian age, Jung proclaimed the way to the Supreme Meaning. This was an important insight in the evolution of the world's religions, when the world had been searching for a new orientation toward an attitude that moved beyond religion toward personal spiritual experiences that might be scientifically verifiable. The vision of unity came to Jung at the age of fifty, during a visit to the Taos Pueblo, in New Mexico, as he reflected on the bloody history of the Church—both Catholic and Protestant—in the Americas. He saw to his horror the way in which Christ's teachings had been completely saturated with violence and evil and human bloodshed throughout the Americas—North, Central, and South. The vision of evil continued to unfold in 1938, where in India, it reached an apex in the Kali Temple. It was there that he found Indian spirituality. Jung's experiences in India helped him solve to some degree the problem of the splits in the three monotheisms, which have all been saturated with the dark deeds of God. He found that the only way to cure the problem of violence and evil was for all of us to take the suffering of God upon our shoulders and carry our own individual Cross, with all of its suffering. This really comes out in the narrative of his autobiography, where the accent on violence and blood is highlighted in his final years. Throughout the 1930s Jung had been wrestling mightily with the problem of the split in the historical Western and Middle Eastern God images. From 1939 until 1944, when he suffered his first major heart attack, Jung was subject to momentary bouts of overexertion. But Jung's trip to India and his heart attack changed him. At the end of World War II, Jung wrote a letter to P. W. Martin on August 20, 1945, that shows how very much his method is a psychology of spiritual experience:

> It always seemed to me as if the real milestones were certain symbolic events characterized by a strong emotional tone. You are quite right, the main interest of my work is not concerned with the treatment of neuroses but rather with the approach to the numinous. But the fact is that the approach to the numinous is the real therapy and inasmuch as you attain to the numinous experiences you are released from the curse of pathology. Even the very disease takes on a numinous character.[64]

It is important to add that the period of Jung's fights with his father over the subject of faith and traditional doctrines of the church coincided exactly with the establishment of the Parliament of World Religions in Chicago in 1893, where Vivekananda emerged as the most eloquent voice at the conference. Jung was only eighteen years old then, yet he was already rehearsing for his rightful place in history as one of the most revolutionary religious thinkers of all times. In the previous passage, Jung shows clearly why his psychology of individuation is so controversial today, even in our major teaching institutions. By "symbolic events characterized by a strong emotional tone" Jung means the inexplicable things that happen to us that are beyond our sense of willing. They simply happen. Events cross our paths that violently disrupt our ways of life, and these trials alter us. We suffer them out because we have no choice. If Jung's psychology of individuation is not focused on the treatment of the neuroses, but the approach to the numinous, then we have to ask what he means by *numinous*. This will require a broadening of the general understanding of the term. When many of us think of the word *numinous,* we typically think of positive emotions. Yet Jung just said that violence too is a numinous experience, as are terror, horror, and fear. By enduring the violence of instincts and their emotional corollaries, the archetypes, inwardly, grace came and with it the *healing emotions*—happiness, ecstasy, and bliss. Jung was exceedingly cautious in his word selection, for he did not say *Bliss Absolute;* he said that *the approach to the numinous is the real therapy.* One needs to be cautious, in other words, in handling transpersonal emotions. Only through careful consideration of symbolic events characterized by strong emotion can the transformation of consciousness truly occur in individuals. Numinous experiences can release us from the curse of pathology. We have to find curative ways to walk on toward our own individual Self-path—a path that can only be found through an ongoing dialogue with the inner voice, the Self within.

NOTES

1. Jung, interview in *Good Housekeeping Magazine,* December 1961; quoted in Edinger *Ego and Archetype,* 101.
2. Jung, *Nietzsche's Zarathustra,* vol. 2, 1251.
3. Jung, *MDR,* x, vi.
4. Jung, *MDR,* 50.
5. Jung, *MDR,* 8.
6. Jung, *MDR,* 9.
7. Jung, *Nietzsche's Zarathustra,* vol. 1, 61.
8. Jung, *MDR,* 10.
9. Jung, *MDR,* 9.

10. Jung, *MDR*, 12.
11. Jung, *MDR*, 11.
12. Jung, *MDR*, 15.
13. Jung, *MDR*, 15.
14. Jung, *MDR*, 49.
15. Jung, *MDR*, 12.
16. Jung, *MDR*, 19.
17. Jung, *MDR*, 18.
18. Jung, *MDR*, 18.
19. Jung, *MDR*, 30.
20. Jung, *MDR*, 32.
21. Jung, "A Psychological Approach to the Trinity," CW 11, ¶233.
22. Jung, *Nietzsche's Zarathustra*, vol. 2, 1368.
23. Jung, *Nietzsche's Zarathustra*, vol. 1, 449.
24. Jung, *MDR*, 3.
25. Jung, *MDR*, 4.
26. Jung, *MDR*, 4.
27. Jung, *MDR*, 14.
28. Jung, *MDR*, 14.
29. Jung, *MDR*, 15.
30. Jung, *MDR*, 12.
31. Jung, *MDR*, 17.
32. Jung, *MDR*, 22.
33. Jung, *MDR*, 19.
34. Jung, *MDR*, 23.
35. Jung, *MDR*, 21.
36. Jung, *MDR*, 31.
37. Jung, *MDR*, 32.
38. Jung, *MDR*, 39.
39. Jung, *MDR*, 47.
40. Jung, *MDR*, 48.
41. Jung, *MDR*, 55.
42. Jung, *MDR*, 47.
43. Jung, *MDR*, 56.
44. Jung, *MDR*, 40.
45. Jung, *MDR*, 41.
46. Jung, *MDR*, 45.

47. I believe the son remained alive in Jung for the remainder of his life, in an archetypal way, as an activated image or symbol of the rebellious pursuer of his own inner way in relationship to religious authorities. James must have come as a breath of fresh air to Jung in 1909, in a similar way as Eckhart did in 1890. Both emerged in his life at crucial developmental stages, when he was fifteen and thirty-four years old, respectively.
48. Jung, *MDR*, 47.
49. Jung, *MDR*, 40.
50. Jung, *MDR*, 45.
51. Jung, *MDR*, 55.
52. Jung, *MDR*, 55.
53. Jung, *MDR*, 57.
54. Jung, *MDR*, 62.
55. Jung, *MDR*, 59.
56. Jung, *MDR*, 68, 69.
57. Jung, *MDR*, 69.
58. Jung, *MDR*, 89.
59. Although Jung's comments on Yoga are covered later in brief, I will not elaborate too much on this subject in the book, except insofar as his views relate to James's views on Yoga and Swami Vivekananda in what follows. Jung's objections were both about the naïve application of the philosophy of Yoga and also the physical practices. In Jung's view, the two must not be separated. Oftentimes in Yoga classes in the West the asanas are stressed and also some breathing and meditation techniques. Jung was classically educated in virtually all subjects he was called to address, Yoga included. Therefore, he started with the philosophy of Yoga, the Vedas, Puranas, Upanishads, Bhagavad Gita, and Kundalini. And he also studied Vedanta. Vedantists teach that the physical forms of Yoga are of the lower type, whereas the mental types are the highest. Also, they caution that Yoga must be practiced with a skilled teacher. Therefore, Jung thought that Yoga must be practiced with caution, because breathing methods, such as pranayama, can induce states of mental instability or present physiological dangers.
60. Jung, *MDR*, 91–92.
61. Jung, *MDR*, 93.
62. Jung, *MDR*, 98.
63. Jung, *MDR*, 98.
64. Jung, *Letters,* vol. 2, 377.

Chapter 7

FIELDS OF CONSCIOUSNESS

In the middle of June 2011, I jotted down some notes in the margins of an essay that was written by Aniela Jaffé regarding C. G. Jung's thoughts on the subject of parapsychology, a field of research that preoccupied Jung for most of his lifetime. The focus in my notes was on the phenomenon of the Arab Spring, which was going on at the time and which served as the catalyst for the writing of my book *Spiritual Democracy*.[1] To my mind, the question then was whether a series of *waves* passing through the collective bodies of individuals who are moved to resist autocracies and speak up for democracy might have been set in motion by a spiritual principle in the human psyche—*fields of action, consciousness, and thought* in the World Soul. I had intuited something like this might happen long before the events happened in reality. My usual way of thinking about such matters didn't seem to work in this particular situation. Something more than an exclusively psychological approach was needed. A new nomenclature was called for. In traditional Jungian parlance, we generally speak of the collective unconscious as the objective psyche. Jaffé's opening chapter in *From the Life and Works of C. G. Jung* gave me a new metaphor.[2] The term *transpsychic reality,* used by Jung in relation to the subject of parapsychology, suggested that events occurring in the world might have been set in motion from a reality plane transcending the unconscious, a *field* Jung called the *transpsyche*. Calls for democracy were being released from deep instinctual forces in many people who were insisting on change within large groups in Tunisia, Morocco, Syria, Libya, Egypt, and other nations. Such transnational events might be structured, I thought, by an *organizer;* and this, according to Jung's 1948 hypothesis, may well be an archetype of order, an archetype I called spiritual democracy.

"What is the transpsychic reality behind the events of the Arab Spring?" I wondered. According to Jung's hypothesis, it was probably an instinctual image, a portraiture of a *typos* of some kind, an archetypal urge toward equality in the *unus mundus*. The egalitarian instinct for democracy has a goal, a purpose, a *telos*; it needs a channel through which to realize itself *consciously* in any tribe, culture, or nation. Spiritual democracy is its aim: the essential oneness of all religions, ethnicities, cultures, and groups. This is one of the many possible meanings of the movement we were witnessing at that time. In his essay "The Psychological Foundations of Belief in Spirits," Jung said he was convinced in 1919 that parapsychic phenomena are "exteriorizations" of "unconscious complexes."[3] Yet, he later added this in a footnote:

> After collecting psychological experiences from many people in many countries for fifty years, I no longer feel as certain as I did in 1919, when I wrote this sentence. To put it bluntly, I doubt whether an exclusively psychological approach can do justice to the phenomena in question. Not only the findings of parapsychology, but my own theoretical reflections, outlined in "On the Nature of the Psyche," have led me to certain postulates which touch on the realm of nuclear physics and the conception of the space-time continuum. This opens up the whole question of the transpsychic reality immediately underlying the psyche.[4]

By 1948 Jung added to his theory of psychic patterns of behavior in biology the concept of a "transpsychic" or *psychoid* archetype, which he compared to "the axial system of a crystal, which, as it were, performs the crystalline structure in the mother liquid, although it has no material existence of its own."[5] Thus, the psychoid dimension of the archetype of spiritual democracy became for me a fact of human *knowing*, based on a nonmaterial pattern intrinsic to human evolution that tends toward *equivalence*. This is the energy-field of human democratization I sensed during the Arab Spring, particularly in the uprisings in Egypt: Egyptian exaltation and joyous singing and dancing in the streets of Cairo, three years after Obama's stupendous speech there in 2009.

In his Cairo speech President Obama made it clear at the outset that he came to Cairo to seek a "new beginning" between the United States and Muslims around the world. He insisted that there can be no doubt that "Islam is a part of America."[6] What I find most significant in his speech is his insistence on the need to abandon violence worldwide. He used the Civil Rights marches in the US as an example of "a peaceful and determined insistence upon the ideals at the center of America's founding." He addressed democracy even more directly by saying: "no system of government can or should be imposed upon one nation by another," and no government should abuse "power" by suppressing the "rights" of others. He mentioned the issue of "religious freedom" and praised Islam for its long "tradition of tolerance." Pointing out the fault lines of Muslims, such as the divisions between Sunni and Shia that has led to tragic violence in Islamic countries, especially Iraq, he asserted: "Freedom of religion is central to the ability of peoples to live together," and that "Faith should bring us together," not lead us to senseless killing. Finally, Obama addressed the pivotal issue of war by stating: "It is easier to blame others than look inward." This *inward looking* is a psychological and a spiritual solution, and it was also a central concern, as we shall see, of James and Jung. Obama quoted from the Holy Quran, Talmud, and New Testament and then ended: "The people of the world can live together in peace. We know that is God's vision. Now, that must be our work here on Earth. Thank you. And may God's peace be upon you." Obama ended this speech by essentially blessing the Muslim world with a message of a new beginning of real world peace through spiritual democracy and nonviolence. By turning to the first principle of our Constitution of the United States—Freedom of Religion—Obama essentially put the United States on the map as the first democracy to promote religious equality as the basis of its political and economic liberties. This, I find, to be extraordinary in the history of nations.

To my mind events such as the Arab Spring signaled that the moment of the archetypes coming-into-consciousness from the *psychophysical* realm was on the verge of being perceived on a large scale. I had the opportunity to experience this excitement firsthand while I was teaching a course entitled "Walt Whitman's Global Vision of Spiritual Democracy" at the International House at the University of California, Berkeley, on the eve of the celebration in Egypt. It was delightful to witness. Many nations have predicted and known that there is an archetype of order that can unite the world—such is the symbolism of the United Nations.

Rather than any one religion serving as an endpoint for religious evolution across the globe, it seemed that the "miracle effect" of the psychoid archetype was occurring not only in events in isolated individuals, but also in the world—in the consciousness of individuals who witnessed the events on international television, or on Twitter, Facebook, or the Internet. Unfortunately, these waves of events were short-lived. The forces of oppression once again prevailed over such far-flung visions in the direction of transnational unity and freedom from dictatorship. The time for the archetypes' emergence on a grand scale sadly had not yet come.

I will turn my attention now to William James. Henri Ellenberger gave a rather sensational description, for example, of an archetype that emerged in James's life:

> As an example of an archetypal image released by an exterior event we might quote William James' experience of the San Francisco earthquake of 1906... For James it rather had the quality of an individual being... This is a wonderful picture of how a man experiences the emergence of an archetypal image. In William James' case the archetype was projected under the impact of an exterior event. More frequently archetypes are manifested in conjunction with events of one's innermost life.[7]

I will examine James's statements about the 1906 earthquake in-depth shortly. First, however, I must give the reader a brief picture of why I feel James is so pivotal to the field of analytical psychology today. While reflecting on the field notion in modern psychology, Marie-Louise von Franz noted that "The description of the 'field' comes originally from William James."[8] In another important volume, she added:

> The principle of complementarity introduced into physics by Niels Bohr also has an archetypal background. Although it is not known for sure whether Bohr was influenced by William James or whether the idea came to him quite independently, he later referred frequently to James's assertion that conscious and unconscious are complementary.[9]

In his book *Synchronicity*, moreover, Joseph Cambray quotes James as the forerunner of the notion of "fields of consciousness."[10] More recently, John Beebe writes in his book *Energies and Patterns in Psychological Type* that when Jung wrote of the "'functions of consciousness' we encounter the language of William James."[11] Moreover, in her chapter "The Spectrums of Emotion," Beverley Zabriskie devotes several pages to a comparison of James's and Jung's views on emotion.[12] I might add to this list, yet, for brevity's sake, I will now let James speak for himself from *The Varieties of Religious Experience*:

> The expression "field of consciousness" has but recently come into vogue in the psychology books. Until quite lately the unit of mental life which figured most was the single "idea," supposed to be a definitely outlined thing. But at present psychologists are tending, first, to admit the actual unit is more probably the total mental state, the entire wave of consciousness or field of objects present to the thought in any time; and, second, to see that it is impossible to outline this wave, this field, with any definiteness.
>
> As our mental fields succeed one another, each has its center of interest, around which the objects of which we are less and less attentively conscious fade to a margin so faint that its limits are unassignable. Some fields are narrow fields and some are wide fields. Usually when we have a wide field we rejoice, for we then see masses of truth together, and often get glimpses of relations which we divine rather than see, for they shoot beyond the field into still remoter regions of objectivity, regions which we seem rather to be about to perceive than to perceive actually.[13]

I pause here to reflect for a moment on some of the thoughts James put forth in these two paragraphs. First, notice that James treats the words *fields* and *waves* synonymously; these, he says, are impossible to outline with any definiteness. Fields and waves in the total mental state are, therefore, indefinite. They cannot be specified. Second, mental fields succeed one another and fade to a *margin* so faint its limits are unassignable. The fields or waves of consciousness are limitless—some being narrow, some wide. He also brings into this discussion the emotion *rejoice* when the field is widespread enough for expanded consciousness, for then, masses of *truth* can be seen together and we get glimpses of *relations* we divine in our field of mental vision. Third, he says, when such large glimpses of relations are divined, they can shoot far beyond the field and its margin to still remoter regions of *objectivity*. *Objectivity is, therefore, what one gains in remoter regions of the fields of consciousness*. James goes on to say:

> Different individuals present constitutional differences in this matter of width of the field. Your great organizing geniuses are men with habitually vast fields of mental vision, in which the whole program of future operations

will appear dotted out at once, the rays shooting far ahead into definite directions of advance. In common people there is never this magnificent inclusive view of the topic.[14]

Such passages reveal what the highest function of the mind is in James's analysis of religious conversion: the function of *visioning*. Fourth, connected to visioning is *vista*—a sky-wide view from above, encompassing many fields of mental vision in the Self. Here James describes what is clearly a function of consciousness, or a combination of functions working together, with *rays shooting far ahead in sure guidelines of advance*. By directions of advance he means *futurity, prospection, development*. Such individuals are about to perceive something objectively, something real. For James reality is in the future, beyond the margins of ordinary experimental psychology, and this is the magnificent inclusive view that James's psychology is after. Elsewhere, he calls it his theory of Truth, which is indeterminable: "The important fact which this 'field' formula commemorates is the indetermination of the margin."[15]

James's vision into remoter regions of objectivity moves readers to look beyond the margins of ordinary experiences. When consciousness alters into its successor, a fourth and Higher Self, above the Body Self, Social Self, and Spiritual Self, can be awakened: the consciousness of a metaphysical *Knower* above the Spiritual Self. The *Higher Self* is a term Jung introduced in his *Dream Seminars*. I capitalize it here to equate it with a transcendental factor in the objective psyche that is transpersonal, or above, the subjective sphere of empirical awareness of our ego and can only be known through states of psychic objectivity through the narrow doorway into metaphysical reality. Few people in history have attained such high levels of visionary consciousness in which the Spiritual Self is able to think and see and know scientifically and mystically at the same time what is just around the corner of our empirical awareness. James and Jung possessed this visionary capacity in complementary measure.

Before these two pioneers in the field of psychology emerged, there were earlier ancestors; one of the most important to James was Fechner, who introduced the term *higher consciousness*. As James writes in *A Pluralistic Universe*, "Where there is no vision the people perish. Few professorial philosophers have any vision. Fechner had vision, and that is why one can read him over and over again, and each time bring away a fresh sense of reality."[16] What made reading Fechner so fresh for James is the nondual vision he attained, his equal embrace of material and spiritual reality. "In few of us," James said in "The Energies of Men," "are functions not tied-up by the exercise of other functions":

> G. T. Fechner is an extraordinary exception that proves the rule. He could use his mystical faculties while being scientific. He could be both critically keen and devout. Few scientific men can pray, I imagine. Few can carry on any living commerce with "God." Yet many of us are well aware how much freer in many directions and abler our lives would be, were such important forms of energizing not sealed up. There are in everyone potential forms of activity that actually are shunted out from use.[17]

James makes it clear here that there are *functions* inside each of us that can be freed up from the excessive exercise of other functions. Fechner's nondual *scientific and mystical functions* were able to operate in a complementary way so that the most vital forms of *energizing of his total potential activity* were not sealed up or shunted from use, but intensified to the highest degree, through the visionary faculty of his mind.

Jung also noted Fechner's contributions. In his paper "New Paths in Psychology," Jung traced the history of the experimental psychology movement to Fechner: "The father of this movement was the dual-minded Fechner, who, in his *Elemente der Psychophysik*, dared to introduce the physical point of view into the conception of psychic phenomena."[18] In his essay "Depth Psychology," Jung wrote further: "With Theodore Fechner, the unconscious becomes an empirical concept."[19] In the former statement, Jung uses the term *dual-minded,* meaning Fechner could hold both the view of a physicist and an experimental psychologist equally.

Fechner's influence on the life and work of William James is simply incalculable. For this reason, I must say more about him before discussing Jung's psychology and its relationship to James. Fechner was a German philosopher and the founding father of psychophysics. He was a pioneer in the field of experimental psychology. He studied medicine at Leipzig University and later took up an interest in physics. By 1830, he had published more than forty papers in physics. During his experiments on afterimages and their complementary colors in 1840, Fechner sustained an eye injury after staring too long and intently at the sun. He thereafter withdrew from his professorship at Leipzig University, as well as from most social activities in the world. After three years of seclusion in which he wore a mask on his face to shut out the light and lived in a darkened room, the walls of which were painted black, his depression and physical condition became precarious. Near the end of his long seclusion, he had a dream in which he viewed the number 77, and which he understood to mean that he would be cured on the seventy-seventh day after he had been fed a dish of some strongly spiced ham cooked in Rhine wine and lemon juice that a lady friend of the family had prepared for him. Fechner says that his cure happened on the seventy-seventh day after he began eating this dish in small portions on a regular basis. The three-year period of isolation was followed by one of elation and a return to social life. Wilhelm Wundt (1832–1920), his student and follower, described his euphoria as having been transmuted suddenly into a philosophical concept, the *Lustprinzip,* or principle of pleasure, from which Freud took his term the *Pleasure Principle:* "Opening his eyes in his garden for the first time after his three years of darkness, he was struck with the beauty of flowers; he understood that they had a soul and this led to his book *Nana, Or the Soul-Life of Plants.*"[20]

Fechner returned to Leipzig University as a professor of philosophy in 1848. His psychological studies set out to prove the theory of panpsychicism, which maintains that the entire universe in all of its vastness is spiritual in character and the whole phenomenal world is the external manifestation of an immense panoply of unlimited spiritual reality. According to Fechner, the material universe is inwardly alive and teeming with consciousness and the earth itself is a living being with a soul. James concurred:

> The entire earth on which we live must have, according to Fechner, its own collective consciousness. So must each sun, moon, and plant; so must the whole solar system have its own wider consciousness, in which the consciousness of our earth plays one part. So has the entire starry system as such its consciousness; and if that starry system be not the sum of all that is, materially considered, then the whole system, along with whatever else may be, is the body of that absolutely totalized consciousness of the universe to which men give the name of God.[21]

One of the reasons why Fechner is so important to our contemporary discussions about the nature of the psyche and matter in analytical psychology today is that he posited a *collective consciousness* within his notion of the unconscious. This, of course, raises a question of what consciousness really is as an empirical datum of experience. Fechner appeared to believe that a higher consciousness is absolutely universal, and this universal reality is a superior kind of intelligence in the Cosmos, to which James ascribed the word *complexity*: "Complexity in unity is another sign of superiority. The total earth's complexity far exceeds that of any organism, for she includes all of our organisms in herself, along with an infinite number of things that our organisms fail to include."[22] This idea is central to what is being discussed in light of contemporary complexity theory. *Complexity in unity suggests a kind of high-level order in psyche and matter, an intelligence that Jung, using an alchemical term, called the* Unus Mundus, *or what James saw as the Many in the One* in his book *A Pluralistic Universe.* In this larger Fechnerian vision, we individual humans are merely the many "sense organs of the earth's soul."[23]

James advanced Fechner's theories to support his own views on religious experiences; in his analysis believers feel they are continuous with a wider Spiritual Self from which saving experiences flow in. Such individuals have had a *vision*, James says; they *know* and this sense of *knowing* is all they need. "One may therefore plead," James asserts, "that Fechner's ideas are not without direct empirical verification."[24] This is precisely the issue I'll explore in the chapters ahead, for it is on the question of consciousness that Jung and James differed as regard to the world of pure experience. Not only is this a question in this book on pragmatism and analytical psychology, but it also is a subject for current scientific research in the area of transpersonal psychology.[25]

Jung said that his scientific duty was to examine the condition of human consciousness. He viewed consciousness as a tool with which the unconscious can be investigated. But a question of whether consciousness is relative to the ego, or already exists in the streams of consciousness within, is a question for further analytic research into the functions, energies, and nature of the human psyche. "By consciousness," wrote Jung, "I understand the relations of psychic contents to the ego. Relations to the ego that are not perceived as such are *unconscious*."[26] According to Beebe, if anything, consciousness would seem to rise out of what Jung described in a talk with students as "the peculiar intelligence of the background."²⁷ By this Jung meant an intelligence of instincts made conscious of themselves through archetypal images, or thought-forms of experience that may be *known,* as James said, by their relations.²⁸ The aim of Jung's method of dream analysis, amplification, and active imagination was not only to awaken the various functions of consciousness at key moments in time, but also to use the imaginal faculty and scientific faculty in an equivalent manner, something Fechner, James, and Jung all excelled in and lived out in their own unique ways.

The methodological study of paths of access to the great sums of psychic energy or streams of consciousness passing into the psyche from the Self is a main question I will pursue here. For a long time, I've had a hunch that the way to untap the streams of energy in the Self is through the *doorway* of the inferior function. For instance, while I was writing this book, I got into the habit of planting and watering redwood trees in the hills behind our home. This physical activity connected me to my inferior function, which is extroverted sensation. In this way, I was able to perhaps feel into and sense what Fechner and James meant by panpsychism in their works. The soul-life of plants is something that was conveyed to me directly from my experiences of walking among ancient redwood trees in the hills of California; these trees, I learned, are living ecosystems with ancient roots. This weekly habit contributed to the strengthening of my superior function of introverted intuition, a connection Beebe says creates the "spine of consciousness that gives a personality backbone."²⁹

NOTES

1. For a quick overview of the meaning of this notion see Chapter 20, "Eight Principles of Spiritual Democracy."
2. Jung, *From the Life and Works of C. G. Jung.*
3. Jung, "Psychological Foundations of a Belief in Spirits," CW 8, ¶600.
4. Jung, CW 8, fn. 15.
5. Jung, "Psychological Aspects of the Mother Archetype," CW 9i, ¶155.
6. "Text: Obama's Speech in Cairo," *The New York Times,* June 4, 2009, https://www.nytimes.com/2009/06/04/us/politics/04obama.text.html.
7. Ellenberger, *The Discover of the Unconscious,* 706.

8. von Franz, *C. G. Jung: His Myth in Our Time,* 124, fn. 9.
9. von Franz, *Projection and Re-Collection in Jungian Psychology,* 64.
10. Cambray, *Synchronicity,* 42.
11. Beebe, *Energies and Patterns in Psychological Type,* 21.
12. Zabriskie, "The Spectrums of Emotions," 88–91.
13. James, *Writings 1902–1910,* 213–214.
14. James, 214.
15. James, 214.
16. James, 705.
17. James, 1125, 1126.
18. Jung, "New Paths in Psychology," CW 7, ¶407.
19. Jung, "Depth Psychology," CW 18, ¶1144.
20. Wundt cited in Ellenberger, *Discovery of the Unconscious,* 216.
21. From *A Pluralistic Universe,* Lecture IX, "Concerning Fechner," in James, *Writings 1902–1910,* 699.
22. James, 701.
23. James, 707.
24. James, 770.
25. Herrmann, "William James & C. G. Jung."
26. Jung, *Psychological Types,* CW 6, ¶700.
27. Beebe, *Energies and Patterns in Psychological Type,* 24.
28. James, *Writings 1902–1910,* 1152.
29. Beebe, *Energies and Patterns in Psychological Type,* 130.

Chapter 8

ERICKSON AND JUNG ON JAMES

In his book *Identity, Youth, and Crisis,* Erik Erickson made an initial attempt to sketch out a framework for a biographical interpretation of William James's life, based on his notion of a "protracted identity crisis" in James's history, coupled with the "emergence of a 'self-made' identity" within "the new and expansive American civilization."[1] His analysis examined the *unity* of James's *personal and cultural identities,* which Erickson believed were "rooted" in "fate," through a *"psychosocial relativity"* that included subjective and objective reality.[2] Erickson's idea of "crisis" and emergence is in alignment with contemporary Jungian thought about the nature of psychological phenomena—although his hypotheses need to be taken further toward a higher understanding of the human personality, a broadening of scope, which includes James's own authentic experiences of *vista*. Erickson speaks further of the "stubborn selfhood" that resembles "extreme individualism" (so typical in our rough American character), against a larger, more open, and spacious "surrender to some higher identity," which is reflected in James's *integrity*.[3]

Rather than seeing James's crisis at midlife in such a limited way, I will look at his youthful identity that was sloughed away as a dissolution of his old personality structures, followed by a more expansive *emergence of the Self*, which involved an enlargement of his consciousness to include the Spiritual as well as the Body and Social Selves. James himself provided ample evidence for such a view through his own theoretical formulations and self-understandings. In Murray Stein's brilliant book *Transformation: Emergence of the Self* we can see, furthermore, how transformations take place in people during periods of deep structural change that involve a more total metamorphosis of character inclusive of the imaginal.[4] According to Stein, Jung's self-concept created the basis for a linkage between analytical psychology and spiritual ideas of transcendence.[5] In a further paper, Stein asserted that Divinity, Divinization, or Divineness, *die Göttlichkeit*, "forms and shapes (*ausdrückt*) the self as a *coincidentia oppositorum*...The self mirrors the Divinity (at least to some degree)."[6] Divineness and the self-concept are not identical, in Stein's view; but as the ground of all human images and ideas of Deity, the self appears to be "grounded in and fused with Divinity."[7] At certain times of *transitus* in life, neither ego nor the subjective self of an individual ever becomes the Absolute but may, indeed, feel fused with Divinity. The apparent *fusion* may well be due typologically to an emergence of a higher synthesis of the functions of consciousness in a Consciousness of Self that transcends them, a superior *Intelligence of spirit and instinct* in the background. In some intricate way the Self, Divineness, and psyche are inextricably intertwined in a transparency of the reflecting mind. This mind is always limited, however, by its containment and supersession by the Infinite.

Erickson concluded his interesting analysis of James's biography with an examination of a series of *dreams*, which James reported while he was staying at Stanford University prior to the 1906 San Francisco earthquake. In his meditations on these dreams James spoke of feeling that his "I" "was losing hold on my 'self.'"[8] This kind of loosening is not atypical during states of liminality when old structures of identity are being dissolved so that a new image of the personality can soar, to use Stein's metaphor, out of the outgrown chrysalis.

The psychoanalytic understandings Erickson was left with after his close reading of James's account is that "in his eagerness for and closeness to transcendence, he ended by feeling that his dream had been dreamed 'in reality'—by another 'I,' by a mysterious stranger."[9] In my view, the other "I" that dreamed these dreams was not a stranger, but rather, the familiar big *S Self. It was the Self that crystallized the new identity structure* that was psychologically aware of *Itself* in psyche and Cosmos. James had already formulated a concept for it. He called it the *Spiritual.* Yet, the outcome of James's realization that Jung would criticize in 1921 as a mere "makeshift" did not stop with his thoughts in *Pragmatism*.[10] James's transformations continued to undergo successive evolutions, which neither Erickson nor Jung were aware of. The later stages of James's metamorphosis are to be found in his more holistic and experiential book, *A Pluralistic Universe,* which focuses on an exegesis and extension of Fechner's works on psychophysics to the field of modern psychology.[11]

In his review of *Pragmatism,* in his 1921 book *Psychological Types,* Jung zeroed in on a problem in James's theory of types when he stressed that James's descriptive terms "tough-minded" and "tender-minded" were "onesided and at bottom conceal a certain prejudice."[12] It seemed clear to Jung, from James's characterizations of the opposites, that he was dealing with the same types that Jung termed *introverted and extroverted*. To be sure, James leaned in *Pragmatism* toward an empirical attitude, which suggests his preference for a more tough-minded scientific approach to philosophy and religion, yet this may have been what the *zeitgeist* was calling for in America and Europe. In my view he followed this call toward its apotheosis in his final work. In *A Pluralistic Universe* we can see the emergence of a new structure of identity in James, the transformed self-structure that transcended his previous prejudice of empiricism: *the psychological united with the psychophysical*.[13] In his late work, James became much more attuned to a plural view of psyche and matter and was increasingly open to a more *tender-minded* view of the consciousness that may be found in the Earth-Soul, the environment, trees, plants, Cosmos, and all of Nature. I take these later transformations to be characteristic of the American cultural identity at its highest stages of spiritual evolution, such as we find, for instance, in the writings of Thoreau, Whitman, Melville, Dickinson, and Muir.

As we'll see, Jung's views on *religiousness* were strongly influenced by James's understandings of *devotion* to a scientific temperament, upon which the school of analytical psychology was forged. Extending James's thoughts, Jung wrote incisively:

> Instead of reverence for "eternal" ideas, the empiricist has an almost religious belief in facts. It makes no difference, psychologically, whether a man is oriented by the idea of God or by the idea of matter, or whether facts are exalted into the determinants of his attitude. Only when this orientation becomes absolute does it deserve the name "religious"...At any rate, absolute surrender to facts can never be described as irreligious from the psychological point of view.[14]

Following the earthquake, James was in a state of *passionate intensity* that resulted in a tremendous release of psychic energy: "James himself lived through the rest of 1906 on a cresting excitement, on a sort of spreading contagion of enthusiasm."[15] Thus, Jung was right when he noted in his analysis of *Pragmatism* that "we must once again assume that James was thrown off the rails by his emotions, as can happen all too easily."[16] Part of his being thrown off the tracks into the expansiveness of his *personal and national identity* toward a higher and more spacious *transnational integrity* may have been due, at least in part, with the writers whom James had been reading and citing in *Pragmatism,* for he quotes Whitman as well as Swami Vivekananda and Josiah Royce extensively, during his heated feuds with the Absolute. He was clearly searching for his own personal myth, which I believe he found in the years prior to his death. Jung concluded positively that "James deserves credit for being the first to draw attention to the extraordinary importance of temperament in coloring philosophical thought. The whole purpose of his pragmatic approach is to reconcile the philosophical antagonisms resulting from temperamental differences."[17] This reconciliation in philosophy no doubt helped Jung form his own understanding of the inevitable disagreements that can crop up in psychoanalysis, such as the typological differences he analyzed in 1917 between Freud, Adler, and himself.

NOTES

1. Erickson, *Identity, Youth, and Crisis,* 20.
2. Erickson, 23.
3. Erickson, 153.
4. Stein, *Transformation*; Herrmann, "Murray Stein: The Transformative Image."
5. Stein, *Transformation.*
6. Stein, "'Divinity Expresses the Self'... An Investigation," 310.
7. Stein, 316.
8. Erickson, *Identity, Youth, and Crisis,* 206.
9. Erickson, 207.
10. Jung, *Psychological Types,* CW 6, ¶540.
11. James, *William James: Writings 1902–1910.*
12. Jung, CW 6, ¶517.
13. James, *William James: Writings 1902–1910*
14. Jung, CW 6, ¶529.
15. Richardson, *William James: In the Maelstrom of American Modernism,* 478.
16. Jung, CW 6, ¶530.
17. Jung, CW 6, ¶539.

Chapter 9

JAMES'S EXPERIENCE OF THE SAN FRANCISCO EARTHQUAKE: THE OPENING OF A DOOR

This chapter is composed in four sections. In the first section, I will provide the reader with an overview of William James's experience of the San Francisco earthquake in 1906. In section two, I will look at the question of whether this violent shaking of the earth might have provided an experiential opening for James into a fourth dimension of the Self that he had conjectured earlier in 1890 was outside the domain of his empirical psychology. In section three, I will discuss the limits of empirical knowledge. In section four, I will explore the question that is central to my book's research methodology: dreams of destiny. I will provide a personal dream of my own that I had about Emily Dickinson to ground my discussion. The destiny dreams section will provide a preface to "Part IV: The Future of Analytic Psychology."

A Violent Shaking
In the opening chapter of his book *Pragmatism,* published in 1907, James pointed out that the esteem for facts and science had become "almost religious. Our scientific temper is devout... He [modern men and women] wants facts; he wants science; but he also wants a religion."[1] According to James, what had to go when *Pragmatism* was published was the notion of a theistic God, an abstract intellectual notion that had been localized to the various God-images of the world's religions, with their competing theological claims to what James was ever-fond of fighting against, namely what neo-Hegelians (such as his friend Josiah Royce) and other philosophers called the Absolute. Who was Royce?

Josiah Royce was born in Grass Valley, California, on November 20, 1855, the same year Longfellow published his epic poem "The Song of Hiawatha." Royce's parents had come out West to California as American pioneers during the Gold Rush era of 1849. Royce received his bachelor's degree from the University of California, Berkeley, in 1875, where he subsequently taught English, literature, and rhetoric. He then received his PhD from Johns Hopkins University and taught there for a short while before finally settling at Harvard to teach philosophy while serving as a sabbatical replacement for William James. James was on leave after the loss of his parents and his spiritual godfather, Ralph Waldo Emerson, in 1882; all three died in the same year. Royce remained a close personal friend of James and his chief antagonist. They sharpened their swords against one another, but never used them to inflict violence, which could have cost them their friendship. In 1898, James gave a series of talks at UC Berkeley, moreover, that launched the pragmatist movement on Royce's home turf in the Golden State. As I'll discuss, James returned to California eight years later to encourage the development of American philosophy, and it was roughly at this time that he coined the term *transpersonal* psychology. "When I departed from Harvard for Stanford University," wrote James in 1906, "almost the last good-bye I got was that of my old California friend B.: 'I hope they'll give you a touch of earthquake while you're there, so that you may also become acquainted with *that* California institution.'"[2] Several months after he arrived in Palo Alto, James was in for a shock.

After visiting the Grand Canyon and arriving in Palo Alto on January 8, 1906, James began a one-semester appointment at Stanford University. He was sixty-four years old and now the most famous American psychologist. At a few minutes after five o'clock in the morning, on April 18, the great earthquake of 1906 shook the crust of America's Western plates from its epicenter in San Francisco. The earth's trembling rippled all the way to Palo Alto. As James said in an essay titled "On Some Mental Effects of the Earthquake," his bed began to "waggle." The terrible force of Nature shook for forty-eight seconds, according to data from Lick Observatory. Then, it was all over, save for aftershocks and the destructive fire and panic that consumed much of the city of San Francisco and left many homeless. Most of the First Growth Redwood trees, the world's tallest organisms, some measuring over 400 feet, had been logged between 1850 and 1855 in the Oakland hills and sent across the Bay to provide wood for frames and panels, furniture, and shingles for roofs—most of which went up in flames and smoke. James's first conscious emotional response to the massive quake that rocked the Bay Area was one of "gleeful recognition of the nature of the movement." "'By Jove,' I said to myself, here's B.'s old earthquake, after all!' And then, as it went *crescendo,* and a jolly good one it is too!' I said . . . I felt no trace whatever of fear; it was pure delight and welcome . . . '*Go* it,' I almost cried aloud, and go it *stronger*."[3] This is a clear example of James being captured by his emotions, a risk anyone who attempts to approach the unconscious faces.

What is perhaps most curious about this narrative description of what was for many a horrifying event is the complete absence of fear and the delight James felt during the awe-inspiring shaking. As I mentioned in Chapter 7, Ellenberger described the earthquake as an example of an archetypal image released by an exterior event, with the quality of an individual being, a wonderful picture of *how an individual experiences the emergence of an archetypal image at an emotional level*. But, for James, it was more than an image of an archetype. The earthquake was a living agent, a conscious being, or power in the Earth that he felt personally called to write about in his narrative description as best he possibly could, given Nature's superior powers; the 1906 earthquake shook James into mythopoetic awareness of the vast immensity of God's being in the immeasurable Cosmos.

> First, I personified the earthquake as a permanent individual entity. It was *the* earthquake of my friend B.'s augury, which had been lying low and holding itself back during all the intervening months, in order, on that lustrous April morning, to invade my room, and energize the more intensely and triumphantly. It came, moreover, directly to *me*. It stole in behind my back, and once inside the room, had me all to itself, and could manifest itself convincingly. Animus and intent were never more present in any human action, nor did any human activity more directly point back to a living agent as its source and origin.[4]

Many people James consulted in the acrid city gave an account of their experiences when he interviewed them the following day. To him, "It," the earthquake, "wanted simply to manifest the full meaning of its *name*. But what was this 'It?' To some, apparently, a vague demonic power; to me an individualized being, B.'s earthquake, namely."[5]

Note the accent James placed on the word *meaning* here, an *individualized meaning* concerning B's augury, or a sign of what might happen in the future, before he headed West, an omen that had been lurking as a consciousness in the Earth. Today a modern-day Jungian analyst might understand such an experience of an event that calls strong *significance* and numinosity to itself a meaningful *coincidence, chance,* or *synchronicity.* For James, who lacked the concept of such a fourth principle in modern science, it was accompanied by a sense of *knowing* in the context of his relationship with B. It energized him, connected him to his inferior function of extroverted feeling, what Beebe would call the vertical axis of his spine function. It made him jump up straight up out of bed and filled him with an emotion of sheer *delight.*

Was James in his right state of mind? James himself said, in an 1896 Lowell Lecture on Exceptional Mental States, that "The prevailing opinion of our time supposes that a psychopathic constitution is the foundation for genius."[6] We have to accept the possibility, therefore, that James was in a transnormal state, having a mystical-scientific experience, characterized by strong excitement and *ecstatic* emotion. No doubt, James was a genius. Perhaps one of the greatest intellectual giants America has produced. Something extramarginal was happening in him, something he called in 1906 "transpersonal." In a footnote, while discussing Eckhart on Blissfulness, Jung quoted a line from William Blake's "The Marriage of Heaven and Hell," where the visionary poet writes: "Energy is eternal delight."[7] To be sure, in this instance, James was feeling delight—energized, alive, in touch with the eternal in his own finite existence.

For James the earthquake was the very confirmation he'd been searching for to disprove, once and for all, the Hegelian notion of the Absolute's perfection. It freed up the pluralistic hypothesis in him, gave him evidence by way of an immediate fact of his empirical experience. A couple years later, he wrote in a chapter "Hegel and His Method":

> The absolute is identified as the ideally perfect whole, yet most of its parts, if not all, are imperfect… It [the absolute] creates a speculative puzzle, the so-called mystery of evil and of error, from which a pluralistic metaphysic is entirely free… I believe the only God worthy of the name *must* be finite.[8]

For James the mental facts of his experience convinced him of the notion of a higher consciousness enveloping his empirical Self. He tapped into a center of personal *energization*, the hot fiery core of his vocation, something he'd written about earlier as "the hot place in a man's consciousness, the group of ideas to which he devotes himself, and from which he works, call it *the habitual center of his personal energy*."[9] This personal center of energy is what I've referred to as the nucleus of the *vocational archetype*.[10] To express it one needs to come into possession of one's own psychological truth, one's own myth. To what degree Jung's myth was influenced by James is uncertain, yet one thing is certain: they both took on the concept of the Absolute by storm. Jung has given us perhaps one of the clearest definitions:

> "Absolute" means cut off, detached. To assert that God is absolute amounts to placing him outside all connection with mankind. Man cannot affect him, or he man. Such a God would be of no consequence at all. We can in fairness only speak of a God who is relative to man, as man is to God … this urge to regard God as "absolute" derives solely from the fear that God might become "psychological." This would naturally be dangerous. An absolute God, on the other hand, does not concern us in the least, whereas a psychological God would be *real*. This kind of God could reach man.[11]

For both Jung and James, the idea of God was at the center of their sources of psychophysical energization. They were each called to give the world their own answers to the problem of human existence and meaning. As Jung wrote, "Consciousness needs a center, an ego to which something is conscious."[12] For James consciousness needs a center, a Self to which something is conscious, a Self that *knows*. The language may be different, for instance James's use of the word *subconscious*, rather than *unconscious*, and his preference for Fechner's views toward consciousness over Wundt's more sterile experimental language. Such differences need to be kept in mind. But if we can remember that they are different psychological types—Jung an introverted intuitive with auxiliary extroverted thinking and James an introverted thinker with auxiliary extroverted intuition—then we may be able to grasp their complementary psychological types, based on the variety of aptitudes and ways of knowing and sensing and feeling and seeing they each possessed. The key to grasping such complementation is the inferior function. As Marie-Louise von Franz asserted, "The inferior function is the door through which all of the figures of the unconscious come into consciousness. Our conscious realm is like a room with four doors, and it is the fourth door by which the shadow, the animus, and the personification of the Self come in."[13]

This comment by von Franz is not anything new in Jungian psychology, as Jung had already said the same basic thing in his 1939 essay "Concerning Rebirth," while discussing at an *Eranos* conference in Ascona, Switzerland, the phenomenon of psychological possession that can arise from captivation by the anima and shadow.

> I should only like to point out that the inferior function is practically identical with the dark side of the human personality. The darkness which clings to every personality is the door into the unconscious and the gateway of dreams, from which those two twilight figures, the shadow and the anima, step into our nightly visions or, remaining invisible, take possession of our ego consciousness. A man who is possessed by his shadow is always standing in his own light and falling into his own traps.[14]

An Opening of the Doorway

The metaphor of the gate or the doorway, however, which both James and Jung were so fond of using and that I am borrowing as a subtitle for my book, is actually found in the Old and New Testaments. Meister Eckhart gave special significance to this symbol of the gateway, or doorway, in one of his most important Sermons, Sermon number 35 in Miss Evans's English translation of Franz Pfeiffer's original 1857 text, which Jung read and which Eckhart began by quoting Jeremiah 7:2. "Stand in the gate of God's house and preach the word, declare the word!" By "stand in the gate," Eckhart said, "He means that the highest part of the soul should always stand erect."[15] The highest part of the soul that should stand erect in the gate according to Eckhart was intuition, which was, as it was for Jung, his superior function, or highest power of the soul. The Dominican gave special theological significance and preference to intuition as the highest of the soul's agents. Like Jung, Eckhart believed this gateway was found in darkness, which he called the primal Ground, *Grunt*, or Godhead. The gate was also the place of "primal eruption": "But the primal eruption where truth breaks forth and originates, there in the doorway of God's house, the soul should stand and pronounce and declare God's Word."[16]

What interests me here is the connection between James's emotional reaction during the 1906 earthquake and what Eckhart said, 700 years earlier, about the doorway as being the place of the *primal eruption* in the foundation of the soul. It seems apt in my discussion, therefore, to mention this passage here, as what James was about to put forth was a pronouncement of his own personal theory of truth, his declaration of the Word of God, as best as he possibly could formulate it in *Pragmatism*. For Eckhart, what was highest was also always lowest, and what was lowest was always highest in the soul; earth and heaven were interconnected by virtue of our callings from the Word, or our vocations. Thus, we can use Jung's theory of the inferior function to understand James's captivation and excitement by his anima, his standing in his own light, being a lecturer in philosophy, which may have made it difficult for him to see his own shadow—that is, the lack of empathy, compassion, feeling, for the sentient human beings who had just either died, were traumatized, or lost so many physical possessions, whether friends, homes, or loved ones. During the powerful 7.9 earthquake that rocked the Bay Area, 3,000 people died and 80 percent of San Francisco was destroyed. On the other hand, it would be an error to assume that James's apparent joy did not also have a place to play in his individuation of the higher intuitive and intellectual powers of his anima and Self, the breaking forth from the primal eruption of his theory of the truth through which he attempted as best he could to bring great Light to the world. In this higher sense, the earthquake to him personally was a godsend because it increased his connection to deeper insight, or Wisdom.

The question of whether the inferior function is the only door to the personal and collective unconscious is an interesting one to consider here, or whether there are many doorways that can be passed through via other functions of consciousness. James viewed consciousness as a "river" or "stream" of thought in our subjective life.[17] He preferred the plural view. Jung may have been aware of James's metaphor of the subliminal door, which I will examine in a later chapter, but the earlier source for the metaphor of the doorway seems to have been Eckhart[18]:

> The art of letting things happen, action through non-action, letting go of oneself as taught by Meister Eckhart, became for me the key that opens

the door to the way. We must be willing to let things happen in the psyche. For us, this is an art of which most people know nothing. Consciousness is forever interfering, helping, correcting, and negating, never leaving the psychic process to grow in peace.[19]

Jung dropped hints that it was Eckhart who gave him the key that opened the door to the way. Shamdasani noted the fact that Jung was reading Eckhart at fifteen, long before he read James. The symbolism of the doorway that opens up to the objective psyche is a recurrent metaphor for Jung. In speaking of the process of active imagination, for instance, Jung cautioned that the deepest danger of the method is a state of "godlikeness," in which an individual "feels as though he possesses a key that opens many, perhaps even all, doors."[20] In his seminars on Nietzsche's Zarathustra, Jung said further: "God is forced to go through that narrow doorway, the gate of man, in order to become God. That is the teaching of Master Eckhart, and that is also the meaning of the Christian mystery, that God first became man and underwent the most miserable fate in order to become God."[21]

For Eckhart the highest and most noble power of the soul was intuition, the "forerunner" of the other soul's agents: "Intellect is a matter of pure being. Intuition, its forerunner, goes ahead and penetrates to what is born there: God's one begotten Son ... Intuition, with the key of Peter, unlocks and goes in and finds God face to face."[22] Eckhart was undoubtedly an intuitive type, so intuition was the highest function of consciousness for him. Among the early German philosophers, such as Fichte, intellectual-intuition was viewed as the way to gain access to the Higher Self. Like Hartmann and Freud, Jung preferred the term *unconscious*, however, over *subconscious*, which was James's preference, and he wrestled for much of his career life with the notion of a "supraconsciousness," which he attributed to Fechner and the Schelling school.[23]

Typically, when people hear the word *supraconscious,* or *higher Self,* they think of the Absolute, God, or Ultimate Reality. Many of us have been conditioned by empirical psychology to limit ourselves to the Relative. Yet, I believe the Absolute may be examined scientifically. Consider the dreams that simply cannot be understood until later in life, when a dream of destiny is mirrored through events in a person's external life. During such moments the doorway between the Relative and the Absolute may swing open in the most miraculous ways and leave the question about the ego's involvement in the destiny pattern in a state of perplexity. At such moments there is only one possible answer: It was the Self that constellated this! My ego played the minor role, whereas the major role, the predestined part, was orchestrated by the Self.

I believe there must be an agent in the soul that perceives events in time from a place of timelessness or trans-temporality in the unconscious that can be foreseen but not directly known. There are places of knowing that the soul can enter into during sleep that are so deep that non-ordinary visioning becomes possible. Destiny is communicated to us through the doorways in the unconscious, not in images, but in lightening-flashes of intuition, which are so rapid the ego cannot convey them in words.

On the Limits of Empirical Knowledge
In a section of the chapter "The Self," in *Psychology: A Briefer Course,* James speaks of the I as "the *Thinker*; and the question immediately comes up, what is the thinker?"[24] Later he draws a line of distinction between the I and the Me. The problem of who the transcendental *Knower* is, James says, is a "metaphysical problem," and psychology as a natural science needs take no account of its source and origin.[25] This kind of demarcation of the limits of empirical psychology sounds very much like the epistemology of Jung.

Jung knew that when the going gets tough on the way of individuation, it is the Self that becomes the guiding factor, and letting go of oneself is the best way forward. As he wrote in "Introduction to the Religious and Psychological Problems of Alchemy," "The right way to wholeness is made up, unfortunately, of fateful detours and wrong turnings. It is a *longissima via,* not straight but snakelike, a path that unites the opposites in the manner of the guiding caduceus, a path whose labyrinthine twists and turns are not lacking in terrors."[26] This is why we need a resilient ego to endure life to the end, because if we are not careful, our emotions can get the better of us. Getting a handle on wild emotions can be life-preserving and life-saving. This is why Jung placed such a great importance on the integration of the shadow and on healing the split in individuals, groups, and nations. Fateful detours typically come to us from outside events that are beyond our control. During such times we may fall into hopelessness or despair. When great loss comes, death approaches us with its messages of doom. We panic. We may get anxious or depressed. We cannot predict when death will come, any more than we can predict the weather patterns a year or even a month in advance. Yet regardless of any outer blows of fate that may cross our paths, if we stay true to our destiny, then we will fulfill our calling, our vocation to wholeness, in the end.

Dreams of Destiny
Destiny dreams come from the deepest strata of our being, our nerves, muscles, organs, and blood—our entire Body Self, not just our brains. They appear to come from the deepest urgings of the "inner voice" within us. They call us to take creative actions in the world. By infusing us with energy and determination, they may lead us into unintended difficulties and entanglements, good fortune or bad fortune. But regardless of how difficult it is to understand them pragmatically, it is our responsibility to try to do so. What destiny dreams intend, in an external way, may be clarified through a series of miraculous coincidences that are unsought, unexpected, and often seem uncanny. Such signs are pointers to our destinations. For our destinations are not usually reached through causal means; it is only revealed through clarity of mind or careful consideration over a long period. *Dreams of destiny give us a picture of Reality, a portrait of our Self-path, which we can trust.*

Typically, one dream of destiny cannot tell us much about who we really are. More may be learned by studying them in an extended series over time—over two or three decades, for instance. They tend to come in waves, or energy-vectors, through doorways in the collective psyche, with the aim of awakening us. Their timing is mysteriously patterned by what physicists' call "the *complementarity of energy and time.*"[27] Energy is an important concept to consider psychologically here. Too often we lose our energy, momentum, or motivation when fate dupes us. We fall apart, give way to destructive emotions, succumb to despair, hopelessness, or lose faith in the Universe. But the vectors of destiny cannot be destroyed. They are Universal. Like the Self, destiny's energies are indestructible. We can destroy the ego, or even the body, but the routes of the Self cannot be destroyed. They are the eternal trajectory elements that forever beckon us onward toward greater and greater sums of consciousness. Since "indestructible energy" in quantum physics and the *"appearance of energy in space and time"* tend to *"correspond to two contradictory (complementary) aspects of reality,"* then a qualitative analysis of destiny dreams might demonstrate empirically that matter and spirit are one and the same reality.[28]

In 1995 I was sent by my analyst, Donald Sander, to see the analyst and author John Beebe for editorial consultation about an essay I'd written on Emily Dickinson. When I first entered John's office, I stepped through a doorway that felt numinous to me. Dickinson spoke of a doorway inside herself, where she wrote wild poetry, and a literal door to her room in her Homestead in Amherst, which she sometimes kept ajar. Dickinson had a number of destiny dreams I write about in my book *Emily Dickinson: A Medicine Woman for Our Times*. My destiny to write about her began in Don's office. It was crystallized further when I encountered John Beebe. When I told him about my paper, he entered a reverie and began to recite by memory: "Dare you see a Soul *at the white heat?* / Then crouch within the door—" (J 365).[29] Where does our motivation to write come from? I wondered. What is its source? One answer that came to me is that it comes from the Self. Another is that it might come through a doorway in the supraconscious. Both might true I believe. But I must qualify this hypothesis by adding, in my case, the words "American Self."

When we ask ourselves the question, "What is the meaning of a destiny dream in the context of my life as a whole?", we may be surprised by answers that arise from the unconscious and synchronicities that may emerge along the way; such coincidences emit a phosphorescence that is unmistakable. An event like the one about my calling to write on Emily Dickinson suggests that entanglement happens for unknown reasons. One hypothesis is that the Higher Self orchestrates it.

I believe that destiny dreams (such as Jung's dream of the cave with two skulls) need to be carefully studied from a theoretical and pragmatic standpoint, only then can they show us *why* they are so important to the overall outworking of our lives. They may instruct us, for instance, on ways we may take creative action in the world, *right now*, and may be of some lasting benefit to future generations in an increasingly complex global society. Destiny dreams contain an absolute foreknowledge that is inborn in the psyche, a certainty in a goal, or our journey's end. They tell us that we are all going somewhere. Whether we are aware of it or not, we all have a visionary purpose in life, a calling. Destiny dreams are facts of the environment, Nature, and the World in which we live. To penetrate the meaning of destiny dreams, it is best to start with ourselves. We must make a careful record of the facts of our own dreams. Jung gave us a language for how to analyze our dreams in his *Dream Seminars,* in "Symbols and the Interpretation of Dreams" in the popular book *Man and His Symbols,* and in his semi-autobiographical book, *Memories, Dreams, Reflections.* Let me give you an example from my own life. On December 19, 2002, nine days after Emily Dickinson's birthday, I had the following dream:

> *I find myself at a university campus in Amherst, Massachusetts. My wife Lori and I have gone to Amherst to get a recommendation from a Dickinson scholar-professor there for my application to the San Francisco Jung Institute's analytic training program. I ask him personally for a copy of the recommendation. When we meet, he tells us he has recommended me highly, and he thinks I should get into the Institute. He is very encouraging and supportive. Then, Lori and I revisit the steps at the University where Emily Dickinson once walked. I see many women there, all in pairs, having animated conversations about her. I go with Lori and others (mostly women) on a tour to trace the sacred places where Emily once stepped. We enter some old buildings and the guide (a female Dickinson scholar) talks about the meaning of the "Step" and "Door" as metaphors for the transport in Dickinson's art. Suddenly a flow of ideas come rushing into me as I step on one of the sacred steps. One of them in particular, a marble step, is one Emily had definitely stood upon; it is white, like alabaster. I realize in the dream I suddenly know more about Emily than our guide knows, or the pairs of women who are having lunch and animated discussions about her there, and that I have something important to teach them. This is what the scholar-professor had seen in my work, and this is what he remarked on in his recommendations to the analytic training program. I recall that he'd written something in his recommendations about my Jungian commentaries on the meaning of Dickinson's words: the "Soul's Superior instants / Occur to Her alone." "This absolute knowledge," I say, before I awaken, "the knowledge of the supraconscious is difficult to gain and inner than the bone."*

By "Soul's Superior instants," I take Dickinson to mean moments in time when *supraconscious* knowledge (Jung called it *transconscious*[30] to distinguish it from the Vedic concept of the supraconscious) is transmitted to dream-ego-consciousness. It comes in through my soul via a doorway of the Self, during dreaming sleep. In Jungian terms this is a doorway to the objective psyche. The dream statement that supraconscious knowledge is *difficult to gain and inner than the bone* is a conjunctive sentence, constructed from two of Emily Dickinson's poems: "Superiority to Fate" (J 1081) and "Of all the Sounds dispatched abroad" (J 321). The latter poem speaks of an inner "Inheritance" that comes to us by way of individuation and evolutionary biology, in other words through instinctive knowing. One doesn't gain this kind of Superiority to Fate, she says in the poem, one earns it, like Emily did, through right effort, right work, and right toil. Furthermore, supraconsciousness[31] in which the soul's superior states occur in an instant, in the Now, is *inner than the bone*, which means psychologically that hereditary knowledge is inborn, transtemporal, eternal, and innate. It is in the carbon, DNA, bone marrow, life-blood, or wisdom-Body. On the other hand, it may also be outside the body in a sphere that is never completely knowable because, as James says, "*The simplest thing, therefore, if we are to assume the existence of a stream of consciousness at all, would be to suppose that things known together are known in single pulses of that stream.*"[32] Knowledge of destiny, when looked at scientifically, therefore, is biological knowledge and spiritual knowledge interfused: material and spiritual at once, pulses of a single stream. No distinction. That I would get a recommendation from an inner Dickinson scholar for my application to analytic training shows how much I value the kind of psychobiography I wrote in my book about her and in this book's brief historical sketches on James and Jung.

Notes

1. James, *William James: Writings 1902–1910*, 492.
2. James, 1215. It is unclear who B. was in James's narrative description; historians have not answered this puzzling question. I'm left to conjecture here, based on my psychobiography of James, that it was actually Josiah Royce at Harvard, since James so often used him as a springboard and foil for his philosophical and psychological arguments.
3. James, 1215.
4. James, 1216.

5. James, 1216.
6. Taylor, *William James on Exceptional Mental States*, 149.
7. Jung, *Psychological Types,* CW 6, ¶422, fn. 159.
8. James, *Writings 1902–1910,* 686–687.
9. James, 183.
10. Herrmann, *William Everson: The Shaman's Call.*
11. Jung, "The Relations between the Ego and the Unconscious," CW 7, ¶394, fn. 6.
12. Jung, "Conscious, Unconscious, and Individuation," CW 9i, ¶506.
13. Von Franz and Hillman, *Lectures on Jung's Typology,* 67.
14. Jung, "Concerning Rebirth, CW 9i, ¶222.
15. Walshe, *The Complete Mystical Works of Meister Eckhart,* 207.
16. Walshe, 208.
17. James, *William James: Writings 1878–1899,* 159.
18. Let me explore the James's and Jung's connections through Eckhart further: Royce published *Studies of Good and Evil: A Series of Essays upon Problems of Philosophy and Life* in 1898. Chapter 10 of this book included a study on Meister Eckhart. James read this book and quoted a short passage from Eckhart's sermons and several from Royce's *Studies of Good and Evil*, footnoted in *Varieties of Religious Experience* in the chapter on "Mysticism" (James, *Writings 1902–1910,* 376). James then discussed Jacob Boehme and Angelus Silesius, who Jung also quoted. James did not discuss Royce's work on Eckhart at any depth, however, such as Jung does in *Psychological Types.* Eckhart is the missing link, nevertheless, between James and Royce and Jung and James. Eckhart was the greatest thinker of his Age (1260–1328). He is certain to have given James and Royce a greater vision of knowledge, as he did Jung, through his remarkable powers of intellect and intuition, for his fields of wider seeing into the depths and heights of Self are, in essence, nondual. It was in Eckhart's theology of the Word and his brilliant scholasticism as a professor at the University of Paris, in fact, that the division between the subjective self and objective Self was transcended in a sky-wide firmament of intellectual vision that opened the door to a unity of understanding between Judaism, Christianity, Islam, Hinduism, Buddhism, and Vedanta in modern and post-modern studies in comparative religions.
19. Jung, "Commentary on the Secret of the Golden Flower," CW 13, ¶30.
20. Jung, "The Relations between the Ego and the Unconscious," CW 7, ¶224.
21. Jung, *Nietzsche's Zarathustra,* vol. 1, 723.
22. Pfeiffer, *Meister Eckhart,* vol. 1, 74–75.
23. Jung, "On the Structure and Dynamics of the Psyche," CW 8, ¶352.

24. James, William James: *Writings 1878–1899*, 191.
25. James, 208.
26. Jung, "Introduction to the Religious and Psychological Problems of Alchemy," CW 12, ¶6.
27. Wolfgang Pauli cited in Meier, *Atom and Archetype*, 184.
28. Pauli cited in Meier, 185.
29. For a full analysis of the poem, see Herrmann, *Emily Dickinson*, 206. The *J* stands for the Thomas Johnson edition of *The Complete Poems of Emily Dickinson*, originally published in 1955.
30. For a more detailed discussion, see Chapter 38, "The Transpsyche."
31. I will return to this discussion in Chapter 44.
32. James, William James: Writings *1878–1899,* 195.

Chapter 10

Movement Toward a Psychological Attitude

In 1997, I published a two-part essay in *The San Francisco Jung Institute Library Journal* that I titled "The Visionary Artist: A Problem for Jungian Literary Criticism." Most helpful to me in writing that article were some observations from a personal conversation I'd had with the late San Francisco analyst Joseph L. Henderson. Readers of this book may be aware that in 1980, Henderson published a book called *Cultural Attitudes in Psychological Perspective* where he asserted that *all true philosophic attitudes arise from the archetype of the shaman.*[1] When I first read Henderson's book in 1997, I enjoyed it immensely. It gave me an understanding of how a Jungian analyst is called today to remain sensitive to different shifts in attitude in analytic conversation and how a psychological attitude can hold differing perspectives with diversity.

When we attempt to understand the problem of Jung as a religious philosopher, it might be difficult to grasp at first the great complexity of this issue, due to Jung's mistaken cultural identities. We might at first, for instance, be tempted to conjecture that it was Jung's reading of German philosophers and poets, such as Kant, Schopenhauer, Hartmann, Goethe, Schiller, Nietzsche, that helped Jung break away from the one-sided and reductively conceived psychology of Freud to found his own school of analytical psychology. Based on my research into the writings of James, I don't think this is an accurate way to portray Jung's influences. I believe a primary source for the philosophic and psychological attitudes Jung maintained throughout his professional lifetime was actually less European than it was quintessentially American. William James cannot be excluded from his gallery of influences. Here, I must admit that my hunch is mostly speculative, for it is a difficult hypothesis to substantiate based on available historical data.

Yet, seldom is the large impact of James's psychology on Jung's analytic attitude really noted. In 1892, *The Principles of Psychology* was abridged and rewritten for a one-volume text, *Psychology: Briefer Course*. In the second paragraph of his introductory chapter to that shortened text, James said explicitly: "Psychology is to be treated as a natural science in this book. This requires a word of commentary. Most thinkers have a faith that at bottom there is but one Science of all things, and that until all is known, no one thing can be completely known. Such a science, if realized, would be Philosophy."[2] In Chapter 12, moreover, James spoke of "The Self" as being made up of several *constituents*: a material me, a social me, and spiritual me—the Body Self, Social Self, and Spiritual Self of which I've spoken earlier. "By 'spiritual me,'" he said, "so far as it belongs to the empirical self, I mean no one of my passing states of consciousness. I mean rather the entire collection of my states of consciousness, my psychic faculties and dispositions taken concretely."[3] These three selves are arranged in a hierarchical scale, according to James, with "*the bodily me at the bottom, the spiritual me at the top, and the extra-corporeal material selves and the various social selves between.*"[4] This hierarchical ordering of the various selves into an ascending order (Material/Body, Social, and Spiritual), with the bodily self at the bottom and the supremely precious Self at the top—and not one mention of sex in the index of this 444 page book!—would surely have been an anathema to Freud. Not to Jung, however, who was about to posit the concept of the spiritualization of the libido in *Wandlüngen*.

We have Eugene Taylor and Sonu Shamdasani to thank moreover for having made significant headway in providing a Jamesian view of Jung's work.[5] And there is also the unpublished chapter on Theodore Flournoy and William James that never made it into C. G. Jung's autobiography, *Memories, Dreams, Reflections*. This chapter will show how vitally important James actually was in mediating between the young man Jung, who had lost his soul through the rigors of experimental psychology inaugurated by Wundt in 1902, and midlife Jung, whose mature conversations with Philemon took place in 1915 once his soul was rediscovered. This omitted chapter was curiously supposed to have been inserted directly after Jung's chapter on Freud, but the editors of *MDR* and his publisher decided for unclear reasons to leave it out. The Countway Library of Medicine (CLM) manuscript is at Harvard Medical School and is currently available for research. I had, by a stroke of good luck, an opportunity to make a close reading of it, which I will outline for the reader in my own words later in Chapter 33, "The Influence of William James."

Shamdasani, who did the yeoman's work of researching this text, informs us that in the CLM manuscript, Jung credited Flournoy and James with providing the methodological presuppositions that helped him formulate some of the intellectual ideas that contributed to the founding of his school of analytical psychology. In the manuscript, Jung says that he was highly influenced by James's work on the psychology of religion. In addition to Shamdasani's work on the James-Jung relationship, Eugene Taylor also brings to light that William James had a significant impact on "the intellectual destiny of Carl Gustav Jung."[6] Both Shamdasani and Taylor make it obvious how much Jung was indebted to James as both a philosopher and as the father of an analytic psychology that complements Jung's. To be sure, Jung's psychology owes a great deal of debt to James who wrote in "The Stream of Consciousness": "The order of our study must be analytic."[7]

In "A Contribution to the Study of Psychological Types," a lecture delivered at the Psychological Congress in Munich, in September 1913 (the last time Jung and Freud met), Jung said further, "So far as my limited knowledge goes, we have to thank William James for the best observations in this respect. He lays down the principle 'Of whatever temperament a professional philosopher is, he tries, when philosophizing, to sink the fact of his temperament.'"[8] This is an interesting statement in light of what I've said about the movement toward a psychological attitude. Jung continued:

> And starting from this idea, which is altogether in accord with the spirit of psychoanalysis, he divides philosophers into two classes: the "tender-minded" and the "tough-minded," or, as we might also call them, the "spiritually-minded" and the "materially-minded." The very terms clearly reveal the opposite movements of the libido. The first-class directs libido to the world of thought, and are predominately introverted; the second direct it to material things and objective reality, and are extroverted.[9]

Jung then paraphrased James for two pages. "The tough-minded man is empirical 'going by facts.' Experience is his master, facts are his guide and they color all his thinking. It is only tangible phenomena in the outside world that count. Thought is merely a reaction to external experience."[10] After this "tough-minded" and "spiritually-minded" exposition on the importance of James's thought for modern psychology, Jung ended his masterful exposition on *Pragmatism* with a famous quote by James: "But our esteem for facts has not neutralized in us all religiousness. It is itself almost religious. Our scientific temper is devout."[11]

In *Memories, Dreams, Reflections,* Jung noted that it was during this congress in Munich that someone turned the conversation to Amenophis IV (Ikhnaton). The argument was made that behind Amenophis's destruction of his father's cartouches and the creation of a monotheistic religion was a father complex, which irritated Jung who said that "other pharaohs had replaced the names of their actual or divine forefathers . . . feeling that they had the right to do so since they were incarnations of the same god."[12] Jung then pointed out to Freud that the Egyptians had neither "inaugurated a new style, nor a new religion":

> At that moment Freud slid off his chair in a faint. Everyone clustered helplessly around him. I picked him up, carried him into the next room, and laid him on a sofa. As I was carrying him, he half came to, and I shall never forget the look he cast at me. In his weakness he looked at me as if I were his father . . . [Yet at] . . . the time Freud frequently made allusions indicating that he regarded me as his successor.[13]

What Jung said about James's typology in *Psychological Types* provides support for my hypothesis that James was pivotal to his development as a psychoanalyst. Although Jung criticized James's type theory in *Psychological Types*, his comments about James's views as a religious psychologist are laudable, for they reveal transparently his sources for some of his most important ideas about the collective psyche. For instance, consider the significance of what Jung said about James during his 1936 lecture at Harvard University on his sixth trip to America: "It was [James's] far-ranging mind which made me realize that the horizons of human psychology widen into the immeasurable."[14] By immeasurable, Jung means boundlessness, spaciousness, the infinite expanse of the human psyche.

If we take Jung's statement as preliminary data that he took James's far-ranging mind as a *model* for the horizons of human psychology, then we would be wise to extend the range of our understandings about James in Jung's inner development as someone who made him realize that the vistas of psychology are infinite inside of him. This realization suggests something significant about psychology's future: its scope is limitless. James himself had said so much in his lectures IV and V of *Varieties of Religious Experience,* which he called "The Religion of Healthy-Mindedness," where he spoke of "wonderful inner paths to a supernatural kind of happiness." To augment what he meant, he made references in literature to the figure of Walt Whitman as a restorer of what he called the eternal natural religion. A passage that is sure to have spoken to C.G. when he read it is this one on the systematic way of being healthy-minded.

> Systematic healthy-mindedness, conceiving good as the essential and universal aspect of being, deliberately excludes evil from its field of vision ... When happiness is actually in possession, the thought of evil can no more acquire the feeling of reality than the thought of good can gain reality when melancholy rules. To the man actively happy, from whatever cause, evil simply cannot then and there be believed in.[15]

Although James's thoughts about healthy-mindedness were accurate as they pertained to the *Zeitgeist* in which he was writing, his analysis of Whitman is unfortunately superficial and cannot, therefore, stand the test of empirical verification, for Whitman, like Melville and Dickinson, had an uncanny ability to stare evil in the face, particularly during the agonizing ordeals of the Civil War, which left him a half-paralytic. (I've taken up this subject previously and will not go into it here.[16]) Nevertheless, James was spot on in his diagnosis of what he foresaw in his time as a sort of religious movement in America, a sort of "religion of nature," as he said, "which has entirely displaced Christianity from the thought of a large part of our generation. The idea of a universal evolution lends itself to a doctrine of general meliorism and progress which fits the religious needs of the healthy-minded so well that it seems almost as if it might've been created for their use."[17] Later he added:

> We are now just witnessing—but our scientific education has unfitted most of us for comprehending the phenomenon—a very copious unlocking of energies by ideas, in the persons of those converts to "New Thought," "Christian Science," "Metaphysical Healing," or other forms of spiritual

philosophy, who are so numerous among us to-day. The ideas here are healthy-minded and optimistic; and it is quite obvious that a wave of religious activity, analogous in some respects to the spread of early Christianity, Buddhism, and Mohammedanism is passing over our American world.[18]

What James foresaw here, and quite accurately, I believe, with his introverted thinking and extroverted intuition, is what has been called *New Age Religion*.[19]

The pragmatism of William James has become a modern standard for present-day people seeking a personal destiny in an age lacking a spiritual focus in a Self that combines and transcends the opposites, just as C. G. Jung's vision of analytical psychology is a vision of the Self that is grounded in a truly global collective unconscious and is perennially inspiring to an American audience. "Variety within diversity," vast "complexity in unity," or "Many in the One," is an idea, moreover, that also spoke to James, the father of a distinctly American psychology. In 1865 James went on an expedition to South America, where he assisted in collecting specimens for Harvard's Museum of Comparative Zoology. Being away for nine months enabled him to access ideas he didn't have time to fully explore amid the hustle of ordinary life. Although his scientific understanding increased on the exhibition, he also knew he was not cut out for zoological research. Instead, he brought back a foundational intuition for what would become the pivot around which religious lives revolve, the nuclear idea of the individual in his or her *private personal destiny, The Varieties of Religious Experience.*[20] With James, the intuition of spiritual democracy[21] first entered the field of American academic psychology as a notion that sought to form a bridge between philosophy, science, theology, and spiritual experience. *The Varieties of Religious Experience* was based on James's famous Gifford Lectures on natural religion at the University of Edinburgh, in 1902 and 1903. In this American masterpiece, which is now an international classic, James viewed the subconscious Self in a similar way as Jung did: as a *doorway* to authentic spiritual realization. James brought a pluralistic, pragmatic, and empirical attitude into academic psychology that surveyed the world's mystical poetry and gave examples from many of the world religions. For instance, he cited a passage from Luther: "I saw the Scripture in an entirely new light; and straightaway I felt as if I was born anew. It was as if I had found the door of paradise thrown wide open."²² James's views had a direct impact on Jung's psychology. James illuminated something extremely important for Jung's extension of the vision of spiritual democracy, namely his astute inspection of the world religions and mystical experience as a whole. His ideas were expressed succinctly in a letter written to a friend in Edinburgh:

> The problem I have set myself is a hard one: *first*, to defend ... "experience" against "philosophy" as being the real backbone of the world's religious life. ...and *second,* to make the hearer or reader believe, what I myself invincibly do believe, that, although all the special manifestations of religions may have been absurd (I mean its creeds and theories), yet the life of it as a whole is mankind's most important function.²³

The function of spiritual democracy is, therefore, in James's view, *the very backbone of the world's religions as a whole, and humanity's most important function is a spiritual purpose present in everyone, a determination to give voice to one's personal destiny.*

One of James's most seminal contributions to the history of religious ideas is his insistence that the type of religion he calls "healthy-mindedness" is one that "deliberately excludes evil from its field of vision," and for this very reason it can be highly dangerous.²⁴ Deliberately minimizing evil from one's intuitive visionary field can become a form of blindness, insensitivity, and blatant disregard toward the darker aspects of the objective reality of things in the social and political world and in relationship to Nature.

I've emphasized this *exclusionary principle* because Jung's project to rehabilitate global religion toward a spiritual democracy ultimately argues for the inclusion of evil as well as good into our *Weltanschauung,* our own philosophy, mythology, or personal theology of life. James brought a *vision of evil* into his psychological discussions on religion in a way no European had before Jung. He helped us see that evil is as much a function of God as good is.

James asks us to consider: "How *can* religion on the whole be the most important of all human functions?"²⁵ For James the "subconscious self" was the real seat of religious experiences.²⁶ By religious function, James meant *feeling*. "I do believe that feeling is the deeper source of religion, and that philosophic and theological formulas are secondary products, like translations of a text into another tongue."²⁷ Note the accent he places on *feeling* here. This is because feeling is James's inferior function and, as such, it is what Beebe calls the basis of his "spine" or "backbone."

In his "Conclusions," James wrote:

> You see now why I have been so individualistic in these lectures, and why I have seemed so bent on rehabilitating the element of feeling in religion and subordinating its intellectual part. Individuality is founded in feeling; and the recesses of feeling, the darker, blinder strata of character, are the only places in the world in which we catch real fact in the making, and directly perceive how events happen, and how work is actually done. Compared with this world of living individualized feelings, the world of generalized objects which the intellect contemplates is without solidity or life.²⁸

In the 1986 lecture, "C. G. Jung's Rehabilitation of the Feeling Function in Our Civilization," Marie-Louise von Franz penned a powerful essay that became the subject of a *festschrift* in *Jung Journal: Culture & Psyche* for the Fall edition in 2009.²⁹ Yet, the earlier rehabilitation of feeling for world culture was made by James. Jung, to his credit, went much further than James did in clarifying the distinction between the feeling function and emotions, which James sometimes mixed up. But James gave us the tools (prior to Jung) to analyze the most pernicious problem in the history of religions, namely the problem of evil. In an 1896 lecture on exceptional mental states, given in Lowell, Massachusetts, James zeroed in on the phenomenon of the witch-hunting epidemic that had swept through Bavaria, France, and Cape Cod, Massachusetts. James showed his audience that the epidemic, which began in 1250, really began to heat up in 1484, eight years before Columbus's "discovery" of the Americas, with the issuing of a papal bull (proclamation) by Pope Innocent VIII, which intensified investigations against magicians and witches. This was followed by the 1486 publication of the infamous *Malleus Maleficarum,* or *Witches' Hammer,* a treatise on the prosecution of witches by the German Catholic clergyman Heinrich Kramer. The *Malleus* helped spread the vicious witch-hunting epidemic to France, England, Italy, Ireland, Scotland, Mexico, North America (Salem, Massachusetts), and to many other parts of the world. James told his audience: "a curious, gruesome, rathole feeling exuded from it."³⁰ Notice, again, the rehabilitation James was attempting to accomplish through his accent on the words *rathole feeling*. In this lecture James scrutinized historical evidence of the German Inquisition and found that most of the women accused of witchcraft were really hysterics. Furthermore, he found that the torturers themselves were possessed of a certain morbidity of mind, soul, and spirit resembling clinical morbidity and madness. James pointed to the repressed sexuality of monks, who, struggling with their own vows of celibacy, projected their own hatred, unlived desires, and stifled impulses onto the female sex and tortured these poor women mercilessly.[31] Such a searing analysis has clinical and cultural and religious relevance today following the contemporary epidemic of pedophilia in the Catholic Church. James asserted: "There is no worse enemy of God and man than zeal armed with power and guided by a feeble intellect."[32] The feebleness of the intellect comes from the lack of connection to sympathetic human *feeling*.

Notes

1. Henderson, *Cultural Attitudes in Psychological Perspectives*.
2. James, *Writings 1878–1899*, 11.
3. James, 178.
4. James, 186.
5. Taylor, "William James and C. G. Jung"; Shamdasani, *Jung Stripped Bare by His Biographers, Even*.
6. Shamdasani, *Jung and the Making of Modern Psychology*; Taylor, "William James and C. G. Jung," 157.
7. James, *Writings 1878–1899*, 152.
8. Jung, *Psychological Types*, CW 6, ¶864.
9. Jung, CW 6, ¶684.
10. Jung, CW 6, ¶667.
11. Jung, CW 6, ¶689.
12. Jung, *MDR*, 157.
13. Jung, *MDR*, 157.
14. Jung, "Psychological Factors Determining Human Behavior," CW 8, ¶262.
15. James, *Writings 1902–1910*, 86.
16. For a full discussion of my thoughts on James and Whitman and the problem of evil, see Herrmann, *Walt Whitman: Shamanism, Spiritual*

Democracy, and the World Soul.
17. James, *Writings 1902–1910,* 89.
18. James, 1238.
19. Wouter J. Hanegraaff, *New Age Religion and Western Culture.*
20. James, *Writings 1902–1910,* 439, 440.
21. See Chapter 20: "Eight Principles of Spiritual Democracy."
22. James, 344, 345.
23. James, *The Varieties of Religious Experience,* 17.
24. James, 101.
25. James, 66–67.
26. James, 245.
27. James, 419.
28. James, 483.
29. See Herrmann, "Colloquy with the Inner Friend."
30. Taylor, *William James on Exceptional Mental States,* 117.
31. Taylor, 118.
32. Taylor, 129.

Chapter 11

JAMES ON INSTINCT, EMOTION, AND THE SIGNIFICANCE OF LIFE

I will begin this chapter by clarifying some of the subtle ways in which James viewed instinct, emotion, and the significance of life. First, in brief, Jung viewed *archetypes as images of instinct,* which are charged with a unique kind of *numinosity*, a term he borrowed from Rudolph Otto in his book *The Holy*. Jung's methods for liberating the images contained in the emotions was through various ways of working with the self-portraits created in dreams, active visioning, or any of the expressive arts—literature, poetry, philosophy, or science. For James *emotion* was what he called "a tendency to feel," whereas he viewed *instinct* as a "tendency to act" when in the presence of a certain object in the environment. But emotions also have their bodily expressions, which may involve strong muscular activity. James gave the examples of fear or anger. Fear is both an instinct and an emotion because fear often arises from an instinctive reaction and the two, impulse and affect, cannot, therefore, be theoretically separated into precise scientific categories in chapters of a textbook on the principles of psychology. Therefore, he asked the question: "Shall fear be described in the chapter on Instincts or in that on Emotions?"[1]

James was a physiological psychologist first and foremost and, in 1890, very little had been written about the emotions in the emerging field of psychology; most writing was merely descriptive. James took it upon himself to follow the guiding principle that the beauty of all truly scientific work is to get to ever deeper levels of experience. "Is there no way out from this level of individual description in the case of the emotions?" he asked. "I believe there is a way out if one will only take it."[2] The way out for him was empirical, scientific, and psychological. Its basic axiom was this: emotions, like instincts, are indefinite and tend toward uniqueness in individuals. Of emotions, he wrote: "*We immediately see why there is no limit to the number of possible different emotions which may exist, and why the emotions of different individuals may vary indefinitely*."[3] James's description of instinct was just as precise: "*Instinct is usually defined as the faculty of acting in such a way as to produce certain ends, without foresight of the ends, and without previous education in the performance.*"⁴

Thus, when transposing James's definitions of instinct and emotion to the field of analytical psychology, his insights invariably led to the principle of free will. Here he recognized, with Jung, that there were limits to understanding the question of free will solely on the basis of empirical psychology. Whether Jung willed the thought of God befouling his Church in adolescence, for instance, whether it was an act of free will or not that the thought entered him, is difficult to determine psychologically. The thought forced itself on his consciousness against his will and, therefore, we need to take the metaphysical factor into consideration here: Does God as a function in the human psyche act autonomously at times to enforce upon us certain actions and achievements that are simply above our heads and come from a place of non-ordinary knowledge, outside the sphere of ordinary awareness? Free will, I argue, is the place in between for Jung, the area of his conscious ego, or self, that created an opening for the Self's thoughts to come through. This view is in alignment with James's assertion: "*The fact is that the question of free-will is insoluble on strictly psychological grounds.*"⁵

In 1895 James gave an address to the Harvard Young Men's Christian Association, or YMCA, called "Is Life Worth Living?" As a scholar on the subject of American poetry, I am quite interested in James's opening remarks in response to this question. Here is where he began to present his hypothesis regarding the question of life's worthiness or unworthiness. He posited that a certain type of "temperamental optimism" can make some people so incapable of believing that "anything seriously evil can exist" that they simply live in a kind of sufficiency, life being significant in the present moment, a sense of being significant just as they are. He gave an example of what he meant by referring to "Our dear old Walt Whitman's works" as being a standing textbook for this kind of optimism, where the mere "joy of living" is so immense in "Whitman's veins" that it completely "abolishes the possibility of any other kind of feeling."⁶ James later used Whitman, rightly or wrongly, as a central actor in his chapter "The Religion of Healthy Mindedness" in *The Varieties of Religious Experience*. But the seeds for this chapter had been planted at least twenty years prior. Consider his address delivered to the Unitarian Ministers' Institute at Princeton, Massachusetts, in 1881, called "Reflex Action and Theism." There he said, "to awaken our loyalty happens to be one of God's functions."[7] Loyalty is what leads to the opening of the Self's doorways: "The floodgates of the religious life are opened, and the full currents can pour through."[8] This pouring through of the God-function into Whitman's life and poetry is what we might call today going with the flow, being mindful, or living in the Now.

What James meant by it is in alignment with what Jung meant when he spoke about the importance of loyalty to one's calling in promoting personality development. Whereas for Jung, image, myth, and meaning took on absolute significance in his hypothesis of individuation, for James, it was the arrival at a theory of truth that was penultimate in his psychology. "What kind of being would God be if he did exist?"[9] James asked the Unitarian ministers to consider, then responded, "May not the *knowing of the truth* be his absolute vocation?"[10] For both Jung and James the only truth that would suffice is a subjective response to life's meaninglessness or insignificance, a myth to live by, or theory of truth. Being an introverted thinking type, truth was penultimate for James. Getting to know the *Knower,* above one's thoughts, was the ultimate truth, the higher goal and aim of life.

In an essay called "What Psychical Research Has Accomplished," James gave an example from the *Proceedings* of clairvoyance, taken from an article by a Miss X., on "Crystal Vision." This is a fascinating account of an experience of crystal-gazing in which the subject saw, while staring into a crystal, a newspaper printing about the death of a lady of her acquaintance. Startled by her clairvoyant vision, she looked at the *Times* from the previous day for verification of the fact and among the deaths in the obituary column were the identical words she'd seen in her vision.[11] This is the same essay in which James gave his famous description of Mrs. Piper, the medium who so interested Jung; he called her his "white crow":

> If you wish to accept the law that all crows are black, you must not seek to show that no crows are; it is enough if you prove one single crow to be white. My own white crow is Mrs. Piper. In the trances of this medium, I cannot resist the conviction that knowledge appears which she has never gained by the ordinary waking use of her eyes and ears and wits. What the source of this knowledge may be I know not, and have not the glimmer of an explanatory suggestion to make; but from admitting the fact of such knowledge I can see no escape.[12]

In his "Talks to Students" James again invoked the example of Whitman, who in his poem "Crossing Brooklyn Ferry" celebrated the divine in each face he met among the diverse population. Again, James used his familiar trope of *feeling* to get at the experience Whitman had while merging happily with people: "He felt the human crowd as rapturously as Wordsworth felt the mountains, felt it as an overpoweringly significant presence."[13]

One has to look long and hard through James's writings to find evidence for moments of *opening* in which some thought-transcending experiences of the *Knower* in him broke open the doorways to his own sense of democratic individuality, as a carrier of his own subjective truth, just as Jung carried with him his own myth of meaning. Yet, James's psychology of the Self is a psychology of action, of social, political, and *spiritual activism*, which democratizes psychology as a contemporary science of human character and as transmitter of the meaning of a Higher Self to move humanity as a whole toward freedom.

In his essay "What Makes Life Significant," James told a personal story during his talk to students about a happy week he'd spent during a summer at the famous assembly grounds on the borders of Chautauqua Lake. There, he says, he got "a foretaste of what human society might be, were it all in the light, with no suffering and no dark corners."[14] He realized while he was there on sabbatical that "all of the ideals for which our civilization has been striving: security, intelligence, humanity, and order," all of these goals, had been superficially attained in a sort of superficial Utopia. He meditated on the fact that at "Chautauqua there was no potentiality of death in sight anywhere, and no point of the compass visible from which danger might possibly appear." He went on: "What our human emotions seem to require is the sight of the struggle going on." In Chautauqua there was no struggle to be seen. James then concluded: "An irremediable flatness is coming over the world."[15] Flatness suggests no vertical dimension to connect us to our Higher Self, only the objects of our lower instincts, passions, and emotions, which can easily lead us astray.

With all his thoughts and criticisms about the artificial city of Chautauqua on his mind, he then told students another story, of being on a train speeding toward Buffalo, and seeing the sight of a workman doing something on the dizzy edge of a sky-scaling iron construction, which brought him to his senses suddenly and made him pay particular attention to what he was feeling. He'd never noticed the great fields of heroism lying roundabout him. He thought of the heroism of the innumerable democratic individuals that make up our vast nation, who pick up a scythe, an ax, a pick, or a shovel every day, and sweat and toil with powers of patient endurance for hours upon hours of strain. All of this heroic life all about him and the toils of untold masses of humanity doing their daily jobs woke him up suddenly from his Chautauqua illusion, and the scales fell from his eyes. Suddenly, "a wave of sympathy greater than anything I had ever before felt with the common life of common men began to fill my soul."[16] *A wave of sympathy, he says, with the common life of common men.* This is what Whitman had conveyed from his crossing of Brooklyn Ferry. "Divinity lies all about us, and culture is too hidebound to even suspect the fact."[17]

Now this, I would argue, is a quintessential example of what makes American psychology different than European psychology, with its focus on the extraordinary individual and his or her place of paramount significance in the evolution of the social compact. Democratic individuality is, in essence, a democratization of Self-experience within all of us. This, finally, is what makes James's *Varieties of Religious Experience* so very special as a sequel to his *Principles of Psychology*. The link between the two, the common denominator that links American psychology to the psychology of religious experience worldwide, is propounded by the *sympathy he felt* in a true Whitmanesque idiom for his fellow humans. As the wave washed over him and he rested with a feeling of peace that day, "a sense of widening of vision" occurred, and "with it what is surely fair to call an increase of religious insight into life."[18] The insight was the truth that we are all the same really, despite our vast differences as human beings. What makes us all the same, equals, is the liberty we each have through free will, deep feeling, and the higher intellect or intuition to follow our vocation in life, in the wider existence of the infinite Cosmos.

NOTES

1. James, *Writings 1878–1899*, 350.
2. James, 351.
3. James, 357. Italics in the original.

4. James, 366. Italics in the original.
5. James, 423.
6. James, 480.
7. James, 547.
8. James, 558.
9. James, 547.
10. James, 559.
11. James, 691.
12. James, 694, 695.
13. James, 851.
14. James, 863.
15. James, 864, 865.
16. James, 866.
17. James, 867.
18. James, 867.

Chapter 12

Doorways to the Self

One of the most brilliant contributions to the subject of modern psychology was William James's *inclusion of feeling as a religious function that all human beings must keep in touch with, if we are to advance toward a true spiritual democracy of love, equality, and compassion during the Aquarian Age, when the Self reigns supreme over all God-images in human history.* This includes not only our religious tolerance for others, but also, shockingly, an acceptance of the shadow[1] of our *religious intolerance, hate, envy, and evil* as part of the full inventory of our hereditary and evolutionary makeup. Martin Luther, for instance, is an example of the reverse of this hopeful ideal of staying mindful of our shadow. Although Luther could state in earnest, while immersed in God-consciousness, "I felt as if I was born anew. It was as if I had found the door of paradise thrown wide open," *this doorway to paradise also has a splenetic shadow.*[2] Luther was, unfortunately for all Lutherans, a publicly proclaimed anti-Semite. This is why it is difficult to celebrate him uncritically today in the spirit of equality-making that I'm putting forth here as a hard-won psychological ideal. We typically don't suspect evil to appear in our own person and to project it, unconsciously, onto our sisters and brothers. In doing so, our subjective destiny may paradoxically turn into a tragic fate. Such was the sad situation with regard to Luther's reputation as a religious reformer by the time of the five-hundredth anniversary of the Reformation last fall in 2018.

Today, most people in the United States have forgotten the tragic history of the Thirty Years' War, or perhaps they never even realized or considered its significance to the present day. This war is still in the blood of Americans of white European and Anglo Saxon descent as a religious complex, in heredity and history, a living horrendous legacy, when eight million Europeans were killed over a religious controversy. Luther's vulgarity and violence against the Jews, Muslims, and Catholics are living proof he was no Spiritual Democrat at heart. His anti-Jewish rhetoric in his 1543 book, *On the Jews and Their Lies,* became a blueprint for Nazi propaganda. In it, he advocated the burning of synagogues, seizing of Jewish property, and smashing of their homes. He has the respect of many for standing up to the economic evils of the papacy, for paving the way toward spiritual liberation of our individual consciences, and for translating the Bible into German and making it widely available to people in vernacular; yet, his theology of the Word is, unfortunately, as much toned by *a feeling for evil,* as it is by *a feeling for the good.* His shadow is a blight, and it's here to stay.

> The shadow is a tight passage, a narrow door, whose painful constriction no one is spared who goes down to the deep well. But one must learn to know oneself in order to know who one is... But if we step through the door of the shadow we discover with terror that we are the objects of unseen factors. To know this is decidedly unpleasant, for nothing is more disillusioning than the discovery of our own inadequacy.[3]

When experience democratizes us, on the other hand, if the "doors of perception" are mystically "cleansed," as the poet William Blake once wrote, we are open to the "infinite."[4] But here's the rub and Blake knew it: evil can also rush in during such moments of opening! When asked how the inferior function connects with the collective evil in the world, Marie-Louise von Franz had this to say: "There remains what I call the devil in the corner. This is only the personal devil, the personal inferiority of an individual, but with it collective evil comes in as well. The little open door of each individual's inferior function is what contributes to the sum of collective evil in the world."[5] For Luther the devil in the corner was the evil he could not swallow in himself.

Like Luther, James was quite fond of the metaphor of the *doorway*, which for him was essentially a universal archetype with Biblical, Upanishadic, and Sufi roots. As James wrote, for instance, while meditating on the subject of *prayer*:

> So when one's affections keep in touch with the divinity of the world's authorship, fear and egotism fall away; and in the equanimity that follows, one finds in the hours, as they succeed each other, a series of purely benignant

opportunities. It is as if all doors were opened, and all paths freshly smoothed. We meet a new world when we meet the old world in the spirit which this kind of prayer infuses.[6]

As James says further in his "Conclusions," while speaking of the religious function that he's been analyzing, by this time, for 450 pages:

> This doorway into the subject seems to me the best one for a science of religions, for it mediates between a number of different points of view. Yet it is only a doorway, and difficulties present themselves as soon as we step through it, and ask how far our trans-marginal consciousness carries us if we follow it on its remoter side.[7]

What James means by "difficulties" is that insofar as all religious experiences occur through openings in our "trans-marginal consciousness," each religion attempts to attach *objective significance* to its own particular God-images, creeds, or dogmas, over all other scriptural statements. During such a process of deification of one's own theology books, the science of religion, which is a *personal experience of one's subjective destiny*, loses its objectivity, by the insistence on superiority of one's own creed, which can, in turn, become superseded by bias, shadow, and evil at the cultural, or national, level. Thus, the *rehabilitation of religion as a function of sympathetic feeling* is thereby lost. Yet absolutism, not equality-making, in theology is the order of the day. For such reasons, James complained: "I state the matter thus bluntly, because the current of thought in academic circles runs against me, and I feel like a man who must set his back against an open door quickly if he does not wish to see it closed and locked."[8] The doorway to the Self is, for James, intended to symbolize *hope* in the world's future.

Pluralism for James is an evolutionary principle that, like the universe itself, is unfinished. It needs humanity to help it advance toward *the creation of theories of truth* through which the doors and windows of our house might remain open, not closed, to future possibilities for civilization and world culture—with the caveat that we remain *aware of the evil* that can easily creep in.

James and Jung were democratizers of the World Soul, Body, and Spirit. Each made their individual errors when it came to problems of the inferior function. An example of James's rare oversight and lack of recognition of tendermindedness while his toughminded empirical attitude held sway in him, were his sometimes-exaggerated criticisms of Whitman, Royce, or Vivekananda.⁹ Here is a beautiful passage by Vivekananda, which shows just how Spiritually Democratic he was in his own right:

> In Buddha we had the great, universal heart and infinite patience, making religion practical and bringing it to everyone's door…Science and religion will meet and shake hands. Poetry and philosophy will become friends. This will be the religion of the future, and if we can work it out, we may be sure that it will be for all times and peoples.¹⁰

Of all the psychologists of the twentieth century, however, Jung went the furthest in establishing the ground for a universal understanding of the metaphor of the *door that leads within and without,* an archetypal reality in psyche and cosmos that may be found in all religions: *doorways to the Self.* In "Transformation Symbolism of the Mass" Jung has this to say about Christ or the Self as a door:

> Christ, or the self, is a "mirror": on the one hand it reflects the subjective consciousness of the disciple, making it visible to him, and on the other hand it "knows" Christ, that is to say it does not merely reflect the empirical man, it also shows him as a (transcendental) whole. And, just as a "door" opens to one who "knocks" on it, or a "way" opens to the wayfarer who seeks it, so, when you relate to your own (transcendental) center you initiate a process of conscious development which leads to oneness and wholeness.¹¹

Jung equated the terms *Christ* and *self* as a "mirror" of the empirical human in relationship to the transcendental whole. Christ, as Jung has shown, is an image of the Self; the Self is not an image of Christ, but all images of God mirror the Self as an objective and cosmic reality. In the East, Brahma is also known, not incidentally, as a door. As Joseph Campbell wrote, "The white serpent-goddess Kundalini, 'fine as fiber of a lotus-stalk,' is coiled three and one half times around this lingam, asleep, and covering with her head its Brahma-door."¹²

The Beloved in Sufism is also an open door. Vivekananda reports a wonderful story in this regard:

Figure 12.1 Jung's house in Küsnacht Summer 2008
(Photograph by the author)

There was an ancient Persian Sufi poet and one of his poems says "I came to the Beloved and beheld the door was closed; I knocked at the door and from inside a voice came, 'Who is there?' I replied, 'I am.' The door did not open. A second time I came and knocked at the door and the same voice asked, 'Who is there?' 'I am so-and-so.' The door did not open. A third time. I came and the same voice asked, 'Who is there?' 'I am Thyself, my Love,' and the door opened."[13]

My point about all of these metaphors, while circumambulating around *door symbolism*, is that the doorway is a universal *archetype* that opens the way to the Self-path, vocation, or to what James calls our personal path of individual *destiny*. The paths inward are not easy to walk on; and that's why, in fairytales and myths, the fool, mother's daughter or son, or simpleton is the one who often finds the pot of gold at the rainbow's end or the hen that lays the golden egg. The *Golden egg* is a synonym for *Brahman* in the Upanishads. So, too, in the Old and New Testaments, the door is a metaphor for *God-consciousness*. Psalm 24:7 reads, for instance, "Lift up your heads, O ye gates; and be ye lift up ye everlasting doors; and the King of glory shall come in." Similarly, the Gospel of St. John (10:9) says Christ is *the* door: "I am the door: by me if any man enter in he shall be saved, and shall go in and out, and find pasture." In Colossians 4:3, "God would open unto us a door of utterance, to speak the mystery of Christ." Revelations 3:8 states further: "I know thy works: behold I have set before thee an open door, and no man can shut it: for thou hast a little strength, and hast kept my word, and hast not denied my name." Finally, Revelations 3:20 reads: "Behold, I stand at the door, and knock: if any man hear my voice, and open the door, I will come in to him, and will sup with him, and he with me."

If we can find a *way* that leads inward to the doorways that open up to the Self, Christ, Brahman, "Nature's God," or the Cosmos, we can possess keys to our individual destiny. No one did more in the twentieth century to advance the concept of the Self as a doorway for modern psychology than James and Jung. This is perhaps why one of the largest organizations in the world, Alcoholics Anonymous, gives equal credit to both Jung and James for having opened the door to spiritual experiences for their membership. As Bill Wilson reported fondly in a letter to Jung, for instance, AA "made conversion experiences—nearly every variety reported by James—available on an almost wholesale basis." Later, he said James was a "founder of Alcoholics Anonymous." Wilson gave Jung equal credit for having treated and inspired his good friend Roland H., who sought Jung's help with alcoholism in Switzerland and who Jung helped overcome his sickness by pointing out that what he'd mistakenly done was to misplace a spiritual outlook in life with the poison of "spirits": "When he [Roland H.] asked you if there was any other hope, you told him there might be, provided he could become the subject of a spiritual or religious experience, in short a genuine conversion."[14]

From these introductory passages on doorways, I hope I have made it clear that there are as many doors as there are religions, and there are doorways in Nature that require no transport from any organized religion at all. In fact, spiritual experiences are part and parcel of our own evolutionary nature and democracy. This brings up the controversial question about drug-induced ways to open the doorways to the Self. Jung took on this subject in a letter to the Dominican theologian, Father Victor White, in 1954. White had mentioned he'd been invited to a lunatic asylum to talk to the staff about the religious-archetypal material that patients were producing under the influence of LSD. Jung then brought up the book *The Doors of Perception*, which had been published in that same year by Aldus Huxley. Huxley had taken his title from the passage by William Blake, which Jungian analyst June Singer referred to and which I quoted previously. Jung's response is fascinating:

> I only know there is no point in wishing to *know* more of the collective unconscious than one gets through dreams and intuitions.... Do you want to increase loneliness and misunderstanding? Do you want to find more and more complications and increasing responsibilities? You get enough of it. If I once could say that I had done everything I know I had to do, then perhaps I should realize a legitimate need to take mescalin (sic). But if I should take it now, I would not be sure at all that I had not taken it out of idle curiosity. I should hate the thought that I touched on the sphere where the paint is made that colors the world, where the light is created that makes shine the splendor of the dawn, the lines and shapes of all form, the sound that fills the orbit, the thought that illuminates the darkness of the void... It is really the mistake of our age. We think it is enough to discover new things, but we don't realize that knowing more demands a corresponding development of morality. Radioactive clouds over Japan, Calcutta, and Saskatchewan point to progressive poisoning of the universal atmosphere. ... It is quite awful that the alienists have caught hold of a new poison to play with, without the faintest knowledge or feeling of responsibility.[15]

Clearly for Jung, dreams and intuitions were enough. That was all he needed to open the doorways to the Self. One needn't wish furtively to open all the doors. This letter, little read or commented upon by New Agers, shows clearly that Jung distanced himself from quick fixes to the moral dilemma—the fight with the shadow. Today the radioactive clouds have only increased; we have global warming and climate change to contend with. James and Jung always placed their greatest focus on *what the Self wants from us in terms of action in the world as a destiny to live by, or vocation.* We neglect it at our peril.

Most of Jung's published writing on William James is found in *Psychological Types*. Jung devoted twenty-one pages to James's theory of types in chapter seven of that volume, "The Type Problem in Modern Philosophy."¹⁶ In his paper "Concerning the Archetypes, with Special Reference to the Anima Concept," first published in Leipzig in 1936, Jung mentioned Theodore Flournoy and James. There he concluded: "I owe it mainly to these two investigators that I learnt to understand the nature of psychic disturbances within the setting of the human psyche as a whole."¹⁷

Jung often paid tribute to Flournoy and James together. Between the two, James was by far the most evolved mind, however, in the area of philosophy. One cannot read James without a philosophical attitude. While writing his masterpiece, *Varieties,* however, James sank his temperament as an introverted thinking type and relied heavily on his extroverted intuition and extroverted feeling to outline his sketches of the future of psychology, as functions or doorways through which he set out to analyze religious phenomena.

Another fine example of Jung's attitude as a philosopher of religion was made during his seventh and final trip to America, shortly after delivering his famous Terry Lectures at Yale University in early 1937, at the Plaza Hotel in New York:

> Many people have asked me and doubtless asked you too, whether analytical psychology is really a religion. This sounds like religion, but it is not. I am speaking just as a philosopher. People sometimes call me a religious leader. I am not that. I have no message, no mission; I attempt only to understand. We are philosophers in the old sense of the word, lovers of wisdom.¹⁸

By philosophers, I take Jung to mean empiricists, like James and James's Swiss friend and Jung's mentor Flournoy. Jung was a post-Jamesian philosopher, an analytical psychologist, and a *Spiritual Democrat* at heart, just as James was. As Jung remarked further, during his opening statements at Yale University in 1937: "As I am a doctor and a specialist in nervous and mental diseases, my point of departure is not a creed but the psychology of *homo religiosis,* that is, of the man who takes into account and carefully observes certain factors which influence him and his general condition."¹⁹ For William James the horizon of human psychology could not be fully realized without a synthesis or integration of at least three constituents of the Empirical Self: 1) the Material Self, 2) the Social Self, and 3) the Spiritual Self.[20] The *Spiritual Self* is the Self that opens up to the furthest reaches of religious experience, the vast vista Jung referred to as *immeasurable*. In Jung's 1932 essay "The Development of Personality," he said the same essential thing about individuation: "A whole lifetime, in all its biological, social, and spiritual aspects, is needed."[21] The *1) biological, 2) social, and 3) spiritual corresponds, in Jung's definition, exactly with James's three-tiered hypothesis of hierarchal organization in the Self!*

Through investigations into Jung's total published references to James we know he not only was inspirational to Jung, but also served a function of what Jungian analyst Murray Stein refers to as a "transformative relationship." He may have helped to evoke, along with Flournoy and Philemon, a *transformative image* of the Empirical-Spiritual Self in Jung. We find in his writings, after Jung's two meetings with James in 1909, the emergence of some unique American characteristics: Immensity, vista, and spaciousness.

The extent of James's influence as a transformative figure is not entirely clear. Jung reported no dreams about James. Yet I will piece together a sketch in Chapters 31 and 33, through an overview of Jung's writings about James, which will hopefully provide the reader with a portrait of something that inhabited Jung after his two meeting with James: a new insight into Freud's limitations and a return to his Spiritual Self after the sacrifice of his professional personae (psychoanalyst, lecturer, editor). One thing is clear from my examinations of the psychological nature of their relationship is that Jung's brief encounters with James and his limited reading of his work opened Jung, in *Liber Novus,* to an experience of space.

The attribute of *spaciousness* in the American psyche and its wide vistas and landscape was first clarified by American professor, scholar, and playwright Thornton Wilder, who, in addition to having penned the famous novel *The Bridge of San Luis Rey* and the play *Our Town*, wrote a lesser-known, yet perhaps even more impressive book from a psychological standpoint, *American Characteristics of Classical American Literature*. Jung's pupil and analysand Joseph L. Henderson wrote a fine review of *American Characteristics* that may be found in his collected papers in the volume *Shadow and Self*. Henderson's greatest contribution to the field of analytical psychology may rest—along with his co-authoring of some commentaries on a beautiful alchemical text published with Dyane Sherwood, *Transformation of the Psyche: The Symbolic Alchemy of the Splendor Solis*—in his astute observation of what happens in the mature phases of life, when the hero myth loses its relevance and its leading star, the hero, becomes relativized by a symbolic death that signals an achievement of the initiate's full maturity. Henderson focused specifically on the theme of sacrifice or death of the hero as a necessary cure for his *hubris*: "the pride that has overreached itself."[22] Henderson described what happens when the hero willingly offers himself or herself up as a human sacrifice at an archetypal level during a decisive moment of transcendence: the hero's self-sacrifice symbolizes a liberation of the feminine component of the personality, necessary for a new, cooperative, and more related attitude toward one's social group. When the hero no longer seeks to fight the shadow, but accepts it wholeheartedly, then there follows a transition toward an act of inner and outer "friendship" with the Self. The hero is then "no longer driven to competitive struggle for individual supremacy but is assimilated to the cultural task of forming a democratic sort of community."[23] Only then does the hero become an initiate.

Henderson's focus on the symbolic death of the hero was portrayed mythologically by a return to the *immensity* or *spaciousness* of the archetypal Cosmic Mother: "He must see himself as if he were dead and entombed in a symbolic form (the sarcophagus) that recalls the archetypal mother as the original container of all life."[24] The hero motif applies just as much to the psyches of women as to men. Henderson offered a wonderful example of such a metamorphosis from his own clinical practice. He cited a dream from a middle-aged woman to illustrate what he meant. During the years of her marriage and raising of children, she'd neglected her creative gifts as a writer, with which she'd once made a small yet genuine reputation. In her dream she was given supernatural healing powers. There was a man who was at death's door whom she felt impelled to *cure*. This was her neglected masculine spirit that had undergone a symbolic death and needed revivification to live life fully again. She reported: "I have a kind of quill or perhaps a bird's beak through which I blow air into his nostrils and he begins to breathe again."[25]

Here is the breath of spiritual democracy—the bird's quill or beak, what Henderson referred to as a symbol of transcendence, a transport to immensity. In the dream, his patient was performing an archaic function of *breathing spirit* back into her masculine principle, reviving her calling as an author. The bird is a shamanic symbol and the medicine woman is one who flies about the universe in her visions as a bird, gander, or eagle, representing the highest categories of thought. Thus, the quill or bird's beak (a writing instrument) has a universal amplification as a symbol of transcendence, or transport, to expanded states of consciousness, necessary for winged flight into Self-consciousness, or what James called the Spiritual Self. One needn't practice Yoga, stand on one's head, or use pranayama, to achieve such spiritual transformations. The analytic matrix is itself a Western form of healing, where the natural integrity of the democratic spirit can be aroused in relationship to a skilled analyst, mentor, or spiritual teacher who is conscious of the Self. The pen itself can become a catapult for the Spiritual Self toward higher regions of thought, where psyche gets wings. Poetry, automatic writing as taught by James, or the method of Journaling, as I have used it in my own analytic practice (see Appendix), can launch the mind, in other words, into the furthest reaches of inner and outer space. Henderson was also, like Jung, deeply impressed and inspired by the writings of William James.

> Not so very many years ago, in his *Varieties of Religious Experience*, William James foreshadowed an entirely new psychological relativity towards religious experience. Ignoring theology, he brought to his readers the benefit of an impartial and, above all, accepting attitude to all forms of religious experience. He did not consider some to be higher or lower, better or worse than others.[26]

One of the most important factors Jung took into careful account as an empirical psychologist, in addition to the democratization of the Self, was the pernicious problem of the personal, national, and collective shadow. The shadow, an archetype of the evil that lurks in all of us, cannot be neglected in any complete inventory of the Self. I believe the concept of the shadow, a notion Jung got from his reading of Nietzsche, is one of Jung's most consequential contributions to the field of modern psychology. Without the shadow psyche could have no future, without analysis to assist her, in her efforts to ensoul the world. I will discuss this notion in-depth later, in the chapter "The Fight with the Shadow."

Jung believed wholeness of the personality was the most difficult moral task. Wholeness can only happen individually and collectively when enough people change their conceptions of life and undergo a radical change of heart. By learning to dialogue with our own hidden darkness, we can get to know the Self, as a personal and objective fact of the human psyche.

One aim in what lies ahead is to show that Jung's empirical psychology of the Self was significantly influenced by James and that we cannot properly understand Jung in America without an appreciation for his far-seeing precursor. If James was standing on the shoulders of Emerson, Whitman, Vivekananda, and Fechner, to chart out the immeasurable horizons of human psychology, and Jung was, in turn, standing on the shoulders of William James, then psyche's depths must be vast indeed, as the universal is, and psychology's future would therefore be, without any doubt, scientific.

Jung spoke about the Self as the author of our destinies, whereas James said we have three main Selves, always preferring the plural. Jung knew the Self through his own dreams and experiments with active imagination, his "language experiment," and through the study of tens of thousands of dreams and fantasies from his clinical practice, which is to say that he experienced the Self empirically and objectively through his scientific research. In a letter to Arwind Vasavada, an Indian psychologist and Jungian analyst, Jung wrote in 1954: "You seem to be interested in how to get back to the self, instead of looking for what the self wants you to do in the world... Nobody can be more convinced of the importance of the self than me."[27] Jung's focus on action is consistent with what James called the nuclear constituent of the *acting Self.*

Jung's letter expressed the significance he attached, however, to a *vocation of the Self*.[28] The fact that the Self wants to be incarnated through a vocation to live by, in each of us, is a fact of nature. In order to bring the Self to maturity and birth in the world, one has to have a commitment to an ongoing integration of one's personal and archetypal shadow as well as to the light side of the Self. "The self is brought into actuality," Jung said, "through the concentration of the many upon the center, and the self wants this concentration."[29] Whether one moves toward this center through Yoga, Zen meditation, Kabalistic chants, writing, poetry, the painting of a mandala, art, or active imagination, *the Self gives shape to the various God-images of all cultures. It is the place of convergence toward a central point in the psyche that I've called spiritual democracy, which gives shape in every individual to the vocation of the Self.* As I'll discuss later, Jung was meditating on the Self when he was composing his *Red Book*; he was also reading William James.

Although not generally remarked on, William James strongly influenced Jung's intellectual development. Both his character and his writings had a transformative effect on Jung's consciousness, at a pivotal point in his maturation, during his approach to and entrance into midlife. Both played a pivotal role, therefore, in Jung's inner evolution, as a modern thinker and as the father of analytical psychology.

NOTES

1. This is a Jungian concept I will explore in-depth in Chapter 19, "The Fight with the Shadow."
2. James, *Writings 1902–1910*, 344, 345.
3. Jung, "Archetypes of the Collective Unconscious," CW 9i, ¶¶45, 49.
4. Singer, *The Unholy Bible*, 3.
5. Von Franz and Hillman, *Lectures on Jung's Typology*, 81, 82.
6. James, *Writings 1902–1910*, 425.
7. James, 458.
8. James, 466.
9. See the Preface, page xix. [paragraph beginning "Whereas in Europe Schelling"]
10. Vivekananda, *The Complete Works of Swami Vivekanand*, vol. 2, 140. Hereafter referenced as *TCWSV* volume number, page number.
11. Jung, "Transformation Symbolism in the Mass," CW 11, ¶427.
12. Campbell, *The Mythic Image*, 341.
13. Vivekananda, TCWSV 3, 282.
14. Richardson, *William James*, 531.
15. Jung, *Letters*, vol. 2, 172–173.
16. Jung, "Psychological Types," CW 6, ¶¶505–541.
17. Jung, "Concerning the Archetypes, with Special Reference to the Anima Concept," CW 9i, ¶113.
18. Jung, *C. G. Jung Speaking*, 95, 98.
19. Jung, "Psychology and Religion (The Terry Lectures)," CW 11, ¶15.
20. James, *Writings 1878–1899*, 174–179.
21. Jung, "The Development of Personality," CW 17, ¶289.

22. Henderson, "Ancient Myths and Modern Man," 114.
23. Henderson, 128.
24. Henderson, 132.
25. Henderson, 139.
26. Henderson and Oakes, *The Wisdom of the Serpent*, 3.
27. Jung quoted in Molchanov and Collins, *Jung and India*, 31.
28. Herrmann, "Meister Eckhart and Carl Jung."
29. Jung, "Transformation Symbolism in the Mass," CW 11, ¶427.

Chapter 13

The Call to Vocation

When I think of life's ultimate journey, I think of it as a Self-path—a path to individuation and wholeness. Ideally, I think of my quest for wholeness as being realized through a vocation, or calling in life. I've spoken about this quest in singular form in my book *William Everson: The Shaman's Call*. In considering William James's overall influence on C. G Jung's oeuvre in this book, I will write about the subject in a plural sense, not as one, but as numerous callings to sacred work. Life is too complex to incarnate the Self through a single calling. My re-reading of William James over the past several years has convinced me to revise my understanding of Jung's callings (Jung spoke pluralistically about our callings to the inner life and community) and write about it pluralistically. I speak herein, therefore, about several vocations, as manifested through dreams and fortuitous chance meetings in which the Self's path was illuminated at pivotal points in Jung's life. One of these crucial meetings occurred when Jung met James.

A metaphor I meditate on throughout this book, one that forms a link between James and Jung, is the symbol of an open doorway to the Self-foundation, or an entranceway to Cosmic awareness. This image came to me during my reading of James, but it is one that had long been with me. I had encountered doorway symbolism in Jung's works, life, dreams, and stone architecture. But the significance of the symbol came from this pivotal passage of Jung's 1933 "The Meaning of Psychology for Modern Man." I memorized the passage and used to recite it to my students, as Bill Everson's teaching assistant, when I first read James at the University of California, Santa Cruz, in 1980.

> The dream is a little hidden door in the innermost and most secret recesses of the soul, opening into that cosmic night which was psyche long before there was any ego-consciousness, and which will remain psyche no matter how far our ego-consciousness extends. For all consciousness is isolated;

because it separates and discriminates, it knows only particulars, and it sees only those that can be related to the ego. Its essence is limitation, even though it reach to the furthest nebulae among the stars. All consciousness separates; but in dreams we put on the likeness of that more universal, truer, more eternal man dwelling in the darkness of primordial night. There he is still the whole, and the whole is in him, indistinguishable from all nature and bare of all egohood.[1]

Here we can see the immeasurability of human psychology that Jung realized through his two brief encounters with and reading of James. We can also see the immensity that Thornton Wilder found in his reading of American poetry and that so appealed to Henderson when he was his student. I see *dreams as doorways* into the deeper part of a person, including the archetypal levels of being. *Being* is a psychological and metaphysical category of existence, just as *knowing* is. Whenever a doorway to the Self is opened, dreams may emerge that render empirical and theological distinctions nondual. They become portals, in other words, to locate core elements of the authentic Self, by virtue of our callings. These elements are personal and Cosmic.

Figure 13.1 Doorways at Chaco Canyon, New Mexico, Summer 2011 (Photograph by the author)

Vocational dreams are doorways, therefore, into the Self, psyche, and Cosmos, or God and the Void, in which the inner man or woman, the Self, is bare of all egohood. This is one of those mythopoetic passages in Jung's work that borders on the metaphysical. For Jung the only way to study the eternal man or woman, the Self, was through the doorway of the dream. The streams of consciousness in the unconscious extend into the innermost recesses of the soul through the "little hidden door" of the dream. Only in dreams do we assume the form of our more real Self, the Self who is one with the psyche. Ego consciousness only has access to this deepest level of the Self through dreams and their symbolic language. Whereas in the East, yoga and meditation are ways to awaken the fourth level of supraconscious visioning in the Self, for Jung the Western equivalent of yoga is achieved through dream analysis and active imagination. Not all dreams, of course, are doorways into the cosmic night. Jung refers here to those rare dreams that are so far-reaching that it is no longer the dream-ego that is doing the perceiving; rather, it is the Self and its furthest depths of experiencing and knowing, psyche perceiving psyche.

There have been few attempts to verify the phenomenon of *psychological experiences* of the Higher Self, experimentally and experientially, from within the Empirical Self's door. Typically, we have been conditioned, by experimental and behavioristic research methods, to look from outside the door toward the data of personal experience, not to the vastness of the Self, the inner self within, via dreams, which, Jung said, are bare of all egohood. Dreams, as Jung taught, give us a perspective from the inside and assist in adaptation toward the unification of our twin destinations.

In his 1916 paper "Adaptation, Individuation, Collectivity," Jung wrote, for instance, that individuation is *against* all adaptation to others and resists personal conformity to society and its collective values. What Jung referred to in this paper was a psychological process of individuation that consisted of two primary processes: "1. Adaptation to outer conditions. 2. Adaptation to inner conditions."[2] Both were necessary for full Self-realization, he said. Perhaps more than any other of Jung's unpublished typescripts, this one, discovered after his death in the archives of the Psychological Club in Zürich, speaks most directly to the subject I'll be discussing.

At least for an introvert, the way of individuation leads to a temporary withdrawal or separation from the known world so that new *Self-values* may be discovered. This way is not free of conflict. Rather, it involves intense suffering, equivalent to a symbolic crucifixion of the ego, on the cross of one's individual destiny pattern. Adaptation to inner conditions, Jung said, leads to a tragic *guilt,* which requires *expiation*—the aim of which is to raise the Self and its values to the level of a *new collective function:* the function of a transpersonal calling, or vocation that requires a sacrifice to the generality.[3] Sacrifice is at the heart of the process of Self-realization, and there can be no true individuation without it. Thus, at least for a period of time, the *individuant* (the person undergoing individuation) is a bit neurotic because he or she suffers from a temporary lack of adaptation to outer conditions. In *"neurosis,"* Jung noted, "the adaptation process is disturbed."[4] Tragic guilt is redeemed by the individual if she or he can bring forth "values which are an equivalent substitute for his absence in the personal collective sphere . . . Only to the extent that a man creates objective values can he and may he individuate."[5]

How are new objective values created? Only through *sacrifice* (by which Jung meant a sloughing away of the heroic ego at midlife). The best analogy for this may be in Love. When we are in Love, we give our hearts away completely to our beloved. We become selfless. We become empty of who we formerly were and Love fills us with everything, even the embrace of the Cosmos. The chaos of our former lives may be suddenly transformed into an inner and outer Order, which increases our modesty.

"The individuant has no *a priori* claim to any kind of esteem."[6] By sacrificing our desires on the altar of Love, the Self quickens. *We sacrifice ourselves and our former values to a transpersonal Truth that is higher than ourselves.* Whenever an "exceptionally strong transference" is created in the analytical situation, moreover, one that sparks a "demand for individuation, it means farewell to personal conformity with the collective, and stepping over into solitude, into the cloister of the inner self."[7] We fall in love with our analysts and/or our lovers. We cease to be persons we thought we were. We become much bigger, more spacious. We outgrow our former selves and sense of collective values and adopt our own set of ideals that are thenceforth transmitted from the Spiritual Self to the Self-in-Society and Nature. Then, when the sacrifice of collective conformity is enhanced: "Only the shadow of the personality remains in the outer world. Hence the contempt and hate that come from society. But inner adaptation leads to the conquest of inner realities, from which values are won for the reparation of the collective."[8] "Individuation is a pose," Jung said, "so long as no positive values are created."[9] The central question here is: are the values an individuant creates realizable or not "because society has a right to expect *realizable* values"?[10]

What are the *realizable values* we may create through our individuation when we sacrifice our conformity to society and find the courage to become ourselves by choosing the way of the Self-path? Jung's hypothesis about individuation is as follows. In order to expiate for the guilt of our individuation, we may start by giving our "supreme good, [our] love" to "a human being who stands for [our] soul," or we may project this supreme love, for one human being, and it will thence be transferred from this love to God, Cosmos, or Universal Being, which may then become a new way of collective functioning or a path toward a new relativistic God-concept. Only then may our individuation rightfully be celebrated; for in this act of sacrifice, this generous outpouring of Love onto the Other, the Soul of the World, new values may thence emerge that are truly meant to transform and liberate society. The gift of Selfhood becomes our ransom, our payback, our rightful reparation for the absence; for then we know we were "destined to climb so high that [we] can stand in solitude before God and before [humankind]," as a birth-giver of new objective values for civilization and culture.[11]

By introverting Love we once projected onto our beloved, analyst, or career ideal, we can then begin to "give [our] soul the good" of the Self that we have "received"; and, as Jung added, in this offering of our gift, this birth-giving of the Self through the greater sacrifice of Love to a greater personality, we "will receive it again from God."[12] For it is true that "Individuation and collectivity are a pair of opposites, two divergent destinies": one to the Self, the other to society, two divergent destinies, or *bestimungen* in German—which might also mean "destinations."[13] Both destinies that once diverged now flow into the stream of unity that is the way to Wholeness.

Healing our neuroses, from a lack of adaptation to civilization and culture, then leads to an expansion of the human heart, to a fuller embrace of Love for the *Anima Mundi*. Healing our neuroses leads us on a twisting path of fate—a serpent's path—toward individuation and Wholeness, despite our former selves. Once we are securely on this way, there is no turning back: *We must follow the star of our individual destiny to the Self,* which is our final embrace and terminus.

Vocation is a religious term that needs to be unpacked. Jung viewed it as a calling from an inner *Voice,* from the Latin root *Vocare,* "to be called beyond the known," whether one hears it speak through dreams, fantasies, visions, walks in nature, or active imagination. To get at the foundations of this concept, we need to give a nod first, however, to James. In 1902, James published the *Varieties of Religious Experience.* In this book he tried to find a common variable, a common thread, a democratic denominator of sameness, that all the world's religions have in common with one another. This common variable is what he called *religious experience.* Today we might call it *spiritual.*

Like James, Jung began his studies with research in medicine and the occult. He later returned to his early interests in parapsychology once he'd achieved a greater maturity of age and worldwide fame. By the time he wrote his monograph on synchronicity, in 1951, the empirical and metaphysical, personal and transpersonal domains of the psyche, had been rejoined in his typically nondual and circumambulatory way of thinking. Jung was in quest of *empirical knowledge*, a psychology outside the margins, based solely on experience.

Whereas James called the most important experiences of our lives *religious,* Jung, borrowing a term from Rudolph Otto, called such experiences *numinous,* from the Latin term *numen,* a *nod* from Divinity. The Self nods toward us, in other words, through dreams, poetry, dance, writing, sculpting, sports, or whatever vocation we are called to pursue, once the doorways have been opened and passed through; then we get momentary glimpses of what it actually *feels like* to be on the other side of the doorway.

It is unnecessary, I believe, to separate psychology from spirituality, science from mysticism, as these paths are, in essence, indistinguishable and nondual. James and Jung were both phenomenologists and neither troubled himself much about theology. Jung found, in his old age, the right scientific and mythopoetic language to give voice to his lifelong interests in spirituality and nature, poetry and empirical psychology, as a synchronicity, or a coincidence, a fact of nature that is "just so." The key words in Jung's essay on synchronicity are, to my mind, that it is an "organizing principle." What Jung was always curious about was the hidden and elusive *Organizer.*

Synchronicity is a fourth principle of modern science that is hard to prove. Something is "hidden" behind synchronistic phenomena in the transmarginal field that remains forever mysterious. What I'll say about vocational dreams as doorways to the Self might sound somewhat mystical. I mean it practically and materially and scientifically too, as a complement to outer reality. I entered the Self's doorway a few times in my life in sensate reality; once, when I stepped through the famous doorways at Chaco Canyon, New Mexico. I had it again when I stepped through descending doorways at Yale Divinity School. And again when I entered the door to Jung's house in Küsnacht. A similar experience was manifest at simultaneous levels of cultural experience, in other words, irrespective of time and place: one indigenous and shamanistic, the other two modern and postmodern. But the experiences were essentially the same regardless of the cultural patterns. Each were entranceways into the realm of the sacred.

Figure 13.2 Doorway to Jung's house with inscription about the door, Summer 2008
(Photograph by the author)

Figure 13.3 Inscription above the door: *Vocatus Atque Non Vocatus Deus Aderit* ("Called or not Called, God will be Present") (Photograph by the author)

Jung found in his investigations into the phenomenon of synchronicity that "they can easily be shown to have a direct connection with an archetype," that is, "an irrepresentable psychoid factor of the collective unconscious."[14] Thus, the vocational entranceways to the Self cannot be fully represented. They are portals to the unknown, windows on infinity. I have found in my investigations into the nature of vocational dreams, moreover, that their manifestations lead to one unitary plural calling, the Self, which is cosmic. *Vocational dreams are, therefore, doorways into the Self, gateways to the Cosmos.* Such moments of meaningful reflection are what Jung called "acts of creation in time." They are moments in time when the infinite becomes incarnated in our limited, finite existence in a grounded sense.

We can see this kind of Self-reflection in Jung's comments during his retrospective thoughts in old age in *Memories, Dreams, Reflections,* when he appeared to have perceived the simultaneous ordering of events in his life as part of a *psychoid* or psychophysical process, whereby he was able to consecutively integrate "absolute knowledge," formerly lodged in the nuclei of the Self. Jung was called to be a scientific researcher, whose primary aim in old age was to arrive at *objective cognition*. Such an objective recollection of the Self is one of the central aims of Jungian analysis and individuation.

Jung's psychology teaches us not to project the Self onto any external master, guru, or teacher. This has been a challenge for me as a student in the field of depth psychology and religion. There have been times in my life when I projected the Self onto an outer person for a brief period of time, in order to acquire increased vocational knowledge in my various fields of interest. After doing this for a while, I always returned to the realization that Jung was right; I have continuously been advised by dreams to take my projections back in, to introject them onto my own Self-foundation.

At times, Jung made it sound easier than it actually is to realize the Self. Actually, there was a time in Jung's life when he did not feel as if he could act independently from his mentors and had to look to them for psychological guidance. This is the way it is, I believe, for all of us, and Jung and James were no exceptions to this general human rule.

The two very brief meetings between Jung and James and the psychophysical vocational correspondences for each of them (James at the very end of his life, when his heart was rapidly failing, and Jung at the decline of his psychoanalytic career, just prior to the death of his inner hero) fall within the framework of what Jung called a "coincidence in time of two or more causally unrelated events which have the same or a similar meaning."[15] According to Jung such correspondences were due to the "transgressive" character of archetypes.[16] Philemon was perhaps Jung's most transgressive symbol for the Self, and he emerged in Jung's dream life about five years after James's death. I can't say whether James was a "spiritual" figure in Jung's psyche. I do assert, however, that James played a *mediatory* role to the world of ideas about the furthest depths of human consciousness and that both men ultimately developed their own visions of what it meant to follow the Self-path.

In Jung's example of Philemon, evidence for the probable existence of a supreme inner *teacher and introverted Thinker* was suggested from an epistemological angle. The appearance of Philemon was a prevision of Jung's future and of psychology's future path. When Jung saw Philemon in a dream, he saw him as a winged being, sailing across the sky. Philemon held a ring of four keys in his hands, one of which he clutched, as if he were ready to open a lock of a door.[17] The motif of the four keys is significant in light of what I'll say about *vocational dreams as doorways to the Self.* For Jung, Philemon held four keys to his destiny. What might these four keys represent?

Jung learned from his old fatherly friend, Theodore Flournoy, that dreams have a purposive and teleological role in developing latent faculties of the personality. Flournoy attached great significance particularly to the faculty of the creative imagination that he thought was the "foundation of our being." Thus, Jung's interest in the prospective function of dreams began with Flournoy and the teleological view found its positive apotheosis in the Zürich school.[18] To be sure, Flournoy had a huge impact on Jung's thinking, yet it may have been the American-born, expansive James who opened the doorway to the idea of the collective or transpersonal unconscious. James was the first to coin the word "transpersonal" in 1906. Jung would later use the term in 1917 and then he dropped it. Jung's pupil, the Israeli analyst Erich Neumann, later picked it up, popularizing it more than a decade before there was a transpersonal movement in vogue in the Bay Area of California.[19] In the last decade of his life Jung was less limited by his empirical attitude and increasingly open-minded (following his serious illness in India in 1938 and heart attack in 1944) to investigating metaphysical questions, such as the question of the possible survival of consciousness after death; much of this is found in his "Late Thoughts."[20]

When we attempt to examine synchronistic phenomena from an empirical standpoint, moreover, we're treading on uncertain ground, for we can only prove the existence of *correspondences* if we can discover environmental factors that have a similar resonance, meaning, or pattern. The example of Philemon's appearance in the dream, for example, and the simultaneous discovery of a dead kingfisher in his garden while Jung was engaged with the process of painting the bird-man, is one of the most famous instances of meaningful chance on record. Jung's paintings of Philemon are now known worldwide because of the publication in 2009 of the *Red Book,* which at one time peaked to number 18 on *The New York Times* Bestsellers list, making it Jung's most successful book. Jung also painted a portrait of Philemon in his stone tower at Bollingen, which he called *Philemonis Sacrum,* or "Shrine to Philemon."[21]

NOTES

1. Jung, "The Meaning of Psychology for Modern Man," CW 10, ¶304.
2. Jung, "Adaptation, Individuation, Collectivity," CW 18, ¶1084.
3. Jung, CW 18, ¶1094.
4. Jung, CW 18, ¶1087.
5. Jung, CW 18, ¶1095.
6. Jung, CW 18, ¶1096.
7. Jung, CW 18, ¶1097.
8. Jung, CW 18, ¶1097.
9. Jung, CW 18, ¶1098.
10. Jung, CW 18, ¶1098.
11. Jung, CW 18, ¶1103.
12. Jung, CW 18, ¶1103.
13. Jung, CW 18, ¶1099.
14. Jung, "Synchronicity," CW 8, ¶912.
15. Jung, CW 8, ¶849.
16. Jung, CW 8, ¶964.
17. Jung, *MDR*, 182, 183.
18. Shamdasani, *Jung and the Making of Modern Psychology*, 141.
19. See Herrmann, "Transpersonal Psychology and the Self-Field."
20. Jung, *MDR*, Chapter XII.
21. Jung, *MDR*, 235, fn 5.

Chapter 14

THE MEANING OF THE CROSS

As detailed in Chapter 5, in the dialogue that took place between John Beebe and Sonu Shamdasani in 2010—one hundred years after the death of William James—one of the central questions that emerged in *Liber Novus* is a problematic of Christian theology: "What does it mean to take up one's own cross?" Any attempt to get at the meaning of the symbolism of the cross in Jung's *Collected Works* must start with his first amplifications of the image in his 1912 book, *Wandlüngen*. What we read in *Symbols of Transformation,* volume five of the *Collected Works,* is essentially a reworking of the fourth edition, which Jung rewrote in 1950, with a new preface, and which Rasher Verlag, Zürich, published in 1952. It was later published in America in 1956 by the Bollingen Foundation with an English translation by R. F. C. Hull. The first American printing of the book, however, was the English translation of the 1912 edition in 1916 by Beatrice Hinkle, printed as *Psychology of the Unconscious: A Study of the Transformations and Symbolisms of the Libido.*

To grasp the full significance of the book, I feel that it is best to read volume 5 side by side with Hinkle's edition, for which Jung wrote the first preface. In the "Author's Note to the First American/English Edition," Jung wrote of his task:

> My task in this work has been to investigate an individual fantasy system, and in the doing of it problems of such magnitude have been uncovered that my endeavor to grasp them in their entirety has necessarily meant only a superficial orientation toward those paths the opening and exploration of which may possibly crown the work of future investigators with success... This contribution is addressed to those having similar ideas concerning science.[1]

Jung's initial attempt to chart out the phenomenology of the process he later called *individuation* was originally viewed as a superficial orientation toward paths he hoped would crown the work of future investigators with achievement. This statement shows Jung's scientific modesty, even then. His major revision was done, moreover, in the same year he wrote the foreword to *Aion*, which focuses chiefly on the Christ symbol and its evolution across a two-thousand-year trajectory. In the American edition of *Symbols*, Jung asserted:

> The cross, or whatever other heavy burden the hero carries, is *himself*, or rather *the* self, his wholeness, which is both God and animal—not merely the empirical man, but the totality of his being, which is rooted in his animal nature and reaches out beyond the merely human towards the divine. His wholeness implies a tremendous tension of opposites paradoxically at one with themselves, as in the cross, their most perfect symbol.[2]

In the 1950 foreword to this fourth Swiss edition, Jung talked, furthermore, about the process he went through during the book's first publication, when he entered a dialogue with himself about the nature of his *personal myth, the myth of individuation, the subjective story in which he was living at the time he wrote it*. The book was written in 1911 during Jung's thirty-sixth year, a year after James died of heart failure. It was a critical moment for Jung, marking the beginning of the second half of his life when a "metanoia, a mental transformation, not infrequently occurs."[3] In other words, it happens in all of us whether we are aware of the process of metamorphosis that is taking place in the unconscious, or not. The key is to make the process of change in the unconscious conscious through various techniques. Analysis, of course, can go a long way in helping patients become conscious of the phenomenon of transformation in themselves. Yet the subject of Jung's study, the American poet Miss Frank Miller, relied mostly on her mythopoetic fantasies as her only source of therapy.

At the center of Jung's myth of meaning in midlife is his notion of the empirical God-image, God-complex, or God-symbol, for which the cross is an ideal symbol. It is Supreme because the tension of opposites on the cross, the polarities of shadow and light, masculine and feminine, good and evil, are paradoxically united, as Jung said, on its outstretched beams. The cross is the hero or heroine Himself or Herself, which I capitalize here, to designate it from the ego complex, as the carrier of consciousness.

Jung's task at midlife was to discover his own subjective myth, his truth, his God-image, and uncover its meaning through an investigation of objective facts hidden away in his unconscious. The personal unconscious does not contain the answer to the question of our personal myth, Jung informed us; instead, the collective, or transpersonal unconscious, the domain of primordial images or archetypes, contains our individual secret. Jung's self-analysis, after he finished the book, inevitably led him to a scrutiny of his own dreams all the way back to his third year. This process directed him to suffer out his own inevitable crucifixion on the cross of his two destinies.

For Jung, the meaning of the cross turns up in the second part of *Wandlüngen*, which cost him his friendship with Freud. In *Jung and the Problem of Evil,* published in 1958, moreover, the author H. L. Phillip published a long correspondence between himself and Jung in the form of questions and answers. Jung's views on the meaning of the cross were made explicit in this exchange: "Christ has shown how everyone will be crucified upon his destiny, i.e., upon his self, as he was . . . We are threatened with universal genocide if we cannot work out the way of salvation by a symbolic death."[4]

To believe in Christ and his death on the cross is one thing, in Jung's view, yet to carry the burden of one's own cross, to suffer the fate of symbolic death, outstretched on the crossbeams, the agony of crucifixion, the Self and hero must become one, become identical, during the tension of opposites and their hopeful resolution in an emergence of a new life. The ego paradoxically suffers the fate of the Cross, whereas the hero is sacrificed on the Cross of the Self's destiny. Fate and destiny were recurrent principles in Jung's book, a complementary pair. The concepts of fate and destiny began to emerge fully in chapter 7, "The Dual Mother," in which he discussed the life of Gautama Buddha and the influence of this post-Hindu myth on the fantasies of Miss Miller:

> How right we were in our supposition that what was going on in Miss Miller's unconscious as a battle for independence is now shown by her remark that the hero's departure from his father's house reminded her of the fate of the young Buddha, who renounced all the luxury of his home in order to go out into the world and live his destiny to the full.[5]

Fate and destiny were seen here as the archetypal pattern of the hero's journey and his or her inevitable Self-sacrifice. This sentence was almost identical in Hinkle's translation. I must note, moreover, that Miss Miller was a poet and her fantasies were written in a mythopoetic language. Jung used an American myth to amplify the meaning of Miss Miller's fantasies, *The Song of Hiawatha* by Henry David Longfellow, published in 1855, the same year as Whitman's forty-four-page masterpiece, *Leaves of Grass*. In doing so he attempted to create a theory of mythologems that were said to describe the structure and nature of the human psyche that was more or less the same everywhere in everyone. Keep in mind, though, that Jung's hypotheses were never meant to become Procrustean; his *science of the soul* was meant, rather, to remain open to further empirical investigations. Jung was led to examine the contents of Longfellow's poem because Miss Miller had read the poem and it directly influenced her fantasies.

NOTES

1. Jung, *Symbols of Transformation,* CW 5, ¶xxx.
2. Jung, CW 5, ¶460.
3. Jung, CW 5, p. xxvi.
4. Jung, "Jung and Religious Belief," CW 18, ¶1661.
5. Jung, CW 5, ¶470.

Chapter 15

The Child Archetype and the God Behind the Door

In a case study of a child I presented at the ETH Zürich in 2008, "The Case of Jacob," I recalled this child's traumatic history, which I'll repeat, in brief, here[1]: He was an adopted child with European ancestry whom I started seeing when he was five-and-a-half years old; he was abandoned at birth by his heroin-using biological mother who was a street prostitute and an addict. He suffered from severe emotional trauma; for the first forty-five days of his life, he struggled mightily for his existence in an incubator (he weighed two-pounds) in an Infant Detoxification Unit for drug-exposed babies. Through some miracle of psychic life, he was able to preserve some measure of psychological "health," despite his tragic fate as an addicted baby and an orphan with a stressed nervous system.

In my paper I asked,

> What does the motif of abandonment in infancy mean psychologically and how can it *influence* an orphan's fate, really?
> How might we gain insight into the phenomenon of the orphan's *affective violence*, moreover, and its transformation?
> Is there a middle ground between an archetypal and developmental view toward the abandoned child's fate, his depressions, anxieties, and symptoms in the context of Jungian child analysis?

By paying attention to the products of a child's unconscious fantasy-activity, and by uncovering "self-portraits" in the child's statements, utterances of the "unconscious psyche about itself," Jung indicated that we might arrive at an objective standpoint through which the "*unconscious core of meaning*" inherent in the child's history might be perceived analytically.[2] This meaning is expressed by the impulse toward *increasing consciousness of the personality*, expressed "first and foremost, in metaphors."[3]

One element of metaphorical meaning that may emerge in Jungian child psychotherapy is the theme of the infant's "abandonment and danger through persecution" by malevolent forces and evil, followed by a potentially fortuitous *change* in the child's conscious attitudes in latency and, hopefully, the living out of her creative destiny.[4] Something happens in a child's relationship to fate, in other words, when, by an act of *grace,* a child with such a history is *blessed by life* through *chance encounters with special persons who possess boon-bestowing powers* and who can accept and contain the child's loving and violent fantasies. The reader may know of children whose negative fates have been suddenly reversed by being consecrated in the *temeno*s of the transference/countertransference relationship, whether to a therapist or analyst who has succeeded in helping the child *spiritualize violence* through the vehicle of ritualized symbolizations.

A question arises about how *destructive emotions* and their somatic correlates might best be handled in the field of child psychotherapy. This inquiry does not have any simple answers; what the question yields—clinically speaking, however—is that there are *multiple ways* to treat infantile abandonment-traumas or overanxious and depressive illnesses in analysis. I prefer the plural way prescribed by James, who believed that every vehicle toward knowledge should be considered, and no hypothesis discounted, until it is proven invalid.

A developmental approach to the problem of aggression is fine, but what it often overlooks are the clinical conclusions supplied during the very early stage Jung identified, the *chrysalis stage,* and by what I've added to the field of Jungian analysis, the *transitus,* where violence and the killing-weapon provide a symbolic key to affective transformation through *symbolization*. Jung, as I've said, was not a child analyst himself, yet he conducted a Seminar on Children's Dreams in 1940 during the same year he wrote his paper on "The Psychology of the Child Archetype," so he had observed the autochthonous emergence of the archetype in *actual dreams of children, at that precise moment in time, after the outbreak of World War II.*

Karl Kerényi's inquiry regarding the "orphan's fate" was a bit different than Jung's. His mythopoetic view provided an insight to a science of mythology, but his views could also apply to clinical concerns.[5] Insofar as Kerényi and Jung were analyzing the *true orphan's fate,* which is to say the fate of the divine child and his or her destiny as a culture hero in myth, the mythologem always reveals, Kerenyi asserted, the "triumph of the elemental nature of the wonder-child" over and against the annihilating forces of darkness, violence, cruelty, and evil in the psyche and the world.[6] "The childhood and the orphan's fate of the child gods," Kerényi noted, "have not evolved from the stuff of human life, but from the stuff of cosmic life."[7] I must add—based on what I know about the origins of the Cosmos and the tremendous explosiveness at the center of human consciousness, the great explosion, or Big Bang of Creation, 13.7 billion years ago. So Kerényi and Jung were really on the same page regarding the symbol; I think they were right.

What led Jung to write his essay "The Psychology of the Child Archetype"? I believe it was Jung's friendship with Kerényi and Jung's *religious vocation*. Kerényi immigrated to Switzerland in 1943 to lead the life of an independent humanist and co-founded the C. G. Jung Institute because of his close connection with Jung.[8] The book they cowrote together, no doubt, was a major catalyst for Kerényi's *Essays on a Science of Mythology: The Myths of the Divine Child and Divine Maiden*.

In preparing to write this companion paper to Kerényi's "The Primordial Child in Primordial Times" for this book, Jung had observed the spontaneous emergence of the child archetype in actual dreams of children, as reported by parents or remembered by adults. When the book was published in collaboration with Kerényi, in 1941, Jung was formulating his own hypotheses based on empirical data. I feel his postulates and Kerényi's still hold weight in light of current trends in the field of analytical depth psychology. The essays are an important contribution for anyone interested in questions concerning fate and destiny, whether in science, psychology, religion, philosophy, or art. They are certain to strike a corresponding chord in the reader's mind.

In the opening paragraph of "The Psychology of the Child Archetype," Jung stated that he was asked by Kerényi for a psychological commentary on the subject of his investigations. Kerényi began his opening paper with the following inquiry: "Which came first: solitude in the primeval world, or the purely human picture of the orphan's fate?"[9] This question is still of central importance, not only to a science of mythology, but also to clinical problems experienced every day by psychotherapists who deal in practice with fate and destiny in the lives of their patients.

In his analysis of children's dreams at the ETH in the winter term of 1938/1939, Jung analyzed the dream of a four-year-old girl, for instance, *who dreamed of a wedding carriage and an angel*. Jung made it clear that knowledge about her *vision of the future* was a form of unconscious *knowledge* that was in her potentially from the beginning. Jung then added that with this knowledge, arrived at through the memory of her dream, she came upon the *germ for the ground plan of the development of her personality as a whole, and this development was inborn in her*. From the "sea" of the collective unconscious, the human personality is born, Jung continued, and from "that collective region in which all of human destiny is present in images" the "child has to step out of this primordial world, to be able to really enter into life."[10] If she can actualize the potential in the archetype of the divine child, her destiny is seeded. *A door is opened and the Self may come in*. Jung was not speaking of mere fantasies of fate and destiny here, he was speaking of the world and transpsychic reality. The more archaic and "deeper" such symbols are, Jung concluded, the more collective or universal and, hence, the more "material" they are. In this sense, Jung held Kerényi to be absolutely right that "in the symbol the world itself is speaking." This book is one of the great classics in analytical psychology. It was Jung's destiny, I believe, to write this essay, the destiny of the divine child in Jung as an image of the Self inside the door.

An insight that has been central to my own research, analytic practice, and writing on the subject of Jungian psychotherapy with severely traumatized children is that Jung served a role as a mentor, teacher, and influencer of general interest in the domain of child psychotherapy, a subject that is sometimes overlooked. As the reader may know, Jung had a deep fascination with the subject of children's dreams, elegiac reveries, and mythopoetic rhythms; his first trip to America, moreover, may have signaled the beginnings of this interest in print. The end of his discipleship to Freud, an expert on child psychosexual stages, yet a researcher who unfortunately lacked sufficient scientific understanding into the archetypal background, was foreshadowed then over the issue of dream interpretation.

Jung's interest in children's dreams may have sparked Kerényi's research. Kerényi's analysis of the primordial child and Jung's paper contained an answer to the problem Jung set out to analyze in "The Significance of the Father." Jung saw early on, in his research into children's dreams, that waves, rhythms, and elegies were of prime importance to the field of analytical psychology as a whole.

My focus on the destiny of the child and his or her fate is pertinent to this book because, regardless of whether it was the significance of the mother, or father, in James's or Jung's destiny-patterns, the *healing* of developmental traumas and overcoming of neurosis can take place in a natural way—without the aid of analysis—if the person is lucky. Through a *feeling* of having been selected by a giant hand, Higher Self, or divine voice in the unconscious, James and Jung followed their predestined vocations toward their futures as empirical psychologists after lengthy deliberations, fateful detours, and wrong turns. Once each discovered the *way of natural science*, they followed a destiny-pattern that they affirmed and followed with trustful loyalty to the end. Although a thorough look at the developmental histories of either James or Jung is beyond the scope of this book, it's important to preface my psychobiographical sketch of James with this: despite any wounds to his Body Self or Social Self on an emotional level, James's Higher Self was constellated by early childhood or latency, as he was blessed by a fortuitous family situation, by the giant hand of his destiny. James was "blessed" by his godfather in infancy, Ralph Waldo Emerson, during a visit to the family home in New York City in 1842.[11] Between 1848 and 1854, Emerson was a frequent guest at the James's homestead. Behind the door to the guest room of his house was the insignia proclaimed by James's father: "Mr. Emerson's Room."[12] James's brother Henry said that during his latency, moreover, he was always "drawing and drawing, always drawing."[13] In adolescence William James attended school in Geneva, Switzerland, Jung's home ground. In 1860, at eighteen years old, he said: "I have fully decided to try a career as a painter."[14] In 1866, at twenty-four, he became terribly depressed and even contemplated suicide.[15] James traveled to Switzerland many times. His last trip there was two months before his death, when he visited Geneva, Lucerne, and Zürich.[16] Jung, who had heard an annoying story that his grandfather was a natural son of Goethe, also eventually felt that his destiny was God-sent.[17] James and Jung were each related, therefore, whether through birth-line or familial relationship, with figures of semi-divine authorial power—national literary figures with grandfatherly influence.

My point here is that regardless of whether the child is orphaned, like my patient, or born into a well-to-do family and blessed at birth, like James, there's something miraculous in the child archetype that can switch on during key stages of development. My particular interest has focused intensively on the stage of latency as a child psychotherapist. Yet, whether a child is analyzed or not, what James called *"the impulse towards better cognition"* may be switched on in a child by teachers who constellate *Love* and *curiosity* in the classroom environment: 'The sporadic metaphysical inquires of children as to who made God, and why they have five fingers, need hardly be counted here. But when the theoretic instinct is once alive in the pupil, an entirely new order of pedagogic relations begins for him."[18] (Jung said this theoretic instinct was activated at the age of eleven in himself.) For this reason, James advocated in his "Talks to Teachers" to promote good *habits* in children, and he believed strongly that the greatest thing in education is *"to make our nervous system our ally instead of our enemy . . . For this we must make automatic and habitual, as early as possible, as many useful actions as we can."*[19] A European education in Switzerland certainly helped James with this, but it did not cure his childhood depression. The *medicine*, I think, was his *vocation*. James was elected president of the American Association of Psychologists in 1893, when Jung was eighteen. By this time, he had found his place in the world as a leading authority on the Self.

In his *Dream Seminars,* Jung spoke about the case of a man who was having a difficult time awakening his superior self, superior man, or Higher Self. To paraphrase: *The man had a dream where he was in his bedroom with his wife, and a door that led into another room slowly opened before him. He went immediately to the door and pushed it open the rest of the way. In the other room he found a naked little boy. He carried him into the bedroom, convinced in the dream that he was not a natural boy. In order to prevent the boy's getting out of his arms, the dreamer pressed the boy against himself, and the boy gave him the most remarkable feelings of satisfaction, as if this true thing he was holding were enough to satisfy his longing for intimacy. Then his wife brought in a variety of foods for the child to eat. The dreamer saw black bread and white bread. The child did not want to eat the black bread, but ate the white bread instead. Then suddenly he flew out of the window and beckoned the dreamer and his wife from the air to follow him.*[20]

Jung's analysis of the dream is quite fascinating. Jung interpreted the little boy to be a representation for Eros, or relatedness. The man had become too businesslike and was suffering from a moral shadow, related to his economic greed and illicit behaviors. "His problem can only be dealt with by making an appeal to his higher self," Jung said, "but that appeal would be worthless so long as the man is not his own higher self, so long as his higher values are projected into the father, and he is living the provisional life."[21]

Several pages later, Jung told the seminarians: "Meister Eckhart had a vision of a little naked boy."[22] He mentioned further on a story about Eckhart's vision from the fourteenth century of a visitation he received from a beautiful naked boy who came from God. "Where hast thou left him," Eckhart asked the boy. "In virtuous hearts," answered the boy. "Whither goest thou?" Eckhart asked. "To God." "Where wilt thou find him?" "When I leave all created things." "Who art thou?" "A king." "And where is thy kingdom?" "In my own heart." Of course, Jung said, the boy was God himself who was with Eckhart a little while.[23]

This dialogue with the *naked boy behind the dream door* describes beautifully the natural process Jung called active imagination. By active imagination, Jung meant a colloquy with a content, an image, or a symbol of the collective unconscious. In Eckhart's story, it was an archetype of the Self, the eternal child as the Word of God, that spoke eloquently to Eckhart during his elegiac dream-vision. In the vision, the conversation or colloquy with the Self-as-divine-child spoke back and Eckhart listened; then he answered the child and asked questions of him in a two-way process: question and answer. The naked boy took on an active form of speech and gave voice to the Word of God. Eckhart's vision illustrated what Jung called the birth of the new God-concept: the relativity of God. The God-notion Eckhart gave birth to was Lord Jesus. By speaking God's Word, Eckhart gave birth to a new vision of divinity beyond the Trinity—the Mother of God, or Godhead, a Fourth principal that structured the whole psyche, spirit and instinct, matter and Cosmos. Jung might have first turned to Eckhart to describe the new vision of the indwelling of the Self in the West. Eckhart was so far ahead of his time that he anticipated both James and Jung. Indeed, Eckhart anticipated where we all are today by 700 years!

The naked child of God spoke the Word to Eckhart and the Master took down what he said in the form of a dictation through the technique of vocalism, whereby Eckhart was clearly under instruction from the Word and the inner Child also benefited from the dialogue. One could say that he was channeling the archetype of the divine child as a new God-notion in the collective psyche through the "living symbol" of Jesus that was "pregnant with meaning": "The symbol is alive only so long as it is pregnant with meaning... It is, therefore, quite impossible to create a living symbol, i.e., one that is pregnant with meaning, from known associations."[24]

Jung finished his disquisition by telling the wonderful story of Eckhart's vision of the naked boy. He informed his listeners that when Eckhart said finally to the child, "Take any cloak thou likest," the God-child simply replied, "Then I should be no king," and suddenly He vanished. "So you could say," Jung concluded, "The equivocal quality of the child in this vision is not just a God but a King of the Kingdom of Heaven that is within, within ourselves, not the God without... This god, this divinity, has the appearance of a child. If you do not become as a little child you cannot enter the Kingdom of Heaven, you cannot make true the God within."[25]

Jung essentially gave an Eckhartian address on the relativity of God to his Jungian seminarians. But as an American, William James, during his infancy and through his adolescence, lived this myth out every night that the door was opened to welcome Emerson. In his address at the Emerson Centenary, James said this:

> The point of any pen can be an epitome of reality; the commonest persons act, if genuinely actuated, can lay hold on eternity. This vision is the headspring of all his outpourings... Emerson's wraith comes to me now as if it were but the very voice of this victorious argument.... As long as our English language lasts, men's hearts will be cheered and their souls strengthened and liberated by the noble and musical pages with which you [now addressing Emerson's wraith in the first person here] have enriched it.[26]

The esteem with which James viewed his Master is obvious. He was a man, in James's eyes, who lived the destiny of his Higher Self, the superior man, and who helped to shape the spiritual life of the American Soul. For Transcendentalists and for James, Emerson was for America what Eckhart might have been for Europe. For, as Jung says of Eckhart, "he was the fellow who could have been followed by a great religious movement."[27]

In the same seminar on dream analysis given on March 20, 1929, Jung spoke further, finally, of the dream of Brother Eustachius, a dream reported to Meister Eckhart while he was preaching in Paris. Again, to paraphrase: *In the dream, Brother Eustachius saw that many brethren in the monastery were standing in a circle in the refectory around a beautiful boy, namely Jesus. The little child of Mary demanded a loaf of pure white bread to eat. A humble Brother, Brother Ruopreht, who was in charge of baking, found the divine boy a loaf of simple white bread and Eustachius loved this Brother with all the force of his heart because of his humility.*[28]

What interests me concerning such passages on Eckhart's vision is that Jung's comments all predate his study with Kerényi on the archetype of the divine child in 1939. Eckhart's vision of the naked boy that vanished from the world of created things into Nothingness and who returned swiftly to the Kingdom of Heaven within the Ground of the Godhead, became, I think, fertile material for Jung to consider as he reflected on the empirical recurrence of the child archetype in dreams of adults while treating patients in Switzerland.

In his "Introduction to Suzuki's Zen Buddhism," Jung maintained that Eckhart actually went to a deeper level of the psyche than any Christian theologian before this time.[29] Eckhart's radical and daring new truth-telling of birthing the new God-notion reflected the stature of the man who was standing-in-himself.

Thus, as Jung discussed in the *Dream Seminars,* for the patient in midlife, the Self behind the door was the God within. "In our actual modern mind we cannot explain it like that anymore; we understand it more psychologically than ever before. We explain the little naked boy as a psychological fact. A thousand years hence they may have an entirely new name but it will be merely a new form of expression for the same old fact."[30] The concept of the psychological relativity in the human-God relationship that Jung made explicit in his 1921 essay on the Master, the radically new idea that *God needs humans, as humans need God,* was also realized for psychology, philosophy, and modernity by William James, prior to Jung.[31]

For James life and meaning were always the main things, the constant overflowing of effervescent energy from the Self out of the foundation of ever-ebullient life: "I confess that I do not see," he wrote in *The Will*

To Believe, "why the very existence of an invisible world may not in part depend on the personal response which any one of us may make to the religious appeal. God himself, in short, may draw final strength and increase of very being from our fidelity."[32]

Notes

1. The ETH (Eidgenössische Technische Hochschule) is the Swiss Federal Institute of Technology, located in Zürich, Switzerland.
2. Jung, "The Psychology of the Child Archetype," CW 9i, ¶¶262, 266.
3. Jung, CW 9i, ¶267.
4. Jung, CW 9i, ¶281.
5. Kerényi, "The Primordial Child in Primordial Times," 30.
6. Kerényi, 36.
7. Kerényi, 45.
8. Kerényi's *Dionysos: Archetypal Image of Indestructible Life* contains a great two-page biography that readers may want to peruse, if they have not already.
9. Kerényi, "The Primordial Child in Primordial Times," 30.
10. Jung, *Children's Dreams*, 184.
11. James, *Writings 1902–1910*, 1321.
12. Richardson, *William James*, 153.
13. James, *Writings 1902–1910*, 1322.
14. James, 1324.
15. James, 1327.
16. James, 1348.
17. Jung, *MDR*, 35.
18. James, *Writings 1878–1899*, 741.
19. James, 751. Italics in original.
20. Jung, *Dream Seminars*, 170.
21. Jung, 169.
22. Jung, 175.
23. Jung, 180–181.
24. Jung, *Psychological Types*, CW 6, ¶¶816, 817.
25. Jung, *Dream Seminars*, 180, 182.
26. James, *Writings 1902–1910*, 1125.

27. Jung, *Nietzsche's Zarathustra*, vol. 2, 1487.
28. Jung, *Dream Seminars*, 181.
29. Jung, "Foreword to Suzuki's *Introduction to Zen Buddhism*," CW 11, ¶¶877–907.
30. Jung, CW 11, 183.
31. Jung "*The Relativity of the God-concept in Meister Eckhart*," CW 6, ¶¶407–433.
32. James, *Writings 1878–1899*, 502.

PART II

Spiritual Democracy and the Fight with the Shadow

Chapter 16

C. G. Jung's Vision of Spiritual Democracy

The American psychologist William James first stated in *The Varieties of Religious Experience* that the "real backbone of the world's religious life" was not to be found in any creeds, theories, schools, or books, but in psychological experiences, first and foremost. As a young man, James had traveled with Louis Agassiz, Alexander von Humboldt's student, to South America. Agassiz knew first hand that experience meant experience of the world and engagement in both its present reality and its inevitable geological transformations. James followed Agassiz's example by establishing a foundation for American psychology that was to be treated specifically as a "natural science."[1] In *Varieties* James asserted as a matter of empirical psychological observation that the religious life of humanity as a whole was our "most important function," meaning the function of psychological life.[2] Jung had read *Varieties* and specifically sought James out for a personal meeting on his first trip to the United States in 1909.

For anyone who has read *Varieties*, it is clear that the religious function—the life granted by our psyches to the world's religions as a whole—is also coincident with a cosmic function, part of the natural history of the universe to be observed by an empathically participating psychological consciousness. The trip to Brazil with Agassiz was important for James's own *feeling for the cosmic range of human individuation*. As the founding father of American pragmatism, James found it sensible to unite empirical science and the transcendent intuitions that were grounded in religious experiences because, for him, they belonged to the same universe of thought.

For Jung, on the other hand, spiritual democracy was not just one of the deepest goals of the psyche, it already existed, at least in potential, everywhere around us. Joseph L. Henderson went so far as to say that democracy was the natural state of life and that dictatorships were an "interruption" to the democratic spirit.[3] In his paper "The Inner Vision and Social Organization," Henderson spoke of the move beyond king-ruled society (Hobbes's *Leviathan*) after the end of the seventeenth century: "But this kind of unity began to break up, leaving behind a new diversity represented by a government we call democracy with its blessings and its discontents and interruptions by dictators."[4] Later in the same paper, he said of Jung: "He was an introvert and a more or less conservative Swiss citizen in a country with a long history of functional democracy, uninterrupted by political demagoguery."[5] He then went on talk about Jung's conception of the *Anthropos* ("an image of mankind that transcends ethnic or national forms and embraces the totality of what it means to be human") and how this image appeared among the Naskapi Indians as Mistapeo ("my friend... the Great Man).[6] Finally, at the end of the paper he concluded: "So here we have some real anthropological and psychological evidence for the innate motivation for living in a democratic spirit which is not to be equated with its doubtful corollary: free enterprise."[7]

"True democracy," Jung said, "is a highly psychological institution."[8] Thus, we need a psychology of the depths in order to see what democracy is at a spiritual level and to demonstrate where order and totality may be experienced in conjunction with the natural harmony of material things. Whatever this unity is that embraces everything, it is, without any doubt, what Jung and Nobel-winning physicist Wolfgang Pauli called a *psychophysical reality*, neither wholly physical nor psychic, but a third thing *transcendent of the opposites*. Jung's late theory of the Self suggested that at bottom it is "probable that psyche and matter are two different aspects of one and the same thing."[9] These dual sides of the Self, rather artificially called by us "inner and outer reality," come together as we move forward in accord with our instinctive prerogative to individuate, which is to realize the union of psyche and environment in a spiritual democracy of consciousness that gives equal weight to both.

By spiritual democracy I'm not speaking of democracy at the political or economic levels, but at the individual level, of pure divine experience of the essential equality of the human psyche. "If the collective equality of the psyche were not a primordial fact, the origin and matrix of all individual psyches, it would be a gigantic illusion."[10] The widespread spiritual change in the consciousness of Westerners, Jung continued, set in after the Reformation, which shattered the authority of the Church as a teaching institution. "The inevitable consequence was an increase in the importance of the individual, which found expression in the modern ideals of humanity, social welfare, democracy, and equality."[11] But this kind of democracy is not what Jung meant by spiritual democracy either. *True democracy*—the equality of each individual psyche with the "superior man, his superior self" within—means that we are each a doorway, a gate into an experience of infinitesimal insignificance in the Cosmos really, unless we become who we are.[12] Political and economic democracy were illusory to Jung; what mattered most was the experience of humility and modesty in the face of the Infinite:

> Small and hidden is the door that leads inward, and the entrance is barred by countless prejudices, mistaken assumptions, and fears. Always one wishes to hear of grand political and economic schemes, the very things that have landed every nation in a morass. Therefore it sounds grotesque when anyone speaks of hidden doors, dreams, and a world within. What has this vapid idealism got to do with gigantic economic programs, with the so-called problems of reality?[13]

Nothing really. This is why Jung felt misunderstood in the end. For Jung, spiritual democracy was a narrow doorway that led to an experience of the superior self within. This was not the Big "I" experience of Vedanta, the presumption that "I" and Shiva are One, or Brahma, Vishnu, or Krishna and "I" are One, but the small "I," the common "we," our subjective selves are merely gateways to an experience of *equality* with the psyche of everyone. Only by passing through this passageway of the personal and national shadow of humans at the political and economic levels can we be born anew in the spiritual world through a vocation to live by, one that accepts imperfection, sin, evil, and death of the hero in relation to the first big *Nothing* out of which *everything* is created.

NOTES

1. James, *Writings 1878–1899*, 11.
2. Perry, *The Thought and Character of William James,* vol. 2, *Philosophy and Psychology*, 327.
3. Henderson, "The Inner Vision and Social Organization," 28–33.
4. Henderson, 29.
5. Henderson, 30.
6. Henderson, 32.
7. Henderson, 33.
8. Jung, "Symbols and the Interpretation of Dreams," CW 18, ¶456.
9. Jung, "General Aspects of Dream Psychology," CW 8, ¶418.
10. Jung, "The Meaning of Psychology for Modern Man," CW 10, ¶285.
11. Jung, CW 10, ¶326.
12. Jung, *Dream Analysis,* 168.
13. Jung, CW 10, ¶328.

Chapter 17

Jung's Vision of Spiritual Democracy in *The Red Book* and in *Psychological Types*

In this chapter, I explore the myth of the Cosmic Man in Vedic mythology to help form a bridge between C. G. Jung's hypothesis of the Self and the Self/Selves and streams of consciousness in James. Not enough has been written about the origins of the Self in Jung's early writings, such as in his now world-famous *Red Book*. Jung had an uncanny way of meditating on texts through active imagination, as a prelude to his greatest breakthroughs in scientific formulations. I want to briefly highlight a key passage from *The Red Book*. The passage appears in a section called "Incantations," in which Jung said specifically: "That is the demise of the Gods: man puts them in his pocket. That is the end of the story of the Gods. Nothing remains of the Gods other than an egg. And I possess this egg."[1]

In Part II, Chapter XIII of *Symbols of Transformation*, "The Sacrifice," Jung commented on the figure of *Purusa*, the Primal Cosmic Man, in *Rig Veda*, 10: "It is evident that by this is meant not a physical, but a psychological cosmogony."[2] Who was *Purusa* in Vedic mythology and what is the significance of the egg Jung put into his medical pocket?

In *The Wonder that Was India*, A. L. Basham tells us that in "The Great Hymn of the Primeval Man," *Prajāpati*, "the Lord of Beings," was subsequently called *Brahmā*, the masculine form of the neuter *brahman*. Prajāpati was thought of as a Primeval Man (*Purusa*) who existed before the beginning of the Universe. In Purusa 10.90 (the Purusa-Sūkta, one of the last hymns of the Rig Veda), moreover, we come upon one of the most celebrated hymns of ancient India. Prajāpati is the Cosmic Man who was sacrificed and survived his own dismemberment. It was believed that without regular sacrifices, all cosmic processes of order would cease, and chaos would again come into existence; sacrifice was, therefore, at the center of the Rig Veda. Furthermore, *Brahman* means a sacred word that fills all space and time; Brahman is the primal Ground of all Being, above and below all forms of phenomena. From Prajāpati the whole Universe emerged. Thus, all phenomena arose out of the primal Self as Prajāpati, who is also the individual indwelling of Ātman, World Spirit, "Person," or the Universal Soul as a cosmic essence.[3]

In the Rigvedic period, there was a steady movement toward unity that assumed two primary forms: one looking toward monotheism, the other toward pantheism. This unity of the world was based on the concept of the Cosmic Man, and its multiplicity was traced to the archaic sacrificial Self-dismemberment—an archetype that extends all the way back to shamanism—of Prajāpati. A supreme example of monotheism, according to H. D. Griswold, may be found in the Hiranyagarbha-Prajāpati Hymn, where *Hiranyagarbha* means "the golden germ," or *seed,* that arose in the beginning (10.121). Finally, the dismemberment of the Primeval Man is considered to be a willing and voluntary sacrifice and is an instance of the original creation of Order out of Chaos.[4]

How does the myth of the Cosmic Man form a link between Jung, James, and the carrying of one's own cross? The myth of Prajāpati forms the nucleus of Chapter V, section 3, parts a, b, and c of Jung's book *Psychological Types,* called "The Type Problem in Poetry." This chapter comes directly before the pivotal chapters on Meister Eckhart and William James. The three subsections in section 3 are titled a.) "The Brahmanic Conception of the Problem of the Opposites"; b.) "The Brahmanic Conception of the Uniting Symbol"; and c.) "The Uniting Symbol as the Principle of Dynamic Regulation." These are all key subsections of an analysis that centers on Jung's formulation of the notion of the Self in analytical psychology.

After quoting a line from the Ramanayana—"This world must suffer under the pairs of opposites forever"—Jung commented further: "Not to allow oneself to be influenced by the pairs of opposites, but to be *nirvandva* (free, untouched by the opposites), to raise oneself above them, is an essentially ethical task, because deliverance from the opposites leads to redemption."[5] The key passage here is *to raise oneself above (or over) the pairs of opposites.* This, he claimed, is an *essentially ethical task.* He then added: "Since suffering is an affect, release from affects means deliverance. Deliverance from the flux of affects, from the tension of opposites, is synonymous with redemption that gradually leads to Brahman."[6] In the second subsection "The Brahmanic Conception of the Uniting Symbol,"

Jung said further: "Brahman is also *prana,* the breath of life and the cosmic principle."[7] This passage is crucial because he later said, as I quoted previously, while reflecting on his childhood, "Only in Meister Eckhart did I feel the breath of life."[8]

Jung then went on at length about the sacrifice of Prajāpati, quoting from the Brahmanas and Upanishads. His analysis is quite impressive. Jung equated the concept of Brahman with the libido as a uniting symbol, and he rightly called it "the Absolute" with a capital *A.*[9] Traces of the myth of the Cosmic Man are also quite evident in *Liber Novus,* in the 1920 stone carving of Atmavictu in Jung's garden (see Chapter 18 on Atmavictu), and in "The Type Problem in Poetry." Interestingly, the first penetrating focus of Jung's study of Hindu thought appears to have been, however, during the 1916–1917 period, when he was composing one of the main sections of *Liber Novus.*

Below picture 45 in *The Red Book,* for instance, we find the words inscribed in Sanskrit "*atharva-veda 4, 1, 4.*" In Jung's painting a man holds up a mandala with an egg in the center of it. Below picture 54 is the word "*brahmanaspati,*" the lord of prayer and worship in the *Rig Veda.* Below image 59 is the word "*hiranyagarbha,*" the primal seed from which Brahma was born. In a footnote, Sonu Shamdasani describes a slip of paper in Jung's copy of the Upanishads, in *The Sacred Books of the East,* with a line inscribed in Jung's hand: "And the same Self is also called Hiranyagarbha."[10] Finally, below picture 64 are the words "*catapatha-brahmanam 2, 2, 4,*" in which Prajāpati, the Cosmic Man, reproduced himself through his mouth in the form of Agni, the fire God.

Clearly Jungian psychology is indebted to India for its central concept, the Self. It is important to note, moreover, that Jung was also reading William James. In "Psychology: Briefer Course," James distinguished between the *Material (Body) Self,* the *Social Self,* and the *Spiritual Self.* He divided these Selves into a hierarchy, with the Body Self at bottom, the Empirical Self at the top, and the extracorporeal Material Selves and various Social Selves between. The Empirical Self, Me, or Ego is founded on the harmonious bodily, social, and spiritual functioning of the Self in each person. Jamesian psychology was concerned with helping others center their minds on a nuclear pathway for action in the world. In the two-volume 1890 edition of *The Principles of Psychology,* which Jung read, James put forth a theory of the Empirical Self, comprised of five essential constituents. He also posited a "nuclear Self" in the total structure of the Empirical Self, which I will discuss in some detail, based on my adaptation of James's original diagram:

James wrote about the first level: "The body is the innermost part of

	1.	a. *Material Self*	b. *Body Self*
5. *Empirical Self* (views all four dimensions of being and their two subsets, a and b.)	2.	*Social Self*	
	3.	a. *Spiritual Self*	b. *Central nuclear Self*
	4.	*Transcendental Thinker* (A metaphysical postulate that can only be inferred, not proven to exist empirically)	

the material Self in each of us; and certain parts of the body seem more intimately ours than the rest."[11] So the Body Self exists in the center of the Material Self. The Social Self is how we relate to ourselves and others in the world, whether in success or failure, good or bad fortune, and so on. The Empirical Self, in American pragmatism, is, in a theoretical sense, a principle of dynamic adaptation patterned on processes in a subconscious and the conscious Self of each moment. If the Self exerts an active function in the home, classroom, or community, it may become conscious, in a wider sense, of its ultimate ideals and practical aims on the path toward wholeness in a pluralistic universe.

What concerns me in this chapter are all four levels of the Self, including a Knower, or Transcendental Thinker, which is ultimately a metaphysical principle, according to James, who does not discuss this fourth level of the Self at any great depth in *The Principles*; it is, nevertheless, a primary focus in his final works, which I explore later. Thus, while keeping such distinctions in mind, I will focus on the third strata now—the Spiritual Self—as a doorway between the Material and Metaphysical levels. I refer to this third strata as the doorway to the Self, by which I mean a gateway in the Self that opens up to all four dimensions of our existence in the Empirical Self. James, of course, was not an analyst or psychotherapist; he was a professor of philosophy and president of the American Psychological Association, who also happened to be, like Jung, a psychical researcher. Yet he was perhaps the most articulate mind of his age and his impact on Jung was more significant than most theorists have hitherto suggested.

The Spiritual Self, James wrote, "so far it belongs to the Empirical Me," is a person's "inner or subjective being, his psychic faculties or dispositions, taken concretely ...These psychic dispositions are the most enduring and intimate part of the self, that which we most verily seem to be."[12] The spiritual faculties in the total Self are made up by a "plurality" of dispositions in the entire stream of our personal consciousness. A certain portion of this stream may be "abstracted" from the rest. When this occurs, it is "felt" by all people as "a sort of innermost center within the circle, of sanctuary within the citadel, constituted by the subjective life as a whole." This citadel, James said, is "the self of all the other selves," the "active element in all consciousness."[13]

"It is the home of interest," and from this innermost epicenter of our being, our ideas or incoming sensations are reflected and then pass over "into outward acts." By *epicenter* I mean the most active part of a person. James then inquired about "what the feeling of this central active self consists," and "what we feel when we become aware of its existence."[14] Stop thinking for a moment and allow yourselves to feel into this question and you may become aware of the active Self's existence, whether you're seated in a lecture room, listening to a professor of psychology, reading a work by James or Jung, or in the process of Jungian psychotherapy or analysis. Feeling is a function James stressed when he spoke of this central part of the Self; it is really a feeling of one's bodily activities whose exact nature are mostly overlooked. Since the three lower Selves are all rooted in the body, the central Self is grounded in the Body Self too, in the here and now. Where the Metaphysical Self resides is unknown. Yet the function of feeling is what tells us whether our actions in the world are most authentically our own and where we might become equals on the path toward completeness and complementarity.

The "Self of Selves," James hypothesized further, is our "innermost activity" of which we are "most distinctly aware."[15] It's really a feeling of bodily activities, which, for James are "found to consist mainly of the collection of these peculiar motions in the head or between the head and throat." Such physiological activities in the cerebral and vocal locations of the body were, for James, the domain of the "nuclear part of the Self." Insofar as they become "active" in analysis, or pragmatically in the world, they become "executions" of a "reflex type," meaning they are based on an instinctive foundation.[16] The voice is pivotal in formulating a link, therefore, between James and Jung, for what is found between the head and throat areas, the location for James's *innermost activity* in the Spiritual

Self, is the mouth: the passageway of speech, breath, language, teaching, and analytical discourse.

No doubt this Spiritual Self was already constellated in Jung during his adolescence, when he first tried to comprehend Eckhart's sermons at the age of fifteen. Later, in *Psychological Types,* between the sections on Hinduism and James, Jung examined the works of Meister Eckhart (1260–1328). As Eckhart said:

> A master who has spoken the best about the soul says that all human science can never fathom what the soul is in its ground. To know what the soul is, one needs supernatural knowledge... What the soul is in its ground, no one knows. What one can know about it must be supernatural, it must be from grace. That is where God works compassion.[17]

The Ground in Eckhart's theology of the soul is more than the collective unconscious, for it includes matter and the infinite Cosmos, and it is, therefore, to my mind equivalent with what Jung called the *psychoid*. The problem in analytical psychology, Dominican theology, and modern theoretical physics today is that no one can tell us what precisely the Ground or psychoid really is. Jung aptly called it a *psychophysical continuum* that transcended causality, space and time, and united the dualities of psyche and matter in a *Unus Mundus*. Eckhart said the Ground was beyond the Trinity. It was a Fourth Feminine dimension of being and nonbeing. He added: "Here God's ground is my ground and my ground is God's ground."[18]

Entering such a Ground can be therapeutic because compassion lives there. The goal of analytical psychology is to reunite the mind, therefore, with what Jung, echoing Eckhart and Jacob Boehme, later called the "eternal Ground of all empirical being."[19] Anyone may access this divine Ground through traditional methods of meditation, offered by any of the world's religions. Late in life Jung said succinctly: "But this much we do know beyond all doubt, that empirical reality has a transcendental background."[20]

Eckhart called this background the *Godhead;* Lao-Tzu called it the *Tao;* Emerson, the *Universal Mind*; and in 1947, Jung called it the *psychoid*. The Ground cannot be named, but it can be known experientially. The highest Ground of the soul, according to Eckhart, was the intellectual-intuition:

the place of supernatural *knowledge*. I believe there is no distinction between East and West regarding the notion of the Ground of human experience. It is above and below, high and low, earth-based and sky-based.

In *Aion* Jung made the vital connection between Atman and Christ clear by linking these two symbols of the Self through a comparison between the Vedas and the sermons of Eckhart. He had already created this bridge, more eloquently, in his brilliant 1921 essay on the Dominican in *Psychological Types*. There, Jung wrote beautifully while reading and meditating on Eckhart's words: "We feel ourselves transported back into the spacious atmosphere of the Upanishads."[21] The atmosphere Jung described during his side-by-side readings of the Upanishads and Eckhart is the *spaciousness* that is most remarkable in comparisons between Jung and James. Spaciousness is part of a larger analytic frame for Jungian analysts to inhabit in their work. Eckhart and James and Jung all point the way to such a broadening.

As an analyst I need to explore and struggle with my countertransferences and locate ways to move toward a more spacious analytic attitude. Frequently, such an enlargement of scope comes through the discovery of spiritual practice of some kind. In my analytic training at the C. G. Jung Institute of San Francisco, for instance, I needed to shift at times and become less enmeshed with my patients' struggles and search out ways to hold a more spacious view in my psychotherapy sessions. As I returned to my regular practice of Yoga and meditation, working with some of the psychic prana techniques prescribed by Swami Vivekananda, I felt a spaciousness inside of me around my patients' presenting symptoms, which appeared to allow a few of them to further explore their doubts, depressions, and fears in greater depth and possibly at a higher altitude of understanding.[22] Jung explained how the spiritual and historical analogy he made with the East got into his way of looking at things in a letter written in 1932 to Dr. A. Vetter: "The intrusion of the East is rather a psychological fact with a long history behind it. The first signs may be found in Meister Eckhart, Leibnitz, Kant, Hegel, Schopenhauer and von Hartmann. It is not however the actual east we are dealing with but the collective unconscious, which is omnipresent."[23] James was reading the same basic sources as was Jung.

NOTES

1. Jung, *The Red Book,* 285. Hereafter references to *The Red Book* will be cited as *RB*.
2. Jung, *Symbols of Transformation,* CW 5, ¶652.
3. Basham, *The Wonder that Was India,* 239–252.
4. Griswold, *The Religion of the Rigveda,* 344–350.
5. Jung, *Psychological Types,* CW 6, ¶327.
6. Jung, CW 6, ¶330.
7. Jung, CW 6, ¶334.
8. Jung, *MDR,* 68, 69.
9. Jung, CW 6, ¶336.
10. Jung, *RB,* note 130, 258.
11. James, *The Principles of Psychology,* 125.
12. James, 126.
13. James, 127.
14. James, 127.
15. James, 128.
16. James, 128.
17. Fox, *Breakthrough: Meister Eckhart's Creation Spirituality in New Translation,* 442.
18. Fox, 108.
19. Jung, *Mysterium Coniunctionis,* CW 14, ¶760.
20. Jung, CW 14, ¶768.
21. Jung, CW 6, ¶411.
22. The first psychology, the science of Yoga, begins with the breath, *Prana,* breathing deeply. *Pranayama* can bring the body and mind to a state of peace. Breath work is the beginning. Pranayama does not stop there. Psychic prana is a further state about which depth psychology knows very little. Beginner's mind begins with breath.
23. Jung, *Letters,* vol. 1, 87.

Figure 18.1 Atmavictu in the garden at Küsnacht, Summer 2008
(Photograph by the author)

Chapter 18

Atmavictu: "The Breath of Life"

Atmavictu (first spelled *Atmaviktu*) is an inner mythical figure that emerged in C. G. Jung's *Black Book* 6 on April 25, 1917.¹ In *Black Book* 6 Jung said Atmavictu had been the serpent's companion for thousands of years. He was at first an old man; then he went through a series of four consecutive deaths, passing in theriomorphic form from an old man to serpent followed by his quintessential transformation into Philemon; he transformed into a bear, then an otter, a newt, a serpent conjurer—the kernel of the Self—and finally, into the winged spirit Philemon who taught Jung the method of "psychic objectivity": the "reality of the psyche."² Long before I became aware of Jung's associations to the figure of Atmavictu in *Black Book* 6, as indicated in Sonu Shamdasani's footnotes to Image 117 in *The Red Book*, I wrote a little poem titled "Atmavictu." As a young man, I had read about Atmavictu in Jung's *Memories, Dreams, Reflections,* and his comments about this figure intrigued me. It would be years, however, before I actually traveled to Zürich to deliver a paper at the ETH in the summer of 2008. When I was in Zürich, I went on a walking tour of Jung's house in Küsnacht, and there, in the garden, low and behold, he stood, looking silently at me—Atmavictu! I immediately got out my camera and made my approach.

When I crouched down to photograph him, I felt a stir of the Self speaking to me from the stone, through a sudden rush of excitement and emotion, as I recalled lines from the poem I'd written a decade earlier after a drumming session. The name *Atmavictu* had been drummed into me then, in a series of downward-driving beats, like a dirge, that found their way into free verse. The poem was a sort of chant for Atmavictu to reawaken and speak to us again from the spirit of the depths. It was a primal calling from the Self to give voice to something vital I felt Jung had left behind for us to wonder about. In 1920, he had carved two figures of Atmavictu from branches of wood while in England. Then, he later had Atmavictu reproduced in stone, shown in the photograph on the front cover of this book. The spirit of Atmavictu is well preserved in this stone carving. When I knelt down to look at him, from all angles, a sort of shamanistic cry out of the depths of nature spoke to me again from the spirit in the stone. The pictures I took are the way I experienced him, near the hanging branch of the tree. On our tour of Jung's house and garden, I was asked by someone what the figure's name was. "Atmavictu, Atmavictu!" I replied, repeating the opening verse of my poem. "Who is Atmavictu, and what does the word *Atmavictu* mean?", this interested person asked. "Jung's unconscious called him 'The breath of life,'" I replied. What is more personal in existence than one's breath? Jung meditated on Prāna, among other things, when he composed *The Red Book*. This is why I have inserted a discussion about Atmavictu after Eckhart.

The devotee, who in his or her life has properly meditated on Prāna, is said in the commentaries on the eleven principal Upanishads to enter after death into the world of Hiranyagarbha. In the Kaushitaki Upanishad, there is a wonderful little prayer that shows how vitally important the concept of Prāna is in Advaita, or nondual Vedanta: "I am Prāna; meditate on me as the conscious self (prajnātman), as life, as immortality. Life is Prāna; Prāna is life. Immortality is Prāna; Prāna is immortality… Prāna is consciousness; consciousness is Prāna."[3] Hiranyagarbha is also identified with the Absolute, or the Cosmic Mind of Emerson, Whitman, and Dickinson. In Jung's stone carving of Atmavictu, I wondered why his face looked so old as I reflected on the meaning of the little statue's facial features. As an archetypal image carved into matter, he seemed rather ancient. In the *Chhāndogya Upanishad*, in a chapter called "The Supremacy of the Prāna," I found an answer that satisfied me: "OM, HE WHO knows what is oldest becomes himself the oldest and the greatest. The prāna indeed is the oldest and greatest."[4]

The connection between Jung's concept of the Self and the Vedanta's concept of the Self is beyond the scope of this book. What is important for the reader to grasp, however, is the idea of Hiranyagarbha as the *breath of life*. Knowledge of God in Vedanta is knowledge of Prāna. Prāna is knowledge of the nondual Self. The Indian philosopher Sankarāchārya (788–820) said: "*Outside the Knowledge of the non-dual Self, the complete attainment of the Highest Good [Prana] is impossible.*"[5]

Notes

1. See photo of Atmavictu on the front cover of this book. The *Black Books,* which are soon be published, were Jung's first attempts to document his inner experiences in active imagination. He later transferred the writing from these books, with calligraphic script and illustrated paintings, into *The Red Book.*
2. Jung, *RB*, note 222, 303.
3. Upanishads 3, fn 3. All references to the Upanishads come from Nikhilananda's translation listed in the bibliography.
4. Upanishads 4, 249.
5. Upanishads 4, 107. Italics in original. It is evident to most people today that the very thing humans are panicking about and which is increasing in the news daily with the drum beat of the seemingly endless COVID-19 death count, is a global panic that there will not be enough respirators available in the hospital wards for patients who have contracted Coronavirus and are worried about being able to breathe on their own. At the core of the traumatic complex in the nation and world, therefore, is a fear that infected people might drown in their own liquids, their own fluids, and not be able to breathe the precious oxygen we need for our existence without ventilators. C. G. Jung created Atmavictu following the 1917-1918 Influenza that killed 50,000,000 people world-wide. To my knowledge, Jung did not comment on the pandemic. Although I'm sure it was on his mind. Shortly after the pandemic subsided, Jung's psyche created the healing symbol. Interestingly, this was the symbol I chose from a series of photographs I took in 2008. I selected it for my book's front cover in early 2019, a year before the outbreak in the United States. I will pursue the meaning of Atmavictu as a living symbol and as a subtext via various interconnected thematic meditations interspersed throughout my book's Chapters. For instance, I stress the importance of breath in yogic practice, pranayama, and what James called a "fourth wind," in Chapters 22, 25, 30, and 31. In addition, I end my book, in Chapter 44, with a discussion of the importance of planting Redwood trees as an antidote to climate change. My picture of Jung's statuette on the front piece was originally meant to serve as a *symbol of transition and hope during a crisis point on our planet. The "moral equivalent of war" (James's phrase) today is the war against deforestation, pollution, and climate change.*

Chapter 19

THE FIGHT WITH THE SHADOW

Many images in Jung's *Red Book* and *Memories, Dreams, Reflections* illustrate what he means by the shadow. In analytical psychology, the shadow is what we need to integrate most in ourselves. It is the evil in us that often gets overlooked and projected outward onto individuals, large groups, or nations.

On November 3, 1946, the BBC broadcast a talk Jung gave called "The Fight with the Shadow." It was published in *The Listener* in London, shortly thereafter. In "The Fight with the Shadow" *Jung zeroed in on what a true democracy might look like in the future.* It would begin with a change of heart in each and every one of us. He pointed out that as early as 1918, he had observed in the national unconscious of each of his German patients the emergence of mythological motifs, instinct-types, or *archetypes,* that suggested there was a major chaotic disturbance occurring in the objective psyche of the German nation. This outbreak of violence, as we know, was truly terrifying and tragic, with the loss of approximately 70 million human lives transnationally. Jung put it this way: "the archetypes I had observed expressed primitivity, *violence,* and cruelty."[1] Note the accent Jung placed on the word *violence* here. This emphasis is crucial for Jungian theory and practice: we deny the shadow at our own jeopardy.

Later, Jung said that in his follow-up to a number of German cases, "I could watch these forces as they both broke through the individual's moral and intellectual self-control, and as they flooded his conscious world," and in this very confusion and "chaos of the conscious mind," Jung added, "New symbols . . . then appeared of a collective nature, but this time reflecting the forces of *order.*"[2] Such axial systems as the squaring of a circle, a spiral, or an eight-spoke wheel—like the spiral galaxies from which we have evolved as humans—are what the ancient Hindus of India called in Sanskrit *mandalas.*

In Jung's view dreams were "the facts from which we must proceed."[3] Thus, the collective outbreak of violence was anticipated in dreams through an activation of chaotic uprisings of violent emotions from the national unconscious, and symbols of totality and order (an inner Cosmos of order and meaning in the shape of mandalas) helped him arrive at the "most difficult task, demanding a high degree of ethical responsibility."[4]

In his BBC talk, Jung then spelled out his thoughts on *true democracy* using Switzerland as a model. The Swiss are "inclined to think of democracy as a chronic state of mitigated civil war. We are far from being at peace with ourselves: on the contrary, we hate and fight each other because we have succeeded in introverting war."[5] The ideal of democracy is a model society that has never existed before; it is not a condition of peace alone. It is, rather, an introversion of war inside the subjective sphere. The *introversion of war* starts with the war within. Only when *this* inner "fight with the Shadow" has been successful can one truly engage and fight with others in a compassionate and caring way without resorting to external violence.

Turning chaos into a Cosmos, such as Jung did in *The Red Book,* and perhaps especially when our warlike instincts are involved in domestic quarrels, commonly called "political life," is no easy task for any human being—or nation. Peace is always a supreme state toward which all nations must diligently strive, even though peace is, paradoxically, an "unwholesome delusion." Jung was well aware that states of relative peace could only be arrived at if the world became increasingly *psychological* in its attitudes toward the personal, national, and collective shadow. The problem of the shadow in the evolution of the historical God-image must be accepted as an empirical fact, therefore, if we are to survive as a global society. We are far too naïve about the nature of the shadow, according to Jung. *The greatest danger is not outside, but inside the human psyche.* The shadow is a reality. It is here to stay.

Ideally, peace is possible in any organization or institution, even if it is a delusion because we will never actually get there. Life is too complex. By striving, however, we move toward peace, which may only be found within individuals, or in small groups, never in collectivity nor in the world as a whole. Jung's position was always to begin with individuals, one at a time. Jung continued: "Even our national, mitigated state of war would soon come to an end if everybody could see his own shadow and begin the only struggle that is really worthwhile: the fight against the overwhelming power-drive of the shadow" within.[6] Here Jung admitted that world peace might come about *if and only if* every person fought against his or her own personal and national shadow, stopping the cycle of projection and reprojection.

This, then, is Jung's *best formulation* of the organization of spiritual democracy: *introverting our warlike instincts and transforming chaos into a Cosmos of meaning, relatedness, and ever-greater consciousness of shadow and Self is the only way ahead that makes any kind of sense.*

> Our order would be perfect if only everybody could direct his aggressiveness inwards, into his own psyche. Unfortunately, our religious education prevents us from doing this, with its false promises of an immediate peace within. Peace may come in the end, but only when victory and defeat have lost their meaning. What did our Lord mean when he said: "I came not to send peace, but a sword"?[7]

Jung's prescription of spiritual democracy, therefore, consists of making the darkness of the shadow conscious in each of us. If the world is truly to become conscious of the Self in a natural condition of spiritual democracy, it must begin with the confrontation with chaos, the inner adversary, enemy, or *forces of violence, cruelty, and evil dwelling in our own hearts*. Directing our aggressiveness inward, into our own psyches, toward the chaotic world within, could provide the basis for a new spiritually democratic order of a global society of conscious human beings in the future. If such an ideal is ever to exist in the world, we need to create *order* out of chaos first, such as Jung models for us in *Liber Novus*. "To the extent that we are able to found a true democracy—in a conditional fight among ourselves, either collective or individual—we realize, we make real, the factors of order, because then it becomes absolutely necessary to live in orderly circumstances."[8]

Political life is never a peaceful place in any democracy. This is why spiritual practice is needed today. It needs a psychology, moreover, that places its greatest emphasis on ethical decisions or individual tasks of conscience. It "is surely better to know that your worst enemy is right there in your own heart. Man's warlike instincts are ineradicable—therefore a state of perfect peace is unthinkable... True democracy is a highly psychological institution which takes account of human nature as it is and makes allowances for the necessity of conflict within its own national boundaries."[9]

Jung zeroed in on a definition of what a true democracy might look like at an ideal spiritual level—as a *highly psychological institution*. Spiritual democracy is, in Jung's psychological view, *a matter of the heart*; if the heart does not change, nothing changes. In "The Fight with the Shadow," Jung leaves us with the question of how to deal with violence and war through mitigated internal struggles in our democracies. In *The Red Book,* he demonstrates empirically how this might be done in the interior battleground first.

Here is another salient quote from "The Fight with the Shadow": "The destructive power of our weapons has increased beyond all measure, and this forces a psychological question on mankind: Is the mental and moral condition of the men who decide on the use of these weapons equal to the enormity of the possible consequences?"[10] This responsibility is the ultimate moral task of humankind. Jung added, more optimistically: "But the great Western democracies have a better chance, so long as they can keep out of those wars that always tempt them to believe in external enemies and in the desirability of internal peace. The marked tendency of the Western democracies to internal dissension is the very thing that could lead them into a more hopeful path."[11]

In *Aion: Researches into the Phenomenology of the Self,* Jung warned: "Today as never before it is important that human beings should not overlook the danger of evil lurking within them. It is unfortunately too real, which is why psychology must insist on the reality of evil and must reject any definition that regards it as insignificant or actually non-existent. Psychology is an empirical science and deals with realities."[12] Jung's view of the Self is not like the Hindu concept of the Atman, or the Christian view of Christ, the perfect man, who, for the most part, lacks a human shadow. For Jung the Self, the wholeness of the personality, is an integration of good and evil. This is not a metaphysical concept, but rather a *psychological* reality.

In Chapter 14 of *Aion,* "The Structure and Dynamics of the Self," Jung presented readers with two quaternary structures: an *Anthropos Quaternio* and a *Shadow Quaternio*. The first represented the world of spirit, or metaphysics, whereas the second represented the human being's instinctual disposition, which has its roots in the animal kingdom. The "nadir" of the *Shadow Quaternio* was, in Jung's words, "the cold-blooded vertebrate, the snake."[13] "The second of these quaternios," Jung added, "is the negative of the first; it is its shadow." By "shadow," Jung meant, moreover,

> the inferior personality, the lowest levels of which are indistinguishable from the instinctuality of an animal.... Since the shadow, in itself, is unconscious for most people, the snake would correspond to what is totally unconscious and incapable of becoming conscious, but which, as the collective unconscious and as instinct, seems to possess a peculiar wisdom of its own and a knowledge that is often felt to be supernatural... Its unrelatedness, coldness, and dangerousness expresses the instinctuality that with ruthless cruelty rides roughshod over all moral and any other human wishes and considerations and is therefore just as terrifying and fascinating in its effects as the sudden glance of a poisonous snake.[14]

We know next to nothing about the snake. It is totally unconscious in most people. Therefore, the tendency toward projection of the shadow (snake) is an ever-present reality, particularly in the field of politics and national affairs. Jung spoke further in *Aion* about the "double significance of the serpent" as an "allegory of Christ as well as the devil."[15] "The shadow is on one side regrettable and reprehensible weakness, on the other side healthy instinctivity and a prerequisite for higher consciousness."[16]

Like Jung, James too was not always optimistic about the future of democracy. On the other hand, he was no pessimist either. As a positive psychologist he had the highest respect for the individual, and he was mostly pessimistic about big organizations. He saw perceptively, I feel, that in the United States, "democracy is a kind of religion, and we are bound not to admit its failure." Here is a problem of democracy as part of our national shadow, spelled out for us in unequivocal terms. For in a May 1, 2004, radio address, our former US president George W. Bush proclaimed his administration's mission to "change the world" and pledged to protect democracy's "crusade against evil" in all nations in the Middle East. This "crusade" as he infamously called it after the 9/11 terrorist attacks, was referred to in a February 28 article in the *Washington Post* as the "most ambitious US democracy effort since the end of the Cold War."[17]

Bush's crusade to dispense democracy to Afghanistan and Iraq and to the greater Middle East was one of the chief aims of his administration, and it was a complete failure.[18] Such efforts by big government to launch an appalling religious war were not the kind of "personal religion" James had in mind. Today, we would call James's view an all-encompassing cultural attitude that subsumes the spiritual and its highest ethical ideals in a psychological Self that has integrated the shadow and the worst possibilities of human governance. One of James's most powerful statements on democracy came in his stupendous oration commemorating the memorial to Robert Gould Shaw at the Boston Commons in 1897. There, James said brilliantly:

> Democracy is still upon its trial. The civic genius of our people is its only bulwark, and neither laws nor monuments, neither battleships nor libraries, nor great newspapers nor booming stocks; neither mechanical invention nor political adroitness, nor churches nor universities nor civic-service examinations can save us from degeneration if the inner mystery be lost.[19]

Inner mystery of the Self is the natural condition of spiritual democracy, *free of any tendency toward turning the nation toward dictatorship*. Ten years later, on November 7, 1907, James warned again about democracy's trial:

> Democracy is on its trial, and no one knows how it will stand the ordeal. Abounding about us are pessimistic prophets. Fickleness and violence used to be, but are no longer, the vices which they charge to democracy... Vulgarity enthroned and institutionalized, elbowing everything superior from the highway, this, they tell us, is our irremediable destiny... Now, who can be absolutely certain that this may not be the career of democracy?... Our better men *shall* show the way and we *shall* follow them; so we are brought round again to the mission of the higher education in helping us to know the better kind of man whenever we see him... Individuals of genius show the way, and set the patterns, which common people then adopt and follow. *The rivalry of the patterns is the history of the world...* If democracy is to be saved it must catch the higher, healthier tone. If we are to impress it with our preferences, we ourselves must use the proper tone, which we, in turn, must have caught from our own teachers. It all reverts in the end to the action of innumerable imitative individuals upon each other and to the question of whose tone has the highest spreading power.[20]

By catching the higher, healthier *tone* democracy might be saved today, and by tone, I mean what Jung called the *right affect-tone,* namely the right-toned cultural *feeling* for spiritual democracy. We find such a right-toned feeling in Jung and James and also in some of the writings of the founding fathers of our nation. We all have to work together on our own personal and "cultural complexes" by listening for the higher emotional tones in individuals and political leaders with the loftiest *spreading powers*.[21] With few such leaders in sight, we would be wise to begin with the difficult task of starting with ourselves, which is, indeed, our heaviest burden.

I will focus, therefore, on what I think is a central national complex in the United States of America: the *religious complex*. American psychology began with pragmatism; it began with William James. It began with a plural notion of Divinity. It began with an appreciation for a variety of religious experiences, based on the criterion of subjective feeling. It began with Jung and James in America. As James said in his essay, "The Moral Equivalent of War":

> The war against war is going to be no holiday excursion or camping party...It may reasonably be said that the intensely sharp competitive preparation for war by the nations is the real war, permanent, unceasing; and that the battles are only a verification of the mastery gained during the "peace" interval...I will now confess my own utopia, I devoutly believe in the reign of peace.[22]

We ourselves must use the proper tone, but in turn, we must have caught it from our own teachers. In *Varieties of Religious Experience,* James defined religion as *"the feelings, acts, and experiences of individual men in their solitude, so far as they apprehend themselves to stand in relation to whatever they may consider the divine."*[23] It is in this spirit that I've endeavored to write this book. I owe it to my teachers, Jung and James, to show the proper way to protect the integrity of the Self from the political demagoguery that threatens to ruin the very best that is in us, as nations, a world, and as a global spiritual ecology.

NOTES

1. Jung, "The Fight with the Shadow," CW 10, ¶447.
2. Jung, CW 10, ¶450.
3. Jung, *MDR,* 170, 171.
4. Jung, CW 10, ¶451.
5. Jung, CW 10, ¶455.
6. Jung, CW 10, ¶455.
7. Jung, CW 10, ¶455.
8. Jung, CW 10, ¶456.
9. Jung, CW 10, ¶456.
10. Jung, CW 10, ¶457.
11. Jung, CW 10, ¶457.
12. Jung, *Aion, CW* 9.2, ¶98.
13. Jung, CW 9.2, ¶98.
14. Jung, CW 9.2, ¶370.
15. Jung, CW 9.2, ¶390.
16. Jung, CW 9.2, ¶402.
17. Robin Wright, "US to Push Democracy Initiative," *Washington Post,* February 28, 2004, A, 18.
18. For further discussion on this topic, see Herrmann, "Melville's Vision of Evil," 15–56.
19. James, "Robert Gould Shaw: Oration by Professor William James," 76.
20. James, *Writings 1902–1910,* 1245–1248.
21. See Herrmann, "The Cultural Complex in Walt Whitman," 34–61.
22. James, *Writings 1902–1910,* 1281, 1283, 1289.
23. James, 36.

Chapter 20

Eight Principles of Spiritual Democracy

Principal One

By *Spiritual Democracy,* I mean one's individual Self-path, which can begin in any particular creed, but must ultimately lead to an experience of the *equality* of all religions, a psychological vision based on modern and postmodern analytical science. This is an establishment of a common point of agreement by way of empirical validity, or what Jung called objective cognition between the various God-images. Spiritual democracy can exist only in a social condition when the shadow has been effectively transformed or transmuted in the Self.

Principle Two

We are all, I believe, rooted in a common spiritual bond of cosmic relatedness to the democratic Self within each of us. If we are truly Spiritual democrats at heart, therefore, if we are really to advance toward a new global society in which all people are destined for spiritual freedom, we must listen to what the Self wants from each of us. We must find new ways to speak the Self's transpersonal wisdom out loud and proclaim our own unique visionary truths.

Principle Three

In a psychological age, where the Self governs the whole of the human psyche in an atmosphere of transnational unity and equality, we are all potential vehicles for the Divine voice, whether we want to call that voice God, Goddess, Self, or No-Self. Any creed may help us get there, but at the summit of human consciousness and at its foundation, all faiths meet at a place of spiritual democracy.

Principle Four

If William James's attitude of psychological relativity toward religious experiences is correct and if Jung's intuitions about the God-images of humanity, as equivalents, is also on point, then all creeds must eventually become spiritually democratic, if they are to continue to survive in modernity. Above all an impartial and accepting attitude toward all forms of religious experience, tolerance, and compassion is the best way ahead. Neither James nor Jung considered some religions to be higher or lower, better or worse than others. They each saw all religions as equal.

Principle Five

If the Self as an archetype of totality in the psyche is to be awakened spiritually, then the projection-making factor must be quieted. We can only become conscious of the potential meaning inherent in our destiny-pattern if shadow projections stop. In Jung's view, there was essentially no difference between the outer figureheads of various world religions and what lay intrinsically waiting to be Self-realized potential in each person.

Principle Six

Jung taught that the main difference between the psychology of individuation and the path of Vedanta, or Christian mysticism, is that analytical psychologists do not lose ego identity in their dialogues with the Self. For Jung, this meant he had to remain true to his own national mythos, namely the Christian dispensation, while embracing a transnational myth of the Self, which included all other images of Divinity at the same time. It is basic to the teachings of James and Jung that all knowledge of the Self is based on subjective experiences, and we must acknowledge the bias of our "personal equation."

Principle Seven

In the same way that William James was an American, in a spiritual sense, Jung was interested in dreaming his own national myth onward. Jung taught us not to identify with but to dialogue with shadow and Self, thereby avoiding the problem of becoming swept up into a personal, or a national inflation.

Principal Eight

Whereas other nations of the world have tended to cling to particular images of Divinity to help resolve the problem of national complexes, with the founding of the US Constitution this tendency was and still is protected against today by our First Amendment: The Freedom of Religion. This law of governance in our Constitution prevents any preferential treatment of one image of Divinity over another in its national forms of worship, and although it is self-evident that Christianity was and continues to be the predominant religion of many American citizens, the United States, as one Nation of many plural States, has attempted to work out its own destiny and move toward a natural design of democracy in a psychological age—despite the interruptions by the tendency toward dictatorship. In my readings of James and Jung, I've found a common synchronous thread, one that forms and informs the same basic psychological notion. This is the pattern of the Self James and Jung identified for us as the central-most theoretical thread of their "analytic," pragmatic, or empirical psychologies.

Chapter 21

Transnationality

After his trip to the United States in 1925, Jung moved toward a new model of the collective unconscious by saying that the mind was "a *system of adaptation determined by the conditions of an earthly environment.*"[1] He added that archetypes were "the roots which the psyche has sunk not only in the earth in the narrower sense but in the world in general."[2] Jung said further in "The Structure of the Psyche" that the unconscious "appears to consist of mythological motifs or primordial images, for which reason the myths of all nations are its real exponents. In fact, the whole of mythology could be taken as a sort of projection of the collective unconscious."[3] Later, Jung hypothesized that the collective unconscious was affected by "psychological conditions of the earthly environment" that gave "rise to *archetypes,* as I have termed myth-motifs in general."[4]

As Jung's reflections on the nature of archetypes expanded over time, he began to make room for developments in modern physics to open a way forward toward his theory of synchronicity. By 1946, in "On the Nature of the Psyche," Jung began to account for *transcendent factors* of which nothing may be known empirically. During rare moments of intuitive apprehension, Jung conjectured, human beings were capable of penetrating the "flimsy threshold that separates us from the unconscious contents of the psyche."[5] This might be done, he posited, by means of various methods or techniques that enabled human beings to access the inborn "images," "thoughts," or "insights" that lay *above or below* consciousness.[6] Jung included *above* in his hypothesis, not only what is *below*. He went further by formulating at this pivotal time a hypothesis of a "superconsciousness" coexisting with ego-consciousness. He called this *superconsciousness* "*psychoid.*" Jung used the term *psychoid* with one reservation, namely that it be used as "an adjective, not as noun."[7]

The fact that Jung used the term *psychoid* as an adjective suggests that it cannot be located in any one person, no matter how enlightened he or she may be, in any place, or in a thing. A particular mind, therefore, may have *psychoid qualities*; these qualities cannot be quantified by exact science or measured, like the speed of light at 186,000 miles per second, for the quality of psychoid awareness is faster than that. It is timeless. It cannot be measured in terms of causality, space, or time.

We've been conditioned to think of the psychoid as below, or inside us, but we might just as easily think of it as above, or outside us. We enter transpsychic qualities of mind through time—as that is the only medium in which the psychoid can reflect itself qualitatively. But the qualitative experience is transtemporal, transmarginal, infinite. The psychoid is a quality that might best be called cosmic. Whatever the psychoid is, it is transcendent. The myths of all nations have tried to give voice to it in their national mythologies or religions, and their images have shaped the world's national identities across history.

Transnationality is finally where the religions of the world meet and where the humanoid quality of the psychoid achieves its term, at the place of worship where ego consciousness reflects the *Unus Mundus*. Jung and James meant that there is a *transnational religious function in the psyche of every person that can, in fact, be accessed through the development of various psychological, or spiritual, techniques*. They used the terms *transcendent* and *infinite* similarly to connote a movement beyond and above the myths of various nations.

In the following chapters, I will endeavor to state what I believe James's message truly was and how it shaped Jung's attitudes and theoretical ideas. James's vocation was, in some respects, similar to Jung's. *Psychology, if it is to be truly scientific, or empirical, and with the widest reaching effect, must be treated as a natural science.* The Self has its roots not only in virtually every religion of the world but also in every human being living on this planet. This is why Jung used the Self as a general concept in his psychology of individuation, similarly to James. The Self can be found everywhere. It is a universal word or image for the factor of human wholeness. The Self is a transpersonal notion, moreover, that evolved from Jung's simultaneous reading of the Upanishads, Eckhart, and James. Arthur Schopenhauer, too, had been deeply inspired by his reading of the Upanishads. In his later years the old philosopher-sage wrote: "In the whole world there is no study so beneficial and so elevating as that of the Upanishads. It has been the solace of my life; it will be the solace of my death."[8] In order to understand the differences between the Hindu notion of the Self, and the

Self or Selves as James and Jung understood it, I will now take the reader on a brief look at what James had to say about the state of Samadhi.

NOTES

1. Jung, "Mind and Earth," CW 10, ¶49.
2. Jung, CW 10, ¶53.
3. Jung, "The Structure of the Psyche," CW 8, ¶325.
4. Jung, CW 8, ¶334.
5. Jung, "On the Nature of the Psyche," CW 8, ¶362.
6. Jung, CW 8, ¶362.
7. James, CW 8, ¶368.
8. Upanishads 1:11.

Chapter 22

SWAMI VIVEKANANDA, WILLIAM JAMES, AND SAMADHI

The Hindu monk Swami Vivekananda met William James at Harvard in 1894 and again in 1896, when he twice lectured there.[1] Vivekananda's book Raja Yoga and the meetings between the two men influenced James's thoughts for the 1901–1902 Gifford Lectures, which were later published as Varieties of Religious Experience. To be sure, Vivekananda was a missionary of a democratic vision of spirituality, Vedanta, yet his calling was to teach the way to Samadhi (a high form of spiritual enlightenment that he'd been taught to practice directly from his master and teacher, Sri Ramakrishna) wherever he went and, like James and Jung, to unify the world's religions under an idea of Oneness. In Varieties, James quotes Vivekananda at length on the entrance of the mind into the state of Samadhi:

> That the mind itself has a higher state of existence, beyond reason, a superconscious state, and that when the mind gets to that higher state, then this knowledge beyond reasoning comes. . . . All the different steps in yoga are intended to bring us scientifically to the superconscious state or Samâdhi... Just as unconscious work is beneath consciousness, so there is another work which is above consciousness, and which, also, is not accomplished with the feeling of egotism. . . . There is no feeling of I, and yet the mind works, desireless, free from restlessness, objectless, bodiless. Then the Truth shines in its full effulgence, and we know ourselves—for Samâdhi lies potential in us all—for what we truly are, free, immortal, omnipotent, loosed from the finite, and its contrasts of good and evil altogether, and identical with the Atman or Universal Soul.[2]

Neither James's nor Jung's teachings agreed with Vivekananda's about the importance of Samadhi for modern psychology, however. Jung wrote, for instance: "Therefore the individual who wishes to have an answer to the problem of evil, as it is posed today, has need, first and foremost, of *self-knowledge,* that is, the utmost possible knowledge of his own wholeness."[3] Wholeness and Samadhi are not the same thing. By wholeness, Jung meant a knowledge of the Self that included a consciousness of the human and divine shadow. Jung knew the passage by Vivekananda concerning Samadhi before he wrote out his own theory of the unconscious in 1916 and 1917. From the start of his project to revolutionize modern psychology as a natural science—before he gave his first definitions of the Self—the postulation of a superconscious level in the unconscious was in Jung's mind as a theoretical notion. James was preoccupied by religious unity in vast effervescent variety, by pragmatism and pluralism, and with the concept of monism. James refuted Vivekananda's claim about the One—*Samadhi*—to which defeat, wounding, and vulnerability can't happen. "This is Vivekananda's mystical One," James asserted. "This is Reality with a capital R, reality that makes the timeless claim, reality to which defeat can't happen."[4]

For Jung, as we've seen, the defeat of the hero at midlife was the most important thing in the transition to old age. The passages from Vivekananda's book about the superconscious state of Samadhi that James quoted from suggested that it is a potential in each of us, yet psychology as a natural science cannot neglect to focus on the human shadow. All aspects of the Self that James and Jung identified must be included in our psychic inventory if wholeness is to be achieved.

Compare Vivekananda's statement about Samadhi with a letter James wrote in 1905 to a correspondent who told him that he had achieved great improvements in his health after practicing Hatha Yoga:

> Your Yoga discipline and its effects are interesting, I've read Vivekananda's book and looked through the Hatha Yoga. But my temperament seems rebellious to all these disciplines, and I fear I shall have to die unsaved. At least I could only be saved by a Guru with first-rate pedagogic powers... I knew Vivekananda, when he was here, have read both his book and one on Hatha Yoga, and did then try (some 6 or 7 years ago) to practice some of the breathing exercises. But I am a bad subject for such things, critical and indocile, so it soon stopped.[5]

22 - Swami Vivekananda, William James, and Samadhi

James, like Jung, found other ways to have what Abraham Maslow called peak experiences. *Samadhi* is a synonym for higher states of mind known to the mystics of all world religions. Another term for this state might be *Satori,* or *Buddha Mind.* There is also the *Christ Mind,* or Teilhard de Chardin's "Cosmic Christ."[6] I would argue that such states of mind are complementary, although religious psychologists and theologians might dispute that such states of mind are different. Samadhi is about the higher realization of religion. *One has to experience It to know It.* Experiencing it, however, does not free us from the shadow.

In psychological and scientific terms, I believe Vivekananda meant there is a "religious function" in the psyche of every person that can be tapped into through practical methods, and when one has gained sufficient access to the Self, one might begin to know what religion really is as a genuine psychological experience. No one, I believe, can persuasively argue that India has not offered the world one of the greatest spiritual jewels received from the mind of God. But William James, who was a great writer of prose, went on at length about his concerns about Vedanta, such as in a commentary on a lecture that Vivekananda gave in the United States. He described, in some detail, his critique of the kind of elevated enlightenment Vedanta taught:

> Where is any more delusion for him who sees this Oneness in the universe, this Oneness of life, Oneness of everything? . . . he knows the reality of everything, the secret of everything. Where is there any more misery for him? What does he desire? He has traced the reality of everything unto the Lord, the center, that Unity of everything, and that is Eternal Bliss, Eternal Knowledge, Eternal Existence. Neither death nor disease nor sorrow nor misery nor discontent is.[7]

James's criticisms of Vivekananda, scathing though they may sound to the more finely tuned ears of modern students or adherents of Vedanta, were based on his subjective experiences and critical thinking as a philosopher and psychologist of religion who sometimes did not pull any stops. James's Self was, like Jung's, *psychologically aware of Yoga's blind spots.* Although I'm much impressed with James's criticisms of Yoga, Jung's attempts to understand Yoga went much further, although he was not a practitioner of such techniques either. Nevertheless, James's tough-mindedness as a philosopher of religion had an influence on Jung's thinking and possibly (this is purely speculative) inspired some of his cautionary statements about Yoga.

Neither James nor Jung would agree that to become religious is to attain Samâdhi. This may have been a qualitative variable in Vivekananda's life and destiny-pattern, which he sincerely believed was true for him and others from a cultural standpoint, due to his religious training. Yet identifying with any archetype of the transpersonal psyche can be dangerous psychologically; being conscious of the shadow is perhaps a more modest way to achieve a wider consciousness of the wholeness of the personality.

James did, however, make use of experiential techniques, such as meditation and Yoga, in his exploration of the Subconscious Self, and he lamented that a lack in American education of introspective approaches to children's learning was working on us "grievous national harm."[8] In my clinical practice as a Jungian I have noticed an increasing number of children who are learning the practices of Yoga and mindfulness meditation, both at home and in the classroom, a phenomenon James appeared to have been calling for over a century ago. How much James actually owed to Vivekananda in the development of his own thinking about Yoga has not been adequately described by other researchers, even to this day.

Although I cannot go into this subject in any great detail here, one of the ideas James did borrow from Swami Vivekananda's book *Raja Yoga* is the notion of a *fountain-head in the subconscious*, a metaphor that is essentially synonymous to my mind with his notion of a mother-sea, or subliminal doorway, which I return to in Part III. In a letter to Harry W. Rankin he wrote, for instance: "In these lectures the ground I am taking is this: The mother-sea and fountain-head of all religions lie in the mystical experiences of the individual, taking the word mystical in a very wide sense. All theologies and all ecclesiasticisms are secondary growths superimposed …Something, not our immediate self, does act on our life!"[9]

Notes

1. James encountered Vivekananda a second time at Harvard on March 25, 1896, when the swami lectured on "The Vedanta Philosophy."
2. James, *Writings 1902–1910,* 361.

3. Jung, *MDR*, 330.
4. James, *Writings 1902–1910*, 602.
5. Quoted in Norris, "William James and Swami Vivekananda," 49.
6. Herrmann, "Teilhard de Chardin: Cosmic Christ."
7. James, *Writings: 1902–1910*, 552–553.
8. Taylor, *Consciousness beyond the Margin*, 63.
9. Taylor, 90–91.

Chapter 23

INDIA'S MISSION: TO PROMOTE WORLD SPIRITUALITY

Regardless of their differences, Vivekananda, James, and Jung all taught that our ideas about religion were far too small to encompass the truths of spiritual democracy. They all felt we needed to open our concepts of religion to subsume the vast variety of God-images. Such a synthesis could only come about through Self-realization. "Realization is real religion, all the rest is only preparation—hearing lectures, or reading books, or reasoning is merely preparing the ground; it is not religion."[1] "Thus it is clear," Vivekananda added, "all the religions of the world have been built upon that one universal and adamantine foundation of all our knowledge—direct experience."[2] This kind of thinking appealed to James.

Yoga, in addition to being a practice of meditation, is a method for stilling the mind. It is therefore, most importantly, a vehicle of an ancient science—the *science of psychology*. Vivekananda's estimation of psychology as *the* science of all sciences of the past, present, and future is abundantly clear in his lecture, "The Importance of Psychology," in which he wrote eloquently: "The idea of psychology in the West is very much degraded. Psychology is the science of sciences."[3]

Psychology and religion are complementary paths to the same goal—Self-realization of the unconscious. Yet, it is important to clarify what the Self means for Western psychology and how it differs from Eastern psychology. I find passages from Vivekananda's book *Raja Yoga* to be exquisite. Sometimes, however, I wonder if his thoughts were also shaped by the spirit of the West, whether he'd tapped into the wellsprings of the American mind to help shape some of his most objective statements.

The study of religions, in Jung's view, must be based, not on a creedal foundation, but rather on a phenomenological one. "This standpoint is exclusively phenomenological, that is, it is concerned with occurrences, events, experiences—in a word, with facts."[4] To Vivekananda's mind, India's mission was and continues to be to promote world spirituality and teach the way to Samadhi. Jung's view was that an idea is "objective in so far as that idea is shared by a society—by a *consensus genitum*."[5] According to Jung, great ideas, when they come to a person, simply happen. They create themselves spontaneously, independently of causality, time and place, migration, and tradition. "They are not made by the individual, they just happen to him—they even force themselves on his consciousness."[6]

Spiritual democracy in the United States, and the movement in the major world religions toward a spiritual center of unity and peace, can be found in Hinduism, Buddhism, Judaism, Christianity, Taoism, Sufism, Islam, Native American spirituality, and in Emersonian Transcendentalism. All of these creeds or systems are what the Parliament of World Religions has attempted to synthesize and integrate into one unitary organization, not unlike the United Nations. The religions of the world appear to be tending, in other words, toward some kind of center of unity and general agreement—despite the fact that there is still much division and disagreement among certain faiths and for which the attempts of the Parliament have only been preliminary. What is needed today, I believe, is a radical revisioning of a psychological and theological solution that insists on the efforts of single individuals, whether within religious groups and/or more generally in politics and global society, in insisting on a withdrawal of projections of evil and hatred onto "others" and a recognition of violence and hatred as reflections of one's own hidden away darkness, occluding the doorway to one's own heart.

Notes

1. Vivekananda, *The Complete Works of Swami Vivekananda*, vol. 1, 232. Hereafter referenced as *TCWSV*, volume, and page number.
2. Vivekananda, *TCWSV* 1, 126.
3. Vivekananda, *TCWSV*, 6, 28, 30.
4. Jung, "Psychology and Religion (The Terry Lectures)," CW 11, ¶4.
5. Jung, CW 11, ¶4.
6. Jung, CW 11, ¶5.

Chapter 24

A FEW REFERENCES FOR THE TERM SPIRITUAL DEMOCRACY

In addition to pointing out some of the similarities between Yoga, pragmatism, and analytical psychology, I will stress some of the differences. Here is a problem with some of the great teachers of Yoga, as I see it. *We need a language of analysis to properly understand the attainment of Samadhi, or the Higher Self. Otherwise it sounds New Age. We also need an experience of our darkest shadows and evil to become conscious and sensitive, as feeling human beings who are simply doing our best to introject our own fight with the shadow and attempting to transmute its darkness in the personal and political domains by immunizing ourselves from the power complex of evil.* We would be wise, therefore, if we were to follow Jung's instructions to begin with an exploration of the shadow—the shadow of nationalism, the shadow of race-relations, and the shadow of evil in ourselves. We must see that if we are to evolve toward spiritual democracy, we need to adopt a psychological and spiritual attitude side by side with a social and material earth-based attitude.

Vivekananda meditated on the democratic notion I've been discussing thus far on April 8, 1900, in San Francisco, in a lecture he called "Is Vedanta the Future Religion?" In this address he essentially asked whether Vedanta was the religion of coming humanity: "You want to be democratic in your country. *It is the democratic God that Vedanta teaches.* . . . There is a chance of Vedanta becoming the religion of your country because of democracy."[1] I find this talk to be extraordinary; he challenged his audience with the task of becoming more spiritually democratic, by which he meant Self-realized. By practicing Yoga, he said, one will see that the *democratic God* is in every religion. It all begins with the awakening of the Self within.

From the beginning of his career as a modern psychologist, William James formed a concept of a Higher Self. He did not mean one of the many passing states of consciousness in the lower self; rather, he meant *the entire collection of states of consciousness*; James positioned the Higher Self at the apex of the hierarchy of Selves, a Body Self, a Social Self, and *Spiritual Self, or supreme Me, with which the lower two are continuous.*[2] This shows not only how far ahead of his times James was but also how contemporary he still is today.

Although the Higher Self has been known transnationally, across all cultures, and assigned various names, it only entered American psychology with James's *Principles* in 1890. Earlier, Ralph Waldo Emerson had coined the term *Oversoul* to describe this level of consciousness in the Self. But psychology was rapidly becoming a laboratory science that paid little interest to spirituality. Eugene Taylor addressed this context in his book *William James on Exceptional Mental States:* "Increasingly disenchanted with a scientific psychology in America that restricted itself more and more to the laboratory and to the filtering of reality through a clouded lens of statistical analysis, James sought to extend the discipline by including within it the study of psychic phenomena, the subconscious, and religious experience."[3] In the 1896 Lowell Lectures, for instance, James began Lecture IV, "Multiple Personality," with the following statement: "We are by this time familiar with the notion that a man's consciousness need not be a fully integrated thing. From the ordinary focus and margin, from the ordinary abstraction, we shade off into phenomena that looks like consciousness *beyond the margin*. Hypnotism and automatic writing have been our means of approach."[4] The aim of automatic writing, which James employed and recommended to his audience, aimed to connect *subliminal* mentation to *supraliminal* or *transliminal* dimensions of mind. In an essay for *Scribner's Magazine* in March 1890, "What Psychical Research Has Accomplished," James gave credit to the French researchers Janet and Binet for demonstrating the simultaneous existence of *two different strata of consciousness in the same person.* He spoke of "an 'extra-consciousness,' as one may call it," which "can be kept on tap, as it were, by the method of automatic writing. This discovery marks a new era in experimental psychology, and it is impossible to overrate its importance."[5]

James was a personal friend of Frederick Myers, who coined the term *subliminal self,* which James designated as *ultra-marginal consciousness* within the spectrums of the Self. James spoke in a wonderful way about consciousness as a spectrum between ordinary and extra-ordinary reality.

"The ordinary consciousness Mr. Myers likens to the visible part of the solar spectrum; the total consciousness is like that spectrum prolonged by the inclusion of the ultra-red and ultra-violet rays. In the psychic spectrum the 'ultra' parts may embrace a far wider range, both of physiological and psychical activity, than is open to our ordinary consciousness and memory."[6] This vision of a *total consciousness* likened to the color spectrum anticipated Jung's positing in 1948 of a *psychoid* continuum in the collective unconscious, extending from the subconscious to the supraconscious.

Automatic writing facilitated for James an opening of the doorway from the subliminal to the supraliminal states of mind, for the "ultra" parts of the spectrum of consciousness were where the Higher Self could be *acted* on in the "now" of the moment. James enjoyed walking in the Adirondacks, and he once stated that the discipline of *writing* was his form of *Yoga*.[7]

James's ability to practice this discipline of writing as a Yoga—a means to connect with his Higher Self—was evident in his "Conclusions" sections to *Varieties,* where he spoke of accessing "higher powers." He described a "common nucleus" to which all the world's creeds bear testimony unanimously as a stage:

> [where a woman or] *"man identifies his real being with a germinal higher part of himself... He becomes conscious that this higher part is conterminous and continuous with a MORE of the same quality, which is operative in the universe outside of him, and which he can keep in working touch with, and in a fashion get on board of and save himself when all his lower being has gone to pieces in the wreck.*[8]

James's ruthless honesty here about the inherent link between genius and psychopathology is captured beautifully in this ironic statement of his style.

Several pages later, he spoke of the supreme reality of the Higher Self by the natural appellation of God: "I will call this higher part of the universe by the name of God. We and God have business with each other; and in opening ourselves to this influence our deepest destiny is fulfilled . . . God is real since he produces real effects."[9] The Higher Self is where the concept of spiritual democracy comes from, from a place of visioning that Whitman called Vista. Only when this third level of democracy has been attained through a breakthrough into the vistas of the Spiritual Self, can a person truly be of service to democracy on a political or economic level. Then we become, as James says, the "yeast-cake" for democracy with high spreading power:

> If we are to be the yeast-cake for democracy's dough, if we are to make it rise with culture's preferences, we must see to it that culture spreads broad sails. We must shake the old double reefs out of the canvas into the wind and sunshine, and let in every modern subject, sure that any subject will prove humanistic, if its setting be kept only wide enough.[10]

James was strongly influenced prior to and during the writing of *Varieties* by Vivekananda.

Notes

1. Vivekananda, *TCWSV* 8, 125, 126. Italics mine.
2. James, *Writings 1878–1899*, 178, 186.
3. Taylor, *William James on Exceptional Mental States*, 2.
4. Taylor, 73.
5. James, *Writings 1878–1899*, 178, 186.
6. James, 692.
7. Taylor, *William James on Consciousness beyond the Margin*, 65.
8. James, *Writings 1878–1899*, 454.
9. James, 461.
10. James, *Writings 1902–1910*, 1247.

Chapter 25

C. G. JUNG'S VIEWS ON YOGA

Jung was not an avid student of Śaṅkarācārya, the foremost exponent of Advaita Vedanta (788–820), although he reported a fascinating story in *Memories, Dreams, Reflections* of a meeting he had in 1930 with a friend of Mahatma Gandhi, a highly cultivated elderly Indian gentleman who told him that his guru was Śaṅkarācārya! "You don't mean the commentator on the Vedas who died centuries ago?" Jung asked him. "Yes, I mean him," the man replied. At that moment, Jung said he thought of his personal inner guru, Philemon, a living figure of superior insight and wisdom with whom Jung conversed through active imagination and who taught him "psychic objectivity, the reality of the psyche."[1] For Jung, the guru was found within. To project the Self onto an outer personage was, in his view, problematic to individuation. In "Yoga and the West," Jung ended his essay (published in *Prabuddha Bharata* in February 1936) by saying with dutiful sincerity: "In the course of centuries the West will produce its own yoga, and it will be on the basis laid down by Christianity."[2]

As a Jungian analyst, I cherish no illusions about the psychological nature of evil. I think a psychological view of conscience helps us better accept our imperfections. If one's God-image is perfect, one's teachings can sound, at times, as if they are infallible. Wholeness releases us from perfection's myth and gives us Liberty to follow our own the Self-path. Then all arguments about whose God-image is the "highest" ceases and all may be valued equally for their own unique variety and diversity.

There are movements afoot to call Islam and Hinduism nations based on spiritual democracy, but there is a problem with this in both India and Pakistan, especially when it comes to the translation of democratic principles based on religious ideologies into the political domain. No Hindu or Islamic nation, nor really any nation, can truly be democratic, I believe, if it claims itself to be a religious polity. *For a nation to claim its God to be truly democratic, it would have to leave the question of its national identity free* *of any creedal affiliation.*³ The early American visionaries, James and Jung chief among them, were determined to fight for religious liberty, and set an example as philosophers and empirical psychologists with a high potential for impressing people with their proper spreading tones, which they, in turn, caught from their own teachers. Vivekananda, of course, had his own spiritual tone with a great ability to influence people.⁴ The only problem with a tone such as Vivekanada's, for the future of psychology, however, is that it is too heroic. *By Spiritual democracy, I mean a nonjudgmental form of psychological equality that neither places any one God-image above the liberty of the individual, nor places one religion above another.*

Spiritual democracy, as James and Jung taught, is not a creed, but a science of psychological experiences that is transnational and nondogmatic in its principles of equality-making. As a whole, the United States does not compete with any nation on earth, nor preach any message of national superiority with regard to religion, because it has no God-image to preach.⁵ American Liberty rebels against any religious prophet that might attempt to convert her and declares independence from any presumption of creedal preeminence.

Religions tend to engage the public in a collective form of active imagination around an idealized figure, who embodies one of the world's great God-images. Such a figure can become the center of one's religious preoccupations: one prays, worships, and recites verses of the Guru, or Prophet, as if they were the Word of God. This collective dream offers people a great deal of meaning in life, but it can also lead them away from their authentic Self-path. The Self-path comes, not from without, but from within, and the Self is not localized in any one nation; it is transnational in scope. The destiny of our world is not to preserve the nations of the globe by infusing them with any religion, as a new dispensation of a global spirituality. The Shadow of religion is the dark side of the Self, represented by the rejection of the desires of the body, the Material Self. This is among the greatest dangers we face today, along with the Self's hostile brother: the political and economic rape of the planet constellating climate change.

In his essay "Yoga and the West," Jung was wise to remain silent on what Yoga meant for India, but he was clear that he had an intellectual understanding of Yoga methods.

> In its training of the parts of the body, it unites them with the whole of the mind and spirit, as is quite clear, for instance, in the pranayama exercises,

where prana is both the breath and the universal dynamics of the cosmos. When the doing of the individual is at the same time a cosmic happening, the elation of the body (innervation) becomes one with the elation of the spirit (the universal idea), and from this there arises a living whole which no technique, however scientific, can hope to produce. Yoga practice is unthinkable, and would also be ineffectual, without the ideas on which it is based. It works the physical and the spiritual into one another in an extraordinarily complete way.[6]

I believe Jung's prescriptions to his students and readers in Switzerland, the United States, and Europe not to practice Yoga should be read, therefore, with an open mind, holding in mind everything he said about the human Shadow: "I say to whomever I can: 'Study yoga—you will learn an infinite amount from it—but do not try and apply it, for we Europeans are not so constituted that we apply these methods correctly, just like that.'"[7] There is certainly some truth to what Jung is saying here. Yoga is a viable spiritual practice, however, no matter where a person lives, no matter in what country or region, and no matter what a person's ethnicity or cultural background might be. For anyone who is interested in the practice of Yoga, I do not hesitate to recommend it as a physical and spiritual practice. On the other hand, there are possible dangers involved, if one does not have a proper teacher, or if one lacks an understanding of the emotions and images that may arise through the practice of Yoga. Jung ended his essay "Yoga and the West" by saying in this regard: "If I remain critically so averse to yoga, it does not mean that I do not regard this spiritual achievement of the East as one of the greatest things the human mind has ever created. I hope my exposition makes it sufficiently clear that my criticism is directed solely against the application of yoga to the peoples of the West."[8] Keep in mind, Jung also taught the way of active imagination, which can be risky without proper preparation and therapeutic guidance. Jung warned in this regard that active imagination is not a "plaything for children" and an analyst must pay considerable attention to the "dangers of this method."[9]

Jung knew a great deal about the religious psychology of the East. He'd seen correctly in 1939 that there was a Universal Mind, yet asserted that in the West it is a metaphysical postulate that cannot be proven to exist scientifically; Jung broadened the validity of this view by including synchronicity or "mind-matter" correlations later, leaving the door open for further empirical inquiry into the nature of the psyche.[10] He was well aware of the differences between *personal* aspects of the Self and the Cosmic and metaphysical qualities of the *suprapersonal* Atman in the philosophy of the Upanishads;[11] he spoke, moreover, of the characteristics of the "Hindu Cosmic Man" in the Rig Veda.[12]

In his commentaries on "The Tibetan Book of the Great Liberation" written in 1939, Jung made it clear that the transformation of the personality that he had in mind as the task for analytical psychology was spacious enough to include the darkness of the human Shadow and instinct. "I would not advise anyone to touch yoga without a careful analysis of his unconscious reactions. What is the use of imitating yoga if your dark side remains as good as a medieval Christian as ever?"[13] Jung wrote this in 1939, when the national Shadow of Germany was about to break out into one of the worst psychic infections the world has known. In "The Psychology of Eastern Meditation," written in 1943, Jung remarked further: "And I wish particularly to warn against the oft-attempted imitation of Indian practices and sentiments. As a rule nothing comes of it except an artificial stultification in our Western intelligence. . . . So, let us first attempt, with the head, to find or build that hidden bridge which may lead to a European understanding of yoga."[14]

Here, I'm attempting to build a bridge between East and West by keeping Jung's concept of the personal and national Shadow in mind. Being mindful of the Shadow means being mindful of the Self. Jung's cautionary words about the dangers of minimizing evil are sobering, a wake-up call for the world to deal with, if people have the patience and endurance to read him. I agree with James and Jung that psychology is a science and not a religion. Nevertheless, unlike James and Jung, I've practiced and continue to practice Yoga, and I can vouch for its benefits as a Westerner.

We do not know much about Jung's use of Yoga techniques during his confrontation with the unconscious while he was engaged in writing *The Red Book*. Though he did, indeed, find Yoga helpful during that time:

> I was frequently so wrought up that I had to do certain yoga exercises in order to hold my emotions in check. But since it was my purpose to know what was going on within myself, I would do these exercises only until I had calmed myself enough to resume my work with the unconscious.

As soon as I had the feeling that I was myself again, I abandoned this restraint upon the emotions and allowed the images and inner voices to speak afresh. The Indian, on the other hand, does yoga exercises in order to obliterate completely the multitude of psychic contents and images.[15]

He also left some clues in *The Red Book* that we can draw inferences from to supplement what we may never know for certain. Such literary and artistic facts are largely poetic and pictorial. In "Liber Secondus," there are two paintings (#51 and # 125) that depict a yogi seated in semi-Lotus postures. In both of these pictures, the yogi's eyes are closed. In a dream from 1944, *he was walking through a hilly landscape; the sun was shining and he had a view in all directions. Then he came to a small wayside chapel. The door was ajar and he went in. The yogi he saw in the chapel on the floor of the altar appeared to have been meditating or dreaming with his eyes closed.* When Jung awoke from this dream, he thought: "Aha, so he is the one who is meditating me. He has a dream, and I am it." He then added: "I knew that when he awakened, I would no longer be."[16] The yogi with Jung's face was in deep meditation and seated in a lotus posture.

"In India," Jung was "principally concerned with the psychological nature of evil."[17] We learn more about this from perusing his comments in "The Psychology of Eastern Meditation," in which he said: "Only the man who goes through this darkness can hope to make any further progress. I am therefore in principle against the uncritical appropriation of yoga practices by Europeans, because I know only too well that they hope to avoid their dark corners. Such a beginning is entirely meaningless and worthless."[18]

He then went on to say that "Our Western psychology has, in fact, got as far as yoga in that it is able to establish scientifically a deeper layer of unity in the unconscious . . . On account of the remarkable agreement between the insights of yoga and the results of psychological research, I have chosen the Sanskrit term *mandala* for this central symbol."[19] Jung then asked a very important question in light of the themes I've been exploring subsequent to his 1944 dream of the yogi: "But what has our empirical psychology to say about the Buddha sitting in the lotus? Logically one would expect Christ to be enthroned in the center of our Western mandalas."[20] Was Jung's dream of the yogi in the chapel a compensation for a possible one-sidedness regarding his European understanding of Yoga techniques?

Whether Christ or Buddha appears in modern mandalas anymore is not what interests me here. Jung's unconscious placed a yogi seated in lotus posture in 1944 as his own representation for the Self, and this image spoke deeply to him in a complementary way, like some of his key paintings in *The Red Book*. What interests me is the question he asked himself in India: "What is the psychological nature of evil?" Let me give one more example from Jung's essay on Eckhart to help the reader understand why the integration of the Shadow is such an important part of the individuation process, and without which, if I read Jung correctly, the whole world may be destroyed: "Therefore do I turn once more back to myself, there I find the deepest places, deeper than hell itself; for even from there does my wretchedness drive me. Nowhere can I escape myself! Here I will set me down and here I will remain."[21]

Jung's point about the importance of integrating the Shadow, therefore, is vital. *The only way to achieve world peace is by each and every individual taking a moral inventory of his or her own Shadow and evil.* No method, whether yoga, active imagination, mindfulness practice, or praying five times a day toward Mecca, is a cure-all for the problem of evil that has infected the world's heart and soul. This is the main point that Jung and James have to teach East and West, Middle East, Near East, Far East, the Americas, and Africa too, as we take this next journey forward during a time of increasing degradation of our democracies and damaging climate change, which may prove to be more lethal to human survival than all wars on earth combined, unless we act fast.

Spiritual democracy offers a way forward beyond creeds, beyond religious beliefs, beyond faiths, beyond books. In the words of Islamic scholar Shagufta Begum, lecturer of philosophy at the University of the Punjab in Lahore-Pakistan,

> According to [Allama] Iqbal, spiritual democracy is the ultimate goal of Islam. He saw a beam of hope for entire humanity in establishing this kind of democracy … Iqbal views man as a unity … Iqbal rejects nationalism… He says: … "Let the Muslim of today appreciate his position, reconstruct his social life in the light of the Ultimate principles and evolve out of hitherto partially revealed purpose of Islam that spiritual democracy which is the ultimate aim of Islam."… In the case of Islamic Spiritual Democracy the Holy Quran is the main source of the law.[22]

Whatever the future of spiritual democracy may be, it is an idea that the world has not caught onto yet in any big way. It seems to be emerging through different religious sects, slowly, one creed at a time, and appears to be becoming increasingly transnational. Whitman and the early American poets and visionaries, James and Jung especially, did not stand for any creed. They got outside the need to quarrel about priority with any religion. Their ideas were free, as the United States is free and as Switzerland is free.

In lecture three of his Seminars on *Nietzsche's Zarathustra,* dated November 2, 1938, Jung said to his audience about Ramakrishna: "For example, there is a statute of Sri Ramakrishna in the temple of Belur Mutt, made from a photograph which was taken of him quite against his will. He is clearly in what we would call a state of *ekstasis*—a somnambulistic or hypnotic condition—and they call it *samadhi*."[23] In addition to Jung's criticisms to White about LSD, he was highly critical of ecstasy-seeking as an end in itself. He said *ecstasy is dangerous and calling it by beautiful names is cultivating a dangerous state of unreality.*[24] Jung defined *ecstasy* as experiences of transport that can throw a person completely out of the body; this, he felt, was what made such experiences so risky psychologically. Stepping outside of the body and becoming a spirit, or a soul, denotes a kind of *ekstasis*, which is highly inflationary, he cautioned.[25] I will examine a change in attitude in Jung in regard to ecstasy in a later chapter. Now, however, I will turn to the life and works of William James.

Notes

1. Jung, *MDR,* 183, 185.
2. Jung, "Yoga and the West," CW 11, ¶876.
3. I'm using the United States as a model, even though I know it is only an ideal to be striven toward and what is needed is a psychological point of view provided by James and Jung.
4. James, *Writings 1902–1910,* 1245–1248.
5. Ideally, the constitution doesn't attach itself to a creed, but we are in danger of moving away from this. There's a strong urge toward Christian religious authoritarianism that wasn't present when Jung and James were alive.
6. Jung, CW 11, ¶866.
7. Jung, CW 11, ¶868.

8. Jung, CW 11, ¶876.
9. Jung, "Prefatory Note to 'The Transcendent Function,'" CW 8, p. 68.
10. Jung, "Psychological Commentary on the 'Tibetan Book of the Great Liberation,'" CW 11, ¶759.
11. Jung, "Individual Dream Symbolism in Relation to Alchemy," CW 12, ¶137.
12. Jung, "On the Nature of the Psyche," CW 8, ¶395.
13. Jung, "Commentaries on 'The Tibetan Book of the Great Liberation,'" CW 11, ¶802.
14. Jung, "The Psychology of Eastern Meditation," CW 11, ¶934.
15. Jung, *MDR*, 177.
16. Jung, *MDR*, 324.
17. Jung, *MDR*, 275.
18. Jung, "The Psychology of Eastern Meditation," CW 11, ¶939.
19 Jung, CW 11, ¶945.
20. Jung, CW 11, ¶948.
21. Jung, *Psychological Types*, CW 6, fn 166.
22. Begum, "Iqbal's Concept of Spiritual Democracy," 24.
23. Jung, *Nietzsche's Zarathustra*, vol. 2, 1373.
24. Jung, *Nietzsche's Zarathustra*, vol. 1, 517.
25. Jung, vol. 1, 351; vol. 2, 1433.

Part III

---

*Radical Empiricism
and the Dream
of Philemon*

Chapter 26

The Radical Empirical Psychology of William James: An Overview of the Problem

William James is central to understanding important aspects of Jung's analytical psychology because he played a pivotal role in influencing Jung's views on parapsychology, instincts, emotions, the empirical method, the fringe of consciousness, transpersonal unconscious, psychological types, religious experience, philosophy, Yoga, the Self, God, the problem of evil, expansion of consciousness, the extramarginal field, bursting point, monism, the Absolute, and spiritual democracy. For readers of Jung it seems clear James's critiques of Vedanta may also have influenced Jung's cautionary attitudes toward its application by Westerners. "We all have some ear for monistic music: it elevates and reassures. We all have at least the germ of mysticism in us . . . The mystical germ wakes up in us on hearing the monistic utterances."[1] In 1896, James published *The Will to Believe,* where he specified what he meant by "radical empiricism": "I say 'empiricism' because it is contented to regard its most assured conclusions concerning matters of fact as hypotheses liable to modification in the course of future experience; and I say 'radical' because it treats the doctrine of monism itself as an hypothesis."[2] This is the same year, interestingly, that James met Vivekananda for a second time at Harvard University. James asserted then that "the difference between monism and pluralism is perhaps the most pregnant of all the differences in philosophy."[3] He repeated this idea in *Pragmatism* and then again in *A Pluralistic Universe.* It shows how pregnant his mind was by this time, with a plural view of God, or the Absolute.

As you will see in the chapters ahead, James did not take the narrow view of religions. Rather, he adopted an empirical and agnostic view that no one theology or symbol of divinity can ever possibly encapsulate the essential totality of the Absolute, God, consciousness, or Transcendental

Reality, which can neither be fully fathomed, nor fully known, except through revelations of spiritual experiences. These experiences are made possible through subjective *feelings* that can expose one to immediate perceptions of divinity through openings of the subliminal door.

The year 1898, moreover, marked a real turning point in William James's life. He was, from the start of his career, a pragmatist and a pugilist. He fought valiantly for the integrity of his vocation as an empirical psychologist and a scientist of the Self. His main business was the study of the psychology of religious experience and the furthest reaches of human consciousness beyond the margins of ordinary awareness.

What had been playing in James's mind ever since he met Vivekananda was the theme of "The One and the Many," which would play such an important part in *Pragmatism* and his other major works. This theme was central to the establishment of a Union in the United States in the Latin phrase *E Pluribis Unum*. For James cross-cultural assertions in the world's religious documents of mystical states of Oneness were at the heart of the notion of Union.

> Mystical states of mind in every degree are shown by history, usually tho not always to make for the monistic view... The paragon of all monistic systems is the Vedánta philosophy of Hindostan, and the paragon of Vedántist missionaries was the late Swami Vivekananda who visited our shores some years ago. The method of Vedántism is the mystical method. You do not reason, but after going through a certain method you see, and having seen, you can report the truth.[4]

James went on at length to quote Vivekananda, after which he commented further:

> Observe how radical the character of the monism here is. Separation is not simply overcome by the One, it is denied to exist. There is no many. We are not parts of the One; It has no parts; and since in a sense we undeniably are, it must be that each of is the One, indivisibly and totally. An Absolute One, and I that One,—surely we have here a religion which, emotionally considered, has a high pragmatic value; it imparts a perfect sumptuosity of security.[5]

To be sure, Vivekananda was a monist, but he also embraced pluralism and the relative, next to the Absolute. He learned this from his master, Sri Ramakrishna. James no doubt had his own spiritual experiences prior to writing *Varieties,* and his most meaningful mystical experience might best be described in James's own words as a "pluralistic panpsychic view of the universe."[6] Panpsychism was not unique to James. It is an old Greek idea, going back Plato, Thales, and Spinoza, and extending from Leibnitz to Fechner to James. It is also found in Vedanta and certain forms of Buddhism. Its basic axiom is that Self-consciousness, soul, or mind is a universal phenomenon inherent in all things and that all minds have a common source. James explored this idea in-depth in *A Pluralistic Universe.*

James's psychology, like Jung's, is founded on a democratic spirituality that speaks out against "Big" government and advocates for individual experience as the most sacred thing in the world and the only principle through which communities may thrive according to Nature's laws. Importantly James's Nature experiences preserved the Divine Feminine in his vision of truth—a relative theory of truth, not Absolute.

After the Gifford lectures were finished, they were published in June 1902 as *The Varieties of Religious Experience,* which sold 11,000 copies in the first year and is by far James's most important book and one Jung mined most deeply in his later writings to help extend his theory of the collective unconscious. Vivekananda died the same year, on July 4, 1902, in Belur, India. In 1905, James made his famous statement: "Damn the Absolute!"[7] This was not a quarrel of hostility toward God, but one of deep and abiding affection for the Absolute. "To give up one's concept of being good," James added in "Reason and Faith," "is the only door to the Universe's deeper reaches."[8] In a letter written to his brother Harry, on April 21, 1908, James went so far as to say ironically that he was "eager for the scalp of the Absolute."[9] James's quarrels with God were not that dissimilar to Jung's.

What I'm after in this chapter is a pragmatic understanding of where James's breakthrough-moment occurred, what he called a *bursting point* (a metaphor Jung liked) that led him to write his Gifford Lectures, the source for his American masterpiece, *The Varieties of Religious Experience.* The nature of this bursting point was also its source. This experience reveals where James fits into a Jungian schema of understanding the psyche. I examine in what follows some empirical evidence for my hypothesis *that James's vocation to teach a psychology of religion in America was essentially evoked by a spiritual experience of polytheism and monotheism united in an indescribable transpersonal embrace of his empirical self with the Spiritual Self of the Cosmos.* This experience, as I argue in the next chapter, had its roots in his childhood experiences.

After delivering his lecture "The Will to Believe" to philosophy clubs at Yale and Brown Universities, James experimented in June 1896 with some government-supplied peyote, which had no hallucinatory effects of any significant kind and only made him vomit violently.[10] James was clearly looking for a religious experience of his own, comparable to Whitman's, Vivekananda's, or his good friend, the neo-Hegelian philosopher Josiah Royce's—but an understandably separate one that was true to his own identity and calling.

A ripe moment occurred in July 1898, when James went with some friends to Keene Valley, a place he liked to hike in the Adirondacks. He had been reading the *Journal of George Fox*, the English seventeenth-century founder of the Society of Friends and was somewhat swept up with his experiences.[11] James read in Fox's *Journal* about what he had called "openings." "It was opened in me that God, who made the world, did not dwell in temples made with his hands . . . but that His people were his temple, that He dwelt in them." For Fox, Christian worship was not an outer event that took place in Church, but an inner happening that could occur to anyone through an experience of "inner light." This opening could happen in a church, but that's not the way it happened to Fox, or James. Fox went "into the orchards and fields" with his "Bible, by myself."[12] Meditating on his words, James began to go on longer and longer hikes. Then, the inevitable happened. He had his most memorable spiritual experience, a real peak experience, where transmarginal perceptions entered him.

As the story goes, James left on a trek with an Adirondack guide toward Mount Marcy in Keene Valley at seven in the morning on July 7, 1898. He hiked most of the day and camped that night. Then he had an extraordinary experience that is frequently commented on by James scholars. Around midnight, when the moon was out and hung about in her shimmering beauty and left only a few of the brighter stars visible in the night sky, "I got into a state of spiritual alertness of the most vital description." This experience of alertness might best be described as "cosmic." It was a clear perception of what he would later call *consciousness beyond the margin.* The experience was a prelude to his most important book.

Robert Richardson comments on this experience in his biography of James: "James was always firm in insisting that he had not himself had mystical experiences; he was scrupulous to claim that he was just a seeker, never that he had found or seen the truth . . . Perhaps it wasn't a real mystical moment, but whatever it was, it seems to have been a triggering, originating, or catalyzing moment for the *Varieties of Religious Experience,* a moment of certain but inarticulate knowledge that real religion is religious feeling, and that it can be experienced by anyone."[13] This experience of spiritual alertness was one of the most memorable experiences of James's life. He called it, in a Goethean idiom, "a regular Walpurgis Nacht."[14] As James wrote to his wife, Alice, "It seemed as if the Gods of all the nature-mythologies were holding an indescribable meeting in my breast with the moral Gods of the inner life."[15] It formed the prelude to his trips to Berkeley, California, in 1898.

On the rail heading west from Montreal to Banff, Canada, James had been reading Herman Melville's book *Typee*. He arrived in San Francisco by August and headed for the great Mariposa Grove of giant sequoias in Yosemite. When he returned from his visit, after seeing some of the largest living organisms on earth, he gave a talk before eight hundred people at UC Berkeley. This talk marked "the beginning of the pragmatist movement."[16] Pragmatism has often been referred to as James's philosophy of life, but it was more than that. It was a *psychology of action,* living intensely, in the most positive sense possible, in the Now, the moment. In his *Talks to Teachers,* James referred to this life activity as *quintessentially democratic because it is based on a reverence for the vocation of the Spiritual Self as the most sacred part of the personality; it is the place where transpersonal consciousness can be experienced:* "The practical consequence of such a philosophy is the well-known democratic respect for the sacredness of individuality."[17]

James's arguments with his friend Royce were mostly over the neo-Hegelian issue of the Absolute. His ongoing dialogues with Royce helped catalyze James's arguments in favor of a relativistic point of view in his Gifford Lectures. James had great admiration for Royce, who he considered "by far the biggest mind I have ever known."[18] James's investment in the course of their long and heated "battle of the Absolute" was located in the post-Christian slant in Royce's statements. He had seen a similar slant in the post-Hindu view in Vivekananda's writings. Both were valid. But there was a subjective factor that proved the Absolute could also be criticized by a science of psychology.

In 1900, after James met with British psychic researcher F. W. H. Myers in France, Royce visited James and gave him a copy of his book *The World and the Individual.* James read the book rapidly and wrote back to Royce that "the Absolute still remains for me a hypothesis to be tested by its uses, rather than as a doctrine to be submitted to for its credentials."[19] James then traveled to Geneva to visit his friend, Jung's later mentor, Théodore Flournoy. The following year James was present at Myers's death on January 17, 1901.

James's influence on Jung's thought has been underemphasized by most of Jung's biographers. These lacunae have recently been filled in the past two decades by Eugene Taylor and Sonu Shamdasani. Following on their trail as a Jungian analyst, I will enlarge on their efforts as historians, with some fresh speculative perceptions from a more clinical point of view.

Jung looked at neurosis as a defense against the healthy aspects of the human personality, which strove naturally toward *wholeness.* In this view, neurosis is seen from a scientific angle to be a pathological development that tells a person when he or she is out of balance with nature and in need of connection to the inner voice of God, psyche, soul, or Self. To heal psyche properly, an inner dialogue with the instincts patterning human behavior, personal and cultural complexes, and transpersonal archetypal images is needed. The Self consists potentially of a plurality of urges—biological drives; a healthy sex life; needs for family relatedness, feeling connections, and communal living; physical and mental health; the healing of traumas; economic stability; evolution of one's highest spiritual potentials; integration of the auxiliary and tertiary and inferior functions, introversion and extroversion; and a synthesis of a cacophony of fantasy expressions, or archetypal representations, personal and collective, that all need to be harmonized around a central nucleus, or center point in the personality. Once the complexes and shadow and anima-animus have been analyzed, dialogues with a chorus of instinctive and spiritual representations may be consolidated into a total structure of the personality; the many voices of the psyche may then be unified into a harmony of ego and Self in relationship to the world and cosmos. Then, neurosis temporarily ceases.[20]

We can be thrown off our Self-path again by inner or outer forces, but at least we know how to reestablish the middle way and find the thread again to the center—the Self. This is not a path of moral perfection but of humanness and completion and imperfection, which includes the defeat of the heroic ego and the shame of failure. The vehicle for such a synthesis of the personality around an instinctive and chaotic center is what's commonly called a *vocation,* or what James referred to as the *acting self* in the human species. This is not a new creed of acting selves, as you will see, but a science of the psyche, which includes a healthy respect and understanding of the human Shadow.

Had the movement in modern psychology followed in the path of Jung's science of the personality after the rediscovery of his soul in 1913 in a *post-Jamesian direction toward a psychology of vocation,* it might have become more empirical rather than experimental.[21] Instead, diagnostics, experimentation, laboratory studies, behaviorism, medication treatment, and cognitive therapy won out. I see this as an interregnum. I believe we are at a major turning point where the science of depth psychology has a chance to prove its merits in research centers in universities, colleges, and medical centers. Untapped human potentials are being released through various techniques that are not necessarily new but have to some degree been overlooked. James was at the cutting edge of this frontier of a more positive psychology that he called *radical empiricism,* which is a psychology of human experience, action, the transmutation of psychophysical energies, balance, and the expansion of consciousness.

In his presidential address before the American Philosophical Association at Columbia University on December 28, 1906, for instance, James delivered a paper titled "The Energies of Men," where he called for a *scientific psychology textbook* to address the most important question of how to help people produce what he called an "efficiency-equilibrium." He spoke about how to increase the amounts of energy available in the nervous system and the neural pathways, long before neuroscience emerged as a field of study in its own right. "To have this level raised," James said, "is the most important thing that can happen to a man, yet in all my reading, I know of no single page or paragraph of a scientific psychology book in which it receives mention." No single paragraph mind you. This is vitally important for practitioners of psychology to understand. Psychoanalysis had already emerged, and James was well aware of Freud's and Joseph Breuer's *Studies in Hysteria,* which focused on the treatment of hysterical symptoms and states of dissociation. What interested James was how levels of energy that had become stuck in the subconscious could be freed up through habits, excitements, ideas, and efforts—how *energy could be transformed.* Jung was also greatly interested in the transformation of energy.

James was well aware, from explorations and experimentations with his own dark moods and depressions, how certain habits, such as hiking in the Adirondacks, could transport him to new levels of energy and thought that he never dreamed of before.

> Most of us feel as if we lived habitually with a sort of cloud weighing on us, below our highest notch of clearness in discernment, sureness in reasoning, or firmness in deciding. Compared with what we ought to be, we are only half-awake… The existence of reservoirs of energy that habitually are not tapped is most familiar to us in the phenomenon of "second wind." Ordinarily we stop when we meet the first effective layer, so to call it, of fatigue… But if an unusual necessity forces us to press onward, a surprising thing occurs. The fatigue gets worse up to a certain critical point, when gradually or suddenly it passes away, and we are fresher than before. We have evidently tapped a level of new energy, masked until then by the fatigue-obstacle usually obeyed. There may be layer after layer of this experience. A third and a fourth "wind" may supervene… beyond the very extremity of fatigue distress, amounts of ease and power that we never dreamed ourselves to own, sources of strength habitually not taxed at all, because habitually we never push through the obstruction, never pass those early critical points. When we do pass, what makes us do so? Either some unusual stimulus fills us with emotional excitement, or some unusual idea of necessity induces us to make the extra effort of will. Excitements, ideas, and efforts, in a word, are what carries us over the dam… Most of us may learn to push the barrier further off, and to live in perfect comfort on much higher levels of power.[22]

Although James clearly relied on his own personal experiences as a teacher, writer, and hiker to give readers insights into subjective ways of discovering their own techniques for transmuting consciousness, here he is talking about experiences of transpersonal levels of psychophysical energy ("higher levels of power") that can be released through an entrance of ordinary consciousness into the *extra-marginal fields*. Of course he is also referring to *endorphins,* mind-altering chemicals capable of producing states of euphoria, in a way not dissimilar to the use of an opioid such as morphine, which inhibits pain and maximizes well-being and ecstasy. Although at the time, James was unaware of the physical production (through vigorous exercise such as hiking or mountain climbing) of endorphins and their psychophysiological effects upon consciousness, the nervous system, brain, and emotions in the Body Self, his idea of a "fourth wind" describes exactly the feeling-states he vocalized for psychology from his own inner experiences.[23]

James loved to hike, so I read the "fourth" wind in Jungian terms, as symbolic for James of the experience of the Spiritual Self: James's entrance into a radiating and uplifting zone of power and energy was probably made possible through the doorway of his third function of sensation: the body.[24] The "fourth" wind can be reached through various methods, whether through automatic writing, psychotherapy, sports, Yoga, Eastern or Western forms of prayer or meditation, but for James, it was the vehicle of his vocation as a "physiological psychologist" and philosopher that carried him over the dam, and it shows beautifully in his verses. He learned well as a son of his father, a Swedenborgian and an eloquent writer himself, and from his godfather, Ralph Waldo Emerson, who blessed him at his birth, how to make his words count to achieve what he called "cash value."

Jung would answer James's call for an academic textbook of sorts in his essay "On Psychic Energy," where he mentioned, at the end of the essay in section IV, "The Primitive Conception of the Libido" the "beginnings of religious symbol-formation."[25] The origins of the energy concept were something James had neglected to explore in his researches into the phenomena of religious experience, but he described it in the concept of the "fourth" wind, by which he meant the breath of the Spiritual Self. The fourth wind, of course, is the physical and spiritual manifestation of prana in Vedanta. It doesn't matter whether one connects to the Self through Hatha Yoga, dance, movement, sports, any of the expressive arts, or painting a mandala. They can all lead to the same goal, which is the Self. But the Body Self, Material Self, Social Selves, and Shadow (Jung's inclusion of a vital aspect of the Self) are necessary prerequisites to arriving at a fourth state that includes the mystical, or what Jung called *numinous experiences.*

All of James's insights in *Varieties* and *Pragmatism* were carried forward moreover in his book *A Pluralistic Universe.* Despite his quarrels with Josiah Royce and occasional criticisms of Whitman and Vivekananda in his earlier books, in his essay "A 'Psychical Researcher,'" James posited, "There is a continuum of cosmic consciousness, against which our individuality builds but accidental fences, and into which our several minds plunge as into a mother-sea or reservoir."[26] James wrote this statement for *American Magazine,* published in October 1909, two weeks before his destined meeting at Clark University, with Sigmund Freud, Ernest Jones, Sandor Ferenczi, and C. G. Jung. It is significant, because it was just at the time Jung was struggling to find his footing as an empiricist and researcher, separate from Freud, in transit toward a new psychology he would call his own. James played a pivotal part in opening Jung to cosmic dimensions.

In his opening Gifford lecture at Edinburgh, on May 16, 1901, James made it clear that while the experience of Americans receiving instruction from books of European scholars was a familiar keynote in academia, what was not so familiar was the receptivity of Europeans listening attentively to American psychologists and philosophers speaking about spiritual phenomena. He said he hoped many of his countrymen in the United States would be asked eventually to lecture in Scottish universities and that we would move toward a global exchange of ideas where personal factors of *religious feelings* would "more and more pervade and influence the world."[27] This transnational study of personal experience is vitally important today during a time of increasing tension in the world regarding which religion has the right or wrong revelation of the Absolute. As you'll see, James and Jung provide an answer: all are equals in the evolution of consciousness, and creating meaning through personal experiences of the Self is the best way forward in a psychological age.

Notes

1. James, *Writings 1902–1910*, 553, 554.
2. James, "Preface" to "The Will To Believe," *William James Writings 1878–1899*, 447.
3. James, 447.
4. James, 552.
5. James, 553, 554.
6. James, 772.
7. James, 457.
8. James, 469.
9. James, 499.
10. James, 1339.
11. George Fox, *The Journal of George Fox*. Fox also had a profound influence on the life and writings of Walt Whitman. As Whitman said of him: "He is the most *democratic* of the religionists—the prophets." See Walt Whitman, *Walt Whitman: Complete Poetry and Collected Prose*, 1221.
12. James, *Writings 1902–1910*, 373.
13. Richardson, *William James: In the Maelstrom of American Modernism*, 375.
14. A German folk belief holds that during *Walpurgisnacht* on the evening of April 30—the eve of the feast day of the Saint *Walpurga*—witches gather on the Brocken mountain, the highest peak in the Harz Mountains, and hold a revel with the devil. The celebration is described as a Bacchanalia of the evil and demonic powers, which are equivalent in Jung's analysis of the Walpurgis Nacht with an "overpowering by the shadow" (See C. G. Jung, "Faust and Alchemy," CW 18, ¶1696).
15. James, 1340.
16. James, 377.
17. James, 381.
18. James, 385.
19. James, 1342.
20. Jung's psychology is a therapy of the healthy personality free from the curse of neurosis. This freedom is relative, not absolute, by which I mean that it does not happen once and for all, but rather when the disturbance by complexes has temporarily ceased. This occurs whenever ego consciousness penetrates through depth-analysis to what Jung called the "secret" of the personality.

This was a breakthrough Jung made during the period of his *Red Book*, which was supervened by the spirit of Philemon. The apotheosis for this Self-development of the personality in Jung occurred theoretically for him in 1932, at the age of fifty-seven, when he delivered his talk "The Development of the Personality" at roughly the same time he was giving his Seminars on Kundalini Yoga. Jung had been searching for a natural nomenclature, a transnational language of the psyche that applied its discipline specifically to a scientific language, one that could potentially unify the sciences around a central image inside the Self. I call this image the *nuclear symbol*. From a transnational angle the task of analysis is to perform a therapy of vocation, where callings become key to freedom from *cultural neuroses*.

21. By *Jamesian* I mean more positive, free from the *vocational complex* and its neuroses. Releasing the psychophysical energy from the vocation complex and its neurotic cores is the goal of every analysis.
22. James, *Writings 1902–1910*, 1224–1227.
23. James, 1223–1241.
24. In "The Energies of Men" James was searching for the very source of vitality itself: a positive psychological solution to the problem of impasse, lassitude, sloth, or drifting, which only a vocation can supervene. The fourth wind connects us to the root-source of the archetype and its representation through *vocational images, aptitudes, and ideas*.
25. Jung, "On Psychic Energy, CW 8, ¶115.
26. James, *Writings 1902–1910*, 1264.
27. James, 11, 12.

Chapter 27

PSYCHOLOGY AS AN EMPIRICAL SCIENCE

William James was born on January 11, 1842, in New York City. His father, Henry James Sr., began studies at Princeton Theological Seminary in 1837. James's father then abandoned his seminary education to devote himself uninterruptedly to the independent study of theology, a life-long interest for him. He turned to the writings of Emanuel Swedenborg and found great solace in them, even writing a number of books that were directly inspired by Swedenborg.[1] The first was *Moralism and Christianity,* published in 1850. Henry James Sr. was also a personal friend of Ralph Waldo Emerson. Emerson met Henry James Sr. shortly before William was born, and he is said to have blessed the baby not long after his birth. This blessing from Emerson would not go unremarked in James's lifetime. Like Jung, James felt he owed a great deal to the dead. James spoke passionately, for instance, about Emerson as his "Beloved Master" in his "Address at the Centenary of Ralph Waldo Emerson," on May 25, 1903. As James said then, Emerson "seems securely destined to exert an ennobling influence over future generations."[2] He concluded with a personal tribute: "As long as our English language lasts, men's hearts will be cheered and their souls strengthened and liberated by the noble and musical pages with which you have enriched it."[3] James could hear the music in Emerson's writings because he had himself a finely tuned ear for poetry, as he had read Whitman and many other poets, including the Sufis and Rishis of India.

This was the cultural context in which James was born. The lineage of his analytic psychology of action and consciousness began with Emerson and his father and their long talks about theology, poetry, and spiritual experiences over the dinner table at the James' home. To be sure, James was strongly influenced by what he heard in his childhood environment. This intellectual environment also influenced his siblings. The most famous of James's siblings was, of course, Henry James Jr., or Harry, who was born on April 15, 1843. Harry became the famous author of such classics as *The American* and *Turn of the Screw*. Between James's infancy and the age of twelve, Emerson was a recurrent guest at James's home. These visits formed a lasting impression on the young brothers' minds, an imprint of the American scholar, which stayed with them for the rest of their lives and helped to shape their sense of a family destiny. The two brothers continued to encourage and inspire one another until William James's untimely death by angina in 1910 at the age of sixty-eight.

In 1855, the year Whitman published *Leaves of Grass*, and twenty years before Jung's birth, William was sent by his father to receive a formal education in Geneva, Switzerland. In Geneva, James and two of his younger brothers, Wilky and Bob, attended a multilingual classroom (English, French, and German). For a time, James believed his vocation was to be an artist. The James family traveled extensively through Europe, and they settled for a time in Geneva, where James studied science at Geneva Academy (now the University of Geneva). Later in his life James would meet the Swiss experimental psychologist Théodore Flournoy who taught at the University of Geneva, and they would form a lasting friendship after their first meeting in Paris in 1889.

In 1861, at the age of nineteen, James abandoned his mistaken vocation as a painter and entered Lawrence Scientific School at Harvard University. There he became deeply impressed by the Lowell Lectures given by the famous American naturalist Louis Agassiz. In 1864 James entered Harvard's School of Medicine. The following year he joined an expedition to Brazil that was organized by Agassiz to collect specimens for his zoological museum. James traveled up the Amazon with Agassiz and collected fish samples, learning a great deal from him about science. When he returned to Harvard Medical School in the fall of 1866, James began to suffer from numerous psychosomatic complaints, felt "loathsome," and contemplated suicide. He suffered from depression and physical problems for much of the rest of his life. The following year, 1867, he read Goethe's *Faust*, and not long thereafter he wrote to his friend Thomas Ward that "perhaps the time has come for psychology to begin to be a science."[4] In 1869, James passed his requirements for his MD at Harvard. At this time, he delved deeply into works of science and literature as well as the works of Johann Fichte and Arthur Schopenhauer, before becoming severely depressed again. At age twenty-eight, as James became increasingly aware of his melancholic temperament, his misery peaked during a moment of panic, a moment of dread, horror, or terror, regarding his possible insanity:

> I have always felt that this experience of melancholia of mine had a religious bearing... I mean that the fear was so invasive and powerful that if I had not clung to scripture texts like "the eternal God is my refuge," etc., "Come unto me, all ye that labor and are heavy-laden," etc., "I am the resurrection and the life," etc. I think I should have grown really insane.[5]

This moment of acute fear marked the period of his awareness of his *spiritual vocation*, and the feelings of terror had, as he said, a distinct "religious bearing." During this tremulous period in 1870, the melancholia seemed to James to be "an acute neurasthenic attack with paranoia."[6] His father had a similar experience at roughly the same age. And, as James observed, the fear seemed to be preparing him for some kind of spiritual activity, or vocation, just as it had for his father, who was led to read Swedenborg and then was further supported by his spiritual friendship with Emerson. Three years earlier, in 1867, James noted in a letter to Ward: "I am going to try and stick to the study of the nervous system and psychology."[7] Hence, the bout of terror may have been an initiatory illness, preparing him for his future vocation in psychology. Today, of course, we who are familiar with what Stanislav Grof called *spiritual emergence,* or *spiritual emergency* in 1989, would recognize it as such from a psychological angle, or, in the language of the 1993 DSM-IV Task Force, as a "Religious or Spiritual Problem."[8]

What this illness did for James was to evoke his calling to "action." His psychological motto was a line from Goethe's *Faust*: "*Im anfang war die tat*" ("In the beginning was the act").[9] Action became the center and circumference of James's pragmatic philosophy and the beginnings of his analytic psychology of radical empiricism. "For the remainder of this year," James wrote in a diary entry, "I will voluntarily cultivate the feeling of moral freedom, by reading books favorable to it, as well as by acting. ...Not in maxims," James added, "but in accumulated acts of thought lies salvation."[10]

Note the importance James attributed to *action* here. From his illness emerged a calling from his inner voice to pursue his passion. "All thought," James said in the same year, 1870, "all emotion which does not tend to action, is morbid and should be suppressed."[11] Suppression suggests that shadowy emotions be kept out of our actions. In other words, we might say today that not to act on emotions in relation to the climate crisis would truly be *morbid,* as the result of inaction, or spreading a sick propaganda of disbelief or doubt that our science is accurate, in the face of increasing and looming evidence of climate change, is certainly shadowy and catastrophic. The nonmorbid or healthy response might be, therefore, to infuse our violent impulses with healthy and positive emotions directed at curbing the use of fossil fuels and global warming through whatever form of creative activities we possibly can.

James's biographer Robert Richardson shows, from an examination of the evidence provided in the marginalia of James's volumes of Emerson's *Essays,* he was captured by his "Master's" thoughts at this time. *James not only read Emerson's* Essays, *but he assimilated Emerson's spirit into his own person, making Emerson's words part of his own natural eloquence and speech of his Spiritual Self.* The image of Emerson, like the legend of Goethe for Freud and for Jung, formed an indelible impress of *vocational energy* that charged his personality with momentary upsurges of creativity, action-potentials filled with creative inspiration, which yielded practical results. In James's copy of Emerson's essay, "The American Scholar" he marked this interesting passage: "Action is with the scholar subordinate, but it is essential."[12] For James, however, *action and consciousness* were primary; scholarship was subordinate. The core of James's pragmatic teachings can be summed up in the following statement: "The knower is not simply a mirror…The knower is an actor."[13] Later, in *A Pluralistic Universe,* he called this knower the *acting self.*

In 1873, at the age of forty-one, James accepted an offer from Charles William Eliot, then president of Harvard, to teach an undergraduate course in comparative physiology. This proposition came as a veritable godsend to James. He taught at Harvard on and off for the rest of his life. In 1874, James helped found the "metaphysical club," devoted to the study of Hegel. In the same year he also opened the first laboratory for experimental psychology at Harvard. From this point onward investigation was central to his psychology of action. In 1875, the year of Jung's birth, James taught a graduate course on the relationship between physiology and psychology, which included the first laboratory work in psychology in the United States. In 1876, James had G. Stanley Hall as a graduate student, and in 1877 he was visited in Cambridge by Josiah Royce, a graduate student at Johns Hopkins University who consulted James about his future career in philosophy. Royce's visit would prove to be meaningful, for he and Royce were to become the best of friends. In 1878 James gave ten lectures on "The Brain and the Mind" and taught psychology at the Lowell Institute of Boston. In 1880, he published "The Association of Ideas" in *Popular Science Monthly*.

James was moving rapidly toward what he'd later call a "bursting point." In "The Sentiment of Rationality" James engaged in what Robertson called his "first skirmish with the Absolute," which was his initial attempt to put the problem of his fight with monism (or the doctrine of oneness) into purely psychological terms: "The Absolute is what has not yet been transcended, criticized, and made relative.... Every thought is absolute to us at the moment of conceiving it or acting upon it."[14] Whitman became a favorite object of James's pen right from the beginning of his quarrels with the Absolute. Later, Royce and Vivekananda would become bigger minds to grapple with.

Like Whitman, who proclaimed Emerson as his Master, James also owed a great debt to the American scholar. No doubt, Whitman and Vivekananda, like Emerson and Royce, woke up the monistic music in James. Having mystical or transpersonal experiences was not the main aim for James, however. It was *activity* that moved James to put forth his new philosophical principle for psychology that would launch an international movement. *One of the hallmarks of this movement is its optimism in one's own personal destiny.* About the subconscious he said: "It is far too little recognized how entirely the intellect is built up of practical interests. Cognition is incomplete until it is discharged in act."[15] James stressed *activity* and *feeling* over philosophical inaction and cognitive processes. After lambasting Schopenhauer for his pessimism, James proceeded to laud "Emerson's creed that everything that ever was or will be is here in the enveloping now; that man has but to obey himself—He who will rest in what he is, is a part of Destiny."[16] James asserted further: "That the course of destiny may be altered by individuals no wise evolutionist ought to doubt."[17]

James was clearly on a mission. At this point in his career, however, his destiny was about to be altered utterly. In 1878, James gave a series of six talks for the Lowell (Institute) Lectures in Boston, which were titled

"The Brain and the Mind." In this series of lectures, James spoke about the activity of cognition as an "action of consciousness." "Every act leaves a trace in the individual... The great thing is to form habits which then leave [the] hemis[pheres] free for higher flights and, in forming habits, to keep them unbroken."[18] This became the starting point for a science of the mind.

The Lowell Lectures prepared his destiny-pattern for a transit to higher spheres of activity in the future. These spheres of action were actually *fields beyond the fringes of his consciousness that were not yet fully accessed as action-potentials,* by which I mean, in Jungian terms, archetypal fields. In 1882, James experienced a series of tragic losses that would eventually lead him through emotional suffering to tap into the source of his own deepest grief: the consecutive deaths of 1) his mother in January, 2) Emerson in April, and 3) his father Henry Sr. in December. All three of these losses opened him, through profound sorrow, into the ground of his very own being and the consciousness of his Spiritual Self. In 1882, James not only said goodbye to his mother and father, but also bid farewell to his beloved spiritual father, Emerson.

After James's mother's death, he had arranged for Josiah Royce to take his place at Harvard so he could recuperate. In September, he traveled to Europe and passed through Germany to Vienna. He attended courses from experimental psychologist Wilhelm Wundt in Leipzig, and then attended lectures by Jean-Martin Charcot in his neurological clinic. In early December, James received word from his brother Harry that Henry Sr. was dying, and he wrote a parting letter to his father that admitted: "All my intellectual life I derive from you."[19] Not long after his father's death, in December, however, James wrote to his brother Harry a line that would become prophetic of his future vocation as an ancestor of analytic psychology: "Father's cry was the single one that religion is real." To his ailing sister, Alice, James wrote further: "You must not leave me till I understand a little more of the value and meaning of religion in father's sense, in the mental life and destiny of man."[20] James's calling to write about the reality of spiritual life was awakened in him strongly by this time. He had heard about such awakenings from his father's inspired books on Emanuel Swedenborg and from his own readings of Goethe, Emerson, and Whitman, but he started to long fervently for an authentic spiritual experience of his own. Nothing really significant was forthcoming, but things were building. Soon, they would boil over.

In early 1883, James had George Santayana as an undergraduate philosophy student. He began to speak at this time about "the wonderful stream of our consciousness."[21] James set out to answer the question of how to tap into the deeper streams of consciousness. Later, he would write in *Principles of Psychology,* "The state of our consciousness is peculiar. There is a gap therein; but no mere gap. It is a gap that is intensively active."[22] James wanted to operate out of the wonderful stream of consciousness and gap of transconscious activity. Early on in his endeavors James experimented with automatic writing. He noted later in an October 1909 essay, "The Confidences of a 'Psychical Researcher'": "The first automatic writing I ever saw was forty years ago . . . Since then I have come to see in automatic writing one example of a department of human activity as vast as it is enigmatic," as it can at times capture the record of "*the presence*" of "*really supernormal knowledge.*"[23]

In January 1884, James wrote in an issue of *Mind,* "The only fundamental quarrel Empiricism has with Absolutism is over the repudiation by Absolutism of the personal and aesthetic factor in the construction of philosophy."[24] It is interesting how vital the empirical method was for James at this time. He even capitalized *Empiricism* here and placed it on a par with *Absolutism.* This fundamental principle of science—*Empiricism* with a capital *E*—would later be adopted by C. G. Jung, without the uppercase or the term *radical.*

Like Jung, James's attitude toward conventional religion was a rebellious one, and his final synthesis would not come without compensation in the direction of empirical one-sidedness. In a famous photograph shot in Chocorua, New Hampshire, in September 1903, for instance, the year after *Varieties* was published, James said famously to Royce: "Royce, you're being photographed! Look out! I say *Damn the Absolute!*"

At least part of the influence in James's heated battle with the Absolute was provided earlier by his father. "Mr. James was one of that band of saints and mystics," James noted in *The Literary Remains,* "whose rare privilege it has been, by the mere example and recital of their bosom experiences, to prevent religion from becoming a fossil conventionalism—and keep it forever alive."[25] Thus, James's father was a breaker with convention. Whereas Henry James Sr. turned to Swedenborg, James turned to Alexander von Humboldt's student, Louis Agassiz, to earn his spurs as a natural scientist. James was now laying the foundation for a science of religion to help moderns and postmoderns arrive at a real experience of God as a "feeling of action" in which the Absolute might be experienced in the subjective domain of empirical reality, which does not leave the relativity of good and evil, right and wrong thoughts, beliefs, and actions out of the inventory of our consciousness.[26]

In 1889, moreover, James attended the International Congress of Physiological Psychology in Paris, where as I previously said he met Flournoy. In 1890, James published the two-volume set *The Principles of Psychology*, which was widely acclaimed and quickly adopted as an academic textbook in many national universities and across the Atlantic in England and other European nations. Jung quoted from *The Principles* in a number of his works, beginning with his doctoral dissertation. By 1892, *The Principles* was abridged and rewritten for a one-volume text, *Psychology: Briefer Course*. In marginalia of his copy of this book, James inscribed at the top of Chapter 10, "Habit," the following ingenious aphorism: "*Sow an action, and you reap a habit; sow a habit and you reap a character; sow a character and you reap a destiny.*"[27] This is exactly what James had done. He was now reaping a destiny through habit and concentrated action and thought.

In James's *Essays in Psychical Research* he wrote in-depth about the works of Frederick W. H. Myers (1854–1920) on the "subliminal self." In his overview of Myers's work, James said, "Each of us is in reality an abiding psychical entity far more extensive than he knows—an individuality that can never express itself completely through any corporeal manifestation. The Self manifests itself through the organism; but there is always some part of the Self unmanifested; and always, as it seems, some power of organic expression in abeyance or reserve."[28] He capitalized the Self in this passage. For James, the Self could never be fully manifested, and therefore, the God-images of any one religion must, therefore, be limited.

While visiting Flournoy and Flournoy's family at Vers-chez-les-Blanc near Lausanne in 1892, James went on a walking tour with Myers, who had helped found the English Society for Psychical Research with Gurney in 1882. In March 1892, James published an important seven-page piece called "A Plea for Psychology as a Natural Science." Jung was not yet seven years old. In this paper James asserted, "All natural sciences aim at practical prediction and control, and in none of them is this more the case than in psychology today ... We live surrounded by an enormous body of persons who are most definitely interested in the control of mind, a sort of psychological science that will teach them how to act."[29]

What such a science of action might look like for the future is still uncertain because we lack experiential grounding in an analytic psychology that can help establish a basis for an educational system that places its greatest emphasis on teaching ways to motivate human *action* and corresponds with what is going on in the transmarginal streams of our consciousness, or higher vistas of our consciousness. As you'll see in the next chapter, this is one of the tasks of a future psychology. James later took up this vital topic in *Talks to Teachers,* published in 1899. In "each of us when awake (and often when asleep) some kind of consciousness is always going on ... The existence of this stream is the primal fact, the nature and origin of it form the essential problem, of our science."[30]

In 1893, James was elected president of the American Association for Psychologists. In 1894 he wrote a favorable notice of Sigmund Freud's and Joseph Breuer's first paper on hysteria for the *Psychological Review*. In the same year, James reviewed with great admiration Pierre Janet's État Mentale des Hystériques. More than any other techniques for the alleviation from emotional and mental suffering Pierre Janet's methods in France seemed to pave the way toward an entirely new psychology for James. Automatic writing had emerged as a method of activating the subconscious mind with the advent of spiritism, but its uses were taken over by scientists, such as Myers and James, and later by Janet, who used it systematically. James felt from the start of reading Janet's research in Paris that he had inaugurated a whole new path of exploration, a shift from laboratory psychology toward clinical and therapeutic psychotherapy, to which James wholeheartedly subscribed. What fascinated James most were Janet's writings on the "fixed ideas" that arise subsequent to "psychic trauma." James wrote incisively: "The nucleus of these subconscious fixed ideas usually consists of reminiscences of the shock by which the mind was originally shattered." James referred to such traumatic shocks as "thorns in the spirit, so to speak. The cure is to draw them out in hypnotism, let them produce all their emotional effects, however violent, and work themselves off."[31] *Thorns in the spirit* suggests, in a Jamesian and Jungian metaphorical way of speaking, that the Self can be "splintered" by what Jung called "complexes."

In 1895 James taught a graduate seminar on the psychology of *feeling*. James was among the first to note that feeling is the way religious experience emerges through the subliminal door. In April 1895, James gave a talk titled "Is Life Worth Living?" to the Harvard YMCA. He began this lecture with a glance at "temporal optimism" and used for his example the poet Walt Whitman, for whom "the mere joy of living is so immense . . . that it abolishes the possibility of any other kind of feeling."[32] In this same talk James added that "Pessimism is essentially a religious disease."[33] James also referred to Schopenhauer's vicious will-substance as being wedded to a pessimistic principle. Here he reversed the trend toward what today is referred to, somewhat appropriately, as *positive psychology*. Yet we have to remember the profound states of despair and recurrence of depressive episodes in James's life that gave this attitude its potential for confident action. "God himself," James said optimistically, "may draw vital strength and increase of very being from our fidelity."[34]

During the fall of 1896, James gave his famous Lowell Lectures on exceptional mental states. He gave eight lectures in total, with the following titles: "Dreams and Hypnotism," "Automatism," "Hysteria," "Multiple Personality," "Demoniacal Possession," "Witchcraft," "Degeneration," and "Genius." Perhaps the most original of the Lowell Lectures was "Genius," where James stated clearly that "a psychopathic constitution is the foundation for genius." James quoted F. W. H. Myers as saying, moreover, that genius was something we might all tap into by gaining access to "an 'uprush' of contents from the subliminal." After James asked each person in the audience to experiment with automatic writing, in Lecture II, he concluded the final chapter "Genius" by asking: "Who shall say absolutely that the morbid has no revelations about the meaning of life? That the healthy-minded view so-called is all? A certain tolerance, a certain sympathy, a certain respect, and above all a certain lack of fear, seem to be the best attitude we can carry in our dealing with these regions of human nature."[35] By this time James appeared to have found a way to transcend momentarily his fears of the unknown.

Notes

1. James, *Writings 1902–1910*, 1321.
2. James, 1119.
3. James, 1125.
4. James, 1327.
5. Richardson, *William James: In the Maelstrom of American Modernism*, 117–118.
6. Richardson, 119.
7. Richardson, 86.
8. Grof and Grof, *Spiritual Emergency*.
9. Richardson, *William James*, 92.
10. Richardson, 121.
11. Richardson, 124.
12. Richardson, 154.
13. Richardson, 183.
14. Richardson, 185.
15. Richardson, 201.
16. Richardson, 202.
17. Richardson, 203.
18. Richardson, 195.
19. James, 1333.
20. Richardson, 232, 233.
21. Richardson, 234.
22. Richardson, 235.
23. James, 1263, 1264.
24. Richardson, 248.
25. Richardson, 251.
26. Richardson, 251.
27. Richardson, 315; italics mine.
28. Richardson, 324.
29. Richardson, 331.
30. Richardson, 341.
31. Richardson, 336, 337.
32. Richardson, 354.
33. Richardson, 355.
34. Richardson, 356.
35. Taylor, *William James on Exceptional Mental States*, 149, 165.

Chapter 28

The Varieties of Religious Experience

I will now review a few passages from *The Varieties of Religious Experience* to give the reader a flavor of how radically empirical James really was. He asked the following question: "What is the character of the universe in which we dwell?" To which he answered: "It expresses our individual sense of it in the most definite way."[1] James was developing a thesis: *there is a doorway in the subliminal Self through which we each may pass into a region of consciousness that is cosmic and, therefore, infinite*. Techniques that have been used by various religions across the globe to gain access to the Spiritual Self may differ, but the universal foundation is the same. "If a creed makes a man [or woman] feel happy, he [or she] almost inevitably adopts it."[2] "In many persons," he continued, "happiness is congenital and irreclaimable. 'Cosmic emotion' inevitably takes in them the form of enthusiasm and freedom… From the outset their religion is one of union with the divine."[3] Notice how he inserted the category of "cosmic emotion" here. What is "cosmic emotion"? Is there one "cosmic emotion," or are there many? A Vedantist, for instance, would say that the Absolute is Bliss. This might be true, but as James knew through his study of emotion, there are many emotions that can express the Absolute, but at bottom these are not monistic expressions, but pluralistic. He, therefore, chose to view such experiences as relativistic, just as Jung would also when describing the *numinous* as a phenomenological category of experience.

> If then, we give the name healthy-mindedness to the tendency which looks on all things and sees that they are good, we find that we must distinguish between a more involuntary and a more voluntary or systematic way of being healthy-minded. In its involuntary variety, healthy-mindedness is a way of feeling happy about things immediately. In its systematic variety, it is an abstract way of conceiving things as good…Systematic

healthy-mindedness, conceiving good as an essential and universal aspect of being, deliberately excludes evil from its field of vision.⁴

This idea of excluding evil by taking a healthy-minded approach to religion spoke directly to Jung who stressed the necessity of including the Shadow and evil. This passage, to be sure, also spoke directly to Jung:

> It is evident that from the point of view of their psychological mechanism, the classic mysticism and these lower mysticisms spring from the same mental level, from the great subliminal or transmarginal region of which science is beginning to admit the existence, but of which so little is really known. That region contains every kind of matter: "seraph and snake" abide there side-by-side. To come from thence is no infallible credential.⁵

That he included seraph and snake in his inventory of the subliminal and transliminal Self is remarkably similar to Jung's vision of the Self in *Aion*.

After an incisive exegesis of Whitman and several other examples of cosmic, or mystic consciousness, James then proceeded to say: "We must next pass to its methodical cultivation as an element of the religious life. Hindus, Buddhists, Mohammedans, and Christians all have cultivated it methodically."⁶ He then cited a quote on the state of *Samadhi,* taken from Vivekananda's 1896 book *Raja Yoga*:⁷ "The Vedantists say that one may stumble into superconsciousness sporadically, without the previous discipline, but it is then impure. Their test of its purity, like the test of religious value, is empirical: its fruits must be good for life."⁸ James then proceeded to give readers some further definitions of the higher states of contemplation in Buddhism and Sufism. Following these interesting and rich discussions and a lengthy quote from a Sufi mystic, James said about the transport: "The incommunicableness of the transport is the keynote of all mysticism. Mystical truth exists for the individual who has the transport, but for no one else."⁹

One of the ideas James championed before he met Jung was an indeterminate "extramarginal" field, or *fields of mental vision,* to which the Empirical Self, during rare moments of mystical seeing, may open to acquire vision. The discovery by James's English friend Frederick Myers of a "consciousness existing beyond the field" led him to postulate that a transmarginal area "lies around us like a 'magnetic field,' inside of which our center of energy turns like a compass-needle, as the present phase of consciousness alters into its successor."[10] This passage comes from James's Lecture X: "Conversion—Concluded."

Experiences, James conjectured, can incubate in the Empirical Self, and the increasing tension of subliminal memories in the transmarginal field may then reach what he called a "bursting-point."[11] Powers in the extramarginal field get into us, moreover, through "the subliminal door."[12] Research into the *fields* of extramarginal consciousness gave James empirical confidence that "We have the beginnings of a 'Science of Religions,' so-called."[13] If psychology could make the objects of transmarginal vision a subject of its empirical investigations through experiential openings in the subliminal door, James believed we might be able to transform the study of religion into a universally convincing scientific paradigm. Note that he was writing about streams of consciousness as fields. As any psychotherapist knows, the field notion is perhaps the most widely held idea in contemporary psychoanalysis and Jungian analysis. Thus, in this metaphor the *science of religion* is the empirical study of interactions in the field. In Lecture XVIII, "Philosophy," James posited, "I do not see why a critical Science of Religion of this sort might not eventually command as general a public adhesion as is commanded by a physical science."[14]

Although James did not believe such a science could ever be an "equivalent for living religion," he nevertheless conjectured that the "pivot" around which religious life revolved "is the interest of the individual in his private destiny."[15] Thus, for James, the way to study the subliminal self was through a door that opened into the mystery of one's deepest destiny-pattern and from which one's actions, practice, and practical considerations came into being. In the nomenclature of analytical psychology, this includes the analyst's insight into her own destiny-pattern in the transference-countertransference field, which is really, if it is extramarginal, a *field between*. James added in Lecture XX, "Conclusions":

> The doorway into the subject seems to me to be the best one for a science of religions, for it mediates between a number of different points of view. Yet it is only a doorway, and difficulties present themselves as soon as we step through it, and ask how far our transmarginal consciousness carries us if we follow it on its remoter side. Here the over-beliefs begin: here mysticism and the conversion-rapture and Vedantism and transcendental

idealism bring in their monistic interpretations and tell us that the finite self rejoins the absolute self, for it was always one with God and identical with the soul of the world.[16]

Here he went far beyond the margins of what most modern psychotherapists might be comfortable with. He then gave readers the quote by Vivekananda, to make his point about the apparent over-beliefs of Advaita, which, as I showed earlier, was a favorite target of his pen. A note about the term *over-beliefs* might be in order here. James specifically names mysticism, conversion-rapture, Vedantism, transcendental idealism, and their monistic interpretations, as four examples of "over-beliefs" that extend beyond the "doorway" of "a science of religions." So by *over-beliefs* he means distant to the conscious mind.

Regardless of whether James is right or wrong about radical empiricism and the Absolute and depending on who is judging what consciousness is, what impresses me most is how deeply his insights go regarding an activity that any one of us might experience if we can find methods to help us step momentarily through the subliminal doorway. James asks us how far our transmarginal consciousness might carry us *if we follow it on its remoter side of the door*, a question he leaves open ended for further field research.

To distill James's hypotheses about religious beliefs, I'll quote a few salient points in his chapter "Conclusions":

1. That the visible world is part of a more spiritual universe in which it draws its chief significance;
2. That union or harmonious relation with that higher universe is our true end;
3. That prayer or inner communion with the spirit thereof—be that spirit "God" or "law"—is a process wherein work is really done, and spiritual energy flows in and produces effects, psychological and material, within the phenomenal world; Religion includes also the following psychological characteristics:
4. A new zest which adds itself like a gift to life, and takes the form either of lyrical enchantment or of appeal to earnestness and heroism;
5. An assurance of safety and a temper of peace, and, in relation to others, a preponderance of loving affections.[17]

I include this further quote: "The less we mix the private with the cosmic, the more we dwell in universal and impersonal terms, the truer heirs of Science we become."[18] Here are three additional questions to ponder: (1) What is the door to the Universe's deeper reaches, which, as James said, the founders of all the world's great religions pass through to arrive at their insights? (2) How can we gain access to this subliminal doorway that opens up to the mother-sea or reservoir of all truly objective thoughts, whether in religion, psychology, big business, technology, or computer science? (3) How might James's insights about Cosmic Consciousness have helped C. G. Jung posit his theory of the collective or transpersonal unconscious?

As we've seen, James was developing a theory of truth in *Varieties*. He stated that there was a doorway in the subliminal Self through which we each may pass into a region of consciousness that is cosmic and, therefore, infinite. Powers in the extramarginal field get into us, he added in "Conversion—Concluded," through "the subliminal door."[19] He suggested it may be democratically possible for anyone to step through this door, as we all come from a larger consciousness and are going always toward it, even if we cannot see it. James asked how far our transmarginal consciousness might carry us *if we follow it on its remoter side of the door*. Of course, in analysis, the extramarginal field is everywhere in the room and in the interactions and sense of presence of something unseen and even numinous in the background of our ordinary awareness. In another salient quote, James wrote: "The hubbub of the waking life might close a door which in the dreamy Subliminal might remain ajar or open."[20]

We might justifiably see the influence of James's metaphor of the subliminal door ajar impressing itself on Jung's thinking. Now, I ask the reader to consider doing a brief journaling exercise.

> *Close your eyes and take a couple of deep breaths at your own pace. Feel yourself sinking into your body and notice if there are any sensations, feelings, images, or thoughts that are present. If you find your mind wandering, just bring it gently back to the present. Take another deep breath and then imagine yourself approaching some kind of a doorway. It may be the doorway to a sacred room of some kind, a Taoist temple, a Buddhist shrine, a mosque, or a church in the United States or Europe, or the doorway to the CEO's office at Google, or Apple, or Twitter, or Microsoft. Any kind of door you might imagine there. Now,*

imagine yourself going through that doorway and see what emerges on the other side. Is there an image or vision? Colors? Textures? What feelings arise for you? Sensations? Allow yourself to engage in an inner dialogue, or in a way you can relate to it, with whatever you experience there. Stay with this experience. When you are ready, pick up your pen and write, or begin typing into your computer, or vocalize whatever words want to flow through you.

NOTES

1. James, *Writings 1902–1910*, 39.
2. James, 77.
3. James, 78.
4. James, 84.
5. James, 384.
6. James, *Writings 1902–1910*, 361.
7. James, 361.
8. James, 361.
9. James, 366.
10. James, 214, 215.
11. James, 218.
12. James, 224.
13. James, 189.
14. James, 409.
15. James, 438–440.
16. James, 458.
17. James, 435.
18. James, 446.
19. James, 224.
20. James, 223.

Chapter 29

Pragmatism

American psychology, as James taught it, is a psychology of religious experience, a psychology of consciousness, a *psychology of action,* of radical empiricism, or *pragmatism.* James borrowed the word *pragmatism* from an 1878 article by Charles Peirce entitled "How to Make Our Ideas Clear."[1] "The term," James asserted, "is derived from the same Greek word πρᾶγμα, meaning action, from which our words 'practice' and 'practical' come."[2] Pragmatism as a path of action and practice breathes life throughout William James's writings. A psychology of action (or *vocation*) is also, not incidentally, at the center of Jung's analytical psychology. The parallels between James's and Jung's psychologies of action, or *callings,* are unmistakable when examining their works side-by-side. The emphasis they each placed on creative *acts* (James) or *callings* (Jung) was primary to both their works. What Jung said about James's typology in his 1921 book *Psychological Types* ("One should not, however, cherish any illusions about its value: pragmatism is but a makeshift" and Nietzsche's "positive act of creation," his "creative act goes beyond the unsatisfying pragmatic solution"[3]) needs to be qualified, given everything else Jung said about James, which I review in Chapter 31.

The pragmatic movement, for which James was best known after his 1898 lecture at the University of California, Berkeley, was originally sparked as a distinctly West Coast phenomenon. The accent James placed on *experience* had a great appeal to a Bay Area mentality, even before the turn of the twentieth century. James's trip to California in 1898 marked the inception point of the "pragmatist movement."[4] I don't mean to exaggerate the significance of California on James's development, but it is possible that the West Coast was ready for the movement for which James is most widely known in philosophical and psychological circles today. This readiness to emergent phenomenon is associated with the Human Potential Movement, alternative therapies and life philosophies, and now transpersonal business and computer science, all of which grew out of the counterculture of the 1960s at Esalen Institute, in Big Sur, California, just south of Monterey. But the earlier movement happened at UC Berkeley, with James as its catalyst.

What the spirit of the times called for, James believed, was an active vision of a new kind of humanism and a psychology of consciousness and field theory that could look at the phenomenon of experience from an objective viewpoint. Through a careful study of psychic facts—free of restrictive dogma, doctrine, or theology—a new methodological foundation was constructed to provide a platform for ongoing scientific research that hopefully will become more and more transnational in the present and future. For James, this required an earth-based psychology that was, at the same time, *scientifically grounded in spiritual and material facts*.

What helped James immensely in his thinking, from 1900 onward—the last decade of his life—were the writings of the German physicist, aesthetician, and founder of modern psychophysics, Fechner. According to Eugene Taylor, Fechner believed that the various states of our limited consciousness to which we are subject throughout our lifetimes form parts of "simultaneous fields of experience of wider scope."[5] Fechner conceived of an "Earth-Soul" in all humans, a kind of higher or superior consciousness that humans will merge with after death.[6] Psychophysics corresponded well with what James needed to help further his empirical view. Fechner's psychophysical philosophy was materially grounded in physics.

James argued, "The more absolutistic philosophers dwell on so high a level of abstraction that they never even try to come down." He then continued:

> And the theistic God is almost a sterile principle...The God of the theistic writers lives on as purely abstract heights as does the Absolute... What you want is a philosophy that will not only exercise your powers of intellectual abstraction, but that will make some positive connexion with the actual world of finite human lives.[7]

By shifting emphasis from abstract theism to *transcreedal feelings of the Divine*, James made the variety of spiritual experiences practical and relevant to anyone. The question was, during James's day, how to develop a method through which an individual could put him- or herself in attunement with the rhythms of the wider Self through which saving experiences come. For whoever touched spirit at its fiery energetic core, according to James, touched the living body of the world, Fechner's Earth-Soul; opening the individual to the consciousness of the universe touches the Many. "Not only Walt Whitman could write 'who touches this book touches a man.' The books of all great philosophers are like so many men."[8]

Writers like Emerson, Whitman, Maurice Richard Bucke, Theodore Flournoy, and Frederick Myers all inspired James to posit (in "A 'Psychic Researcher'") a "cosmic environment of *other consciousness* of some sort." If a person can find a way to tap into such an environment, or field, "individuations" may occur "in the psychic sea"—a metaphor that corresponds nicely with Jung's collective psyche—where the larger "psycho-physical world" intersects; a person might then begin to manifest his or her own theory of truth, or meaning, through individual *acts* that are as natural as they are spiritual in origin. What James was interested in investigating with the tools of modern science was the principle of *individuation* (like Nietzsche, James also used the word before Jung) taking place pluralistically in the cosmic environment of expanded consciousness. James asked: "What are the conditions of individuation or insulation in the mother-sea?"[9]

Although Socrates and many philosophers prior to James had used the pragmatic method, it was only during James's lifetime that the empirical method was applied systematically in modern psychology to the furthest depths of what Flournoy and Myers, at roughly the same time as Pierre Janet, had called the "subconscious" or "subliminal self."[10] This subliminal formula helped James make sense of parapsychological phenomena, the world's religions, and pathological states in a methodical way that had cash-value, practical results, or empirical validity, giving him the lever of criticism that he needed to take on the Absolute claims of any of the great world religions that might proclaim its God-image to be final. James insisted that the Absolute was merely a hypothesis, until proven otherwise.

In the "Preface" to "The Meaning of Truth: *A Sequel to 'Pragmatism*,'" James wrote the following:

> Pragmatism asks its unusual question: "Grant an idea or belief to be true," it says, "what concrete difference will its being true make in one's actual life? What experiences [may] be different from those which

would obtain if the belief were false? How will the truth be realized? What, in short, is the truth's cash-value in experiential terms?" The moment pragmatism asks this question, it sees the answer: *True ideas are those that we can assimilate, validate, corroborate, and verify. False ideas are those we cannot.*[11]

The emphasis on *value* rests, therefore, on an idea or belief being practical and realizable and concrete enough to manifest itself in an individual's meaning of truth as pragmatic because it can be assimilated, validated, corroborated, and verified by science. These are all criteria of a science of religion, which James championed, and as I shall describe in the chapters ahead, this empirical approach, in turn, influenced C. G. Jung.

The pragmatic method, although used in philosophy for many centuries, needed to be generalized in a radically empirical way so that pragmatism's *destiny* could become conscious of itself in individuals as a "universal mission." This is the movement James inaugurated at UC Berkeley, one he believed in and proclaimed as a doctrine of his own: "There is absolutely nothing new in the pragmatic method," James admitted with appropriate scientific humility. "Not until our time has it generalized itself, become conscious of a universal mission, pretended to a conquering destiny. I believe in that destiny, and I hope I may end by inspiring you with my belief."[12] Notice James's modesty; he used the word *pretended* because he knew full well that no final truth would ever be uttered about God in a post-heroic age of depth psychology, other than to state affirmatively that God is an indisputable spiritual *reality* that needs individuals to help make Itself conscious within the democratic equality of the many, who in the future will work toward keeping the subliminal door ajar through individual Self-knowledge.

James saw, like Jung, that theories were instruments for unstiffening pre-arranged beliefs and their fixed ideas, so as to arrive at our own individual theories of truth. "Pragmatism unstiffens all our theories, limbers them up and sets each one at work ... Meanwhile the word pragmatism has come to be used in a still wider sense, as meaning also a certain *theory of truth*."[13] Whereas James preferred the word *truth*, Jung used the word *meaning*. He adapted this word from Lao-tzu and translated it in the *Red Book* as the "Supreme Meaning."[14] In Jung's paper on "Synchronicity," he quoted Lao-tzu as saying "I do not know its name, / But I call it 'Meaning.'"[15]

Meaning, therefore, is another translation for *Tao*. Tao is not the Truth Absolute, but the middle way of the superior person who follows the way of the opposites, yin and yang, toward wholeness of the personality in alignment with the spiritual integrity of the community. James's psychology appealed to Jung, as did pragmatism's philosophical views.

To be sure, by the time James arrived in Palo Alto, California, in 1906, he had already found his own theory of truth—pragmatism and its pluralistic viewpoint. "In short," James said in "What Pragmatism Means," "she widens the field of our search for God . . . She will count mystical experiences if they have practical consequences."[16] By this time his theory of truth had become his muse. "Compared with what we ought to be," James wrote in "The Energies of Men," "we are only half-awake . . . Conscience makes cowards of all of us. Social conventions prevent us from telling the truth . . . Our scientific respectability keeps us from exercising the mystical portions of our nature freely."[17]

In *Varieties,* as we've seen, James presented data of various types of religious experiences in an effort to wake readers up to their mystical natures via an extensive cross-cultural presentation, making him our first *transpersonal psychologist*, or the spiritual grandfather of Jung's more eclectic analytic psychology. Jung would do the same thing at Yale University when he defined religion as the *numinous*. Later he added that real therapy was provided by experiences of the *numinosum* at key moments of life, or the observances of *coincidences, chance happenings,* or *synchronicities* as facts filled with mysterious inklings of meaning.

By remaining neutral toward assertions made by any theologian about the truth of the Absolute, moreover, *James widened the field of modern psychology's search for God, Consciousness, and Spirit*. The wider consciousness that Fechner (whose philosophy also had an impact on Freud's metapsychology) called the "collective consciousness" was living proof for James that psychology's search for God extended to the infinite Consciousness of the Cosmos beyond the margin.[18] James's love for his theory of truth was a conjunctive relationship that, applied universally, does not have an end in any person's lifetime, for it is always co-continuous with a wider life of changing experiences in the mother-sea of the subconscious or unconscious. Individuations that take place in this infinite sea give us our sense of individual meaning and creative destiny. James taught, like Jung, that the "evidence for God lies primarily in inner personal experiences."[19]

In his overview of religious experience in *Pragmatism*, James took up the ancient question of the One and the Many again. He considered it to be the most "pregnant" of all philosophical problems. James's aim was to take neither variety nor unity simply, but totally: to subsume monism and pluralism in a new spiritually democratic movement he named *Pragmatism*.[20] This is no mere "makeshift," as Jung euphemistically called James's theory of types, but a motherlode, his own unique scientific religious psychology of a plurality of principles.

James was critical of Vivekananda in *Pragmatism* because he believed that for Vedanta generally, "There is no many."[21] James went on to quote Vivekananda verbatim once more:

> When man has seen himself as One with the infinite Being of the Universe, when all separateness has ceased, when all men, women, all angles, all gods, all animals, all plants, the whole universe has been melted into that oneness, then all fear disappears. Whom to fear? . . . What can cause me sorrow? I am the One existence of the Universe.[22]

A better target for James to grapple with the Absolute could not have appeared at a more synchronous moment. It helped shape his ideas in the direction of a pluralistic and more modest view of humankind's place in the Universe. Pluralism's *doctrine* is the hypothesis of a world imperfectly unified. Jung later took up this standpoint as the striving for completeness. For James, it was enough to be a pioneer who blazed a trail of radical empiricism toward an ever-more psychological path with pragmatic results. "*True ideas,*" James emphasized, "*are those that we can assimilate, validate, corroborate and verify. False ideas are those we cannot . . .* Truth *happens* to an idea. It *becomes* true, is *made* true by events. Its verity *is,* in fact, an event, a process: the process namely of its verifying itself, its very-*fication*. Its validity is the process of its valid-*ation.*"[23]

For James and Jung, theories of truth (or meaning) were worthless unless they could be married with empirical facts—only then might a psychological theory really be said to be relatively true and meaningful. If it worked, according to the method of verification, it might then be, in James's words, a theory of truth: "The marriage of fact and theory is endlessly fertile."[24]

Another concept in *Pragmatism* that complements Jung's psychological-empirical attitude is expressed in James's resolute statement: "Truths emerge from facts; but they dip forward into facts again and add to them; which facts again create or reveal new truth (the word is indifferent) and so on indefinitely. The 'facts' meanwhile are not *true*. They simply *are*."[25] Thus, for pragmatism, as for Jungian psychology, reality is never readymade and complete for all eternity; it is a *reality of consciousness* that is co-continuous with individuations that happen in the wider depths of the total mother-sea of the Cosmos. *Our individual consciousness is forever in the making. It awaits its completion in the ever-present now and the future through ever-changing human experiences.*[26]

In James's pragmatic psychology and empirical philosophy, which Jung assiduously studied, the monistic view of the psyche was characterized by what James called the "tender-minded" perspective of reality. I have quoted his hard-hitting criticisms of Vivekananda's view of Reality with a capital *R*. In one of James's even more critical moments, he added: "And this, exactly this" is what the "tough-minded" pluralists "find themselves moved to call a piece of perverse abstraction-worship. The tough-minded are the men whose alpha and omega are *facts*."[27]

I get a distinct feeling here that the pragmatist protests too much, however, that he could have been much more grateful to Vivekananda, for having opened his mind to a wider view of personality and more transpersonal cross-cultural Consciousness, which is possible to attain in higher regions of the Universal Mind. In his chapter "Pragmatism and Religion," moreover, James cited a long poem by Walt Whitman called "To You." Interestingly, rather than making Whitman into his monistic target, as he did the Swami, he showed readers how Whitman's poem might be interpreted in a monistic or pragmatic way, illustrating how pragmatism can be used effectively to synthesize opposing viewpoints. Whitman, James suggested, accepted instinct as a vital part of his experience of a pluralistic unity, while seeing the Many from a higher perception of Oneness in the spiritual realm, where high and low (pluralism and monism) are *integrally* made conscious for us.

In the last pages of *Pragmatism,* James said, finally, if the hypothesis of God works satisfactorily in the widest sense of the word, it is *true*; he then added that, although he could not start on a whole new theology, at the end of his lectures, he reminded his audience that he had already "written a book on men's religious experience, which on the whole has been regarded as making for the reality of God."[28]

Thus, James ended *Pragmatism* by returning to a theory of truth he had been waiting to unpack: God *exists* as an internal and external *reality*. James thought he had already proven that God exists. He then finished *Pragmatism* with a flourish: "I firmly disbelieve, myself, that our human experience is the highest form of experience extent in the universe. I believe rather that we stand in much the same relation to the whole of the universe as our canine and feline pets do to the whole of human life . . . So we are tangent to the wider life of things."[29]

This view may have been influenced by Fechner, who, according to James "is considered by some to have laid the foundations of a new science . . . All Leipzig mourned him when he died." For according to Fechner, "the whole universe in its different spans and wave-lengths, exclusions and envelopments, is everywhere alive and conscious."[30] To some extent James shared Fechner's views.

After Hartmann and Freud, Jung advanced the notion of a collective or transpersonal unconscious as a correction for Fechner's notion of "collective consciousness." In an article called "Depth Psychology," Jung wrote in 1948 that "F. H. W. Myers and William James . . . stress the importance of an unconscious psyche."[31] Yet James preferred the terms *subconscious, consciousness,* and *co-consciousness* and criticized "Hartmann's wicked jack-of-all-trades, the Unconscious"; in "Cognition," James added that the subconscious Self "is incomplete until it is discharged in act."[32]

Acts were not unconscious to James. They were simply waiting to be discovered in the activities of the subconscious, which, bursting forth from the outer margins or transmarginal fields, were highly active. For James it was neither sex and Eros (Freud) nor numinous experiences and their meaning (Jung) that counted most across a lifespan, but *consciousness of one's acting self outside the margins of ordinary experiences*. As James thought, it is not an unconscious psyche (as Hartmann, Freud, and Jung all postulated), but *a subconscious field of intense energy, creativity, and activity, with which we may at times become co-conscious of an existence of a higher cosmic Intelligence.*

The conscious self of the moment, the central self, is probably determined to this privileged position by its functional connexion with the body's imminent or present acts. It is the present acting self. Tho the more that surrounds it may be "subconscious" to us, yet if in its "collective capacity" it also exerts an active function, it may be conscious in a wider way, conscious, as it were, over our heads.[33]

Notes

1. Peirce, "How to Make Our Ideas Clear."
2. James, *Writings 1902–1910*, 508.
3. Jung, Psychological Types, CW 6, ¶¶540, 541.
4. James, *Writings 1902–1910*, 376.
5. Taylor, *William James on Consciousness Beyond the Margin*, 137.
6. James, *Writings 1902–1910*, 138.
7. James, 494–495. By *connexion,* James surely meant "connection."
8. James, 502.
9. "A 'Psychic Researcher'" was published in *American Magazine,* October 1909—only a month after Jung's destined meeting with James at Clark University, in Worcester, Massachusetts.
10. Ellenberger, *The Discovery of the Unconscious,* 318.
11. James, *Writings 1902–1910*, 823.
12. James, 508.
13. James, 510.
14. Jung, *The Red Book,* 229.
15. Jung, "Synchronicity," CW 8, ¶918.
16. James, *Writings 1902–1910*, 522.
17. James, 1225. Thus, I urge readers to break out of convention and follow your vocation, by speaking up. The transpersonal mythos is a mythos of vocalizing your own truths. Its epicenter is in the San Francisco Bay Area. The exploration of prenatal and mystical states has, for instance, been a central research interest of Stanislav Grof (1931–present), the founding president of the International Transpersonal Association, established in 1977, and a faculty member at the California Institute of Integral Studies, or CIIS, in San Francisco. San Francisco has been a central place of emergence for the field of transpersonal psychology

since 1900, when Swami Vivekananda founded the first Vedanta center in the Bay Area.
18. James, *Writings 1902–1910*, 699.
19. James, 534.
20. James, 542.
21. James, 553.
22. Vivekananda, *The Complete Works*, vol. 2, 252, 253; quoted in James, 553.
23. James, 573, 574.
24. James, 578.
25. James, 585.
26. James, 599.
27. James, 602.
28. James, 619. His eight Lowell Lectures on "Pragmatism" were given between November 14 and December 8, 1906, and again at Columbia University between January 29 and February 8, 1907, with over one thousand people attending.
29. James, Ibid.
30. James, 697.
31. Jung, "Depth Psychology," CW 18, ¶1144.
32. James, *Writings 1902–1910*, 201.
33. James, 762, footnote 1.

Chapter 30

A Pluralistic Universe

In *A Pluralistic Universe* James was interested in providing what he called a *via media* between the absolutely rational and absolutely irrational views. Alongside this, he also considered the problem of the Many and the One and its pregnancy and birth in a plural and unitary consciousness of an inner and outer Cosmos that does not split the opposites.[1] In his chapter "Hegel and His Method," James made the idea of religious diversity widely known in his own clarifying statement, "The God of our popular Christianity is but one member of a pluralistic system."[2] This relativization of the Christ-image made pragmatism threatening to dogmatic creeds, doctrines, and prejudiced theologies in America and Europe during James's day. He essentially deconstructed the Christ-image—as one among many—a single specimen, or scientific fact of God—not *the* fact of God, but one pluralistic fact that has proven to be true by its fruits across numerous centuries.

This shows not only James's particular preference for a plurality of God-images, but also a systematic hypothesis that was more than merely his subjective truth. James then proceeded to deconstruct the Christian God-image in the New Testament—and the Old Testament God-image as well. He wanted readers to take a wider, as opposed to a limited view, toward the religions of the world. This wider view was closer to the truth of what God really was in His or Her cosmic sense, he thought, and considering the fact that James had faith in a greater transmarginal empirical reality, to which the *acting Self* had access through the subliminal doorway, he ascertained that the Absolute claimed by any one theology was an "improbable hypothesis."[3] This revolutionary move in the development of a science of religion paved the way for Jung. In so doing, James punctured the inflation of not only Christian and Jewish and Muslim theologians, but also orthodox Hindus as well.

James believed that he had evinced sufficient evidence to posit that in a post-Hegelian world of pure phenomenal experience, where the only way to verify a theory was through a provision of a volley of empirical facts, that it was time to "let the absolute bury the absolute, and to seek reality in more promising directions, even among the details of the finite and immediately given."[4] He also added with scientific modesty that if his words sounded to any members of his audience "sacrilegious," then he admitted, now with compassion and humility, "I am sorry."[5]

Let us linger for a moment on this remarkable statement: "let the absolute bury the absolute." If *Q equals Cosmos* in all religions, then what would be left after the relativity of the Gods is a radically empirical view of reality where all *q's* would be right about the nature of the Self, because *It* is felt to be so by their founders. Like Jung, James believed there could never be finally One Absolute because it was an endless calculation.

One of James's champions of the pragmatic viewpoint was Fechner. Fechner believed humankind was moving in an evolutionary way toward a "higher consciousness," and that such a movement might continue until "an absolutely universal consciousness is reached."[6] This might best be called *Cosmic Consciousness,* a term coined by Richard Maurice Bucke, who James quoted in *Varieties* as saying: "The prime characteristic of cosmic consciousness is a consciousness of the cosmos, that is, of the life and order of the universe."[7] James then repeated what he said in *Varieties* concerning the *transmarginal field*:

> My present field of consciousness is a center surrounded by a fringe that shades insensibly into a subconscious more ... What we conceptually identify ourselves with and say we are thinking of at any time is the centre; but our full self is the whole field ... Every bit of us at every moment is part and parcel of a wider self.

In a footnote to this comment he added, "The conscious self of the moment, or the central self," is also "the present *acting* self."[8]

Our *full* self is the whole field, the fourth complete Self in the field of the eternal now, in other words; although we do not know it, we are part and parcel of the wider Self of the Cosmos. James then repeated his hypothesis, stated somewhat differently:

The absolute is not the impossible being I once thought it. Mental facts do function both singly and together, at once, and we finite minds may simultaneously be co-conscious with one another in a superhuman intelligence . . . Fechner treats the superhuman consciousness he so fervently believes in as an hypothesis only . . . He talks not only of the earth-soul and of the star-souls, but of an integrated soul of all things in the cosmos without exception, and this he calls God just as others call it the absolute.[9]

James did not give Fechner the last word. He went further by asserting his own belief that there is no "absolutely totalized all-enveloper."[10]

Post-Jungian analysts would agree with this assessment, although most theologians might still argue that their God is All, whether they want to call it the Cosmic Brahman, Cosmic Christ, Cosmic Buddha, or Cosmic Allah. These are all representations for the same universal trans-marginal Reality. For James, "abnormal and supernormal facts" gave him the "strongest suggestions in favor of a superior co-consciousness being possible."[11] This possible "co-consciousness" might be, he continued, the "only door to the universe's deeper recesses."[12] What I take from this statement is that the door to the universe's deeper recesses, where all religions are equal, can be entered through any creed, or through no creed at all. Whatever this spiritual environment might be with which the empirical self may become co-conscious, James concluded that the outlines of the suprahuman field-consciousness "may be polytheistically or it may be monotheistically conceived of."[13] In stating this, he made room for both polytheism and monotheism, monism and pragmatism, to exist side-by-side. In "Conclusions," James was well aware, moreover, that pragmatism had by that time become a movement in modern psychology in its own right, and he wrote in glowing terms of "the great empirical movement towards a pluralistic panpsychic view of the universe."[14]

James then modestly stepped forward and asserted his own personal belief that his own age was on the verge of the birth of a new psychological attitude toward religion that could truly change the world. Such a pregnancy in philosophy and modern analytic psychology was to become the birth place of a method of analysis and careful observation of the facts of spiritual experience, which C. G. Jung inaugurated. "Let empiricism once become associated with religion," James said, "and I believe that a new era of religion as well as of philosophy will be ready to begin."[15] If such an era based on empirical research methods ever emerges, it will "tend to connect men in imagination."[16]

NOTES

1. James, *Writings 1902–1910*, 667.
2. James, 680.
3. James, 680–681.
4. James, 689.
5. James, 680–689.
6. James, 700.
7. Bucke, *Cosmic Consciousness: A Study of the Evolution of the Human Mind*, 2; quoted in James, 359.
8. James, 761.
9. James, 764.
10. James, 764.
11. James, 766.
12. James, 769.
13 James, 773.
14. James, 772.
15. James, 773.
16. James, 774.

Chapter 31

C. G. Jung's Psychology of the Self

In this chapter, I present overview of Jung's published statements on William James, using only primary sources as my justification for supporting my hypothesis that he was pivotal to Jung's mature development of thought and individuation, rather than merely a minor figure. So the reader can follow my argument in what follows I want to clearly state my methodology first as a Jungian. My methodology is taken from a review I did, two decades ago now, of Murray Stein's *oeuvre*. Titled "Murray Stein: The Transformative Image," it was published in *The San Francisco Jung Institute Library Journal*.[1] I still contend today that Stein's 1998 book *Transformation: Emergence of the Self* is the most outstanding book on Jungian psychology that has been written to date. In my review, I discussed how radical dissolutions of old personality structures can lead to the eventual emergence of a new, more resilient image of identity. Such a dissolution involves a crossing over from one psychological mode of consciousness to another during an entrance into what Stein called midlife *liminality*. During such a time of floating, identifications with former self-images may be temporarily or completely liquidated. During the rapid changes that follow, a fresh configuration of Selfhood can emerge, a newly formed structure of the personality, or what Stein referred to as a *transformative image*. Such an image of change can arise out of the sacrifice of one's former persona on the cross of one's predestined vocation. In such a passage at midlife a person can become temporarily identified with someone else, typically an older person of advanced maturity, a sage-like figure who embodies the predestined image of one's own potential transformation in the direction of one's authentic Self. This process, I contend, is the psychological metamorphosis Jung underwent *after* his trip to the United States with Sigmund Freud.

Moreover, any great changes in Jung were also happening in the field of psychology. Jung was highly influenced by Wilhelm Wundt's experimental laboratory at Leipzig, during his earlier tentative years at the Burghölzli. Prior to Jung's transit to the US, a cultural division was happening in the field of psychology in European and American teaching institutions. The German experimental laboratory tradition was in firm place by the time Jung entered his psychiatric career in the mental institution. Across the vast Atlantic Ocean, in 1878 James had already given the first PhD in American psychology at Harvard to Granville Stanley Hall, who invited Freud and Jung to America thirty years later.[2] Hall was the first to receive his doctorate in psychology under James's tutelage, and he was the founder of the Child Study Movement in the United States and of the *American Journal of Psychology*. However, as Eugene Taylor informs us, Hall was the first American student of Wundt's to return to United States in 1888 and the first to publicly repudiate the reigning Jamesian psychology.

My hypothesis in what follows, therefore, is that when Jung arrived at Clark University with Freud, he encountered, for the first time really, and at the age of thirty-four, a towering figure in American psychology, who placed *pure experience* at the center of psychology's evolving domain. In this sense, being thirty-five years Jung's senior, James became an idealized figure for Jung, a breath of fresh air, to be sure, from the heady and sterile research-laboratory atmosphere of the German Wundtian lab in Leipzig. The Wundtian laboratory was highly influenced by German idealism, which was far more analytic and much less religious than experiential, or personal, in its experimentation.[3]

Jung had been well aware of James for over a decade before he arrived in the US, as he had read *The Principles of Psychology*. With a close reading of the primary sources, therefore, James's role as a *transformative figure for Jung* would be hard *not* to recognize by anyone who considers seriously the parallels between James's vast works and Jung's more mature and expansive thoughts on the human psyche.

Jung mentioned James in his first major work, "On the Psychology of So-Called Occult Phenomena," where he cited James's 1890 book *The Principles of Psychology*.[4] Jung took careful note of the example of two cases James cites: the itinerant preacher, Ansel Bourne, who had repeated attacks of unconsciousness, and the case of Mary Reynolds, published by Weir Mitchell, who underwent a complete change in character after she entered a "second state" of consciousness.[5] In the "Forward to the First Edition" of *The Theory of Psychoanalysis,* delivered to the medical school of Fordham University, New York, in September 1912, Jung had this to say, fully aware of the schism that had emerged between the Leipzig school and James's more progressive American psychology:

> It has been wrongly suggested that my attitude signifies a "split" in the psychoanalytic movement. Such schisms can only exist as matters of faith. But psychoanalysis is concerned with knowledge and its ever-changing formulations. I have taken as my guiding principle William James's pragmatic rule: "You must bring out of each word its practical cash-value, set it at work within the stream of your experience. It appears less as a solution, then, than as a program for more work, and more particularly as the indication of the ways in which existing realities may be changed. Theories thus become instruments, not answers to enigmas, in which we can rest. We don't lie back upon them, we move forward, and, on occasion, make nature over again by their aid."[6]

Theories as instruments of analysis and academic research was very much in line with Jung's later approach to dreams and visions, as he modeled in his ETH lectures. In the first edition of Jung's "Prefaces to 'Collected Papers on Analytical Psychology,'" moreover, published in London and New York in 1916, Jung made a clear distinction between the Viennese School of Sigmund Freud and his own Zürich School. In his call for a more objective standpoint that took the subjective view of the theorist's psychological types into consideration, he again gave a nod to the late William James: "The Zürich School, recognizing the existence of these two types (also remarked by the late Professor William James), considers that the views of Freud and Adler are one-sided and valid only within the limits of their corresponding type. Both principles exist in every individual though not in equal proportions."[7] Twenty years later, in the last paragraph of his lecture at Harvard, "Psychological Factors Determining Human Behavior," delivered in Cambridge, Massachusetts, in 1936, Jung remarked further:

> In my survey, far too condensed, I fear, I have left unmentioned many illustrious names. Yet there is one I should not like to omit. It is that of William James, whose psychological vision and pragmatic philosophy have on more than one occasion been my guides. It was his far-ranging

mind which made me realize that the horizons of human psychology widen into the immeasurable.⁸

Here is the American characteristic of immensity or spaciousness that I mentioned earlier. This was without doubt a great tribute to a man (James) who Jung only met twice, for about an hour or so, on two separate evenings, while Jung was lecturing at Clark University in 1909. James spoke to Jung about his shortness of breath and irregular heartbeats. Yet Jung's thinking about the immeasurable depths and horizon of human psychology shifted considerably between 1909 and 1912. How much this change in Jung's thinking can rightfully be attributed to James is not entirely certain. Nevertheless, the threads from these primary sources confirm Jung's psychology of the collective psyche owed a debt of acknowledgement to James.

An earlier reference to James appeared in "Two Kinds of Thinking," the opening chapter of Jung's 1912 book *Symbols of Transformation*. In a footnote, he said, "The element of adaptation is particularly stressed by William James in his definition of logical thinking. . . : 'Let us make this ability to deal with *novel* data the technical differentia of reasoning. This will sufficiently mark it out from common associative thinking.'"⁹ Several pages later Jung added: "William James regards non-directed thinking, or merely 'associative' thinking, as the ordinary kind . . . We can supplement James's definitions by saying that this sort of thinking does not tire us, that it leads away from reality into fantasies of the past or future . . . We have, therefore, two kinds of thinking: directed thinking, and dreaming or fantasy-thinking."¹⁰

These opening remarks on two psychological types and two kinds of thinking reveal how much Jung was, indeed, indebted to James's 1890 formulations in the *Principles* and also to his 1906 book *Pragmatism* for an increase in his vision as a psychoanalyst. Jung delivered anther seminal lecture at the Psychological Congress in Munich during September 1913, this one called "A Contribution to the Study of Psychological Types." Here Jung said clearly: "So far as my limited knowledge goes, we have to thank William James for the best observations in this respect [the existence in literature of two distinct personality types]. He lays down the principle 'Of whatever temperament a professional philosopher is, he tries, when philosophizing, to sink the fact of his temperament.'" Jung then went on to quote from James's book *Pragmatism* for two pages, ending his overview on the two types with a Jamesian saying he was quite fond of quoting: "But our esteem for facts has not neutralized in us all religiousness. It [the empirical attitude] is itself almost religious. Our scientific temper is devout."[11] Thus, Jung learned from James how to think about religious phenomena scientifically and to see the spiritual attitude as a kind of devotion to a religious dimension of the psyche that is in its very ground psychological.

Now, let us move on to Jung's 1917 work *Two Essays on Analytical Psychology,* wherein he clearly laid out the foundation stone for his method of analytical psychology. Again, he credited James in "The Problem of the Attitude-Type," right after he singled out two opposite types, which he called "introverted" and "extraverted": "William James [in *Pragmatism*] had already been struck by the existence of both these types among thinkers. He distinguished them as 'tender-minded' and 'tough-minded.'"[12] In the chapter "The Relations Between the Ego and the Unconscious," Jung noted examples of mental illness, creative inspiration, and conversion phenomena and informed his readers: "A wide range of material is contained in William James's *Varieties of Religious Experience.*"[13]

In a 1916 lecture called "The Structure of the Unconscious," delivered to the Zürich School for Analytical Psychology, Jung said further: "Although it may not be at all to the taste of the scientific mind, psychology will nonetheless have to recognize a plurality of principles and accommodate itself to them. It is the only way to prevent psychology from getting stranded. In this matter we owe a great deal to the pioneer work of William James."[14]

In addition to James's contributions to Jung's notions of two kinds of thinking, adaptation, and type theory, Jung also drew from James's writings in *The Principles* on a "plurality of instincts" in his 1917 essay "Instinct and the Unconscious": "William James therefore calls instinct, not unjustly," Jung then quoted, "a mere excito-motor impulse, due to the pre-existence of a certain 'reflex-arc' in the 'nerve-centers.'" He concluded, "William James is of the opinion that man is swarming with instincts."[15]

The majority of Jung's published writings on James are found in his 1921 book *Psychological Types.* Jung devoted twenty-one pages to James's theory of types in chapter seven of that volume, "The Type Problem in Modern Philosophy." This seminal chapter was broken into three sections:

1. "William James' Types,"
2. "The Characteristic Pairs of Opposites in James' Types"
3. "General Criticism of James' Typology."

In the second section, Jung listed eight characteristic pairs of opposites as follows:

a. Rationalism versus *Empiricism*
b. Intellectualism versus *Sensationalism*
c. Idealism versus *Materialism*
d. Optimism versus *Pessimism*
e. Religiousness versus *Irreligiousness*
f. Indeterminism versus *Determinism*
g. Monism versus *Pluralism*
h. Dogmatism versus *Skepticism.*"[16]

Notice that he included Monism; Jung was well informed, therefore, about James's ongoing battle with the Absolute and with his criticisms toward Whitman and Vivekananda.

Eight years later, Jung delivered an important lecture called "The Aims of Psychotherapy," on April 12, 1929, at the 4th General Medical Congress for Psychotherapy in Bad Nauheim. In a discussion on the importance of the creative imagination, Jung said:

> All the works of man have their origin in creative imagination. What right, then, have we to disparage fantasy? In the normal course of things, fantasy does not easily go astray; it is too deep for that, and too closely bound up with the tap-root of human and animal instinct. It has a surprising way of always coming out right in the end. The creative activity of imagination frees man from his bondage to the "nothing but," and raises him to the status of one who plays.[17]

In the footnote to this quote, Jung's editors wrote, "The term 'nothing but' (*nichts als*) denotes the common habit of exploring something unknown by reducing it to something apparently known and thereby devaluing it ... The expression is borrowed from James, *The Varieties of Religious Experience*."[18]

In the 1930 *Visions Seminars*, moreover, Jung told his audience to watch out while letting a free flow of imagination take over the rational or empirical mind during the process of visioning. In the seminars, he examined the case of Christiana Morgan, friend, lover, and mistress to Harvard professor Henry A. Murray: "But when you are not prepared, visions like these may come with such force as to change your whole life. Read *Varieties of Religious Experience* by William James. There you will find examples of such visions. The most famous is the vision of Paul that caused his sudden conversion; he had just one vision and that was enough."[19]

In 1934, Jung published a review of a book by Hermann von Keyserling: "Keyserling brands American pragmatism as 'profoundly unspiritual' (I hope, by the way, he doesn't mean William James!)."[20] This passage shows the deep respect Jung had for James. Both James and Jung placed the highest value in the individuation of the Spiritual Self as the author of one's destiny and meaning. In "The Tavistock Lectures," delivered in London, from September 30 to October 4, 1935, Jung ended his first lecture, moreover, with a discussion on the James-Lange theory of emotion, a theory of emotion advanced by James and the Danish physiologist C.G. Lange:

> If you study emotions you will invariably find that you apply the word "emotional" when it concerns a condition that is characterized by physiological innervations. Therefore you can measure emotions to a certain extent, not the psychic part but the physiological part. You know the James-Lange theory of affect. I take emotion as affect, it is the same as "something affects you." It does something to you—it interferes with you. Emotion is the thing that carries you away. You are thrown out of yourself; you are beside yourself as if an explosion had moved you out of yourself and put you beside yourself.[21]

In the "Discussion" section, Jung was then asked about the possible *causal* significance of an emotion affecting a person from the body or mind; here is his reply:

> You know that the James-Lange theory says that affect is the result of physiological alteration. The question of whether the body or the mind is the predominating factor will always be unanswered according

> to temperamental differences. Those who by temperament prefer the theory of the supremacy of the body will say that mental processes are epiphenomena of physiological chemistry... All we can know empirically is that processes of the body and processes of the mind happen together in some way which is mysterious to us. It is due to our most lamentable mind that we cannot think of body and mind as one and the same thing; probably they are one thing.[22]

Jung then proceeded to advance his theory of *synchronicity* in an attempt to solve the matter.[23] Here, again, Jung relied on the guidance of James's "far-reaching" mind to give his audiences a unified picture of the human experience of emotion or affect and relate it to the Body Self.

In his paper "Concerning the Archetypes, with Special Reference to the Anima Concept," first published in Leipzig in 1936, the location of Wundt's experimental laboratory, Jung also mentioned James:

> Biographical descriptions of psychic phenomena, going beyond the strictly medical field, were represented chiefly by the work of the philosopher Théodore Flournoy, of Geneva, in his account of an unusual personality. This was followed by the first attempt at a synthesis: William James's *Varieties of Religious Experience* (1902). I owe it mainly to these two investigators that I learnt to understand the nature of psychic disturbances within the setting of the human psyche as a whole.[24]

Coming from Jung, this statement demonstrates in itself—without my having to say much more to prove my hypothesis of James's pivotal place in Jung's psychological development—how much his own method grew organically out of what he learned from Flournoy and James.

Jung's next significant reference to James was on June 23, 1937, during his seminars on *Nietzsche's Zarathustra*. He discussed with his audience, shortly before his trip to America and later India, the *sense* of an objective presence in the psyche:

> There is an interesting chapter about the experience of the unknown presence in William James' *The Varieties of Religious Experience*. This experience means: I am aware of the fact that I am not alone in this room;

there is a presence and an unknown one. This is the experience of the objectivity of the psyche, an experience of the reality of the unconscious.

The passage Jung referred to is in James's Lecture III, "The Reality of the Unseen," in *Varieties:* "It is as if there were in the human consciousness a sense of reality, a feeling of objective presence, a perception of what we may call 'something there.'"[25]

Several months later, in October 1937, Jung gave his famous Terry Lectures at Yale University. In the opening talk, "The Autonomy of the Unconscious," Jung discussed the use of the term *religion*. He distinguished clearly between creeds and the "word *religio,* which means a careful consideration and observation of certain dynamic factors that are conceived of as 'powers.'" Jung then tipped his hat once more to James: "William James, for instance, remarks that a scientist often has no creed, but his 'temper is devout.'"[26]

In 1938, Jung published a "Commentary on 'The Secret of the Golden Flower,'" where he mentioned the case of Mrs. Piper, a medium previously studied by James. Jung was discussing the animus in the psyche of women as a form of an inferior "plurality" of "preconceived opinions." "A good example of this," he noted, "is the 'Imperator' group in the case of Mrs. Piper."[27] Here Jung borrowed from James's books the notion of a plural psyche in a woman, the masculine principle in a female, to support his hypothesis of the animus, which has since gladly been commented on, criticized, and corrected as a clinical and cultural phenomenon by many recent post-Jungians of a feminist persuasion.

On October 19 of the same year, 1938, after his return from India and not long before the outbreak of WWII, Jung made an astonishing statement about the attitude of modern science. He characteristically mentioned James:

> Of course from a dogmatic point of view we are different, but as William James said in speaking of the natural science of our time, our temper is devout. The temper in which we live and work is the same as that of the Middle Ages only the name is different; it is no longer a spiritual subject, but is now called science.[28]

I believe Jung was trying to say that any calling—to psychology, philosophy, or science—can become dogmatic. What is needed is devotion of a *spiritual attitude* via a vocation to live by. In the fourth seminar of *Children's Dreams*, delivered in 1940, Jung again mentioned the well-known case of James's medium, Mrs. Piper, and her "special group of controls, called the 'Imperator group' by her."[29]

James showed up in Jung's writings in his 1946 essay "On the Nature of the Psyche." This composition reveals traces of Jung's most in-depth rereading of James since his book *Psychological Types*. In section "2. The Significance of the Unconscious in Psychology," Jung reproduced in a footnote a long quote from James's *The Varieties of Religious Experience*:

> I cannot but think that the most important step forward that has occurred in psychology since I have been a student of that science is the discovery, first made in 1886, that ... there is not only the consciousness of the ordinary field, with its usual center and margin, but an addition thereto in the shape of a set of memories, thoughts, and feelings which are extramarginal and outside of the primary consciousness altogether, but yet must be classed as conscious facts of some sort, able to reveal their presence by unmistakable signs. I call this the most important step forward because, unlike the other advances which psychology has made, this discovery has revealed to us an entirely unsuspected peculiarity in the constitution of human nature. No other step forward which psychology has made can proffer any such claim as this.[30]

This was Jung's first reference to James's concept of the *extramarginal field*. Field theory, now a common trope in psychoanalysis and analytical psychology, grew out of modern physics, but James was already writing about it in psychology in 1890! In a further reference in this same work, Jung noted: "Thus far the unconscious is 'a fringe of consciousness,' as William James put it."[31] In the footnote to a passage in section "5. Conscious and Unconscious," Jung returned to the notion of the margin, fringe, or field notion posited by James to broaden his concept of the collective psyche: "James speaks also of a 'transmarginal field' of consciousness and identifies it with the 'subliminal consciousness' of F. W. H. Myers, one of the founders of the British Society for Psychical Research." Jung then went on to quote James at length about the "field of consciousness":

> The important fact which this "field" formula commemorates is the indetermination of the margin. Inattentively realized as is the matter which the margin contains, it is nevertheless there, and helps both to guide our behavior and determine the next moment of our attention. It lies around us like a "magnetic field" inside of which our center of energy turns like a compass needle as the present phase of consciousness alters into its successor. Our whole past store of memories floats beyond this margin, ready at a touch to come in; and the entire mass of residual powers, impulses, and knowledges that constitute our empirical self stretches continuously beyond it. So vaguely drawn are the outlines between what is actual and what is only potential at any moment of our conscious life, that it is always hard to say of certain mental elements whether we are conscious of them or not.[32]

Magnetism was a common trope in modern physics at the time James wrote this, and Jung would later write at length about the magnet as a Self-symbol in his book *Aion*.[33] Later, in section, "7. Patterns of Behavior and Archetypes," Jung described the emergence in certain patients of a climax of a concentrated spiritual and psychic effort toward greater awareness, achieved through the method Jung called active imagination. Such a *synthesis* he defined through the Jamesian metaphor of a "bursting point" into consciousness: "That is to say, the synthesis can also be prepared in advance and brought to a certain point—James's 'bursting point'—unconsciously, whereupon it erupts into consciousness of its own volition and confronts the latter with the formidable task of assimilating the contents that have burst upon it."[34]

In a letter sent to Jung by Virginia Payne, who was writing her doctoral thesis at the University of Wisconsin and asked Jung for his recollections of the Clark University Conference in 1909, Jung had much to say about James, in a reply dated July 23, 1949, which I already cited in Chapter 3.

Jung's next significant mention of James came in an interview he gave to J. P. Hodin, a British art critic and art historian of Czech origin. Jung received him at his house in Küsnacht on June 17, 1952. Hodin mentioned before beginning the interview that in England, Jung's psychology was continually being attacked for being too "unscientific." Jung's reply was animated, ironic, and direct: "Unscientific! There are only a few heaven-inspired minds who understand me. In America it was William James. But most people are ignoramuses. They take no pains to find out the essential things about themselves. It requires too much Latin and Greek!"³⁵ (As well as speaking English, French, and German, James—like Jung—also spoke Latin and Greek)! Jung's outrage revealed his own "bursting point" when it came to clinicians who failed to plumb the depths of human nature and realize their full potential. The essential things, according to Jung, were the facts of one's psychological nature, the Self in its totality, whereas the rest of his contemporaries who neglected to include a Spiritual Self in their inventory of science were simply "ignoramuses!" Here Jung, in his old age and with much less control over his emotions, appeared to have momentarily flown off the rails himself, as he once had said about James, revealing his own psychological wholeness and awareness of his shadow. Jung was overly sensitive, perhaps in a complex about the failure of most people who had just read his sensational book *Answer to Job*. Understanding how his careful exegesis of the Books of Job and Revelations could possibly have anything to do with analysis would take a visionary mind. Only a few "heaven-inspired" psychologists, such as James, could have made a link between Jung's writings on religion and modern psychotherapy. The essential thing to Jung in his old age was our relation to the infinite, which he said he was taught by his careful and close reading of James, the forerunner to his own insightful critique of Western religion. In James's conclusions, following an insightful study of the book of Job, he made the following ironic statement: "We must, therefore, I think, bid good-bye to dogmatic theology."³⁶

In a further letter to Adolph Keller, dated September 1956, Jung wrote about the difficulty some readers were still having with the publication of his controversial book *Answer to Job*. In this letter, Jung said humorously, which revealed that he had by then moved beyond his complex into the relaxed poise of his halcyon days: "I entirely agree that for unprepared readers *Job* is a hard nut to crack. Anyone who finds in the problem of Job—which William James also tackled—too much scorn, irony, and suchlike rubbish had better leave the book alone."³⁷ In the footnote to this comment, Jung cited a James quote from Lecture XVIII of *The Varieties of Religious Experience*: "It's a plain historic fact that they [Kantian idealists] never have converted anyone who has found in the moral conception of the world, as he experienced it, reasons for doubting that a good God can have framed it ... No! the book of Job went over this whole matter once and for all definitively."[38] So said William James.

Jung's *Memories, Dreams, Reflections* was begun in the summer of 1956, at Kurt Wolff's request. Wolff was the founder of Verlag Leipzig. (He would later emigrate to the United States and publish the first Pantheon edition as the director of Pantheon Books.) Wolff had been pestering Jung to write an autobiography for several years. He pressed Jung specifically to write a full-length chapter on William James, so the book might appeal to a broad English-speaking American audience. Jung finally agreed to write the book. He spoke to his secretary, Aniela Jaffé, for two years about a variety of thematically arranged subjects. From the stenographic material taken down by Jaffé, all that has survived concerning Jung's impressions of James is the Countway Library Manuscript (CLM), which is only a couple of pages long, but nevertheless significant for understanding James's influence on Jung, which I cover in depth in Chapter 33.

In a letter dated June 17, 1958, Jung wrote to Kurt Wolff about the book. Here the subject of the missing document, the Countway Library Manuscript comes in, I think for the first time in print. Jung was emphatic and even empathically explicit:

> As for my meeting with William James, you must remember that I saw him only twice and talked with him for a little over an hour, but there was no correspondence between us. Apart from the personal impression he made on me, I am indebted to him chiefly for his books ... I admired his European culture and the openness of his nature. He was a distinguished personality and conversation with him was extremely pleasant. He was quite naturally without affectation and pomposity and answered my questions and interjections as though speaking to an equal.[39]

Jung's equal admiration for James's American culture and his spaciousness, expressed by his openness to nature, was apparent. *Equality* was an American characteristic of James's spiritual democracy, and during their two meetings there was no hint of any exaggerated affectation. His speaking to Jung as an "equal" must have meant a great deal to a Swiss man verging on midlife, a man who was the age of James's grandson!

> Aside from Theodore Flournoy he [James] was the only outstanding mind with whom I could conduct an uncomplicated conversation. I therefore honor his memory and have always remembered the example he set me ... If I were to write an appreciation of James from my present standpoint it would require an essay in itself, since it is impossible to sketch a figure of such stature in a few words. It would be an unpardonable exercise in superficiality if I presumed to do so...I am what I am—a thankless autobiographer![40]

Such an essay, although never written, can be sketched in a speculative way by a close reading of the CLM as a principal source. *Memories, Dreams, Reflections* was originally meant to include the chapter on Flournoy and James, but it was left out for unclear reasons. From my perusal of the historical documents, I can only say the reasons for this omission are uncertain, yet Jung was left feeling near the end like a "thankless autobiographer!" The chapter omitted obviously meant a great deal to Jung.

During Jung's final year, 1961, he nevertheless penned one of his most beautiful and eloquent essays in fluent English (seven of them in total) for the opening chapter for the popular book *Man and His Symbols*. It's one of my favorite essays by Jung, the first one I read at the age of twenty, called "Symbols and the Interpretation of Dreams." In section "3. The Language of Dreams" Jung turned one final time to give his old friend and "example" a lasting tribute and salute: "It is exactly this halo or 'fringe of consciousness,' as William James called it, which gives a colorful and fantastic aspect to the primitive's world."[41] Jung paid many tributes to James during his professional lifetime. From his first published book to his last, Jung credited and cited James.

Jung traveled to Taos, New Mexico, in 1925 and was influenced directly by the immensity of land, the Rockies, and vastness of the earth and firmament, but his expansion of the concept of the collective unconscious to its immeasurable depths was indebted to the writings of James. As James posited in a chapter called "The Stream of Consciousness" from *The Principles*:

Now the immediate fact which psychology, the science of mind, has to study is also the most general fact. It is the fact that in each of us, when awake (and often when asleep), some kind of consciousness is always going on. There is a stream, a succession of states, or waves, or fields (or of whatever you please to call them), of knowledge, of feeling, of desire, of deliberation etc., that constantly pass and repass, and that constitute our inner life. The existence of this stream is the primal fact, the nature and origin of it form the essential problem, of our science ... It must be frankly confessed that in no fundamental sense do we know where our successive fields of consciousness come from, or why they have the precise inner constitution which they do have. They certainly follow or accompany our brain states, and of course their special forms are determined by our past experiences and education.[42]

Is this not what we explore, every day, in our psychotherapy offices, in dream research, or in the classroom setting? The existence of this stream of consciousness, or streams in a plural sense, James said, is the *primal fact*, and the nature and origin of it form the "essential problem, of our science."

Notes

1. Herrmann, "Murray Stein: The Transformative Image."
2. Granville Stanley Hall was the first to receive his PhD at Harvard under James's tutelage in 1878, and he was also the founder of the Child Study Movement.
3. Taylor, *Consciousness Beyond the Margin*, 98–101.
4. Jung, "On the Psychology of So-Called Occult Phenomena," CW 1, ¶20.
5. Jung, CW 1, ¶107.
6. James, *Writings 1902–1910*, 509–510. Jung is quoting from the 1907 original: James, *Pragmatism*, 53; quoted in Jung, "The Theory of Psychoanalysis," CW 4, 86.
7. Jung, "Prefaces to 'Collected Papers on Analytical Psychology," CW 4, ¶676.
8. Jung, "Psychological Factors Determining Human Behavior" CW 8, ¶262.
9. James, *Principles of Psychology*, II, 330; quoted in Jung, *Symbols of Transformation*, CW 5, ¶11, fn 3.
10. Jung, CW 5, ¶¶18, 19, 20.
11. James, *Writings 1902–1910*, 492. Here Jung is quoting from the 1911

edition of *Pragmatism:* James, *Pragmatism: A New Name for Some Old Ways of Thinking,* 15; quoted in Jung, *Psychological Types,* CW 6, ¶869.

12. Jung, "On the Psychology of the Unconscious," CW 7, ¶80.
13. Jung, "The Relations Between the Ego and the Unconscious," CW 7, ¶270.
14. Jung, "The Structure of the Unconscious," CW 7, ¶483.
15. James, Principles of Psychology, vol. II, 391; quoted in Jung, "Instinct and the Unconscious," CW 8, ¶¶167, 271.
16. Jung, CW 6, ¶¶505–541.
17. Jung, "The Aims of Psychotherapy," CW 16, ¶98.
18. Jung, CW 16, ¶98, fn 5.
19. Jung, *C. G. Jung: The Visions Seminars,* vol. 2, 365.
20. Jung, "Reviews of Keyserling's *America Set Free,*" CW 10, ¶941.
21. Jung, "The Tavistock Lectures," CW 18, ¶46.
22. Jung, CW 18, ¶69.
23. Jung, CW 18, ¶70.
24. Jung, "Concerning the Archetypes, with Special Reference to the Anima Concept," CW 9i, ¶113.
25. James, *Writings 1902–1910,* 59; James, *The Varieties of Religious Experience,* Lecture III; quoted in Jung, *Nietzsche's Zarathustra,* vol. 2, 1176, note 5.
26. Jung, "Psychology and Religion (The Terry Lectures), CW 11, ¶8.
27. Jung, "Commentary on 'The Secret of the Golden Flower,'" CW 13, ¶60.
28. Jung, *Nietzsche's Zarathustra,* 2, 1351.
29. Jung, *Children's Dreams,* 317.
30. James, *Varieties,* 233; quoted in Jung, "On the Nature of the Psyche," CW 8, ¶356, fn 23.
31. Jung, CW 8, ¶383.
32. James, *Writings 1902–1910,* 214, 215; James, *Varieties,* 232; quoted in Jung, CW 8, ¶382, fn 47.
33. I can feel into such magnetic energies of the Self in my clinical work with children, who are sometimes attracted to me like a loadstar, particularly when there has been some kind of a trauma, such as a divorce in the family. There have been recent discussions in psychoanalysis and analytical psychology about field dynamics in the transference and countertransference to which we are privy, in the accumulating literature on what constellates affect-attunement and aliveness.
34. Jung, CW 8, ¶413.

35. Jung, *C. G. Jung Speaking*, 221.
36. James, *Writings, 1902–1910*, 402.
37. Jung, *Letters*, vol. 2, 330.
38. James, *Writings 1902–1910*, 402; quoted in Jung, *Letters*, 2, 330.
39. Jung, 2, 452, 453.
40. Jung, 2, 453.
41. Jung, "Symbols and the Interpretation of Dreams," CW 18, ¶465.
42. James, *Writings 1878–1899*, 722.

Chapter 32

Kundalini Yoga and Analytical Psychology

Jung's thoughts on Kundalini Yoga are among his most important reflections on the limits of analytic psychology and spiritual experience. These comments are found in his seminars, beginning with his 1932 lectures "Psychological Commentary on Kundalini Yoga," given between October 12 and November 2, 1932. The seminars consisted of four short lectures in which Jung spelled out his basic hypotheses about Kundalini Yoga in relationship to analytic practice, the interpretation of dreams and visions, somatic symptoms, and transference phenomena from a theoretical standpoint. He continued to expand his comments on Kundalini, or Tantric Yoga, in *The Visions Seminars*, his seminars on *Nietzsche's Zarathustra*, and in the four seminars on *Children's Dreams*. Most of Jung's reflections on Kundalini harken back to the initial four lectures given in the fall of 1932; they contain the seeds for his later ideas about the psychology of the East.

In Lecture One, from October 12, 1932, Jung gave a precise definition of the Sanskrit word *klésas,* which he defined as "natural instinctive urges" in which the libido first appears out of the unconscious. He specifically named the *klésa* of discrimination in Western philosophical terms as the "urge or instinct towards individuation."[1] This *klésa* contained the "germ of personality" as a central aspect of individuation, or the instinct to complete Self-realization.[2] According to Jung, the instinct of individuation was found in the lowest center of the Tantric system, in the first *chakra* called *muladhara*. Chakras are psycho-physical locations in the body, from the base of the spine to the crown of the head. *Muladhara,* translated literally "root-support," is in the region of the perineum.

Jung told his audience that this lowest center was the place where the seed or germ of the personality, the psychological non-ego, or Spiritual Self (to borrow James's term), was asleep—in the roots, in the earth on which we stand, and in our ordinary conscious world.[3] The *muladhara* is the most banal place in the world, Jung remarked; it's our everyday awareness in a railway station, at a theater, in the family, or in a professional situation: these are places in our mundane experiences where the Self is sleeping. This ordinariness, said Jung, was *muladhara*.[4]

The color of this root chakra is the color of dark passion, the color of blood.[5] Jung was emphatic that the Western mind could not build a Hindu system of psychology without "poisoning" itself.[6] Notwithstanding, Jung had the highest regard for Tantric Yoga and made liberal use of it in his seminars. Kundalini was the divine urge, he said, the urge for divination in the human, the urge for Self-awakening, without which there could be no ascent to the higher registers of consciousness.[7] On the other hand, Jung hypothesized that in the East the unconscious was above, whereas with Westerners it was below.[8] This has been a point of heated contention between Jung and his followers and Eastern scholars.

In Lecture Two, Jung said the symbol for *muladhara* was the earth, with the carrying power of the elephant as its transport. *Muladhara* was the transitory place of beginnings, where the higher extramarginal consciousness was inactive. Jung's thoughts on *muladhara* were quite remarkable. He had a unique insight into this lowest lotus center because he came to it through direct personal experience, I believe, in the earliest years of childhood. He understood it intimately through deep bodily experience. He must have known from a very early age the dangers of identifying the ego with the impersonal non-ego, for he advised seminar participants to keep the impersonal contents of their psyches outside the domain of their ego identity, detached, as it were, at a place where they could observe the nonhuman archetypal contents objectively as an empirical reality, a basis for facts.[9]

In the first lecture Jung meditated on the way of Yoga or the philosophy of Yoga as a method that had been kept *secret* for millennia.[10] He made a great deal about this. When he spoke about the secret of Yoga, he was probably reflecting on his own personal secret as well—his first childhood dream at the age of three of an underground phallus, which, had he decided to speak about it, would have most likely been misunderstood. What Jung's dream reveals for us is the extraordinary nature of his calling as a religious thinker—a calling to link an Eastern religious symbol (*linga*) with a Western symbol of the Self (phallus). The linga is located, in the Kundalini system, at the base of the spine; it's a spiritual emblem for the creative and destructive energies of Brahma or Lord Shiva. The *linga* in the *Muladhara* was a mere germ, whereas in the sixth chakra, *ajna*, the *linga* was in the ether.[11] Jung's reflections on the root-support were perhaps his most important thoughts on the nature of what might be called the *elephant-Ground,* or *muladhara*. The *white elephant* was its primary animal symbol. *Muladhara* was the lotus chakra of Jung's greatest intuitive genius, or insight, into the nature of the psyche.

In Lecture Two, Jung presented his prescription to Europeans and Americans in attendance that analysis was, for him, a sort of *Western medicine*: We must believe in this world, he said, "make roots," make our life real with "almost religious conviction," leave our signature on the world, our track, put our personal spark in the *Ground*. In this way, our impersonal shoots, the germ seed of individuation, can come to full fruition, full maturity, full bloom.[12] *Muladhara* is equivalent with the Ground of Meister Eckhart, or what Jung later called the *psychoid*.

The second chakra is *svadhisthana*, the sexual zone, symbolized by the sea and the huge Leviathan that threatens the ego with annihilation.[13] Chakra three is *manipura*, the source of fire, located in the solar plexus or region in the abdomen where the emotions are centrally located.[14] Chakra four is defined as *anahata* and is in the region of the heart. In *anahata*, Jung said, we are in a condition of being lifted up from the earth. There, we behold *Purusa*, the Supreme Self. This is where the instinct of individuation begins to unfold consciously from the seed; it emerges from the germ through the first three chakras into a fourth state of Awakening.[15] In *anahata* the Self is exceedingly impersonal, objective, spiritually Awake.[16]

In Lecture Three, Jung introduced the concept of the *visuddha* center, the fifth chakra, a level beyond the four elements—earth, water, fire, and air. *Visuddha*—the throat chakra—is where one achieves a level of abstraction beyond the empirical world. It is the lower level of the Absolute, which is completely objective and nonpersonal.[17] Collectively, Jung said, humans had not yet successfully crossed the span between *anahata* and *visuddha*.[18] I believe Jung himself was able to traverse this distance impersonally because of his ongoing dialogues with his inner guru Philemon, an idea to which I will return in my discussions on the CLM in the next chapter. In *visuddha,* he said, the world became one's subjective experience, a reflection of the objective psyche. Whereas *anahata* was represented by the element air where one could breathe deeply and easily, in *visuddha* one reached airless space, where there was no chance for the ordinary individual to breathe freely.[19] It would be like trying to summit Mt. Everest without an oxygen mask.

Here, again, the symbol of the white elephant appeared as a power that held up one's objective thoughts, psychic realities, abstract theories, and so on, which were not merely speculative ideas but *facts* based on pure *experience*.[20] Philemon, as Jung's inner guru, was Jung's link between *anahata* and *visuddha*, for he could breathe the psychic atmosphere where Jung's ego couldn't, and he had the wings to transform abstractions into practical realities, or cash-value (James).[21] In *visuddha* we are completely out of breath.

Jung posited the sixth chakra, *ajna*, was completely beyond the reach of Westerners, and he stressed that we should not even try to reach it.[22] *Ajna* is the third eye, located in the center-point between the two eyes. In *ajna* the *linga* was fully illuminated in a blazing white light, fully Self-realized, as a symbol for the spiritualized libido in its higher states of spiritual transformation. The unconscious germ that was once in a dormant state in *muladhara* was now fully awakened. God, the germ seed of the Spiritual Self, or the individuating urge in the personality in route toward the highest Consciousness, was now wide Awake. In *visuddha* the white elephant sustained the reality of the psyche, but in *ajna* the psyche had wings: "Here you know you are nothing but psyche," Jung said. Importantly Jung had a negative view of *sahasrara*—the seventh chakra, the thousand-petaled lotus—because he saw it as merely a philosophical concept with no substance whatsoever for Westerners because it was simply beyond possible experience. Nirvana was dormant, he thought, "without practical value for us."[23]

Jung's thoughts on the chakra system have great practical value for the practice of Jungian analysis. The seven chakras are symbols, portraits for the transformations of the libido, which may help clinicians understand dreams, fantasy symbolisms, symptoms, and the transference dynamics of patients.[24] Analytical psychology as an empirical science stops short at *visuddha*, the level of abstraction. It has nothing to do, to Jung's mind, with the upper two centers, which are about the attainments of higher consciousness in a Cosmic or metaphysical sense.[25]

32 - Kundalini Yoga and Analytical Psychology

Jung's critique of Yoga practice for Westerners actually began in the Dream Seminars, which took place from November 7, 1928, to June 25, 1930. There he provided an important correction to Eastern attitudes toward the Self in Hinduism, with the following insightful words: "I am not God himself who knows everything; I must keep to my psychological world."[26] James drew a similar kind of limitation in relation to the concept of the Absolute put forth by Vivekananda and by Royce. In the fourth lecture of the Dream Seminars, given in February 1929, Jung said the analytical procedure produced Western forms of what in the East was called Yoga. Jung added that very few people in Europe knew anything about Yoga, and it was his calling to attempt to construct a bridge to the East from a Western standpoint: "A real knowledge of yoga practices is very rare in the West. I felt quite small when I became acquainted with these things."[27] Notice Jung's modesty here, an attitude of the noninflated ego. He was quite conscious of the practice of Hatha Yoga, but he acknowledged how small he felt next to the Absolute: "Hatha yoga has particularly to do with breathing exercises, they try to spiritualize themselves through deep breathing."[28]

Jung's comments on Kundalini continued in the *Visions Seminars* (November 5, 1930, to March 21, 1934), where again he cautioned Westerners against the practices of Yoga. The aim of analysis was not to go higher and higher, beyond the heart and throat chakras. Jung believed we must form a connection between what is above and below, integrate the opposites, by maintaining a relationship to our earth center, the lower elephant-Ground in *muladhara*, the root-support, *not become* the elephant. We can be fully related to the infinite, however, via techniques of dream amplification and active imagination.

> So you see the great mistake that people make when they imitate the Eastern Yoga practices, for they serve a need which is not ours; it is the worst mistake for us to get higher and higher. What we ought to do is to establish the connection between above and below. But we take eagerly to the Yoga practice which, of course, does not work ... because our need is just the contrary one.... I never have seen a case [of Yoga practice] that was not applied with the wrong purpose of getting still more on top—to acquire more power or more control, either of their own body, or of other people, or of the world.[29]

This is an incisive and searing critique of what today is known as new age culture, which tends to gravitate euphemistically at times toward spiritual bypass, rather than remaining grounded, in one's ego, body, and matter. Jung's psychology is a psychology of the roots, the earth, the Ground, in which the self/Self is situated firmly in material reality. Only then can the spirit take wing. Analytical psychology is not the psychology of the Higher Self that has been popularized by Eastern gurus who have migrated to the West to spread their teachings of Yoga discriminatively, or undiscriminatively, to the naïve and uninitiated. This does not mean Jung was averse to the applications of Kundalini Yoga to analytic practice; on the contrary, he knew we could see the Kundalini system at work in its archetypal manifestations in the analysis of dreams, visions, symptoms, and projective dynamics in the transference.

Jung gave a wonderful analysis, for instance, of the transition from *manipura* (third chakra) to *anahata* (fourth chakra) in the relationship to the analytical process of transforming primal emotions of rage and anger boiling within the abdomen. By containing them in consciousness, an individual could arrive at a higher objective view of the affective system. Jung said that if a person could take all of the fire in the third chakra and use it constructively, then he or she could change it ultimately for the good of a higher virtue and that this was a sacrificial act.[30]

Jung's analysis of Kundalini Yoga continued in his seminars on *Nietzsche's Zarathustra*. In the winter term of 1935, he made a brilliant connection between the fourth chakra and the archetype of the wise old man, which, for Jung, as you've seen, was personified by the winged-figure Philemon: "That is the self that dwells in the *anahata chakra*, the heart center, and it would of course be the archetype of the old wise man. For to one who is attained only to *anahata*, the archetype of the wise old man still covers the symbol of the self."[31] This would presumably be the place where he encountered Philemon. Philemon was Jung's link to *visuddha*. Jung spoke further in the Seminar on Children's Dreams of the *muladhara* chakra as the *earth lotus*, where the Kundalini serpent, the highest essence of the personality, slept, coiled three-and-a-half times around the *linga* of Lord Shiva.[32]

Perhaps Jung's most concentrated examination of the Kundalini system in analytic process appeared in a decisive paper, delivered at the Second Congress for Psychotherapy, in Bern, Switzerland, on May 28, 1937, prior to his trip to Yale University that summer and to his trip to India in December of that year. As indicated in his clinical paper, one of the most impressive dreams his patient reported was a *dream of a white elephant that was coming out of her genitals*! Soon afterward, she developed uterine ulcers. Jung referred her to see a gynecologist. She was so impressed by the white dream-elephant that she tried to carve it out of ivory. The white elephant was found in both *muladhara* (first chakra) and *visuddha* (fifth chakra), although in the dream the Kundalini energies were stuck at the root-support, developing into serious somatic symptoms requiring medical intervention. Not long afterward, Jung discovered the book *The Serpent Power* by Arthur Avalon, and to his complete astonishment, it helped him understand all of her dreams and symptoms and her transference projections, which had constellated a psychic infection in both the patient and in Jung in the countertransference.[33]

Perhaps the most famous of all of the stories told about Kundalini Yoga and its relevance to analysis from Jung's clinical practice came during the Houston Films in 1957, when Jung recalled the case of an incredibly intuitive girl who suddenly came out with the statement that she had a *black snake in her belly!* "Well now," Jung said in the interview:

> That is a collective symbol. That is not an individual fantasy, it is a collective fantasy. It is well known in India. She had nothing to do with India, but though it is entirely unknown to us we have it too, for we are all similarly human. So, I even thought in the first moment that perhaps she was crazy, but she was only highly intuitive. In India the serpent is at the basis of the whole philosophical system, of Tantrism; it is Kundalini, the Kundalini serpent. This is something known only to a few specialists, generally it is not known that we have a serpent in the abdomen. That is a collective dream or a collective fantasy.[34]

Notes

1. Jung, *Psychological Commentary on Kundalini Yoga. Lectures One and Two—1932*, 1.
2. Jung, 2.
3. Jung, 8, 9.

4. Jung, 10.
5. Jung, 12.
6. Jung, 13.
7. Jung, 14.
8. Jung, 12.
9. Jung, 19.
10. Jung, 20.
11. Jung, 15.
12. Jung, 21.
13. Jung, 12.
14. Jung, 26.
15. Jung, 29.
16. Jung, 31.
17. Jung, *Psychological Commentary on Kundalini Yoga. Lectures Three and Four—1932,* 1.
18. Jung, 6.
19. Jung, 10.
20. Jung, 14.
21. James, *Writings 1902–1910,* 823.
22. Jung, 16.
23. Jung, 17.
24. Jung, 21.
25. Jung, 30.
26. Jung, *Dream Analysis,* 116.
27. Jung, 118.
28. Jung, 397.
29. Jung, *The Visions Seminar,* Vol. 1, 231.
30. Jung, *The Visions Seminars,* Vol. 2, 322.
31. Jung, *Nietzsche's Zarathustra,* Vol. 1, 394.
32. Jung, *Children's Dreams,* 353.
33. Jung, "The Realities of Practical Psychotherapy," CW 16, ¶551.
34. Jung, *C. G. Jung Speaking,* 322, 323.

Chapter 33

THE INFLUENCE OF WILLIAM JAMES

In "The Meaning of Psychology for Modern Man," a lecture Jung gave in February 1933, he said: "The dream is a little hidden door in the innermost and most secret recesses of the soul."[1] Where is the "little hidden door" to the spacious and timeless reality of the dream Jung spoke about? Is there a key that opened the door to the dreamtime for Jung? If so, where might we find such a key to nontemporal reality in Jung's writings and in his everyday life? Did Jung actually possess such a key?

The quote came after a number of significant citations from Part II of Goethe's *Faust*. In addition, Jung wrote in a letter during the same month and year: "we know that a door exists to a quite different order of things from the one we encounter in our empirical world of consciousness."[2] Thus, from these two passages we know that the key and door symbol was on Jung's mind. After Jung finished his Kundalini Seminars, he extended a tower-like annex to his spiritual retreat at Bollingen. In 1931, he wanted a room where he could exist for himself alone. He had in mind what he had seen in Indian houses, an area where they meditate for an hour or so and do Yoga exercises. This second tower was his shrine to Philemon.

> In my retiring room I am by myself. I keep the key with me all the time; no one else is allowed in there except with my permission. In the course of the years I have done paintings on the walls, and so have expressed all those things which have carried me out of time into seclusion, out of the present into timelessness. Thus the second tower became for me a place of spiritual contemplation.[3]

Anyone might naturally draw a hypothetical conclusion, based on the available textual evidence, that Jung borrowed the metaphor of the key and doorway to the inner sanctum sanctorum of dreams from Goethe's *Faust*. This is the logical counter-hypothesis to my hypothesis that Jung borrowed the metaphor from James's book *The Varieties of Religious Experience*. We must not be too quick then to draw any causal conclusions. In fact, one of the most memorable references to the key motif in Jung's entire oeuvre is found in the Introduction to Part II of *Symbols of Transformation,* where Jung again quoted Goethe as his primary source: "The key unlocks the mysterious forbidden door behind which some wonderful thing awaits discovery. One thinks, in this connection, of 'The Mothers' in *Faust*."[4] To be sure, Goethe's metaphor of the "Mothers" played a crucial role in Jung's thoughts about the transpersonal layers of the unconscious. It gave him a key to unlock a central doorway to the transtemporal dimensions of the psyche. But was it the only key?

Jung also gave a nod to James for having drawn a clear distinction between two kinds of thinking: directed thinking and fantasy thinking. I want to draw the reader's attention again to the significance of Jung's transformative relationship with William James—a friendship that was mostly impersonal, not intimately personal, as in the case of his paternal friend Flournoy. James's influence on Jung's inner development during his crucial passage through midlife came not so much from their two brief meetings at Clark University in 1909, but rather from James's writings.[5] A key moment for Jung occurred during the writing of *Symbols of Transformation,* which inevitably led him to face the problem of finding his own Self-path into the vertical dimensions of the psyche. These dimensions could only be accessed through the imaginative faculty, as Jung indicated in his 1925 seminars on analytical psychology.[6] As Jung recalled, after his break with Freud, most of his students around the world, including some in the United States, left him for Freud. Jung consequently found himself completely isolated. Such seclusion, nevertheless, had a distinct advantage for Jung as an introvert. It encouraged him to follow the "vertical movement of the libido" into the furthest regions of inner space. Cut off from the horizontal movement that activity in the outside world would bring to anyone operating from the extroverted functions, Jung was driven to investigate fantasies deep within himself that he had been unaware of. When he finished writing *Psychology of the Unconscious,* he observed: "I had a particularly lucid moment in which I surveyed my path as far as I had come. I thought: 'Now you have the key to mythology and you have the power to unlock all doors.' But then something within me said: 'Why unlock all these doors?'"[7] This statement eventually found its way into *Memories, Dreams, Reflections,* in an altered form. The word doors was replaced in the Pantheon Books edition with the word "gates."[8] This replacement brings up the issue of probable "interference" by Aniela Jaffé and Kurt Wolff, the American publisher, in the handling of the book.

In *Jung: A Biography,* Deidre Bair cited an interesting letter from Kurt Wolff as proof of probable meddling by Jaffé. The brief was dated June 19, 1958. In it, Kurt Wolff discussed the issue of Jung's "declining my request for a few pages on William James." Wolff then thanked Jaffé in the letter for "[seeing] a way" to answer his request, and he was "optimistically looking forward to [her] happy solution."[9] From exchanges like this, Bair arrived at the conclusion that "all the writings about William James were Jaffé's and not CGJ's."[10]

From my own reading of the Countway Library Manuscript, I think this is most likely an invalid conclusion, as the language and ideas in the CLM on Flournoy and James sound very much like Jung speaking.[11] The CLM on Flournoy and James is, in my view, a collaborative effort that arose from the oral discussions that took place between Jaffé and Jung. I'll summarize some of Jung's most pertinent statements from the CLM in what follows.

First, what about the coincidence that James was also similarly influenced by Goethe before he wrote his own passages concerning the door in the subconscious? As Richardson pointed out in his biography, James read a great deal of Goethe's works, including *Faust,* Eckermann's *Conversations with Goethe,* the Goethe-Schiller correspondence, *Warheit und Dichtung,* and other volumes.[12] I believe what influenced Jung most from his readings of James, however, was his capacity for introverted thinking, which was not Jung's strongest function. Jung was, by nature, an introverted intuitive type with extroverted thinking, and he kept his most introverted thoughts locked up in his citadel. While discussing the book *Psychological Types,* for instance, Jung said, "A man centers his power in his thinking and proposes to hold it as a solid front against the public, particularly against other men. He thinks if he tells the truth in this field it is equivalent to turning over the keys to his citadel to the enemy."[13] Where were the keys to Jung's citadel? Who gave him these keys? Goethe? Eckhart? James? Philemon? What interests me is the importance of the door metaphor in both men's writings and Jung's extension of the metaphor in a spiritual and material way, as a key between the empirical and metaphysical domains.

According to the chapter "Confrontation with the Unconscious" in the text of *MDR,* Philemon, the being with fisherking's wings who flew across the sky and had in his possession four keys, appeared to Jung in a dream.[14] Jung painted several portraits of him and held in-depth conversations with this inner sage while in his garden and tower. Philemon flew above Jung's first three chakras, dictating his thoughts from anahata and visuddha. Philemon's scope of vision extended further, however, to the infinite, the Transcendental Self, which is to say the third eye: Ajna. During the process of active imagination, Philemon became Jung's interlocutor, or inner guru, who transmitted to him psychic objectivity, or what he called the "reality of the psyche."[15] Yet this attitude of psychic objectivity was present five years earlier during his discussions with Flournoy and James.[16] In other words, James and Flournoy also possessed this objective attitude in their own methods of psychological observation, and they modeled it for Jung—before he extended it into his own unique techniques for the field of analytical psychotherapy. Psychic objectivity is a leitmotif throughout much of Jung's entire mature work, and it is also present in the CLM in Jung's descriptions of what he learned from these two great men.

To be objective about the nature of the psyche is to be scientific; psychic objectivity means that one takes fantasies and dreams from the stream of consciousness as real. Fantasies are facts of experience. They are facts that can be verified. Philemon, Jung's wise inner teacher of superior insight, demanded a commitment to pragmatic truths, not unlike James's attitude in his book *Varieties of Religious Experience.* Like Flournoy, James had a calling to psychology and philosophy. The same was true of Jung, only Jung took modern psychology much further toward a science of the psyche. Jung made liberal use of James's impartial and all-embracing attitude toward all forms of spiritual experience. Jung learned firsthand from his readings that James made no value judgements about which experiences were better or worse, lower or higher, superior or inferior. Such detached impartiality in James's books helped Jung develop a uniquely spiritually democratic attitude. Although this attitude was transmitted to Jung by James mostly through his writings, it was also conveyed during their three encounters in the United States. An important fact that emerges in the CLM is that Jung visited James a third time, when he came to the United States in 1910, which suggests that Jung highly valued this relationship with James because he sought him out on his own. During this meeting, they apparently discussed parapsychology, the psychology of religious experience, and James told Jung he could hear his heart beating: "When I was in the United States again in 1910, I saw him once more, and we went on a long walk together. During this walk, he told me that he could feel his heart beating. That same year, he died."[17] James died of heart failure several months after this last visit. Jung could see that he was ill at this time, and he did not press James to say too much. Yet this is an important fact because I did not learn about the third visit until I read about it in the CLM.

Here are a few more treats. When Jung first stepped foot in the United States, he had not yet found his inner authority, his own unique voice, the mature and authentic voice of his true vocation. James's appearance, at a crucial turning point (1909–1910) in Jung's development, enabled him to begin connecting deeply with his secondary personality in a new way that left a distinctly American imprint on his psyche. As an idealized figure, James became an outer representation, a transformative relationship, for an archetypal aptitude that was activated through *evocation* in the relationship. What ultimately crystallized out of their relationship, I conjecture, was a metamorphosis of a more spacious Spiritual Self, the great teacher of insight and wisdom in Jung, that influenced the emergence of the figure Philemon who offered Jung increased insight and healing and vocational guidance during a vulnerable time in his life.

I hypothesize that Jung's high regard for James as a scientific researcher and thinker was a projection and recollection of a partially unrealized scientific-spiritual aptitude within Jung that had not yet been fully awakened psychologically. By 1909, Jung had begun to question Freud seriously and was struggling to overcome his self-doubts. The CLM reveals that Flournoy and James helped Jung overcome these doubts and develop an attitude of scientific detachment: "Under the influence of Freud I acquired knowledge, but not clarity. Flournoy taught me to look from a detached distance at the object . . . He was professor of philosophy and psychology, and was strongly influenced by Jamesian pragmatism . . . In both men I found a friendly receptivity toward my doubts, uncertainties and scruples—something that I did not encounter in later life under similar circumstances."[18] It then took Jung a couple of years to consult his own inner authority, the Spiritual Self within. In relationship to James, Jung was free to explore his motivations toward theology more deeply than ever before. The composition of *Liber Novus* helped Jung a great deal with this. Furthermore, reading James helped him see Freud's limitations and discover his full Self-sufficiency as a renowned psychologist on world religions.

Moreover, Flournoy and James shared Jung's quest for an empirical attitude. Like Jung, James began his career as a natural scientist. He also graduated with his degree in medicine, but James was more of a professor of psychology by vocation than a doctor, as Jung was. James was less of a healer in a medical sense and more of what we might call today a cultural healer through his teachings, lecturing, and writings.

Based on my overview in the last several chapters, James clearly played a pivotal role as an organizer of some of Jung's mature thoughts about psychology and religion, psychological types, the Book of Job, Yoga, Samadhi, the supraconscious, and the collective or transpersonal layers of the unconscious. James was thirty-five years Jung's senior. He was more like a grandfather than a fatherly friend. According to the CLM, there was an numinous atmosphere around James, moreover, that attracted Jung. This atmosphere impressed Jung greatly. Despite their differences in age, James treated Jung as if he were his *equal*. This *equivalence* was not found in Jung's relationship with Freud.

When I came of age reading Jung's autobiography, I was at first a bit smitten with the spell of Freud's charisma on Jung. But after reading Shamdasani, who led me to the Countway Library Manuscript, I have seen that this was due, in part, to Kurt Wolff's interference. Freud did not have a democratic attitude toward Jung; rather, he presumed his superiority, the "authority" he said he could not risk. James had already penetrated to the archetypal core of the American cultural psyche and discovered its secret: the psychological principal of Spiritual Democracy. I believe this democratic attitude toward the variety of religious experiences is what spoke most directly to Jung's fantasies. James was a spiritual democrat at heart. He was nonchalant and down-to-earth. He was pragmatic to the bone. The spiritual parity that James exuded and transmitted to Jung is, at its best, quintessentially American.

Whereas Jung's relationship with Flournoy was personal and affectionate, Jung's relationship with James was more idealized, scientifically detached, and spiritual. James was more of a *transcultural mentor figure* to Jung, a *spiritual grandfather* of sorts, or a distinguished and elderly American friend. Jung had never had such a mentor before they met—even though they did not spend much time together and never really got to know one another on an intimate basis. With James, Jung said the *atmosphere* around him seemed to be more spiritual, owing to the expanded capacity of his mind. What fascinated Jung about James, in particular, was his breadth of spiritual vision.[19]

James's "extroverted intuition" helped Jung to see the direction of psychology's future in a less-pathologically colored light. Moreover, James placed feeling on an elevated scale of human values where religious experiences were concerned. Jung commented that he did not get the same sense of personal warmth from James that he received from Flournoy. Nevertheless, Jung must have been warmed when he saw James throw his arms around the shoulders of Ernest Jones at Clark University and declare: "The future of psychology belongs to your work."[20] By this, James meant the whole group of psychoanalysts who were present that day, including Jung. My sincere hope is that the *higher destiny of the Spiritual Self that James and Jung spent many years writing about will become a central part of this future.*[21]

In this book I've postulated that the "acting self" in James and Jung was *spiritually democratic* at its core. It was not founded on illusions of shallow political or gluttonous economic democracy, but on deep spiritual values, which may give hope to society and offer healing—personally and culturally—to individuals, groups, and nations in chaos. Jamesian pragmatism and Jungian psychology are concerned with helping students, patients, and readers center their minds on a *nuclear center of activity in the Self*. James and Jung aimed to make the central Self conscious of Itself. In this complementary hypothetical view, the Self is a principle of dynamic adaptation patterned on the Self's activities of each moment. The spiritual faculties in the Self are composed of a "plurality" of dispositions in the entire streams of our consciousness, including our most basic instincts and emotions. When proclivities to act are activated from within, all people feel it as "a sort of innermost center within the circle, of sanctuary within the citadel,"[22] the "Self of Selves," or our "innermost activity" of which we are "most distinctly aware."[23] This *innermost activity* in the Spiritual Self are the keys to the citadels of speech, language, poetry, the lecture room, or analytical discourse. The instinct of activity is a doorway through which any teacher, analyst, or writer facilitates a process of *vocalism* whenever they make space for the Self to emerge from its citadel. The Self of Selves in James's work has much to do with a type of transcendent thinking outside the ordinary field of awareness. In the chapter "The Self" in the *Principles of Psychology,* James distinguished between the Me and the I:

> Whatever I may be thinking of, I am always at the same time more or less aware of myself, of my personal existence. At the same time it is I who am aware; so that the total self of me, being as it were duplex, partly known and partly knower, partly object and partly subject, must have two aspects discriminated in it, of which for shortness we may call the Me and the other the I.[24]

The relations between the ego (James's *Me*) and the Self (the transcendental *I*) as a center of spiritual activity in the human psyche emerged in Jung's mind during a seminar he gave to the Guild of Pastoral Psychology in London on April 5, 1939, called "The Symbolic Life."[25] What did Jung mean by the symbolic life and what might the symbolic life have to do with the Self in Jung's spirituality and in Jamesian pragmatism? Can dreams help us live a symbolic existence? What about directed thinking, fantasy thinking, and the role of active imagination? Is synchronicity, or meaningful chance, a part of what Jung meant by living a symbolic life out of the ground of the acting Self?

Like James, Jung was a critic of religion on one hand and a supporter of the world's faiths on the other. But his answer to the spiritual problems of modernity might best be summed up in his notion of the symbolic life:

> Only the symbolic life can express the need of the soul—the daily need of the soul, mind you! And because people have no such thing, they can never step out of this mill—this awful, grinding, banal life in which they are "nothing but." ... These things go pretty deep, and no wonder people get neurotic. Life is too rational, there is no symbolic existence in which I am something else, in which I am fulfilling my role, my role as one of the actors in the divine drama of life.[26]

The term "nothing but" (*nichts als*) is an expression Jung borrowed from William James's book *The Varieties of Religious Experience*. To be an actor in the divine drama, we must find ways to become spiritually active. We must discover how to bring our symbolic life into the world through our dreams, journaling, artistic representations, or active imaginations. This means we have to discover our vocation, our calling, or what James called our theory of truth. How many of us really know our theory of truth? To know it, we must have performed an experiment on ourselves. We have to look deeply within ourselves, to the symbols of our dreams, or our streams of consciousness, to know our story, our personal myth. It is one thing to be a member of a society; it is another thing to become a living and active member. Life is too pressing today to merely be a believer in religious dogmas. We must also become activists. This is what Jung meant by individuation—an experiment conducted through an analysis of the unconscious, followed by moral responsibility and ethical actions of some kind.

Analysis is not for everybody, however, and the way to higher Self-realization is not for everybody either. Nevertheless, whatever our symbolic life might be, our actions can give us a sense of meaning and purpose, whereby we can make sense of the trivialities of life. Then we are at peace, as Jung said: "That gives peace, when people feel that they are living the symbolic life, that they are actors in the divine drama. That gives the only meaning to human life; everything else is banal and you can dismiss it. A career, producing of children, are all *maya* compared with that one thing, that your life is meaningful."[27]

To refer to having children as *maya* is unusual. Yet if we don't have meaning in life, even our vocations as fathers or mothers might seem meaningless at times. We don't often consider this, but in some tragic cases, in which a person has lost his or her sense of meaning, it is sadly true. Having a career might seem, at times, completely senseless when the meaning of life is missing. Anxiety, depression, substance abuse, panic disorders, even suicide may result from situations in which a person feels trapped in a job that is no longer alive and pleasing to the soul. Its dead because the career can no longer feed the longings of the soul for the daily sustenance of the Self's calling, which brings peace.

If we have lost our sense of meaning, how can we find a new situation in which the active Self is enlivened in us? In which the Self is truly *alive* in us *now*? How might we *live a symbolic life* in today, in this very existence, out of the ground of the being? What is the vital thing that should be alive in us that is not living today? The active Self "keeps on stirring, it disturbs you, it makes you restless, and it gives you no peace."[28]

The symbolic life can become a part of our activism, our divine drama, yet it is something we can only bring into community from our ritual practices in quiet and solitude and repose. It is what nobody else touches, nobody knows about; it is our personal narrative. This is what Jung called our subjective story, our personal equation.

Do you know what your myth is? Do you know the myth in which you are currently living? Do you know what your acts in the divine drama are? Are you living them spiritually? If not, why?

Jung gave an example of a Jewish girl who came to him for analysis who was not living the ancestral life of her Hebrew forebears and he admonished her. He told her she was a child of God who should be living the symbolic life, not refusing the secret will in herself, which had once been alive in her family of origin.[29] Jung's insights into the *cure* in this case were provided solely through her dreams, the language of her unconscious. After a withdrawal of her godlike projections onto Jung, she soon began to produce extraordinary figures of Divinity within herself. From Jung's reading into world mythology, alchemy, and religion—and especially from studying the dreams of his patients—he learned that "the modern unconscious has a tendency to produce a psychological condition which we find, for instance, in medieval mysticism. You find certain things in Meister Eckhart; you find many things in Gnosticism; that is a sort of esoteric Christianity. You find the idea of the Adam Kadmon in every man—the Christ within."[30]

Jung's spirituality comes out here. In his view, there would be no new incarnation of a World Teacher, no new revelation of a Global Messiah, or Planetary Dispenser of a Universal Truth to support the naïve need of the masses for a new collective fantasy to gather their energies around. The fantasy of an Earthly Savior, Prophet, or God Man is a thing of the past. Today there are also Wild Women and new Goddess Women about.

What might the symbolic life mean to you, reader? Are you practicing some aspect of the acting Self symbolically in your daily rituals?

Jung insisted that the meaning of the symbolic life was a real event in daily actions—when we live by the myth of meaning within ourselves. If it is alive in us, we can bring it into society. As a post-Christian psychiatrist, for Jung, this meant living the "idea of the Christ within—not the historical Christ without, but the Christ within . . . That is our symbol, that is ourselves; we are all that. And if anyone lives his own hypothesis to the bitter end (and pays with his death, perhaps), he knows that Christ is his brother."[31]

What does it mean to live your hypothesis to the bitter end?

Gandhi and Martin Luther King Jr. come to mind here. Jung's calling was to extend the Christ myth onward toward a new personal equation that could be Self-realized in anyone who was humble enough to hear the calling within and bring it into responsible actions in the world as a myth to live by. Such a hypothesis has to do with the acceptance of the personal and archetypal shadow in ourselves—the poor man, bad fellow, or bad gal in ourselves. We have to accept them, if we are to become truly one with the Self within. Jung went on to say: "That is modern psychology, and that is the future. That is the true future, that is the future of which I know . . . I am only concerned with the fulfillment of that will which is in every individual. My history is only the history of those individuals who are going to fulfill their hypotheses."[32]

What does it mean to fulfill our individual will? By "will" Jung meant the will of God or the Self. By "hypotheses" he meant our scientific experiments in individuation. Jung used religious and scientific terms interchangeably. Analytical psychology began as a science and was greatly influenced, as we've seen, by *The Varieties of Religious Experience,* in which William James put forth a nondual notion of a science of religion. Following James, Jung meant *hypotheses* in the broadest sense possible. He meant we must make our own experiments in whatever walks of life we are called to stride forth upon, whether heroically or nonheroically, whether in success or failure. Our fields of activity are designed by our vocations and become filled with an inner light of meaning. Jung's prescription for meaninglessness and neurosis in postmodern culture, his new medicine, or the panacea that may bring healing to those who can stoop low enough to receive it is to listen with scientific or religious intent to the messages of our dreams. When we truly listen to the messages of the Self, we are enriched by our unconscious with transformative symbols that may change our lives utterly. When we give ear to the inner voice of the active Self, we may never be the same again.

During the discussion period of his lecture to the Guild, Jung was asked what happens if a patient in analysis, or a person of faith, can't go back to the rites and rituals of the Church. "Then there is trouble," Jung answered, "then he has to go on the Quest; then he has to find out what his soul says; then he has to go through the solitude of the land that is not created."[33] When we lose the sustaining inherited structures of faith and their symbol-systems, we fall into what Jung called the frying pan of analysis. Then we are in real trouble. Then we are cooked in an alchemical *calcinatio*, hacked apart in a shamanic dismemberment, or crucified upon our own cross. We must pick up our own cross and be crucified upon it, for it is only through death to our former life and persona, the little *Me*, that we may become truly transformed by the activities of the Divine Selfhood, the *I* beyond the margins.

Jung mentioned the analysis of a famous scientist, Wolfgang Pauli, to illuminate this process. Jung had the good fortune to have analyzed Pauli's dreams in his book *Psychology and Alchemy*.

> He set out to see what his unconscious said to him and it gave him a wonderful lead. That man got into order again because he gradually accepted the symbolic data, and now he leads the religious life, the life of the careful observer. Religion is careful observation of the data. He now observes all the things that are brought to him by his dreams; that is his only guidance.[34]

Jung came up with a new definition for the word *religion*, the surprising statement that religion consists of *careful observation and interpretation of the data of our dreams, which are our only source of guidance*. Therefore, we live our experiment, our hypothesis of individuation, our symbolic life by following with devotion the messages of our dreams and fantasies. Very few of us can live by such a high standard as Jung and Pauli modeled for us.[35]

As a Jungian analyst, I live in Jung's myth and my own post-Jungian version of it. My life as a Jungian is a central part of my symbolic life. There's no escaping it. Jung was too large for any of us who are Jungians to escape his influence entirely. We've even adopted his name! What we

33 - The Influence of William James

may add to what Jung taught us is to bring our own living symbols or theories of truth into the mix and enter the divine drama.

When we contemplate the question of how we might cultivate a symbolic life in our personal lives, it's important to consider a return to the earliest memories and dreams of our childhoods. This is what Jung did after he broke with Freud in 1912. He began to pursue his own individual fantasies and dreams on Lake Zürich. He began playing childhood games again, returning to the symbolic life of his earliest years. It was then that he remembered the dream of the great underground phallus.

In the course of writing this book on James and Jung, I have generated some hypotheses by examining my own dreams in an attempt to deepen my understanding of my personal myth, *my calling*. This led me to the study of destiny dreams. By *destiny dreams,* I mean a series of dreams that have helped me recognize and confirm the intention, conviction, and meaning of my life, through direct unmediated experiences of the Self within. Destiny dreams can motivate a person who has dreamt them to take creative action in the world, to practice right speech, right livelihood, or right purpose. Such actions can lead to good fortune if you are lucky. And if so, you may get a clearer sense of your path ahead, your Self-path, even if you're uncertain where the steps may be taking you. You may hear the voice of the Self speaking, the Self within you, if you take time to listen to your dreams. Destiny dreams are the voice of nature speaking to us in symbolic ways.

I've felt called to be a California writer and a Jungian analyst by destiny and by fate. As it is for everyone, there were outer events that completely entangled me in fateful detours during the process of living a symbolic life. To get untangled, I had to learn as much as I could about destiny dreams, from a source outside analytical psychology, namely from American poetry and Jamesian pragmatism. While struggling to get untangled, I've been enriched by an element of meaning. During my years of waiting, practicing, teaching, and writing as a Jungian, I've never given up hope in my future destiny. The end can never be certain. But the important thing is that I stay true to my symbolic life, regardless of what good or bad fortune the fates may bring me. I'm grateful I have James as a companion on my Jungian journey too!

Notes

1. Jung, "The Meaning of Psychology for Modern Man," CW 10, ¶304.
2. Jung, *Letters,* vol. 1, 118.
3. Jung, MDR, 224.
4. Jung, *Symbols of Transformation*, CW 5, ¶180.
5. Jung saw James twice at Clark in 1909 and met with him again the following year in 1910, according to the CLM. The first two meetings in 1909 were for little more than an hour; the third may have been a bit longer, but they had no correspondence. Apart from these three very brief personal impressions, Jung says he was mostly indebted to the books James wrote.
6. Jung, *Analytical Psychology: Notes of the Seminars Given in 1925 by C. G. Jung*.
7. Jung, *Analytical Psychology*, 25.
8. "About this time I experienced a moment of unusual clarity in which I looked back over the way I had travelled so far. I thought, 'Now you possess a key to mythology and are free to unlock all the gates of the unconscious psyche.' But then something whispered within me, 'Why open all gates?'" See Jung, MDR, 171; italics mine.
9. Bair, *Jung: A Biography*, 839.
10. Bair, 839.
11. Frances A. Countway Library of Medicine, Harvard University, Rare Books (hereafter, CLM). Collection # H MS C29. Permission to paraphrase portions of the manuscript, or brief quotes from the section "Théodore Flournoy and William James" granted by Public Services Librarian on November 1, 2019. The James-Jung portion begins on page 197 of the CLM and is two pages long, single-spaced.
12. Richardson, *William James*, 91, 92.
13. Jung, *Analytical Psychology*, 32, 33.
14. Jung, MDR, 182, 183.
15. Jung, MDR, 183.
16. Jung, CLM.
17. Jung, CLM.
18. Jung CLM.
19. Jung, CLM.
20. Taylor, *Consciousness Beyond the Margin*, 146.
21. One of the doorways we cannot leave shut in this book is Jung's theory of meaningful chance or synchronicity. As I was in the process of working with

my copy editor on the second part of this book, a lesbian woman in her early seventies entered my practice and reported a vocational dream that recurred to her over a half-dozen times in her youth. (She entered my practice in late August 2019). As a young woman, she had come out West on her motorcycle with some friends and remembered her first experience of riding across the Golden Gate Bridge. In her early twenties, she was searching for her proper calling in life. Shortly after arriving in San Francisco, she had the following dream: I'm riding my motorcycle across the Golden Gate Bridge, and I see one door after another. I realize I have three or four doors I can go through. In my dream, I keep opening these doors. They open up into expanse, wide open water, vastness of space. When I asked for her amplifications to the door symbolism, she said: "The first doorway I opened was in business. After I finished my MBA at Golden Gate University, a second doorway opened into the field of computer programming. After I made sufficient money, I returned to my childhood interest in American history, and a third door opened to my profession as a university professor. The fourth door has been caretaking my mother and my family." I don't typically hear dreams about doors (let alone four of them!), so this one struck me as highly significant, since she knew nothing about my archetypal research. I'll have more to say about vocational dreams and synchronicity later.

22. James, *The Principles of Psychology*, 127.
23. James, 128.
24. James, Writings 1902–1910, 174.
25. Jung, "The Symbolic Life," CW 18, 267–290.
26. Jung, CW 18, ¶¶627, 628.
27. Jung, CW 18, ¶630.
28. Jung, CW 18, ¶630.
29. Jung, CW 18, ¶636.
30. Jung, CW 18, ¶638.
31. Jung, CW 18, ¶638.
32. Jung, CW 18, ¶639.
33. Jung, CW 18, ¶673.
34. Jung CW 18, ¶673.
35. We may now read their private conversations in *Atom and Archetype: The Pauli/Jung Letters*.

Chapter 34

THE SUPREME MEANING AS THE BRIDGE TO WHAT IS TO COME

In my view, the aim of Jungian analysis might best be described as the approach to the archetypal "nucleus" of the personality. Once this central nucleus is reached, it can unlock the floodgates of the psyche to a transcendent experience at the core of the Spiritual Self. Once the energy-stream of transcendent consciousness that is Self-aware is freed from developmental disturbances, it can liberate the *voice* of the supraordinate personality and become manifest through sacred works. Its individual "secret" may then become free to express itself vocationally as a unitary carrier of the cosmic whole. This secret is the main business of one's life work. Often its goal has a national purpose, namely to make the national myths by which a nation lives conscious for the generality. Such a personal secret, once made objective, contains an inherited knowledge of "typical myths" that emerge in early life and through which our "racial and national complexes" may be worked out *symbolically*.

From this vantage point, a central aim of Jungian analysis is to help a patient find a proper vocational channel or calling in life, to help unlock the "secret" of his or her personality. Once this personal secret is made conscious, the patient has gained significant psychological insight into his or her personal myth.[1]

It was Jung's calling to make the nuclear forms of the collective unconscious conscious in their archetypal seed-forms. One of these myths, which Jung discovered in his research of American poetry, is the archetype of the Peacemaker. In his amplifications of Miss Miller's fantasies, he explored Longfellow's verses in his epic poem "Hiawatha," which was recited in elementary schools in California when I was a child. Today, we might refer to the positive or creative side of the Peacemaker as the Divine Feminine, Liberty, or Mother of all thought. The very notion of spiritual democracy is based on an archetype, therefore, for "All the most powerful ideas in history go back to archetypes. This is particularly true of religious ideas, but the central concepts, of science, philosophy, and ethics are no exception to this rule."[2] This *vocational* idea had been incubating in Jung's psyche ever since the age of three, when, sleeping soundly in his father's room, he had a dream of an enormous underground phallus—the ambivalent God-image, light and dark, Good and Evil, chthonic and spiritual, Christ and Antichrist, seraph and snake, in the form of the great Lingam of Lord Shiva. The phallus had a single eye on the top of its head with an aura of brightness shining above it.[3] In his personal narrative, Jung explained that before he could even read he used to pester his mother to read to him from "the *Orbis Pictus,* an old, richly illustrated children's book, which contained a rich account of exotic religions, especially that of the Hindus . . . My mother told me later that I always returned to those pictures."[4] The eye on the top of the phallus represented Shiva's third mystical eye, the Ajna center. Shiva is an archetypal expression of individuation. Jung's dream was an expression of his own calling and his role and destiny as a seer.

By 1915, Jung arrived at the cornerstone of what would become his personal myth: the discovery of the "supreme meaning" or process of individuation, as the "*path, the way and the bridge to what is to come. This is the God yet to come. It is not the coming of God himself, but his image which appears in the supreme meaning. God is an image, and those who worship him must worship him in the images of the supreme meaning.*"[5] Spiritual democracy, as supreme meaning, appears to take an individual form in each individual who can make its singular way conscious and live according to its destiny. Jung rode on the same wave currents as Walt Whitman and William James when he emphasized the word *Supreme*. By *supreme meaning,* Jung meant the path or way of what is to come in a personal and a collective sense: individual and cultural individuation. Meaning is *supreme* because it is microcosmic and macrocosmic, finite and infinite, infinitesimal and universal. It transcends all previous God-images in history because it sees them all as *manifestations* of One Supreme. "Why has it been taught that there is only one Supreme?" asked Walt Whitman. "I say that there are and must be myriads of Supremes."[6] By recognizing the *supreme meaning* in the God-images of all cultures, James and Jung were articulating ways of direct religious experience and psychological equality for everyone: a democratic experience of the potentially awakened Self in each person. The archetype of spiritual democracy can be known by the effects it produces; it is an *inherited possibility of ideas that is charged with numinous emotions. Just as there are what Jung called ethnic and national complexes in every country, so too are there national myths that continue to influence each of us.*

For Jung, a supreme meaning transcended any religious creed, denomination, religion, or psychology of the past. Not unlike Whitman, Jung saw that the experience of God was a meaning to live by. Or, as Benjamin Franklin put it pithily, a few days before his death: "I believe in One God, Creator of the Universe."[7] Franklin meant the Self as the organizing principle. He assigned to the Creator the same philosophy, sociology, or theology of the Declaration of Independence, reflected in what Thomas Jefferson called the "American mind."[8]

In 1937, on his seventh trip to the United States, Jung defined *religion* as follows:

> Religion, as the Latin word denotes, is a careful and scrupulous observation of what Rudolph Otto aptly termed the numinosum, that is, a dynamic agency or effect not caused by an arbitrary act of the will. On the contrary, it seizes and controls the human subject, who is always rather its victim than its creator ... Religion appears to me to be a peculiar attitude of mind which could be formulated in accordance with the original use of the word religio, which means a careful consideration and observation of certain dynamic factors that are conceived as "powers": spirits, daemons, gods, laws, ideas, ideals, or whatever name man has given to such factors in his world as he has found powerful, dangerous, or helpful to be taken into careful consideration, or grand, beautiful, and meaningful enough to be devoutly worshiped and loved.[9]

Notice that Jung inserted the word *meaningful* here. *Meaning* and *religion* were synonymous in Jung's lexicon. *Religion* was a peculiar attitude through which meaning was conveyed to the mind, but this was a creedless meaning, coincident with the principle of psychological relativity. If the laws, ideas, and ideals were powerful enough, they brought with them a certain influx of archetypal energies that were numinous in nature. The changed psychological consciousness that ensued from such experience was what really mattered to Jung—the visitation by numinous factors of Self-knowledge. These are archetypes or images of meaning. Like Whitman, Jung made it clear that he did not mean a creed by the word *Supreme*; he meant an attitude that was cosmic, spiritual, psychological, a changed consciousness that had discovered meaning in the plurality of Self-images across all nations. Such a development of consciousness was co-creative with the Creator, as a principle of universal relatedness, independent of any creedal authority.

In Jung's view, a collective religious path can become a way to supreme meaning only if it touches on something transcendent, something that so changes consciousness and opens the mind to include the mystery of the Cosmos. Only through such direct encounter with Divinity does one realize one's significance as a responsibility to God, or vocation to the Body Self, Social Self, and Spiritual Self. Meaning is not something one seeks, moreover. Meaning occurs through chance occurrences and "baffling" coincidences.

By May 1928, Jung had introduced the word *synchronism* as a synonym for his new hypothesis of *synchronicity*. He used the word for the first time in his memorial address for Richard Wilhelm in Munich in May 1930, when he sought to explain the Chinese divinization method, the *I Ching*, or *Book of Changes,* which dates back to the fourth millennium BCE.[10] By 1932, Jung used the term *meaning* in a broader way while reflecting on the practice of psychotherapy in general: "[The analyst's] words are effective only insofar as they convey a meaning or have significance. It is this that makes them work. But 'meaning' is something mental or spiritual. Call it a fiction if you like."[11] *Words are curative only if they convey something spiritual.* By this Jung meant a mental attitude, or psychic state, in the analyst and patient; a vocation, or a calling from the inner voice, *vocatus.* Jung did not distinguish between the analyst's vocation and a calling (in a theological sense) from the Word of God. In his writing, the two terms were interchangeable from a vocational context. What concerned Jung in his 1932 paper "The Development of the Personality" were "fictional and imaginative processes" occurring in the field of interaction between patient and doctor. This spacious interactive field was a mental space that was cosmic, or Universal, in scope.

Thus, by 1932, Jung embraced a world-transforming vision of the interconnectedness of all religions, a relativity of Divinity across East and West, and in order to attempt this he had to go beyond nineteenth-century

34 - The Supreme Meaning as the Bridge to What Is to Come

experimental psychology and science. For only in the twentieth century did meaning begin to preponderate as a factor that really counted, he said. For Jung the premises of nineteenth-century science did "not give enough meaning to life. And it is only meaning that liberates."[12] By 1932, therefore, meaning had become the principal of life in Jung's psychology. In this sense, he answered the call for a scientific understanding of the supreme meaning of God-images, in the same year that he conducted his four seminars on Kundalini Yoga, which I reviewed earlier in Chapter 32.

We have to ask ourselves today whether it is correct to postulate that *only* meaning liberates. If this were true, then what about other ways, laws, and methods of liberation that are charged with the numinous dynamisms of the objective psyche? Relatively few researchers would venture to say that "only" meaning liberates. Yet, Jung was emphatic. His answer to the problem put forth by world religions was a statement of his subjective confession, an epistle of his faith in his personal myth, or fiction, that was given to him during the composition of *The Red Book*. I believe he's saying that, like all religious statements, personal beliefs are based on images of God and that fictional and imaginative processes that are charged with luminosity can be *healing* because they give one a sense of *spiritual significance* and its spaciousness is the main liberating factor.

What matters in the transmission of meaning to a patient are the doctor's words that emanate from his or her instinctive-spiritual foundation, transcendent of any traditional religion, no matter how cosmic or comprehensible it might be; for when words are viewed objectively, that is, from the point of view of psychological relativity based on a science of the psyche, all religious revelations are patterned on God-images. What made Jung's vision of spiritual democracy an advance of previous religious forms was its international scope, its vista of transcendent understanding and seeing. This was the same kind of spiritual vista he had observed in James: a spiritually democratic core of linguistic formations, which are self-governing in nature and embrace the All—psyche and Cosmos—and that this is as certain from an objective point of view as meaning itself. This was why Jung called it "supreme." Like Jung, James universalized Divinity in such a way that its *democratic spaciousness* was open to anyone. Whitman and James could not, like Jung, be satisfied with what had been taught about there being only one Supreme; their aim was to destroy all previous teachers and go beyond them by asserting the ultimate Oneness of humanity. *Meaning thus became for Jung a transcendent state of mind.* By fiction or myth, Jung meant a function (he called it "transcendent") that could transport consciousness to new vistas of seeing; objectively observing the psyche required a strong yet flexible ego.

In *Memories, Dreams, Reflections* Jung referred to this form of reflection as "objective cognition." The analyst's words form myths, and his or her vocalizations activate the state of objective observation in a patient through a kind of spiritual resonance, vibration, or energy, captured in the psychotherapist's language, which is depth-psychology's domain—the language of *living symbols.* "A psychoneurosis," Jung wrote, "must be understood, ultimately, as the suffering of a soul which has not discovered its meaning."[13] We suffer when we lose our capacity for attunement to the natural language of the psyche. Jung embodied meaning empirically in his speech, discovered meaning objectively as he spoke; he spoke meaning's words: *he vocalized.* Jung's words conveyed meaning in his work, for meaning is one way God communicates to humans through vehicles as speech, verbal forms, art, dance, and poetry. Such a mental state was conveyed to Jung in 1915 as supreme meaning—and he thought patients needed to *feel meaning* deeply in an embodied sense. The doctor, teacher, or psychotherapist who is in touch with this spiritual state speaks meaning aloud, or waits quietly for a patient or student to discover it in moments of silence. Jung ceased to be the twentieth-century doctor-scientist at this historical juncture and became a conveyer of *fictional-healing, the meaning-cure*: Jung's "healing fiction" became a "meaning that quickens."[14]

Jung entered new territory in 1932, when conducting his Kundalini Seminars, paving the way for the discovery of synchronicity in the twentieth century via his science of the objective psyche. By meaning Jung meant a mythic understanding of one's place in the world, a vocation to transmit a vision of cosmic relatedness and psychic interconnectedness with everything that *is*. An old Chinese sage, such as Lao-tzu, would certainly have had no trouble understanding Jung's references to meaning. Jung cited Chapter 25 of the *Tao Te Ching,* for instance, as an example of what he meant: "One may think of it as the mother of all things under heaven. / I do not know its name. / But I call it 'Meaning.'"[15]

Jung began his studies of Chinese wisdom texts as early as 1927, yet by 1932, he extended the concept of meaning to include an international audience. His aim was ultimately to reach the world by becoming a bridge between Western and Eastern religions and psychologies. As far as I can understand the evolution of Jung's views on religious relativism, everything began to converge by 1932 on the particular psychic state in the doctor that heals. *Meaning became the cornerstone*: the discovery of Jung's healing fiction became his myth to live by.

Meaning was the main thing from 1932 onward, over and above anything reason or science or any creed might offer. Meaning—supreme meaning—was the cornerstone of Jung's myth. Jung defined further what he meant by "religion" when he asserted what a patient in psychotherapy was looking for, "something that will take possession" of his or her mind and "will give meaning and form to the confusion of his [or her] neurotic soul."[16] Meaning helps us endure to the end. Moreover, meaning cannot be *made;* meaning happens. We are all in a laboratory of meaning.

Only when a psychotherapist conveys the mental state of meaning effectively are his or her words effective. In "Psychotherapists or the Clergy," Jung said even more precisely while reflecting on his empirical data:

> Among all my patients in the second half of life—that is to say, over thirty-five—there has not been one whose problem in the last resort was not that of finding a religious outlook on life. It is safe to say that every one of them fell ill because he had lost what the living religions of every age have given to their followers, and none of them has been really healed who did not regain his religious outlook.[17]

Jung wrote as a scientist of the human soul. He was not speaking as a religious prophet, mystic, or herald of the New Age. Like Whitman and James, his attitude, as a Swiss, was spiritually democratic. In Jung's view, creeds were not seen as consistent with the path, bridge, or way to wholeness—only *meaning* was. Meaning was supreme because it transcended all individual God-images by locating the center of all of them in the cosmic Self. How much Jung was influenced by Alexander von Humboldt's view of science is uncertain, yet Jung mentioned the Prussian explorer's book *Kosmos* as one of his chief reference sources in one passage in *Psychology of the Unconscious*: "According to an observation by Humboldt (*Kosmos*), certain South American Indian tribes call the meteors 'urine of the stars.'" Jung suggested, moreover, a comparison with water flowing from the footsteps of stars: "a comet is a light symbolism for fructifying moisture (sperma)."[18] Jung suggested that star light impregnated libido when it introverted into the unconscious. This metaphor suggested, moreover, that there was an inner and outer correspondence between cosmic meaning and supreme meaning in the psyche. Goethe, too, had invoked the "immensity of space" and the "eternal Void afar" to illuminate the correspondence Jung posited in his theory of synchronicity.[19] Not surprisingly, Humboldt's *Cosmos* provided Goethe with deep inspiration, as it did Emerson and Whitman.

Humboldt's cosmos lectures had their inception on the high slopes of the Andes between 1799 and 1804. Yet the book first began to take shape in 1805 in his *Essay on the Geography of Plants,* which he dedicated to Goethe. Humboldt played an important role in sparking Goethe's vision of the immeasurable Universe and its interconnectedness in his poetry. Goethe hailed the scientist's cosmos lectures at the University of Berlin between November 1827 and April 1828 (sixty-one lectures in total), going so far as to declare that "the immeasurable abyss has been fathomed" and "that the great work, beyond all belief, has truly been done."[20]

Jung's psychology of religion is not a doctrine; it is an empirical method of observing and writing about the psyche, a bridge or gateway to *personal* religious experience. As such, analytical psychology concerns itself first and foremost with problems centering on meaning (and meaninglessness and its attendant symptoms, anxieties, and depressions) during midlife and beyond. This includes 1) the conflict of *vocation* (from the Latin root *vocare*) versus career; 2) conflicts of conscience, the moral confrontation between good and evil; 3) the discovery of one's personal myth, or healing fiction; 4) the solution to problems of neurotic suffering and mental illness through a path of *supreme meaning*; 5) the discovery of a religious outlook on life—the chief concern of world religions and all psychotherapists, in Jung's view; 6) the arrival at objective cognition or the relativity of the God-images at the center and heart of all religions; and 7) Spiritual democracy as the way that is to come.

The way to psychological wholeness involves an acceptance of suffering and momentary death to the personal ego. This mortification of the old personality and its complexes at midlife is followed by rebirth, or resurrection of a newly transformed consciousness that is relatively free of possession by affect-images and sees the meaning of existence in a transpersonal *destiny*. This, of course, is an ideal state that cannot be sustained permanently throughout life, for wholeness includes Shadow and messiness and fits of emotion that can cloud judgment and keep us from learning from our past mistakes. Life includes mistakes and failures. The ego's task is to serve, not one historical God-image, but to expand consciousness further toward a larger embrace with the timeless center of the Cosmos: the Supreme Self as the eternal mystery of being.

This does not mean that Jungian psychotherapists become religious teachers of some particular denominational persuasion or practitioners of an expanded consciousness that marks the analyst out as a superior being. Rather, their words are meaningful, or not, in helping alleviate a patient's perplexity. When the mental state of psychotherapists resonates with a basic truth that underlies their methods, they may begin to help awaken meaning in their patients. Jung said the doctor's words were "only" vibrations in the air; their special quality was due to a "particular psychic state in the doctor."[21]

Many have wrongly assumed that what Jung had in mind was a form of esoteric religion. In my view, Jung's thoughts on religion have not been satisfactorily explained. "My life," Jung wrote in the "Prologue" to *MDR*, and "the way I am and the way I write are a unity"; moreover, "all my ideas and all my endeavors are myself."[22] Jung did not say the "self" here; he said "myself." "Myself" is the only way the Self can be embodied—through an "I," "me," or "you." In order to find out what this life and way to myself or yourself is, Jung said we needed first to acquire knowledge about our vocation.

Jung made clear in *MDR* that all of his books were tasks given to him by "fate": "A book of mine is always a matter of fate."[23] He told the reader further that he was not moved to write *MDR* until he realized that there were "certain objective problems" that called him to closer examination and analysis. These objective problems were all central to his discovery of a path to spiritual democracy: the bridge to supreme meaning. I will now put forth a few postulates for the reader that might better clarify what I mean:

1. The central teaching of C. G. Jung's analytical psychology is "spiritual democracy."

2. The aim of Jung's psychology is to realize the supreme meaning of a new God-image in the individual—the Self—as a reflection of the cosmic consciousness inherent in all world religions.
3. Meaning can only be conveyed through dreams, myths, or fictions that liberate. "What we are to our inward vision, and what man appears to be *sub specie aeternitatus* can only be expressed by way of myth."[24]
4. God is at the center of all of our thoughts, and when we have discovered our supreme meaning, all of our thoughts begin to revolve around the Self like the planets around the sun.

Jung's healing fiction is a myth of meaning. It is his confession of faith, his personal story; his experience of God, revealed through a symbolic death of the hero in favor of the pluralistic *language of myths*. Such a tale is limited by the subjective factor of Jung's being in the new myth when he is creating it. "Thus it is I have now undertaken, in my eighty-third year, to tell my personal myth."[25] In telling readers his myth, Jung exclaimed further: "One must be utterly abandoned to God; nothing matters but fulfilling His will. Otherwise it is all folly and meaninglessness."[26] Thus, when we are true to the will of God, we can be assured of going the right way—the way of equality with everyone.

Obedience to the inner voice, *vocation,* is central to Jung's myth of expanded consciousness, but such obedience can also lead to fundamentalism or fanaticism in the mind of one who is in a power complex. Jung's solution to the problem of neurotic suffering came to him through his discovery of vocation as a healing path, as it might also for each of us, and this is what he offered as the *meaning cure*: "Behind the neurotic perversion is concealed his vocation, his destiny: the growth of personality, the full realization of the life-will that is inborn with the individual. It is the man without *amor fati* who is neurotic; he, truly, has missed his vocation."[27]

Here, in 1932, Jung laid down the foundation of his theory of individuation. He asserted his faith in a vocational principle that was not unique to himself alone, or to analysis, but was intrinsic to the principle of individuation as it evolves in all cultures and nationalities. The way to the supreme meaning is through the living out of our personal destiny in close relationship to the inner voice. Meaning is found in submission to our inner voice (which is identical with the voice of God, or *vox Dei*). In his autobiography, Jung took these ideas further:

Meaninglessness inhibits fullness of life and is therefore equivalent to illness. Meaning makes a great many things endurable—perhaps everything. No science will ever replace myth, and a myth cannot be made out of any science. For it is not that "God" is a myth, but that myth is the revelation of the divine life in man. It is not we who invent myth, rather it speaks to us as a Word of God.[28]

As Jung said to Max Zeller, while discussing a dream of a Jungian analyst, "Yes, you know, that is the temple we all build on. We don't know the people because, believe me, they build in India, and China and Russia and all over the world. That is the new religion. You know how long it will take until it is built? ... about six hundred years."[29] Jung meant the world, the globe; he meant everyone. We are all building on it. Jung modestly suggested that all people and, therefore, all nationalities were building on the new religion—every nation, every culture, all human groups: all were contributing to the construction of the new temple. It was and is a collective endeavor that we can all celebrate.

Moreover, traditional Christianity was, for Jung, the "absence of God," and the Church was a place where he realized he "should not go," for there was only "death."[30] Jung said even more tellingly: "My 'religion' recognized no human relationship to God, for how could one relate to something so little known as God?"[31] "Only in Meister Eckhart did I feel the breath of life."[32]

Although Jung may have intuited the experience of oneness and cosmic relatedness of all religions while reading Eckhart, it was nevertheless only at the end of World War II, after his trip to India, that he felt this unity deeply as a sacred marriage. Jung saw, then, in 1944, that there were no absolutes. There were only myths, fictions, God-images. All religions were emanations of the one myth-making function of human beings, a religious function of the psyche that dreamed the myth onward. Thus, there could be no religious superiority; for, in a true spiritual democracy, religion appears to culminate in an awareness of the immensity of consciousness in an expanding Cosmos.

In April 1939 Jung gave his remarkable lecture called "The Symbolic Life." It was delivered in London to the Guild for Pastoral Psychology. In this talk, Jung was emphatic: we all need a *symbolic life,* and because we do not have it, we get neurotic. Meaning is something that the ego needs to win through its efforts every day: "That gives peace, when people feel they are living the symbolic life, that they are actors in the divine drama. That gives the only meaning to human life; everything else is banal and you can dismiss it. A career, producing of children, are all *maya* compared with that one thing, that your life is meaningful."[33]

Of course, for some being a parent, being married, or having a career *is* their meaning in life. Nevertheless, notice that Jung inserted the word *maya* here. In "The Symbolic Life," Jung responded to a question posed by the group leader about the "next step in religious development." Jung turned the discussion, modestly, I think, to a series of stories from his clinical and personal experiences and the first was "the meditation practices in India."[34] "Religion," he said, "is careful observation of the data."[35] By emphasizing the meditation practices of Hindus and Buddhists and Muslims, Jung sought to bridge the gap between personal and cultural meaning in all nations, to make a "bridge" to the supreme meaning transparent as the way to come.

Jung added a fourth principle to the scientific triad of space, time, and causality that he called *synchronicity* in 1928 in an effort to broaden the base of his empirical understandings about the nature of the psyche and its relationship to matter[36]; he did this by positing a "coincidence in time of two or more unrelated events which have the same or a similar meaning."[37] The element of *meaning* is again crucial.

For Spiritual democracy to emerge in a way in which the personal and national Shadow do not interfere with transnational individuation, a miracle would be required. "Today," wrote Jung, "we are obliged to view the miraculous in a somewhat different light."[38] Miracles are happening all around us, every hour of the day. We only need to pay attention. The great similitude of the Cosmos is everywhere, and it needs consciousness to perceive it. Jung asked: "But why on earth should it be necessary for man to achieve, by hook or crook, a higher level of consciousness?" Today this is a critical question because we are faced with religious fundamentalism all around us. "Instead of a real answer," Jung said, "I can only make a confession of faith: I believe that, after thousands of millions of years, someone had to realize that this wonderful world of mountains and oceans, suns and moons, galaxies and nebulae, plants and animals, exists."[39]

In Jung's formulations shortly before his death what stands out is the accent he placed on *language* as the primary vehicle for effecting the

34 - The Supreme Meaning as the Bridge to What Is to Come

necessary changes that must take place if new world myths are to emerge. These myths are necessary to counter our psychic and political incapacity to control our own evil inclinations, stupidity, and immense egotism, which are currently the greatest dangers to our planet. Jung claimed we had stripped the sacred of its mystery and numinosity and that "nothing is holy any longer."[40]

> I know that the Buddhists would say, as indeed they do: if only people would follow the noble eightfold path of the Dharma (doctrine, law) and had true insight into the Self; or the Christians: if only people had right faith in the Lord; or the rationalists: if only people could be intelligent and reasonable—then all problems would be manageable and solvable. The trouble is that none of them manages to solve these problems himself.
>
> We are so captivated by and entangled in our subjective consciousness that we have simply forgotten the age-old fact that God speaks chiefly through dreams and visions. The Buddhist discards the world of unconscious fantasies as "distractions" and useless illusions; the Christian puts his Church and his Bible between himself and his unconscious.[41]

Because the world's religions have not retained much of their "original numinosity," Jung insisted we needed to return to the personal wisdom of our own "original revelations" to uncover the truths in our own individual Selfhood as a species. By this, Jung meant that "infantile memories" still contained imprints of "archetypal modes of psychic functioning." To open our minds to the primary channels or psychic gateways leading toward "a greater extension of consciousness," we must penetrate to the core of meaning contained in such memories.[42]

Jung described how he did this in *MDR* by drawing attention to his first dream of individuation from his third year, the dream of the underground phallus standing upright on a royal throne. This God-image conveyed to him a supreme meaning, and its eye of consciousness at the top of its head pointed him to the way that is to come. The way to come became, for Jung, the way to expanded consciousness, extending to the vast Cosmos. Thus, remembering our dreams from when we were little children can help us create new fictions that *heal*. Jung was at pains to point out further: "man today is painfully aware of the fact that neither his great religions nor his various philosophies seem to provide him with those powerful ideas that would give him the certainty and security he needs in face of the present condition of the world."[43]

As any change must begin somewhere, Jung believed that only the single individual would undergo it and carry it through. *The change must begin with one sole individual, and it might be any one of us.* "Nobody can afford to look around and wait for somebody else to do what he is loath to do himself. As nobody knows what he could do, he might be bold to ask himself whether by any chance his unconscious might know something helpful, when there is no satisfactory conscious answer anywhere in sight."[44]

When you vocalize the power of spiritual democracy, you're going to be challenged to communicate words from the core of your heart-center. Spiritual democracy is a calling to speak out of the depths of the psychological Self within and without, while remaining empathic during moral considerations. Spiritual democracy is an attempt to treat all religious paths and psychologies as equals. It is not a system of national preferences and arguments about God or psychology based on locality. Spiritual democracy is a way to practice religious tolerance without putting anyone else's religious beliefs or psychological practices down. Spiritual semocracy says: When we disagree about God, politics, or psychology why argue about it? Let's celebrate the supreme in the other person's standpoint and not judge, as if we know whose psychology is right, whose is wrong. The impulse to correct an outer attitude toward religion or psychology is typically patterned on a power motive. Analyze the power problem and let go the argument. Vocalizing the way of spiritual democracy is a psychological calling from the Self in all of us. It exists as a potential in each and every human heart.

The aim of spiritual democracy is to encourage the movement toward peace with three simple words: *liberty, compassion,* and *equality.* American poetry uncovered the roots of spiritual democracy in the religious clauses of the US Constitution, but modern psychology (James and Jung) added to what the founding fathers and poets left out. Spiritual democracy is the *archetype of all archetypes* because it includes all religious ideas and psychologies in an experience of the Self, which transcends all possible categories of thought.

Spiritual democracy is an archetype of compassion and love. It is a God-image of world peace. Poets of America speak out of the same indigenous foundation that shaped the direction of democracy, the writing of the US Constitution and the Bill of Rights. Fundamentalism cannot exist where spiritual democracy is made manifest in the body politic. In a spiritual democracy, there is nothing to argue about. Let theologians argue about God; James and Jung gave no arguments. They did not debate about God; they were silent. They *saw*. Jung advised that as readers we, too, would be wise to look to our dreams and visions and meditations for inner guidance. We need to move beyond belief, beyond faith, to an *experience* of the unity of the Self.

Notes

1. In Jung's lectures in London at the Institute for Medical Psychology in 1935, he spelled out precisely what he meant: "I consider my contribution to psychology to be my subjective confession. It is my personal psychology, my prejudice that I see things in such and such a way... So far as we admit our personal prejudice, we are really contributing towards an objective psychology." See Jung, "The Tavistock Lectures," CW 18, ¶275.
2. Jung, "On the Nature of the Psyche," CW 8, ¶342.
3. Jung, *MDR*, 16.
4. Jung, *MDR*, 17.
5. Jung, *The Red Book*, 229.
6. Whitman, *Notebooks and Unpublished Prose Manuscripts,* vol. 6, 2043.
7. Davis, *Religion and the Continental Congress 1774–1776*, 97.
8. Davis, 99.
9. Jung, "Psychology and Religion (The Terry Lectures)," CW 11, ¶¶6, 8.
10. Jung, "Richard Wilhelm: In Memoriam," CW 15, ¶¶74–96.
11. Jung, "Psychotherapists and the Clergy," CW 11, ¶494.
12. Jung, CW 11, ¶496.
13. Jung, CW 11, ¶497.
14. Jung, CW 11, ¶498.
15. Lao Tzu, from Wayley, *The Way and Its Power;* quoted in Jung, "Synchronicity," CW 8, ¶918.
16. Jung, CW 11, ¶498.
17. Jung, CW 11, ¶509.
18. Jung, *Psychology of the Unconscious,* 300.

19. Jung, *Symbols of Transformation*, CW 5, ¶299.
20. Buttimer, "Beyond Humboldtian Science and Goethe's Way of Science, 114; quoted in Walls, *The Passage to Cosmos*, 217.
21. Jung, CW 11, ¶494.
22. Jung, *MDR*, xii.
23. Jung, *MDR*, vi.
24. Jung, *MDR*, 3.
25. Jung *MDR*, 3.
26. Jung, *MDR*, 40.
27. Jung, "The Development of Personality," CW 17, ¶313.
28 Jung, *MDR*, 340.
29. Zeller, *The Dream*, 2.
30. Jung, *MDR*, 55.
31. Jung, *MDR*, 56, 57.
32. Jung, *MDR*, 68.
33. Jung, "The Symbolic Life," CW 18, ¶630.
34. Jung, CW 18, ¶626.
35. Jung, CW 18, ¶673.
36. Jung, CW 18, ¶958.
37. Jung, CW 18, ¶849.
38. Jung, CW 18, ¶995.
39. Jung, "Psychological Aspects of the Mother Archetype," CW 9i, ¶177.
40. Jung, "The Tavistock Lectures," CW 18, ¶254.
41. Jung, CW 18, ¶262.
42. Jung, CW 18, ¶259.
43. Jung, CW 18, ¶261.
44. Jung, CW 18, ¶261.

Chapter 35

THE RELIGIOUS FUNCTION OF SPIRITUAL DEMOCRACY

The Jungian field is at a crossroads today. In the summer of 2015, I presented my paper "C. G. Jung's Vision of Spiritual Democracy" at the IAAP/IAJS Conference at Yale University, where, in 1937, Jung spoke to a crowd of 2500 people on psychology and religion.[1] A question considered at the 2015 conference was whether Jung's writings on the religious function of the psyche should be revised by contemporary Jungians. In two previous books, *Walt Whitman: Shamanism, Spiritual Democracy, and the World Soul* and *Emily Dickinson: A Medicine Woman for Our Times,* I have shown how this might be done based on the writings of these early American visionaries who charted a way for the journey forward.

In this book, I've shown why: *the religious function is a Cosmic function, a function of the Universal Self.* It is a function of harmonization among all religions of the globe operating in a cooperative way toward the unification of the World Self and ultimate Peace. Jung called it the *transcendent function.* It was not Jung's vocation to extend his hypothesis of the religious function to the United States; that is our task, I believe, as American Jungians. The religious function of the American psyche was shaped by the spirit of the mind and earth. It is the still living function of equality that we must heed today or face the possibility of self-annihilation. The religious function is the Universal principle of Equality that gave birth to all religions. Religions are spiritual realities. Jung's hypothesis of the religious function might be revised accordingly to include an answer not only to the West, but also to Islamic countries, India, Korea, China, and Japan. As Jungians today, we must give a broader answer to humanity. The religious function can come to us from afar, penetrate us through the words of a spiritual teacher, enter our psyches from without. This is what happened when Jung met James. For Nature's God is the religious function and the transcendent function; there is no distinction: the inner and outer are One.

Jung's reflections on the religious function have to be broadened to include the Cosmos and Earth in our scientific theories if we are to advance as post-Jungians to a more all-inclusive view of the nature of peacekeeping in the transnational debates that are building in the world right now. Why should one national power rule the earth? To internationalize religion, in the spirit of democracy, we must establish peace within ourselves first: we must make our homes a living harmony between what is most sacred and what is becoming increasingly profane by the day. Religion, now mostly profane, is becoming more meaningless with the profanity of evil regimes and fundamentalist creeds pretending to be religious. The religious function has little to do with creeds. It is above creeds; it is Cosmic. The Self is the ultimate function. Psyche and Cosmos are One. There is no distinction.

Liberty is the beginning of democracy. *The science of spiritual democracy is derived from the most ancient reservoirs of speech. It will not stand for imitation, only for what is most unique and original in our own personalities.* It is not the God of Judaism, Christianity, Vedanta, or Islam that is supreme over all else; it is the notion of the One, of vast unity in multiplicity; that's the Supreme worthy of the name.

We need to take Jung's project further in the West. Eastern spirituality—Yoga and Buddhism—are quite popular in parts of the United States. In writing of this book I am striving toward a vision of Democratic Spirituality that does not split East and West. From a spiritually democratic point of view, Jung's *Red Book* was an attempt to carve out his own myth. He later called it his myth of meaning. But Jung was not the first to bring spiritual democracy to the United States or Europe. Moreover, Jung was unable to always maintain a spiritually democratic outlook in his writings. My point is that to move toward a notion of spiritual democracy in the United States, we have to shed European biases based on a preference for one myth of God over others. To reach a truly transnational audience that is universally democratic, we have to see that Self-realization can happen in any nation, any land, at any age, regardless of one's place of birth, or the particular piece of earth on which one is living.

In the history of world religions, the time has come to move toward a democratic spirituality. William James's book *The Varieties of Religious Experience* was a first attempt by an American to arrive at a truly democratic attitude of religious experience common to all people. This is a place of universal agreement, a place of commonality, a transnational vista.

Everywhere we look in the Middle East today, whether in Jerusalem, Iraq, Afghanistan, or Syria, we see ongoing religious wars. They call strong attention to the fact that we are not in harmony with ourselves as a species and that the real problem today is not just a psychological and political problem; it's a spiritual problem. No religion can survive in an atmosphere of spiritual democracy if its dogmas and doctrines and politics and economies are based on ignorance and intolerance and war. All human wars must end, as the great Hebrew prophet Isaiah said (Isaiah 2:2–4). This is the land of peace in every nation. This is the place of democratic equality between all human beings, regardless of gender, regardless of sexual orientation, regardless of race, regardless of ethnicity, regardless of culture, regardless of religion.

For spiritual democracy to exist, we need to move, therefore, to a common place of respect and reverential acceptance of the beliefs of others, with one notable exception—those national groups presuming to be religious, those who preach peace but declare Jihad, Crusades, or Holy Wars against the movement of a truly democratic spirituality, which is for the people, by the people, and ultimately the light of universal healing, peace, and prosperity for all people. This is the light ignited by the torch of Liberty.

The new myth that is truly democratic because it is tolerant toward all religions allows for liberty and freedom in the domain of religion. It rejects no religion—and it is founded on the science of the Cosmos. This foundation-stone has the power to transform nations.

Spiritual democracy is the center of peacemaking in each of us as individuals, and it is the same principle that guides the United Nations and the Parliament of World Religions. The keynote is that we are zeroing in on a concept that has the potential to unite all nations. It begins with the fight with the Shadow within, through a turning of our warlike instincts inward, toward the enemy in the psyche of every person; through an introversion of human aggression, malice, and hatred.

When that happens in the collectivity in a true society of democracy, then and only then can spiritual democracy emerge in a global culture where evil gets its due, where envy and viciousness are part of the shadow we must confront, and, because it is in need, of our greatest understanding and compassion too. We must make friends with the adversary within us, as Jung taught, and stop projecting it outward onto other nations, religious groups, and ethnicities. It starts with a psychological inventory, where the shadow is grappled with and wrestled to the ground. It commences with the turning of the sword of violence inward. We must learn to take in the arrows.

At the base of the psyche, beyond the relative and empirical domains, is a much deeper stratum of the Self that extends into the very depths of the Cosmos. Here psyche is the Universe: The Cosmic Deity that created this vast and beautiful order through an initially chaotic Big Bang. When projections are pointed at the Shadow in our own hearts, then the libido may stream downward or upward to the infinite and boundless stretches of a universe that embraces over two billion galaxies, black holes, and endless chaos that is forever being turned into a beautiful Cosmos of order and ultimate meaning.

So, too, in the human soul. For Jung, democracy is a mitigated state of internal civil war, whether in an individual or in nations. Democracy requires constant struggle and negotiations if we are to maintain internal and national peace in ourselves, in the United States, India, Pakistan, Europe, the Middle East, Asia, and other parts of the world. Democracy is a psychological institution first and foremost, and there can be no outer order if individuals who are to lead us are in states of disorder, if their psyches are at war, and if the moral condition of society is in a chaotic state of division and unrest. Democracy does not start with peace; it starts with external and internal civil war. This is a psychic and a political fact; it is also a fact of the Cosmos. Spiritual democracy is in a constant condition of change and transformation, just as it is in all human beings who breathe on this miraculous planet spinning in space around the fireball of a star that is but a wee speck in our Milky Way.

The aim of analytical psychology is to trace the forces of evil inside us to the warlike source of aggression within, to the very impulse of violence in our warlike instincts. We think of the religious function as the transcendent function or God-function that integrates good and evil at a high moral vista, which is a relativistic domain of empirical depth psychology. Yet, the religious function is more than merely relative; it is also, without doubt, absolute. The absolute might become an object of investigation for the field of analytical psychology if its analysis of the world's religions is to reach the masses in a fuller way and if its tools are to be serviceable for science. For creeds as well as those who have lost their faith in religious organizations need the new medicine psychology has to offer. Half the world is still conventionally religious and psychology cannot neglect to speak to the masses who believe.

Our task is to educate the public on the nature of the psyche, which includes Jews and Christians, Hindus and Muslims. Insofar as the individual gives birth to the Self in society, the values he or she creates are objective in this sense: they express individual truths, ideals, beliefs, ethics, and new values.

It is clear that Jung's vision of spiritual democracy is more evolved than anybody else's in the field of psychology. The concept of the collective unconscious and the Self were, however, limited by his myth of meaning in *Answer to Job*.[2] His focus on the transformation of the Judeo-Christian myth was not wide enough to reach the world. That is why we need to revise his ideas about the religious function. The hypothesis of a religious function was subject to a scientific limitation in Jung's calculations. On the other hand, we would be wise to take Jung's prescriptions in his Kundalini Seminars into careful account, so the ego and the body and Shadow and Earth are not left out.

Spiritual democracy is not theology; it is psychology: the only psychology that makes any sense to me of mass shooters driven by supremist ideologies; the slaughter of innocents, in marketplaces and concert halls and schools, at churches and synagogues and temples, whether here in the United States or in the Middle East or the cities of Europe; the rise of nationalism and authoritarianism around the world.

In my view, the world needs the *medicine of spiritual democracy*, which is also Sufi medicine, Hindu medicine, Jewish medicine, Christian medicine, Taoist medicine, Buddhist medicine, and also Native American, Indigenous, and Islamic medicine. This universal medicine is the medicine Jung dipped his hands into when he wrote from the river of peace, which is the Self.

Thus, from a psychological standpoint, God is comprised of many images of the Self and the aim of Jungian analysis is to discover one's own personal image of Divinity. What God is remains eternally unknowable. Together, the God-images of all nations make up the spiritual democracy of humanity.

Kabir says:

> Neither a Hindu
> Not a Muslim am I!
> The god of Hindus resides in a temple;
> The god of Muslims resides in a mosque.
> Who resides there
> Where there are no temples
> Nor mosques?[3]

Notes

1. The IAAP is the International Association of Analytic Psychology and the IAJS is the International Association of Jungian Studies.
2. Jung, "Answer to Job," CW 11. *Answer to Job* was first published as a book, *Anwort an Hiob,* in Zürich in 1952.
3. Kumar, *The Vision of Kabir,* 31.

Chapter 36

Self and Cosmos in Jung's Writing

While preparing some lecture notes for my presentation at Yale University on July 11, 2015, I reviewed some of Jung's references on the Self and Cosmos to clarify how his ideas about the collective unconscious expanded over time to include the infinite.[1] Jung's reading of William James clearly helped him extend his thoughts about the human psyche to include the entire Universe.[2] I present my findings in this chapter to demonstrate why a transpersonal approach to the problem of the Self clarifies how Jung's ideas evolved over time. As Jung wrote in *Memories, Dreams, Reflections:*

> The decisive question for man is: Is he related to something infinite or not? That is the telling question of his life. Only if we know that the thing which truly matters is the infinite can we avoid fixing our interest upon futilities, and upon all kinds of goals which are not of real importance… If we understand and feel that here in this life we already have a link with the infinite, desires and attitudes change.… Our psyche is set up in accord with the structure of the universe, and what happens in the macrocosm likewise happens in the infinitesimal and most subjective recesses of the psyche.[3]

Meaning, therefore, is always ultimately cosmic meaning, a *feeling for the infinite.* Embodying the infinite in our relationships, in our solitude, and in our active life suggests that meaning is really about inhabiting the principle of spaciousness while being bounded to the ego to the utmost, for the infinite is the immeasurable depths of the Cosmos. We must be grounded and limited to manifest our life's callings. In Jung's later writings, Cosmos and Self are One. This is the Supreme Meaning Jung set out to chart in *The Red Book,* although the origins of his quest are not always made transparent.

As I've detailed, he paid a very high tribute to William James. In *A Pluralistic Universe,* James asserted, "We finite minds may simultaneously be co-conscious with one another in a superhuman intelligence" and there was, to his mind, no "absolutely totalized all-enveloper."[4] For James "supernormal facts" provided the "strongest suggestions in favor of a superior co-consciousness being possible."[5] As Jung acknowledged, James's far-reaching mind helped him understand that the unconscious extended to the Cosmos.

In 1950, Jung chiseled a beautiful monument out of stone on Lake Zürich, the Bollingen Stone. Jung's inscription reads: "This is Telesphoros, who roams through the dark regions of this cosmos and glows like a star out of the depths."[6] The image of Telesphoros on the Bollingen Stone is in the form of a mandala (*mandala* is the Sanskrit word for "circle"). The child at the center of this stone structure represents the Self, a traveler through the Cosmos at the center. Obviously, the Cosmos meant much more to Jung than his psychological theories often attest. Without doubt, it formed the *nucleus* of his vision, his sense of *equality* with everything that is—rivers, earth, stones, stars, galaxies, animals, fish, kingfisher, suns, trees, mountains, and air. He created a universe of meaning out of the chaotic forces of meaninglessness that assailed him and much of the world through two devastating World Wars. His conviction that his life in relation to the forces of the collective unconscious had a goal, a spiritual purpose, a *telos* that would eventually emerge in a vision of unitary awareness for the future of humankind preserved him throughout his excursions into the Self. Dreams, drawings, and dialogues with imaginary figures (such as Philemon) created doorways into the Cosmos, which he could no longer distinguish clearly from archetypal fantasies. Fantasy thinking itself seemed, at times, to proceed as if through a window of eternity into his conscious perceptions, and this transparency gave the archetypes a universal significance. "All consciousness separates; but in dreams we put on the likeness of that more universal, truer, more eternal man dwelling in the darkness of primordial night. There he is still the whole, and the whole is in him, indistinguishable from all nature and bare of all egohood. It is from these all-uniting depths that the dream arises."[7]

In the all-uniting depths of night, Cosmos and Self were one indistinguishable whole: an interconnected microcosm and macrocosm. For Jung the Self was a nocturnal atmosphere, an unknown quality of the world that we breathe while we sleep, a universal substrate present in the environment. In a 1948 letter to Canon H. G. England, he wrote, "If you call it the universal consciousness we cannot contradict you, we can only confess our ignorance as to its real state. But if you call it universal consciousness, then it is the universal consciousness of God."[8] Here, Jung appeared to be bordering on a metaphysical definition of consciousness to complement his otherwise relativistic and psychological views as an empirical scientist. The universal consciousness of God is an idea found throughout much of Jung's works from 1911 onward. The link between soul or psyche, Self and Cosmos, was already in the air when Jung emerged on the world scene with his theory of complexes in 1902, the same year James published *The Varieties of Religious Experience*.

As readers of Jung, we've been conditioned to look at the collective unconscious as a place where consciousness enters through dreams—a journey downward into the underworld, a movement of psychic energy inward, or below, into the immeasurable depths within. Yet the way to psyche also leads us upward, into the higher atmosphere above us, far, far aloft our heads, into the very zenith of fathomless space. The word *immeasurable* suggests the infinite, incalculable, endless distances. Yet, in a pivotal passage in Jung's essay "Psychology and Religion," written in English and delivered in 1937 at Yale, he wrote: "The medieval representations of the circle are based on the idea of the microcosm, a concept that was also applied to the stone. The stone was a 'little world' like man himself, a sort of inner image of the cosmos, reaching not into immeasurable distances but into an equally immeasurable depth-dimension, i.e., from the smallest to the unimaginably smallest."[9] Later, however, during his mystical visions in 1944, Jung found himself floating in space, at a height of about one thousand miles, from where he could see the snow-covered Himalayas. From this great height the earth was the most glorious thing he had ever seen. Standing in space with his back to the Indian Ocean, a tremendous block of stone entered his field of vision like a meteorite; it was about the size of his house, or larger, and it reminded him of similar tawny granite stones he had seen off the coast of the Gulf of Bengal, stones that had been hollowed out into temples.[10] He had gone, in other words, from the subjective and relative space of ego-consciousness into a reflection on his entire life in a moment of Absolute Self-Consciousness in the vastness of space.

Jung was aware from his wide readings and his travels to the East that temples in India were miniature representations of the Universe. Yet, in his telling of his personal myth in *Memories, Dreams, Reflections,* we can see that his empirical mind was in search of what his intuition already knew about the infinite and finite, above and below, time and timelessness, inside and outside, Cosmos and Self: the relative and Absolute exist side-by-side. Jung said so when leaving his empirical self behind in "Life After Death": "I have been convinced that at least part of our psychic existence is characterized by a relativity of space and time. This relativity seems to increase, in proportion to the distance from consciousness, to an absolute condition of timelessness and spacelessness."[11]

Jung maintained a life-long interest in parapsychology, theology, Hindu and Buddhist philosophy, Christian mysticism, and matters pertaining to the Absolute alongside his interests in investigations into empirical reality. For Jung, the relative and Absolute formed a pair of complementary opposites, even if he limited himself mostly to studying the empirical self.

In his 1946 essay "The Psychology of the Transference," he wrote similarly about the nondual unity of the Self as it pertained to experiences of individuation in any person undergoing an analysis: "And just as the cosmos is not a dissolving mass of particles, but rests in the unity of God's embrace, so man must not dissolve into a world of warring possibilities and tendencies imposed on him by the unconscious, but must become the unity that embraces them all."[12] We must become, in other words, the empirical unity that embraces the warring possibilities and tendencies imposed on us by the unconscious, just as the Universe rests in the unitary embrace of God.

Jung spoke further of the unconscious as displaying an indisputable "cosmic" character.[13] When he referred to the Cosmic aspect of the Self, therefore, he meant the totality of the infinite within as well as what transcends our conscious vision without, a boundless *transmarginal* experience. "We are not in a position to set any bounds to the self... We may be able to indicate the limits of consciousness, but the unconscious is simply the unknown psyche and for the very reason illimitable because indeterminable."[14] The *indeterminable* is again a Jamesian concept: "The important fact which this 'field' formula commemorates is the indetermination of the margin."[15]

Although the Self has no bounds of depth or height, and although it can never be known directly through our intellect, it can be experienced through *imagination*. As James said, "Empirical methods tend to connect men in imagination."[16] Imagination is the mythopoetic function of the mind that makes the infinite comprehensible; through the imaginative function of the Self, the window on eternity can swing open to give us a view of transcendent Reality, as it did for the alchemists: "The *imaginatio*, as the alchemists understand it, is in truth a key that opens the door to the secret of the opus."[17]

One way to create order out of disorder, Jung said, is by creating a mandala: "As magic circles they bind and subdue the lawless powers belonging to the world of darkness, and depict or create an order that transforms the chaos into a cosmos."[18] In "The Meaning of Psychology for Modern Man," Jung wrote, "At the lowest and most primitive level we would find a sort of generalized or cosmic consciousness, with complete unconsciousness of the subject."[19] Jung's idea that cosmic consciousness is completely unconscious in subjects has been the subject of speculation by Hindu scholars who have attempted to read Jung.

In Sulagna Sengupta's words, however, "Jung's final musings about the East were laden with hope—he remained in anticipation of the as yet undiscovered understanding between West and East and an as yet unrealized psychology that would incorporate the spiritual attitude of East and dynamic Western scientific spirit."[20] Something beautiful is, indeed, happening in the world in our millennial children. It happened in my analytic discussion with an eleven-year-old boy. What he told me was revolutionary as far as the archetype of spiritual democracy goes. He said that although his mother is Jewish and his father is Christian, he sees himself as a Buddhist now. When I asked him how he had come to this realization, he replied, "I think the Buddha was reincarnated into the life of Abraham Lincoln because they both believed that all people are created equal." "Wow!" I thought quietly to myself, "That's spiritual democracy!" He said this while making a sandplay. He knew nothing about my interests in this subject, nothing about what I was thinking or writing about outside of therapy. This is democratic spirituality American style from the mouth of a boy verging on adolescence. He came to this understanding completely on his own, without a priest or rabbi or swami to teach him. He only cited the inspiration of a Japanese novelist he had recently read and did not name, which had led him to embrace Buddhism. Yet no apparent book-knowledge led him to link Buddha with Lincoln around the American ideal of spiritual *equality*. His idea neither was a completely original thought nor was it really new. His innate wisdom spoke directly out of the archetype of the American psyche and the World Soul. Equality among religions, races, and nationalities is the key. Spiritual democracy is in this sense not a faith; it is not a religion; it never will be. It is outside religion, outside psychology, outside politics. It is simply a psychological attitude transcendent of all beliefs. When I asked the boy, "Do you really think Buddha believed all people are equal and capable of Enlightenment?" he said confidently and without blinking, "I think he did!" This is what spiritual democracy means, and he did not need a long-winded theological treatise to prove it.

Child cases such as this have taught me we are all part of a universal consciousness that we share as a human species despite any cultural divisions of race, nationality, or religion.

NOTES

1. My paper "C. G. Jung's Vision of Spiritual Democracy" was presented at the Fourth Joint Conference of the IAAP & IAJS, "Psyche, Spirit, and Science: Negotiating Contemporary Social and Cultural Concerns," at Yale University, on July 11, 2015.
2. On the opening page of *Pragmatism,* James defined a philosophy of life as "our sense of what life really means; it is our individual way of seeing and feeling the total push and pressure of the cosmos." See James, *Writings 1902–1910,* 487.
3. Jung, *MDR,* 325, 335.
4. James, *Writing, 1902–1910,* 764.
5. James, 766.
6. Jung, *MDR,* 227.
7. Jung, "The Meaning of Psychology for Modern Man," CW 10, ¶¶304, 305.
8. Jung, *Letters,* vol. 1, 484.
9. Jung, "Psychology and Religion (The Terry Lectures)," CW 11, ¶155.
10. Jung, *MDR,* 290, 291.

11. Jung, *MDR,* 304, 305.
12. Jung, "The Psychology of the Transference," CW 16, ¶397.
13. Jung, "Individual Dream Symbolism in Relation to Alchemy," CW 12, ¶226.
14. Jung, ¶247.
15. James, *Writings 1902–1910,* 214.
16. James, 774.
17. Jung, "Religious Ideas in Alchemy," CW 12, ¶400.
18. Jung, *Aion,* CW 9ii, ¶60.
19. Jung, CW 10, ¶281.
20. Sengupta, *Jung in India,* 243.

Chapter 37

VOCATIONAL DREAMS AND SYNCHRONICITY

Heeding vocational dreams and outer *synchronistic events* during crucial moments of change can help us move toward the realization of our life's essential purpose, or supreme meaning. As an archetype of destiny, the *vocational archetype* can lead to rapid inspirations and creative renewals that may be life-altering and consciousness-changing. Relief may come with the recognition that we have found a way to stay connected, linked, or attuned to the rhythms of the Self. *Vocational dreams* open new possibilities for relationships with the outer figures in our lives and purposeful channels for sacred work; as such, they can turn existential crises, doubt, and despair into hope through spiritual metamorphosis. Transformation, in a Jungian sense, involves a metamorphosis from a career-orientation to a vocational-orientation, where the aim is placed on ever-increasing Self-awareness, which springs from our deepest and highest sense of well-being. Understanding the relationship between vocational dreams and meaningful chance (what Jung called *synchronicity*) can be of great benefit during the passage from disorder to order during midlife's transformations. Rather than attempt to make metaphysical assertions about the nature of reality, Jung spoke as an empirical psychologist about the "reality of the psyche." From a close reading of *Memories, Dreams, Reflections,* we can clearly see that dreams are primarily how the Self gives voice to the path of destiny.

Jung designated the age of thirty-five to be the onset of midlife. When Jung was thirty-four and thirty-five years old, he traveled to the United States. Using Jung's life as a model, therefore, those years not only corresponded with his first two trips to the US, but also with his two chance meetings with William James. The subsequent transformations in his life followed between 1911 and 1917. Thus, Jung's entrance into midlife led him to advance the field of psychology in a totally new direction. William James was, for Jung, a *Self-figure:* someone in whom the Self had been actualized to a marked degree and in whom its psychological and spiritual vitality was awakened. James gave Jung a spiritual exemplar to look up to in the field of psychology. As Jung's senior by thirty-five years, James embodied an archetype Jung called the *wise old man*. As the father of American psychology, James embodied the archetype of an old philosopher-sage. The year 1909 marked a significant turning point, therefore, in the development of Jung's personality, where the religious function of his psyche that had been seeking to become Self-realized was activated in his outer relationship with William James.

Jung "made a very pleasant impression" on James.[1] Their meaningful moments of meeting at Clark University were itself a synchronicity, a chance encounter with Jung's destiny-pattern as a religious psychologist. Jung, of course, was not looking for a father figure in James, but the meeting may have activated the archetype of the *spiritual grandfather* in Jung.

James was very close friends with Jung's mentor in Geneva, Switzerland, Theodore Flournoy—another important synchronicity. Jung's life and work were directed by a single urge to wholeness. Seen in its totality, the *plurality of patterns of vocational activity* in the Self formed some primary channels through which the latent seeds of Jung's personality could develop into their fully Self-realized forms. How such patterns of vocational activity were lived out and realized *pluralistically* by Jung is a topic for another study. Suffice it to say, Jung's decision to become a psychiatrist emerged, however, after two significant life-events that changed the course of his education in early adulthood and led to the fulfillment of his destined vocation as a medical doctor. The first event, a vocational dream, marked the first chapter of Jung's calling in early adulthood. The second event was his chance meeting with William James.

The first episode was marked by two significant dreams that had a clarifying effect on Jung's future vocational direction. In the first dream, *Jung was digging in a burial mound and found some bones of prehistoric animals in the earth*. In the second dream, *Jung dreamt of a giant radiolarian shimmering with opalescent hues in a dark circular pool of water in a dark wood*. After these dreams, Jung decided overwhelmingly in favor of science; they removed all of his doubts.[2] The second dream was Jung's clearest example of a vocational dream during this transitional period. Another major vocational event in Jung's life consisted of the sudden insight or intuition, which came to him like "a flash of illumination," while reading a book by Krafft-Ebing on nervous disorders. This *numinous* moment confirmed for Jung that his only possible goal was psychiatry.[3]

Both inner and outer events—two vocational dreams and a third outer discovery of a book in his chosen field of study, psychiatry—had a clarifying effect on his future vocation. What interests me here are the *correspondences* between the first two examples of vocational dreams and the third example of an outer event (the chance discovery of a book by Krafft-Ebing—an unmistakable instance of what Jung called *synchronicity*).

Such occurrences crossed Jung's path at precisely the right moment in time: his psyche was ripe for vocational activation, and his consciousness was open to a subsequent vocational clarification. To follow a dream or vision with such instinctive certainty is the only possible way ahead during times of liminality. If a person says "Yes," he or she may be saved from the probability of a bad neurosis. If the person says "No" to destiny, due to the interference of childhood complexes, or conventional one-sidedness stemming from a too-close adherence to the spirit of the times, he or she may become neurotic, and symptoms of anxiety and depression, doubt and despair, loss of soul, and meaninglessness may result.

According to Jung, "By far the greatest number of spontaneous synchronistic phenomenon that I have had the occasion to observe and analyze can easily be shown to have a direct connection with an archetype." Such a connecter "is an irrepresentable, psychoid factor of the collective unconscious."[4] As we've seen, Jung got his idea of the transmarginal psychophysical field from James: "What we conceptually identify ourselves with and say we are thinking of at any time is the centre; but our *full* self is the whole field . . . Every bit of us at every moment is part and parcel of a wider self."[5]

Whenever Jungians speak of different forms of vocational activity in the world, therefore, we're speaking of instinctual patterns of behavior first and foremost, what ethologists have called *Innate Releasing Mechanisms (IRMs)*. IRMs are essentially what Jung called *archetypes,* coinciding with existing *instincts of activity*. Such inner images of instinctual activity are often associated with *acausal instances of meaningful chance in areas of an individual's predestined vocation*. In other words, the full self/Self is the whole field in which synchronicities frequently take place.

Jung was called from childhood to be a religious psychologist first and foremost. This archetype was not switched on fully until he stepped foot in the United States, however. There is often a direct correspondence between images of vocational activity and a synchronistic phenomenon in the world. Such coincidences demonstrate clearly a noncausal parallelism between psychic and psychophysical events occurring simultaneously in time,[6] *or long after such dreams were dreamt.*

You might ask yourself, for instance, when noticing synchronicities: *What does such a meaningful chance correspondence connote? What is its meaning in the overall pattern of my life?*

To enter into an inner dialogue with the Self, we can employ what Jung called *active imagination,* a dialogue with our interlocutor. By addressing questions to various representations of wisdom in the psyche, the Self may provide multiple answers: maybe it means this, maybe it means that. We don't always know at first a vocational dream's implication, yet, an entrance into unknowability, where the rational functions are thrown into confusion and we have to pause awhile in emptiness, quieting the mind's restless activities, can lead to a sudden irrational hunch, or sense of knowing, which springs from a place of grounding in the personality: the place of the Self. *Its calling is to materialize natural patterns of work and significance in the world through a positive and progressive process of psychological spiritualization of the instincts that may lead us eventually and if we are lucky to an experience of wholeness.* Such chance occurrences with figures of destiny may lead to sudden reversals of misfortune; they can change bad luck into good fortune, or awaken an experience of feeling suddenly blessed by God, or Nature.

Jung pointed out that every archetype carries with it a *feeling-toned* quality that results from an intensity of affect or *numinosity* that can be immediately sensed. Whenever this occurs, we can follow, with loyal trust, a guiding light arising from the Self. The dynamic instinctual and spiritual energy-charge operating in the central nervous system from the *Self's vocational activity* is subsequently freed up by emergent images that play a highly important role in helping us confirm our vocational path, particularly when such an experience is accompanied by an inner experience of *knowing.* A foreknowledge of some kind, or a visionary sense of futurity, may sometimes be directly felt in the Body Self.

In *Memories, Dreams, Reflections,* Jung recorded many examples of a miraculous mirroring of a vocational dream, a synchronistic phenomenon in Nature, where the dividing lines between inner and outer reality were completely cancelled out in a *numinous unitary experience* of Oneness. These narrative descriptions captured beautifully his first encounter with his inner guide, wise old man figure, or spiritual guru—Philemon. Philemon came to Jung in a dream state while he was composing his *Black Books*. (Philemon evolved out of the figure *Atmavictu*.) Jung did not understand his Philemon dream at first, so he painted his Spirit in order to etch a portrait of the inner dream-image upon his memory. In the dream, *Philemon appeared to Jung with kingfisher's wings with its characteristic colors*. During the days in which Jung was preoccupied with painting this inner dream image, he found in his garden by the lakeshore a dead kingfisher. Upon seeing this lifeless bird, Jung was "thunderstruck," for kingfishers were quite rare in the Zürich vicinity, and he never again found another kingfisher.[7] Jung's choice of the word *thunderstruck* is telling here, for he was in a numinous state during his passage through midlife. Lightning is a frequent symbol for the Self's sudden emergence.

Jung looked to mentors—Bleuler, Freud, Flournoy—as models for his calling as a medical doctor and psychotherapist prior to his trip to the United States. At Clark University in 1909, he had the good fortune of meeting William James. This fortuitous meeting helped release an inner image of the Sage-philosopher inside of Jung, an archetypal aptitude that had been present since his birth and that he had first found in the figure of Meister Eckhart, the model for his *Spiritual Self*.

Flournoy and James were later models for professors, philosophers, and psychologists who looked at *psi phenomena*—telepathy, extrasensory perception, precognition, clairvoyance, or near-death experiences that fall within the field of parapsychology—from a *detached* place of understanding without being biased by any preconceived theories or notions. Although typically considered a "pseudoscience" by a majority of mainstream academic institutions, at the inception of the field of transpersonal psychology, inaugurated by James and Jung, such phenomena were considered valid functions of study within the wider breadth of psychology's domain. Freud, on the other hand, was biased by his sexual theories; whereas Flournoy and James were interested primarily in objective cognition. These latter two figures played a role in releasing a vocational archetype in Jung's psyche, which had long been slumbering in the innermost depths of his being. This archetype of wisdom emerged as Jung's Spiritual Self, Philemon.

Philemon was an image of Jung's *Psychological Self*, which spoke to him in an objective manner as a conveyer of absolute knowledge of his personality. Jung was at pains to point out in *MDR* that Philemon led him to an awareness of objective cognition or "the reality of the psyche." In other words, Philemon taught Jung to understand that his dreams, visions, and the imaginations were *not* what is commonly referred to as daydreams; *they were far more meaningful than that.* They were links between psyche and world, subjective and objective meaning, Self and Cosmos. Insofar as the instinctive concomitant of the Philemon dream manifested itself in the world of matter (such as in the miraculous appearance of the dead kingfisher in his garden), Philemon was, in effect, beyond the psychic. He was also simultaneously in matter, a psyche-world correlate. As an inner guru and guide to the Spiritual Self, Philemon was a link to what Jung called the *psychoid*.

In my empirical research of vocational dreams at UC Santa Cruz and John F. Kennedy University, in Orinda, California, I came upon this category of psychoid experience: the *vocational symbol*, or archetype, which seemed to suggest a hidden line of correspondence between dreams and environmental reality. The two worlds—inner and outer—appeared to be linked together in a common likeness of metaphor and objective meaning that seemed highly improbable from a statistical standpoint.

For instance, I had hundreds of dreams about California kingsnakes, which I had caught as a boy. I observed them in nature in the hills of Contra Costa County in Northern California. Kingsnake dreams were a frequent subject of analysis with my first Jungian analyst, Donald F. Sandner. In June 1995, when I was driving back from my graduation dinner and diploma ceremony, having obtained my PhD in clinical psychology, I came upon a four-foot-long kingsnake outstretched across the road in front of my car as I was turning a corner, just as the sun was beginning to set in the Orinda hills. I stopped my car and grabbed the snake, taking it home with me to give it some water to drink, after which I let it go. As I carried it, I could hear it breathing rhythmically in my hands. I had not seen a kingsnake in the wild for twenty years! Why it would have made its sudden appearance at such a precise moment in time on my graduation night was simply baffling, incredible really. It is statistically improbable that my dream snake would have materialized in nature at that exact moment of celebration. It can only be understood as a synchronicity, as the kingsnake had been my guardian, or totem animal, for over two decades. I seldom dream about kingsnakes anymore. But for many years, it was a numinous dream symbol for me, an ally, and in nature, a natural predator of the rattlesnake. Such psychophysical *vocational correspondences* fall within the category of what Jung called a "coincidence in time of two or more causally unrelated events which have the same or a similar meaning."[8] According to Jung such correspondences were due to the "transgressive" character of archetypes.[9] *Philemon was Jung's most transgressive symbol for the Spiritual Self; what Philemon had in store for him as the developer of the field of analytical psychology was up to Jung's visioning ego to decipher. Jung is the one who had to translate* The Red Book *into science. Philemon could not do this for him; that was Jung's task.*

Although vocational dreams that *transgress* the division between psyche and matter do not coincide with empirical reality in every detail, they do point in a symbolic way to solutions to very real psychological problems, chiefly surrounding our vocations. Such dreams can leave patients in analysis feeling liberated. For Jung, such liberation was certainly present in 1909 at Clark University. Jung's questions about Freud's psychoanalytic theories were not only his own subjective questions; they were also Flournoy's questions and William James's questions. Such questioning made Jung's inner questioning in the United States ever more significant as an objective event.

Flournoy pointed out to Jung that Freud was biased in his attempts to explicate a psychology of the unconscious scientifically. The flaw in Freud's psychoanalytic science was further augmented during Jung's conversations with James. Thus, the conflict in conscience that Jung had been wrestling with for five years prior to his Philemon dream was how to develop a psychology of the unconscious that was truly objective and therefore scientific. Flournoy's detachment from the data of observation and James's empirical approach to phenomena—his American philosophy of pragmatism and spiritual temperament—paved the way ahead for Jung.[10]

Jung's attitude toward the unconscious was typically empirical and based in the natural sciences. Yet, in his chosen field of study, there was an increasing need for greater vocational clarification for an objective science that could speak up for the transpersonal reaches of human experience.

Through dreams and active imagination experiments, Jung answered the call for a more than personal vocation, which is now commonly known as *Jungian analysis*.

Any of us might have a dream to help resolve a similar work problem, each in our own way, if we are conditioned through habits and discipline, such as the daily habit of recording of our dreams. We have to listen to what the inner voice has to say. "The great thing," James said in his chapter "Habits," "in all education, is to *make our nervous system our ally instead of our enemy . . . For this we must make automatic and habitual, as early as possible, as many useful actions as we can . . . Never suffer an exception to occur till the new habit is securely rooted in your life*."[11] This kind of attentiveness to the habit of recording dreams may become a necessity either at the college entry level (as in Jung's radiolarian dream), or during midlife (as in Jung's Philemon dream). Such "big" vocational dreams foreshadow situations of change in a person's psyche, as if they possessed a hidden *foreknowledge* of an actual goal toward which a person's *acting Self* is striving in its attempts to become increasingly aware. These dreams of vital vocational import are products of the *prospective function* of the psyche. Jung defined this function as an "anticipation in the unconscious of future conscious achievements, something like a preliminary exercise or sketch, or a plan roughed out in advance. Its symbolic content sometimes outlines the solution of a conflict."[12]

Vocational dreams of this sort point the way to wholeness by charting paths of work in the present and future. They do not tell a person which way to go in life in an invariably fixed or predetermined way. Their aim is to convey hints about knowledge in the unconscious, Self-knowledge, which can never be fully known. Yet Jung's example of Philemon provides evidence for the probable existence of a supreme Self, as a dispenser of *his* supreme meaning, from an epistemological angle. For Philemon carried the wisdom of detached observation and the four keys to unlock the secrets to the hidden doorway into an expanding Universe, which is to say, scientific objectivity into the great *equivalence*.

In the last two decades of his life, Jung was less limited by this empirical attitude and increasingly open to investigating metaphysical questions, such as the question of whether consciousness survives after death. Even then, however, he approached his subject from the perspective of what he had been taught by Philemon. When he eventually sat down to write his monograph on synchronicity, he considered all of his experiences as a researcher, including, to be sure, his finding of the dead kingfisher.

When we attempt to examine synchronicity phenomena from an empirical standpoint, we tread on uncertain ground, for we can only prove the existence of vocational archetypes if we can discover equivalent environmental factors to which they correspond materially. The example of Philemon's appearance in a dream and simultaneous discovery of the dead kingfisher while Jung was engaged with the process of active imagination is one of the most famous instances of meaningful chance on record.

Significantly, my conversations with William Everson, the Santa Cruz poet-shaman, took place at his home, which he called "Kingfisher Flat." I borrowed the term *vocational archetype* from Everson, although there's no evidence Everson had Jung's Philemon dream in mind when he named his home. Yet the fact of this coincidence is nevertheless meaningful, I think, because Bill was a Jungian poet and writer. What this coincidence meant for me, as his friend and pupil, is that he embodied some of the characteristics of an American Jungian who had been mentored by Father Victor White, a Dominican, in 1956, the year I was born.

Vocational archetypes are charged with a vitality and power and meaning that can make things happen in material reality through a reshuffling of environmental events. They tend to act themselves out, portray or dramatize themselves in life *purposefully*. Their impact on scientific discoveries, social events, and the environmental movement may be quite profound. Jung's paintings of Philemon are well-known now after the publication of *The Red Book*. Jung painted a portrait of Philemon in his stone tower, moreover, that he called *Shrine to Philemon—Repentance of Faust*.[13]

How people are guided to pursue their natural lines of vocational evolution through such inner and outer correlations or how precisely career choices are made has and will always remain a great source of mystery. Nevertheless, we can be absolutely certain that dreams, active imagination, automatic writing, and visionary experiences are among the best sources of data in the study of synchronicity phenomena. The spirit of the kingfisher was obviously not dead at Bollingen; it was alive in the inner figure of the spiritual Self, Philemon, who spoke to Jung. That a vocational archetype exists in the human psyche, which may be personified as a principle of interior and exterior order in the world, does not mean we can ever prove scientifically what the *vocational Self* is in its innermost essence, in its undifferentiated psychophysical state. For *psychoid* factors are irrepresentable and unknowable and their significances may only be grasped intuitively in hints.

Nor can synchronistic events be predicted in any exact or prophetic sense based on a dream. What we can recognize, nevertheless, are the visible effects that archetypes of vocation may constellate through a mirroring of internal and external happenings; through unconscious modes of apprehension in the psyche, synchronicity can make itself known first through vocational dream states. Such dreams may be worked with aesthetically in an attempt to amplify the meaning of their images, such as I sometimes attempted with my kingsnake dreams. Jung used *amplification* to keep a patient focused on the significance of such dream-images.

When we *amplify* vocational dreams, we may activate the prospective or teleological function. We may get a hunch, for instance, that something is about to occur in our career, and we may suddenly dance, paint, or write a poem about it. While such amplifications of a dream are occurring, some outer opportunity or job may suddenly be available just around the corner, or, perhaps there is an unmistakable sense of trust that the dream's meaning will reveal itself in time. We engage in journal writing to amplify and extend the image first; then, as we work with the dream via aesthetic representations, we may be hit, like Jung was, with a thunderbolt. Something surprising happens that is simply too meaningful to have been merely cause and effect. The dream did not cause the outer event to occur, but *something behind the dream and events that have unfolded arrange correspondences into an unmistakably significant series of transgressive occurrences in time that are quite startling.*

Generally, such dreams and their corresponding synchronicities are derived from acausal happenings in the ego's increasing encounters with the Self. Although vocational dreams point to specific lines of development in a plurality of images, the relative freedom and autonomy of ego consciousness to choose its own way and become helmsman or helmswoman of the ship of our destiny remains one of the great decisive factors in any career-decision-making process.

The reason midlife has often been spoken of as a crisis, moreover, is because *midlife often crosses our path with recklessness and violence and wild abandon, after some major defeat has occurred in our career.* For Jung, this defeat of his ego strivings by the unknown destiny of the Self occurred at precisely such a moment after his rupture with Freud: "Symbols of the self appear in dreams and in active imagination," Jung wrote in *Mysterium Coniunctionis,* "at moments of violent collision between two opposite points of view, as compensatory attempts to mitigate the conflict and 'make enemies friends.'"[14]

What Jung's turn to alchemy produced was the *alchemical gold of his scientific research.* The preparatory ground for this transformation was cleared in 1931 when Jung extended the tower-like annex at Bollingen. He had in mind then what he had seen in Indian houses: a sacred place where Hindus meditate or do Yoga exercises.[15] In this spiritual annex of the tower, Jung painted his beautiful portrait of Philemon and continued to engage in his Western-Christian equivalent of Yoga through the process of active imagination.

Miraculously, then, through an interweaving of an individual's fate, a Spirit of Nature (either a helpful wise old woman or wise old man figure, or sometimes both) may appear simultaneously in dreams and nature, imagination and society, to guide us toward our predestined course to fulfill life's purposes. I call such synchronistic life-events during midlife *miraculous* because encounters with such figures or events, as in my encounter with the four-foot kingsnake, have a transformational quality to them that are ultimately *real.* The myths of all nations point to such destined appearances in the life of its peoples, whether during adulthood, midlife, or beyond, as fortuitous events. Moreover, when great good fortune happens to a person, it seems to come about at a stage of some major transhistorical event in culture that signals a change is about to occur in the collective, where a link between "inside" and "outside" suddenly becomes transparent.

Such times of *transparency* are often spoken about through the language of myth as moments of decisive *callings.* They happen in individuals or in groups through the constellation of calling archetypes. By *vocational archetypes,* I mean symbols of creative activity that pattern a person's sense of profession. They are essentially speech patterns that are inborn and innate. Philemon spoke to Jung and Jung spoke back, in an inner and outer colloquy in his garden. Had Jung decided not to converse with Philemon, where might his life have led him? The significant thing is that he decided to do the unconventional thing by conversing with his interlocutor. We are each faced with a similar choice to pursue our calling and give voice to our archetype.

Our life's destiny is merely a potential that needs to be acted on. The vocational archetypes, callings from instinct and our Spiritual Self, give supreme meaning to our lives. They do not come once in life but occur repeatedly. It is this potentiality in the soul—personal and transpersonal, instinctive and spiritual—that repeatedly calls to us in midlife, and it is to an inner and outer "voice"—the summons—that we must answer. This is indeed a paradox: callings are patterned by vocational symbols of the Self that have to be made conscious by each of us in time. I call such inborn patterns of behavior *archetypes of the Self's vocational activity*. Each archetype is structured in a meaningful way by an ego-Self encounter, by which I mean a channel for communication between the "I" and an objective "Other."

Miracles are all around us. Vocational dreams are probably one of the greatest sources of empirical confirmation for Jung's theory of synchronicity. They may be a primary doorway into the secret of the subject under investigation during midlife transformations, such as when Jung met James.

Another significant synchronicity that occurred in Jung's destiny-pattern, long after his discovery of the dead kingfisher, was his visit with Fowler McCormick and Boshi Sen to the Ramakrishna Mission in Belur, India, in early January 1938. The Belur Math was founded by Swami Vivekananda in 1899. It contains the holy relics of Ramakrishna; Vivekananda; the Holy Mother, Ramakrishna's wife, Sarada Devi; and other disciples of the Master. When Jung entered this sacred site, he saw the marble statue of Ramakrishna seated on a hundred-petaled lotus in Samadhi. This image is sure to have stayed with Jung, during his next major transition into old age at sixty-nine, when he suffered his first heart attack. This was followed by the dream of the yogi in 1944, which, to my mind, marks a significant change in Jung from the archetype of the religious psychologist to the archetype of the wise sage of Western spirituality. In his chapter "Life After Death," Jung reported *a dream about a yogi seated in lotus posture in a church. Where Jung's dream ego expects to find the holy crucifix, Blessed Mother, or Virgin Mary, he sees on the floor, seated across from him, a yogi entranced in deep inward meditation. As Jung looks more closely at this dream-figure, he notices he has Jung's own face. This so frightens Jung that he awakes with a sudden start.* The dream presented him with a reversal—a *reversal* of the relationship between his European ego-consciousness and a transpsychic consciousness in the Self, which was represented by the archetype of a yogi meditating from the East.[16]

Vivekananda had been deceased for thirty-six years, yet his relics were there, as was his spiritual presence. This Spirit no doubt entered Jung's psyche. I say this because Jung thought that the coincidences of the most basic teachings in India were so overwhelmingly great that it meant very little to him whether the author was Ramakrishna, Vivekananda, Sri Aurobindo, or Shri Ramana Maharishi.[17] Nevertheless, synchronicity can be seen in the bilateral vision of Jung's yogi dream. *The figure that confronted him was ultimately real because he had Jung's face.* In the dream, the dual aspects of the unitary world (East and West) were revealed as a oneness of spiritual democracy: the image of the yogi in meditation in a Christian Church. There was an equivalence of meaning, in other words, between internal and external worlds in this dream.

In 1938, Jung entered the Belur Math. In 1944, he dreamt of a yogi meditating in a Christian chapel. Moments of spiritual democracy like this are instances in time when equivalences of meaning and a sense of timelessness preponderate, when experiences of universal equality with everything are revealed in the Now. Such states of mind are often evoked by vocational archetypes.

NOTES

1. Richardson, *William James*, 515.
2. Jung, *MDR*, 85.
3. Jung, *MDR*, 108. The book by Richard Freiherr von Krafft-Ebing was *Lehrbuch der Psychiatrie*.
4. Jung, "Synchronicity," CW 8, ¶912.
5. James, *Writings 1902–1910*, 761.
6. Jung, "Appendix: On Synchronicity," CW 8, ¶995.
7. Jung, *MDR*, 182, 183.
8. Jung, "Synchronicity," CW 8, ¶849.
9. Jung, "Appendix: On Synchronicity," ¶964.
10. Jung, CLM.

11. James, "Psychology: Briefer Course," in *Writings 1878–1899,* 146–147.
12. Jung, "On the Nature of Dreams," CW 8, ¶493.
13. Jung, *MDR,* 235, fn. 5.
14. Jung, *Mysterium Coniunctionis,* CW 14, ¶146.
15. Jung, *MDR,* 224.
16. Jung, *MDR,* 323.
17. Jung, *Letters,* vol. 1, 477–478.

Chapter 38

THE TRANSPSYCHE

In 1946 Jung was rereading William James' *Varieties of Religious Experience.* And it was not until 1946 that Jung included "superconsciousness" in his theory of the Self.[1] The word *psychoid* appeared at this pivotal juncture in Jung's essay "On the Nature of the Psyche." In the essay, Jung introduced the idea of "psychoid" *processes* at both ends of the psychic spectrum[2]: 1) the dynamism of instinct lodged at the "infra-red" pole and 2) the archetypal image located at the "ultra-violet" pole.[3] In a footnote, Jung remarked further:

> Especial exception is taken to this "superconsciousness" by people who have come under the influence of Indian philosophy. They usually fail to appreciate that their objection only applies to the hypothesis of a "sub-consciousness," which ambiguous term I avoid using. On the other hand my concept of the *unconscious* leaves the question of "above" or "below" completely open, as it embraces both aspects of the psyche.[4]

Jung then added: "James also spoke of a 'transmarginal field' of consciousness."[5]

By *transmarginal field,* Jung meant outside the margins of ego awareness. Archetypal contents may enter ego consciousness from either the infrared or ultraviolet pole. Jung posited, "It seems to me probable that the real nature of the archetype is not capable of being made conscious, that it is transcendent, on which account I call it psychoid."[6] By *psychoid* Jung meant the "archetypes, therefore have a nature that *cannot with certainty be designated as psychic.*"[7] Later, while reflecting on what he had just written, Jung said, "This opens up the whole question of the transpsychic reality immediately underlying the psyche."[8]

The words *transpsychic reality* included *above and below* and made plenty of room for the hypothesis of a supraconscious in the objective psyche. Jung also considered whether there would be a new world religion. It is baffling to the scientific intellect to conceive of this possibility, as science has nothing to say about religion. Yet, for Jung, "There is no conflict between religion and science."[9] No problem for him because, to his mind, they were callings from the same Self. The problem of religion could only be answered, in Jung's view, through *myth*. James, Jung, and Pauli all tapped into the archetype of spiritual democracy as a mythology of the World Soul. In his chapter "Life After Death" in *MDR*, Jung spoke of fantasy thinking or "mythologizing" as a way to envision what the future might have in store for us as a species: "Even now I can do no more than tell stories—'mythologize.'"[10]

Spiritual democracy is the a priori meaning of what Whitman mythologized in his poem "Passage to India" and what Melville mythologized in *Moby-Dick*. Jung used an alchemical term to express the same thing—the *unus mundus,* or "one world." Clearly, something had broken through in James's psyche, just as it had in Jung's teachings: the idea of religion as a unitary experience, or the *democratization of the Self*. Jung expanded James's notion of fields of consciousness to include a "real zero-point" field where two points "touch and do not touch" and where psyche and matter meet through an inner and outer mirroring of synchronistic phenomena that occur at the margins.[11]

For Jung religion consisted of the Quest. By "Quest" Jung meant that we have to see what the unconscious has to say, and it will give us a wonderful lead if we listen to the voice of Nature, such as it gave Pauli. As Jung said of Pauli: "That man got into order again because he gradually accepted the symbolic data, and now he leads the religious life, the life of the careful observer. Religion is careful observation of the data. He now observes all the things that are brought him by his dreams; that is his only guidance."[12] Clearly, for Jung there was no distinction between the daily habits of a scientific researcher and religion if he or she was focusing at the same time on the archetypal images in the background through the vehicle of dreams and their proper interpretation. In other words, religions have predicted and known that there is an archetype of order that can unite the world, where there is no conflict between science and religion. Rather than seeing one faith as an endpoint for religious evolution across the globe, James and Jung took *religious experience* as their starting point. According to Jung, psyche was ultimately religious. Psyche needed a religion of science every bit as much as it needed a science of religion to make the psychoid archetype of the world-creating order—the "one world"—conscious of a miracle of human existence through a reflecting consciousness.

The archetype of religious democracy is in the process of becoming conscious of itself as a *miracle,* not only in rare and sporadic events occurring in isolated individuals around the world, but in the world at large, which is currently grappling with the horrific problem of climate change. We had better listen, or Nature will destroy our one-world family. Science and religion are One. We separate them at our hazard.

What these correlations suggest is that significances "exist outside the psyche"[13] and meanings are, in fact, "self-subsistent,"[14] "transcendental,"[15] and "a priori in relation to human consciousness."[16] Such meanings of a pre-established harmony, or Tao, operating in Nature and the world's Oceans presuppose the existence of an objective significance in the Cosmos. This area of psychological research provides a vision through which we can "frame a view of the world which adequately explains the meaning of human existence in the cosmos"[17] and of "archetypal equivalences."[18]

As I've shown, Jung recorded an "archetype of meaning" in *Memories, Dreams, Reflections*, the image of the wise old man, or Spiritual Self—Philemon: "the superior master and teacher, the archetype of the spirit, who symbolizes the pre-existent meaning hidden in the chaos of life."[19] Finding the dead kingfisher in his garden after he met James gave Jung the vision he needed, and this perception later evolved into his scientific essay on "Synchronicity." Jung described such double vision beautifully in a letter he penned to Pauli in December 1956, where the one world (*unus mundus*) can be seen in its transcendental and cosmic aspects as a simultaneous literary function that unites science with a new spiritual worldview:

> The important thing about the dream of 26 December 1956 is the double vision. This is a distinctive characteristic of a human being who is at one with himself . . . if man has united the opposites within himself, there is nothing to stop him perceiving both aspects of the world in an objective manner. The inner psychic split is replaced by a split world-picture, and this is inevitable, for without this discrimination, conscious perception would be impossible. It is not in actual fact a split world, for facing the person who is united in himself is an unus mundus.[20]

This is a *weltanschauung* I've called spiritual democracy, and I will go on to show that it was represented symbolically in the minds of James and Jung.

Notes

1. Jung, "On the Nature of the Psyche," CW 8, ¶356.
2. Jung, CW 8, ¶368.
3. Jung, CW 8, ¶414.
4. Jung, CW 8, ¶369, fn. 35.
5. Jung, CW 8, ¶382, fn. 47.
6. Jung, CW 8, ¶417.
7. Jung, CW 8, ¶439.
8. Jung, "The Psychological Foundation of a Belief in Sprits," ¶600, fn 15.
9. Jung, "The Symbolic Life," CW 18, ¶692.
10. Jung, *MDR,* 299.
11. Jung, "On the Nature of the Psyche," CW 8, ¶418.
12. Jung, CW 18, ¶673.
13. Jung, "Synchronicity," CW 8, ¶915.
14. Jung, CW 8, ¶944.
15. Jung, CW 8, ¶915.
16. Jung, CW 8, ¶942.
17. Jung, *MDR,* 373.
18. Jung, CW 8, ¶964.
19. Jung, "Archetypes of the Collective Unconscious," CW 9i, ¶74.
20. Meier, *Atom and Archetype,* 156, 157.

Chapter 39

SYNCHRONICITY AND THE PSYCHOLOGY OF GROUPS

In Jung's seminars on dream analysis, he made his first public reference to the term *synchronicity*: "I have invented the word *synchronicity* as a term to cover these phenomena, that is, things happening at the same moment as an expression of the same time content."[1] In a 1928 seminar Jung spoke further of "waves" being set forth as a reaction from the Self, *waves* that might be activated in any group as upon a stormy sea.[2] Jung then advanced a hypothesis in his third seminar in which he spoke about psychic energy and *waves*: "Now when people have been disturbed by a reaction of the unconscious, there is always a medicine man who has a dream concerning the matter."[3] The medicine man or medicine woman was a person who had immediate access to waves of the transpsyche through various techniques. Here, Jung set forth his hypothesis about the collective unconscious. Whenever someone in a group had done something wrong, he noted, "waves" were released in "baffling circumstances" in the "surroundings."[4] For this reason "the advice of the medicine man is valuable," Jung said.[5] In Jung's life, the constellation of inner and outer events around the interpretation of dreams seemed to him to have produced "waves" in the collective unconscious of the group. These waves were not causal. They simply happened.

What Jung modeled in the seminar group was a new collectivity in the making. By providing an analysis of the shadow in groups, he charted a way forward toward a unitary picture of our common human equality, where group members have to face the inevitable fact of their wholeness as the goal of interactional life in groups, not moral perfection but completeness. Jung's intuitions about the unconscious shadow dynamics came through in successive waves from the sea of cosmic intelligence in the psyche of the group. He was modestly moved by the unconscious shadow dynamics and was looking to participants' dreams and his own internal reactions for answers to the question of what the particular disturbance was. He did not see himself as the great medicine man who had all the answers; he looked rather with humility, to the Self-in-the-group, for a solution to what was creating an impasse in their working together toward an understanding of dreams and their various types of functions in analytical psychotherapy. This meditation on a process in his seminar group is important in discussing the concept of the psyche because it opens the way for a discussion of the concept of meaningful *coincidence*.

> We are moved by the dreams, they express us and we express them, and there are coincidences connected with them. We decline to take coincidences seriously because we cannot consider them as causal. True, we would make a mistake to consider them as causal; events don't come about because of dreams, that would be absurd, we can never demonstrate that; they just happen ... The East bases much of its science on this irregularity and considers coincidences as the reliable basis of the world rather than causality. Synchronism is the prejudice of the East; causality is the modern prejudice of the West. The more we busy ourselves with dreams, the more we shall see such coincidences—chances.[6]

Notes

1. Jung, *Dream Analysis,* 417.
2. Jung, 81.
3. Jung, 35.
4. Jung, 77.
5. Jung, 37.
6. Jung, 44–45.

Part IV

*The Future of
Analytical Psychology*

Chapter 40

PSYCHOLOGY AS A NATURAL SCIENCE

In his Preface to the first edition of *The Theory of Psychoanalysis,* Jung argued: "It has been wrongly suggested that my attitude signifies a 'split' in the psychoanalytic movement. Such schisms can only exist as matters of faith ... I have taken as my guiding principle William James' pragmatic rule: 'You must bring out of each word its practical cash-value, set it at work within the stream of your experience.'"[1] He made it explicit that he viewed such "splits" in psychology to be matters of "faith," based on the guiding principle "nothing but," which he took directly from William James's 1907 book *Pragmatism.* Although Jung's experience as a psychiatrist differed markedly from Freud's, he saw himself as a colleague of Freud and a champion of psychoanalysis in a wider sense, as seen in his 1911–1912 concept of the libido and its transformations. Jung preferred a plural view of the psyche, pluralism over monism or the monistic view, as James had before him. Thanks to James's idea of complementarity, Jung also saw clearly how contradictions in modern psychology could be reconciled through a *complementarity* of principles. Jung would later write, in collaboration with Pauli, about the notion of complementarity in his essay on "Synchronicity."

Jung began in 1912 to advance a teleological view of dreams and inner experiences over "nothing but" reductive approaches. Jung also referred to mental states in his later writing as "fields," as did James. James, however, was quite critical of Hartmann's concept of the "unconscious," as I've pointed out, and preferred to speak of different states of consciousness in the "subconscious," or the Self.

Radical empiricism, in James's view near the end of his life, viewed pragmatism as *psychological* in nature, because it placed *pure experience* at the center of all knowing about the nature of the universe and our modest place within it. All states of human consciousness in this sense existed in a plurality of *interconnected fields.* The metaphor of the field allowed James to break new ground and move toward a more expansive view of the *meaning of life* as a complexity of mental states in a unity of being and nonbeing, which he defined singly by using the simple algebraic symbol q. By q, James meant that cognition as a function of consciousness implied the existence of changing *qualities of a plurality of feelings of q.*[2] As I've noted, when a theorist attempts to describe feelings of q as the only criterion of his or her god, it will form, in the mind of a philosopher, theologian, or psychological researcher, the entire universe. Thus, for James, the Absolute was always merely an assumption. "The quality of q so far, is entirely subjective fact which the feeling carries so to speak endogenously, or in its pocket." He called this the "feelings *dream.*" But, he continued, "For the feeling to be cognitive in the specific sense, then, it must be self-transcendent; and we must prevail upon the god to *create a reality outside of it* to correspond to its intrinsic quality q."[3]

So great a value did James place upon feeling as a criterion of religious experience that he transferred what he learned about religion to all fields of knowledge. Seeing the Absolute from the criterion of a subjective god, as he put it, or as a quality of feeling, allowed James to undergo "a real change of heart, a break with absolutistic hopes" when he took up the "inductive view of the conditions of belief."[4]

The pragmatist way of seeing things enabled James to break down old notions of scientific truth that had held since the time of Humboldt and Darwin, Emerson and Dickinson, Whitman and Melville. Since 1850, all the exact sciences had believed in the expression of truths that formed exact copies of definite codes of nonhuman realities in the realm of nature. James felt, I believe rightly so, that he had experienced a bursting point in his heroic attempts in *The Principles* to create the basis for an experimental psychology, post-Wundt, that could revolutionize the field notion. He later criticized this view as lacking sufficient acknowledgment of the subjective factor of meaning. His attempts at a grand theory in 1890 were then replaced in "The Meaning of Truth," the sequel to *Pragmatism,* with a new view that only experience can create our own meaning of reality in the cosmos.

In the old view, theories were expressions of gods (i's for *infinities*), which were believed to be inherent in the very structure of nature's laws. In James's later and more nonheroic view, these archetypes of experience were not seen as static; they were, as Jung would theorize, symbolizing principles that were only alive when experienced psychologically. "So also of the 'laws of nature,'" James wrote in "Humanism and Truth": "physical and chemical, so of the natural history classifications—all were supposed to be exact and exclusive duplicates of pre-human archetypes buried in the structure of things, to which the spark of divinity hidden in our intellect enables us to penetrate."[5]

How things can be known together in the same mental state is one of those vexing problems that has led to countless unnecessary splits, not only in the field of psychology as a whole but also in psychoanalysis and Jungian analysis, too. Yet, despite the warring difficulties that may at times beset psychology's field, James and Jung were both in quest of a "field" theory that could synthesize the various disciplines, including neurology, mathematics, philosophy, and physics, into a common science of the human soul or psyche. James began his 1894 Presidential Address at Princeton, "The Knowing of Things Together," with the following statement: "The nature of the synthetic unity of consciousness is one of those great underlying problems that divide the psychological schools. We know, say, a dozen things singly through a dozen different mental states. But on another occasion we may know the same dozen things together through a single mental state."[6]

In this lecture, James presented a number of "failed" attempts to offer a *synthetic* explanation for the unity of consciousness, one of which was the notion of the *World Soul* of the New England transcendentalist school of Emerson and Thoreau. "Transcendentalism," he said, "explains things by an over-soul of which all separate souls, sensations, thoughts, and data generally are parts," but in which *everything else in the world* may be known together in the *Over-Soul*. For transcendentalists, he continued, "this is the true condition of each single thing, and to pass into this condition is for things to fulfill their vocation."[7]

James's pivoting upon the idea of vocation is significant. James was strongly influenced by the figure of Emerson as a transformative relationship or destiny figure internalized within his own soul. By 1894 James had already met Vivekananda. Using a now common metaphor from the field of music, James said, in essence, *our brains are the organ pipes of the infinite*. He then proceeded to inform his audience that he could see no abstract reason why transcendentalists might not go into psychology to erect a "psycho-physical science of the conditions of more separate and less separate cognition which would include all the facts that psycho-physicists in general might discover."[8] Using himself as an exemplar for one who had successfully gone beyond the hero myth toward a new psychological attitude that had not been born yet, a true initiate into the mysteries of a transpersonal psychology, James then said ironically and with wit and modesty: "You will agree with me that I have brought no new insights to the subject, and that I have only gossiped to while away this unlucky presidential hour to which the constellations doomed to me at my birth."[9] On the verge of his fifty-third birthday James had let the hero myth pass. He had let go of his career as a laboratory psychologist who authored *Principles*. In the summer of that same year James met at Harvard a young thirty-year-old man (Vivekananda) who had demonstrated how things can be known together through the science of Yoga. This must have startled him, for it took him eight more years to integrate what he learned from this Hindu monk and to synthesize it for the field of modern psychology. In all humility James admitted:

> My intention was a good one, and a natural science infinitely more complete than the psychologies we now possess could be written without abandoning its terms. Like all authors, I have, therefore, been surprised that this child of my genius should not be more admired by others—should, in fact, have been generally either misunderstood or despised …. I am going to make things more harmonious by simply giving it up. I have become convinced since publishing that book that no conventional restrictions can keep metaphysical and so-called epistemological inquiries out of the psychology-books. I see, moreover, better now than then, that my proposal to designate mental states merely by their cognitive function leads to a somewhat strange way of talking of dreams and reveries, and to quite an unnatural way of talking of some emotional states. I am willing, consequently, henceforward that mental conditions should be called complex, just as their objects are, and this even in psychology … For the various fields of which they are parts are integers, existentially, and their parts only live as long as they live."[10]

James added the word *complex* into the mix to augment his understanding of a psychology of action:

> Not till you have dropped the old phrases, so absurd or so empty,... not till you have in your turn succeeded in some such long inquiry into conditions as the one I have just failed in; not till you have laid bare more of the nature of that altogether unique kind of complexity in unity which mental states involve; not till then, I say, will psychology reach any real benefit from the conciliatory spirit of which I have done what I can to set an example.[11]

As James showed in this address to the American Psychological Association, he felt like he had "failed" to formulate a hypothesis of the Self that was broad enough to satisfy the needs of modern psychology for an answer to the conundrum of how complexity might be unified in a *plural cognitive function* that subsumes cognition and emotion, perceiving and knowing, sensing and intuiting, feeling and thinking.[12] This task was left to Jung and to today's Jungians who are gaining a better understanding of how to begin to define how things are *known together* in the same mental state, a single unitary function of the psyche that Jung would call "transcendent." Jung wrote a "natural science infinitely more complete" than psychology possesses even now without abandoning its terms. James came close in his definitions of the World-Soul when he said that transcendentalism explained things by an Over-Soul of which all separate souls, sensations, thoughts, and data generally were parts of things to be known together in unity. For James science needed to be taken at its essence as a method, or technique, to arrive at certain hypotheses, or theories of truth, which are not Absolute, but relative in their plurality of meanings but which ultimately must be inclusive of the data of parapsychology. Science, for James, was a science of personal forces, pluralistic powers, or archetypes that formed the logical basis for symbolic understandings of the categories of the human personality, the *central categories of vocation* being the various fields of our acting selves and the mental states of complexity in unity being the ways we might fulfill our vocations.

Another brilliant statement of James's, which I particularly like and that is frequently quoted, is as follows: "I wished, by treating Psychology *like* a natural science, to help her become one."[13] This passage speaks volumes because what James was essentially saying is that it was up to him to treat psychology *like a natural science in order for her to become such a science and by this he meant a true science of the human soul,* not a laboratory science that treated the soul as if it were a scientific subject in an experimental study where the soul cannot breathe in the true directionality of the spirit of the times. This is why I left the experimental psychology program at UC Santa Cruz to write my own individual major in "Depth Psychology and Religion." I found experimental psychology stultifying, often going for long walks through the redwood trees on the university campus to contemplate my future. At that time I had the good fortune not only to have been reading Jung for several years, but also to have found William James's book *The Varieties of Religious Experience*, which I loved.

This brings me to the question of the future of psychology as a natural science. If it is to truly be analytic, in a Jamesian and Jungian sense, we must help her—psychology—decide what her direction will be. "While the future is uncertain," James predicted, "whatever it will be it is decided in the *here* and *now*."[14] The *Now* is actually a *field,* James said, a field we can enter into every day, on an experiential basis, whether in our clinical offices or our classrooms, whether while seeing patients or teaching students or writing: "The instant field of the present is at all times what I call 'pure' experience."[15]

For pragmatism, James continued, "*it is still in the making, and awaits part of its complexion from the future.*"[16] Although it was not Jung's project to advance pragmatism any further than it had actually gone in William James's lifetime, I see it as one of my own individual tasks and something I owe to the dead—to bring Jung's psychology into alignment with a Jamesian vision, to advance it in a more experiential direction. As a Jungian, I am only one voice in a cacophony of other voices, an individual, with a single voice among many. But there is a meeting ground, I believe, where we are all one, in the movement of the field of depth psychology. I owe it to Eugene Taylor to have given voice to that higher spreading tone that James left us with, what he called *pragmatism,* which has helped me define what it means to be Jamesian as well as Jungian, for I see them as complementary to one another. "Meanwhile, single personalities exist as a democratic conjunction, each one, to the degree that they accept their social responsibility to do so, a unity-in-the-making." A *democratic conjunction*! This suggests that we are co-creators in our own meaning, whether we identify ourselves as Jamesian or Jungian, or a conjunction of both.

Finally, James was also influenced late in life, and again like Jung, by the writings of Henri Bergson on the élan vital.[17] Taylor concluded that "the most important implication of James's thinking for the future of psychology, in my opinion, remains the problem of consciousness."[18] James, in his more mature thought, was highly influenced not only by the Yoga of Vivekananda, but also by the ideas of Anagarika Dharmapala, who he heard lecture on the major concepts of Buddhism at Harvard. After listening to the Buddhist scholar, James arose from his chair enraptured and exclaimed: "This is the psychology everybody will be studying twenty-five years from now."[19]

As noted previously, Jung was also fascinated as five-year-old boy with the religions of India, particularly Hinduism. At this young age he viewed an illustrated children's book, the *Orbis Pictus*."[20] In 1912, two years after his second meeting with William James, Jung cited numerous quotes from the *Upanishads* and *Rig Veda* in his book *Transformations and Symbols of the Libido*. There are copies in Jung's library, furthermore, of Romain Rolland's *Teachings of Sri Ramakrishna* and Swami Vivekananda's *Ramakrishna, Mein Meister*. Therefore, Jung was well aware of the importance of Vedanta and the Ramakrishna movement. But he seemed to have preferred Buddhism. For instance, Jung said in a letter to Boshi Sen, on February 24, 1938: "The two greatest things of India, in my humble opinion, are the earth of the great mountain in the North and the spirit of Buddha in the South."[21] In another letter, dated December 31, 1949, Jung wrote further to a correspondent who had sent him a book:

> I can perfectly understand your preference for Buddhism. It is something magnificent. I have visited the holy places of Buddhism in India and was profoundly impressed by them, quite apart from my reading of Buddhist literature. If I were an Indian I would definitely be a Buddhist.[22]

These statements all show how prescient James and Jung actually were in outlining a *vision of psychology's future*, for we continue to be informed by various forms of Hindu and Buddhist practice over one-hundred years after James's death and over fifty years after Jung's death. Is it any wonder that Jung celebrated James in his writing and lectures?

Notes

1. Jung, "The Theory of Psychoanalysis," CW 4, 86.
2. Because the letter q may not be clear; therefore, I will replace q with i as a reference to infinity in what follows.
3. James, *Writings 1902–1910,* 834–835.
4. James, 859.
5. James, 860.
6. James, *Writings 1878–1899,* 1057.
7. James, 1072–1073.
8. James, 1073.
9. James, 1073.
10. James, 1075.
11. James, 1076. Italics mine.
12. James, 1075.
13. Taylor, *Consciousness Beyond the Margin,* 114.
14. Taylor, 125.
15. Taylor, 127.
16. Taylor, 133.
17. Taylor, 135. Bergson wrote about the élan vitale: "Consciousness is the vital element that is at the origin of life. Consciousness, which is a *need of creation*, is made manifest to itself only when creation is possible. It lies dormant when life is condemned to automatism; it wakens as soon as the possibility of choice is restored." Bergson, *L évolution créatrice*; quoted in Taylor, 135.
18. Taylor, 143.
19. Taylor, 147.
20. Jung, *MDR,* 17.
21. Jung, *Letters,* vol. 1, 242.
22. Jung, 538.

Chapter 41

THE PSYCHOLOGICAL REDISCOVERY OF ECSTASY

The psychological rediscovery of ecstasy[1] is one of the less familiar chapters in the history of analytical psychology, so it may be appropriate to start my reflections on depth-psychology American style with C. G. Jung's struggle to come to terms with ecstatic emotions as a real and valid psychological experience. Jung's theoretical position, in contrast to James's, was, for much of his adult life, subtly distrustful of emotion *per se*. Jung often said that the task of active imagination—the process whereby psychic energy moved from a "lower" to a "higher" form of energy—consisted in a release of symbols, ideas, and images contained within the emotions. To the extent that he was able to "find the images . . . concealed in the emotions," Jung said he "was inwardly calmed and reassured." If he had left the "images hidden in the emotions," he emphasized he "might have been torn to pieces by them."[2] In fact, so much is made of the image in Jungian psychology that the factor of emotion is often overlooked.

Although there is little indication in the body of Jung's writings published in his lifetime that suggests the experience of emotion held a place of value higher than the image, in *Memories, Dreams, Reflections* Jung described a series of ecstatic experiences that appear to place emotion on at least a co-equal level with imagination. These powerful visions formed the transport for an experience of the *coniunctio*, the mystical marriage that Jung achieved after his near-fatal heart attack in 1944. He lay on his back in a hospital bed for three weeks while being given oxygen and camphor injections to save his life. In describing these experiences, Jung wrote, "*It was as if I were in an ecstasy*. I felt as though I were floating in space, as though I were safe in the womb of the universe—*in a tremendous void, but filled with the highest possible feeling of happiness*. 'This is eternal bliss,' I thought. 'This cannot be described; it is far too wonderful.'"[3] Such states of ecstasy cannot be taught. They can only be *lived* by one in whom the emotion of bliss has been awakened.

"At bottom," Jung continued, "*it was I myself: I was the marriage. And my beatitude was that of a blissful wedding . . . These were ineffable states of joy*."[4] Jung went on to describe these visions as intending to render the imagination to a place below emotion, so that we see him arriving—while reading the message of his own fantasies. This idea, that the reality of the psyche is grounded in emotion, did not enter into Jung's theoretical writings until the very end of his life. It cannot be found in many of his other published works. This is, indeed, meaningful because Jung's experience of these visions, with their "ineffable states of joy," came to him prior to the publication of his final great works. Perhaps he sensed that such experiences could not possibly be described scientifically, within the limits of his empirical psychology. Yet this did not prevent him from trying. Doing so required an artist's vision, a poetic language, an attunement to elegiac rhythm, which both he and James possessed, to portray them properly in image-and-thought form.

> It is impossible to convey the beauty and intensity of emotion during those visions... I would never have imagined that any such experience was possible. It was not a product of imagination. The visions and experiences were utterly real; there was nothing subjective about them; they all had the quality of absolute objectivity. We shy away from the word "eternal," but I can describe the experience only as the ecstasy of a non-temporal state in which present, past, and future are one. Everything that happens in time had been brought together into a concrete whole. Nothing was distributed over time, nothing could be measured by temporal concepts. The experience might best be described as a state of feeling, but one which cannot be the product of the imagination.[5]

To be sure, ecstasy cannot be described as an end in itself, for such supreme states of emotion were *not* the aims of individuation in Jung's view. Rather, it was the crystallization of the transpersonal value, or *vocatus*, which alone yielded the *opus,* the goal of individuation, which appeared to be an amalgam of objective visionary experiences and supreme states of emotionality. All of Jung's greatest works were written after these visions in a matter of about ten years.

> After the illness a fruitful period of work began for me. A good many of my principal works were written only then. The insight I had had, or the vision of the end of things, gave me the courage to undertake new formulations. I no longer attempted to put across my own opinion, but surrendered myself to the current of my thoughts... It was only after the illness that I understood how important it is to affirm one's own destiny.[6]

The peace and the transcendent joy that Jung received from his visions was the peculiar affect that attended this mystical union of opposites, and it came to him at a time of grave illness, when he was forced in a personal way to experience the mystery of healing. At this time aspects of the Higher Self broke into his psyche, as they never had before. Yet how does Jung's notion of the *coniunctio* as a state of bliss relate to the Higher Self?

At the beginning of his career, Jung posited that the "essential basis of our personality is affectivity" and all of our thoughts and actions are "only symptoms of affectivity";[7] in *Aion*, moreover, he wrote that "emotion is the chief source of consciousness. There is no change from darkness to light or from inertia to movement without emotion."[8] These are highly significant statements because Jung's experience of his ecstatic visions healed him. He was first able to arrive at this state—albeit in a much more insulated form—through what he called the "synthetic method" during his "Confrontation with the Unconscious." In 1921 he wrote the following in his essay "The Relativity of the God-concept in Meister Eckhart":

> The synthetic method elaborates the symbolic fantasies resulting from the introversion of the libido through sacrifice. This produces a new attitude to the world, whose very difference offers a new potential. I have termed this transition to a new attitude the transcendent function. In the regenerated attitude the libido that was formerly sunk in the unconscious emerges in the form of some positive achievement. It is equivalent to a renewal of life, which Eckhart symbolizes by God's birth.[9]

Prior to *Memories, Dreams, Reflections,* Jung had written in his paper on Eckhart about ecstasy as a state of "intense vitality" in the psyche. The "feeling of bliss" accompanies "all those moments when one feels born along by the current of life."[10] In his elucidation of the "relativity of the symbol," Jung noted further that "from the empirical standpoint of analytical psychology, the God-image is the symbolic expression of a particular psychic state, or function, which is characterized by its absolute ascendancy over the will of the subject, and can therefore bring about or enforce actions and achievements that could never be done by conscious effort."[11] Clearly Jung understood the emotion of bliss quite well from a *vocational standpoint*. "It was only after the illness," he said later, "that I understood how important it is to affirm one's own destiny."[12] While reflecting on the meaning of Meister Eckhart's play on words "*Gott ist selig* [blissful] *in der Seele* [soul],"[13] he asked himself, sometime prior to 1921, "whence comes this 'blissful' feeling, this ecstasy of love?"[14]

Later, in his final work, "Symbols and the Interpretation of Dreams" from *Man and His Symbols,* Jung spoke of archetypes as "images" that were at the same time "emotions." In this essay, he remarked, "It is a great mistake in practice to treat an archetype as if it were a mere name, word, or concept. It is far more than that: it is a piece of life, an image connected with the living individual by the bridge of emotion."[15] So James and Jung agreed that one chief concern of life is the attainment of what James called a *supernatural kind of happiness* in his chapter "The Religion of Healthy-Mindedness" in *Varieties of Religious Experience*.[16]

Here is another important connection in Jung's essay on Meister Eckhart that took a more positive glance at states of transpersonal bliss:

> It is a state strongly reminiscent of that of the child . . . We can safely say that the restoration of the earlier paradisal state is the cause of this blissfulness . . . "Childlikeness" is therefore a symbol of that unique inner condition on which "blissfulness" depends.[17]

A remarkable change took place in Jung following the blissful experiences that bathed him in a sea of transpersonal happiness or joy during his visions of the sacred marriage. His point of view changed with regard to the priority of the image over emotion. The powerful emotions that then swept through him during the writing of *Answer to Job,* published in 1952, changed his point of view utterly. His empirical reflections on the nature of the God-image and the transcendent function were now *accompanied* by music (feeling), and he channeled the God-function for the transformation of the *World-Soul*. Here the bridge between the symbol, elegiac reverie, and religious emotion, with a capital *E,* had become transparent; the empirical and psychological boundaries of his mind had become united into one mental state in which the metaphysical reality of the Higher Self was now included. During the composition of *Answer to Job,* the Higher Self was active in him as a uniting or God-function for all of the higher cognitions of his empirical science. The entire book was dictated to him through an aesthetic mode of feeling, which was both mythopoetic and empirical. In this one book, the only book Jung said he would not change, he returned to the lyrical style of poetry he had begun during the composition of *The Red Book*, but which he later abandoned in favor of science. He returned to a musical-poetical play with lyrical-inspired emotions, words, and images to characterize the qualitatively multivalent experience of the Self, which sounded through him during the earthquake of *Answer to Job* as both blissful and wrathful, awful and rapturous, at once. Yet what may have been the catalyst for the writing of this book was his experience of the Higher Self. During his visions, he was clearly in the consciousness of the Higher Self in which all things he had known throughout his life were known together in the same experience. "It seemed to me that I was high up in space. Far below I saw the globe of the earth, bathed in a glorious blue light."[18] This is the light at the ultraviolet end of the *psychoid continuum,* where psyche is no longer merely psyche but matter too.

> Something new entered my field of vision. A short distance away I saw in space a tremendous dark block of stone, like a meteorite ... An entrance led into a small antechamber. To the right of the entrance, a black Hindu sat silently in lotus posture upon a stone bench. He wore a white gown, and I knew that he expected me. Two steps led up to this antechamber, and inside, on the left, was a gate to the temple.[19]

Jung then saw a *door* with a wreath of bright flames. He had actually seen such a doorway when he visited the Temple of the Holy Tooth at Kandy in Ceylon. As he approached the steps leading up to the gateway, a strange thing happened to him; it was as if he were now carrying along everything he had ever experienced and done—all of his deeds, experiences, words, and actions, everything that happened to him in his lifetime up to that point. He was everything that he was, and that was *everything*.[20]

To be sure, the black stone, the dark Hindu seated in a lotus posture in deep inward meditation who awaited him, and the *doorway* he approached were all symbols of his Higher Self. Although Jung never made use of his inner experiences from these visions to formulate a concept of the supraconscious, he clearly had sufficient evidence from his own experiences to posit a hypothesis of emotion as an ultimate transcendental quality of *bliss* that he had not only read about in Eckhart, or James's *Varieties*, but which he had now tasted, during his own emotional savoring of the Holy Spirit.

NOTES

1. This is a re-working of a section of my book *Walt Whitman: Shamanism, Spiritual Democracy, and the World Soul.*
2. Jung, *MDR,* 177.
3. Jung, *MDR,* 293.
4. Jung, *MDR,* 293, italics mine.
5. Jung, *MDR,* 295–296.
6. Jung, *MDR,* 297.
7. Jung, "The Psychology of Dementia Praecox," CW 3, ¶78.
8. Jung, CW 9ii, ¶179.
9. Jung, *Psychological Types,* CW 6, ¶427.
10. Jung, CW 6, ¶422.
11. Jung, CW 6, ¶412.
12. Jung, *MDR,* 297.
13. Jung, CW 6, ¶418, Note fn. 157.
14. Jung, CW 6, ¶422.
15. Jung, CW 18, ¶589.
16. James, *Writings 1902–1910,* 77–120.
17. Jung, CW 6, ¶422.
18. Jung, *MDR,* 290.
19. Jung, *MDR,* 290.
20. Jung, *MDR,* 290, 291.

Chapter 42

EMPIRICAL EVIDENCE FOR THE SUPRACONSCIOUS

When he was lecturing at the University of Calcutta in Bengal, Jung was most critical of the belief that in Samadhi ego consciousness was extinguished. As he said in a late talk with Miguel Serrano in 1959:

> I tried to explain to them that if Ramakrishna, for example, had been able to get rid of his consciousness completely in his moments of profound ecstasy, then those very moments would have been non-existent. He would never have been able to remember them or record them, or even to consider them as having any existence at all ... Since the unconscious really means the not-conscious, nobody can gain that state while he is alive, and be able to remember it afterwards, as the Hindus claim ... As for your hypothesis about the superconscious, that is a metaphysical concept and as a consequence outside of my interests. I wish to proceed solely on facts and experiences.[1]

One of the problems Jung had with the concept of the supraconscious was his observation that "The Indian feels himself to be outside good and evil."[2] No one is ever outside the problem of good and evil, not even a saint. By taking practical steps, as taught by Swami Vivekananda, consciousness was said, nevertheless, to achieve the state of supraconsciousness, which, in Sanskrit is called *Asamprajnata*. "When this state, Asamprajnata, superconsciousness, is reached," Vivekananda said "the Samadhi becomes seedless."[3] The highest state of Samadhi was said to be a changeless state, when the seeds are "fried"—.[4] In this view, anyone could potentially become a vehicle for the awakening of Asamprajnata, which was believed to be the fountain-head of all ethics. In the Hindu theory of ethics, a person who'd attained *Asamprajnata* was believed to be able to control ego consciousness and the unconscious. Then war between the opposites of good and evil in the psyche could then be solved. In *Asamprajnata,* the Absolute, however, it was believed that no incipient violence could be found, for religions "all have the very same experience when they transcend the body."[5] But Asamprajnata can only be reached in the Body Self.

For Jung, Samadhi was outside the field of his interests as an empirical psychologist; it had no relevance in the domain of psychotherapeutic practice.

According to Sulagna Sengupta in her book *Jung in India*, Indra Sen's integral psychology was based largely on the writings of Jung and Sri Aurobindo. Sen hypothesized that *the urge for wholeness was not just the basic force of human nature, but the most vital aspect of organic evolution as well.*[6] He believed Jung had gone the furthest of all modern psychologists in advancing the concept of the Self. He also believed Jung had failed to comprehend the idea of the supraconscious properly. In a paper called "Personality, Its Development and the 'Inner Voice': A Study in Jung. What Integral Psychology Can Contribute," Sen pointed to a complex issue in Jung's writings, namely the moral demands that the inner voice placed on a person through his or her vocation or calling. Sen believed Jung's mixed-up understanding of the nature of the inner voice was due to his inability to distinguish between the conscious and supraconscious and their relevance to the development of the human personality as a whole. Sen asserted: "Integral Psychology has an Integral Yoga for its actualization. Does Jungian psychology not need a Jungian Yoga?"[7]

The key to understanding the links between Integral Yoga and Jungian psychology can be found in Chapter 14 of Jung's book *Aion: Researches into the Phenomenology of the Self.* There Jung wrote about the meaning of the double serpent motif: "That the snake, contrary to expectation, should be a counterpart of the Anthropos [Self] is corroborated by the fact—of especial significance—that it is on the one hand a well-known allegory for Christ, and on the other hand appears to be equipped with the gift of wisdom and of supreme spirituality."[8] By making the lower chthonic or instinctive side of the snake symbol conscious in us, we are also making the Shadow conscious and thereby opening ourselves up to the greatest possibility of light. The main question for analytical psychology is whether Asamprajnata can be studied through empirical research.

One of my aims in this chapter is to state my own personal view as a Jungian analyst on the question of whether the transpsyche can be studied scientifically. And, if so, how might we do that?

Recall that Jung said during the Terry Lectures at Yale University in 1937 that his standpoint is "exclusively phenomenological" and "concerned with occurrences, events, experiences—in a word, with facts."[9] In "On the Nature of the Psyche," Jung included the supraconscious in his concept of the "*psychoid*." Jung made room for the supraconscious in his theory of the unconscious. Yet, like Fechner and James, he saw it as a hypothesis only. He found no evidence for it in his empirical studies. This was because he thought it was a metaphysical postulate that was beyond the margins of science. To posit that it was a part of the psychoid continuum seemed to him to be more modest. If the psychoid could be carried over into ego-consciousness, Jung believed it could enormously extend the bounds of our mental horizons.[10] The psychoid is the "*unknown psychic . . . of which nothing can be known directly*."[11] It cannot be explained through any scientific formula. Fechner believed that we may be moving in an evolutionary way toward "an absolutely universal consciousness," which may be "reached."[12]

James and Jung were searching for an understanding of religious experience from a transnational point of view. In order to provide a portrait of what I mean by *transnational study of* Asamprajnata, I must first clarify my psychological view of what the objects of study in the field of analytical psychology are.

Analytical psychology is first and foremost empirical, based upon observations. What comes up in dream analyses and patient-therapist interactions in consulting rooms provides us with clues about the structure and dynamics of the unconscious as well as the central archetype of wholeness in the human personality, the Self. The question of whether Asamprajnata can be studied is not typically the subject of inquiry for an analyst; it is, rather, a question of God-images, archetypal numina that cross our paths. The factors shaping religious beliefs—archetypes—can be deduced through their emotional *numinosity*. What possesses a patient during moments of strong spiritual emotion are what Jung called *complexes and their archetypal cores*. They can be observed, for example, when they *grip* patients and stir them up into numinous states of mind. For the most part, Jung believed that we could not study God, only God-images. He said, moreover, that there was a "religious function" in the psyche that produced God-images and that *religious dreams* might arise during moments of crisis when grappling with an apparently insoluble moral or vocational problem. James and Jung were men with callings to the natural sciences. Their vocations were both scientific and religious in nature, and both viewed themselves as philosophers.

Absolute knowledge of God, Jung believed, was beyond empirical investigation. Late in life, however, Jung expanded his views to include the possibility of an objective knowledge of God. For example, in a 1950 interview John Freeman asked Jung directly, "*Do you now believe in God?*" Jung replied, "Now? [Pause]. Difficult to answer. I know. I don't need to believe. I know."[13] He explained his position further: "You see, the word belief is a difficult thing for me. I don't believe. I must have a reason for a certain hypothesis."[14] We can make hypotheses about God, in other words, but never know the Absolute nature of the Divinity. The Absolute is a metaphysical idea that captures a person or a group. In Jung's view, "one never *possesses* a metaphysical belief but is *possessed by it*."[15] We can be captured by any God-image. The affectivity of the metaphysical conviction tells us that it is objectively real as a psychic phenomenon, a fact that "gives us a sure empirical basis from which to proceed."[16] Jung's standpoint, like James's, was agnostic and empirical. As Jung said in a letter to Evans-Wentz in 1939, "I don't compete with confessions of religious creeds."[17] This is an important letter to consider. Twenty-one years later in 1960, Jung said further: "Agnosticism is never sufficient when it comes to the question of life as a whole."[18]

By this time, Jung had amassed enough scientific proof of God's existence to reverse his original opinion; he had examined the God-images of many cultures, yet where his own wholeness was concerned, he had to pronounce his own hypotheses based on his own Self-understandings. In a talk with Miguel Serrano, Jung said on January 23, 1961: "Man should live according to his own nature; he should concentrate on self-knowledge and then live in accordance with the truth about himself . . . Thus, everyone must live in accordance with his nature, both individually and collectively. The best example of that method is to be found in India."[19] The eighty-five-year-old Jung had the highest respect for Indian spirituality. His trip to India helped him advance a theory of the unconscious that included an above or over-consciousness in the psyche. This is the same place in Jung's theorizing where I began my research on vocational dreams at UC Santa Cruz.

Also in the essay "On the Nature of the Psyche," Jung developed the hypothesis of the *psychoid continuum*: a hypothetical "subconsciousness," or "superconsciousness," coexisting with ego-consciousness.[20] He described his experiences of this state in *Memories, Dreams, Reflections,* as detailed in the previous chapter. His vision was of the great interconnectedness *of his emotional personality with the reality of the inner and outer Cosmos, or the Self.* "At the same time this hypothetical 'subconsciousness,' which immediately becomes associated with a 'superconsciousness,' brings out the real point of my argument: the fact, namely, that a second psychic system coexisting with consciousness—no matter what qualities we suspect it of possessing—is of absolutely revolutionary significance in that it could radically alter our view of the world."[21] Jung's experience of ecstasy in 1944 gave him empirical proof about the nature of the supraconscious.

As I mentioned earlier, Jung reread James's *Varieties* when he rewrote his theory of the collective psyche in 1948. He must have been reading, therefore, passages James quoted from Vivekananda regarding control of psychic prana:

> How to control the Prana is the one idea of Pranayama ... The Prana which is working this mind and body is the nearest to us of all the Prana in this universe ... The Prana is the vital force in every being. The mind can exist on a still higher plane, the superconscious. When the mind has attained to that state, which is called Samadhi—perfect concentration, superconsciousness—it goes beyond the limits of reason, and comes face to face with facts which no instinct or reason can ever know. All manipulations of the subtle forces of the body, the different manifestations of Prana, if trained, give a push to the mind, help it to go up higher, and become superconscious, from where it acts.[22]

Thus, for Vivekananda, Asamprajnata was a scientific fact that could be studied phenomenologically. It was, nevertheless, beyond the limits of reason. Although Jung finally agreed there was a possible supraconscious in the unconscious, he maintained that one's own experiences of it could never be all-embracing.[23] Therefore, if the experience of Brahman is not all-embracing, then Buddha-mind is not all-embracing, nor is Christ-mind, nor Allah-mind, nor your mind, nor my mind. We must all have our own individual experiences of the Self, and these are always limiting. Limitlessness can only be known when we are limited to the utmost. If the *psychoid* is carried over into ego-consciousness, it might enormously extend the bounds of our mental horizons.[24]

About the "*unknown psychic* . . . of which nothing can be known directly," there are numerous explanations.[25] Earlier I remarked that I thought analytical psychology should expand its boundaries to include this boundless domain of the transpsyche in its theory of the Self. Yet Jung did include it, and to take Jung forward we must start there.

The way of the Self, as taught by all religions, the mind of God, cannot be reasoned. Thus, Asamprajnata cannot be mapped; it cannot be explained through any scientific formula. Like Jung, James too appeared to have undergone some kind of a reversal in his theorizing:

> The absolute is not the impossible being I once thought it . . . we finite minds may simultaneously be co-conscious with one another in a superhuman intelligence…Fechner treats the superhuman consciousness he so fervently believes in as an hypothesis only… He talks not only of the earth-soul and of the star-souls, but of an integrated soul of all things in the cosmos without exception, and this he calls God just as others call it the absolute.

James went even further by asserting, again like Jung, that there was no "absolutely totalized all-enveloper."[26]

As a Jungian analyst, I agree with James and Jung. I think we are all in similar boats, as fellow travelers on the currents of the Cosmic Ocean. Ultimately, I believe the Universe is the Godhead: *I = Cosmos*. By capital *I*, I mean an endless calculus of the Infinite. No one can say what Infinity is; it is forever unfathomable. Therefore all God-images are lowercase *i*'s. I also agree with Murray Stein that all God-men or God-women fall short of "full incarnation of the Ground of Being despite theological claims to the contrary."[27] All God-men and God-women are merely incarnations of God-images, and no *i* in history has ever embodied God, the Absolute, and never will. Transpersonal theory and practice would be wise to take the Jamesian and Jungian findings into careful consideration.

Many religious figures in history have become momentarily at-one with the Cosmos. But the door to the universe's deeper or higher recesses is in us all. We may all step through it, for brief moments, and when we do, we are open to oneness or unity of being. Such states of oneness, I think, can and indeed should be studied scientifically. Yet, so far in history, the study of Cosmic Consciousness has typically been descriptive, that is, qualitatively portrayed through personal narrative descriptions. What we need, according to Jung, are dreams and intuitions that can provide more objective facts. Rather than try to present some grand theory of the transpsychic state for future research in analytical psychology, let me conclude, therefore, with a dream of my own, to further illustrate my point. I had the following dream at UC Santa Cruz, on October 12, 1981, while I was writing my thesis on Meister Eckhart, practicing Christian prayer and Iyengar Yoga, and teaching Jung.

> *I find myself walking through the halls of a University campus toward a Roman Catholic Cathedral at the center of the campus. As I near the doorway of the Sanctum Sanctorum, or holy of holies, at the central point, I see my old English professor from Diablo Valley College, Clark McKowen. Clark is extremely friendly, both with me and with several of the other students. He is off to teach his class, but he points out his office to me before he leaves; it is located just outside of the Cathedral. After he is gone, I notice that the door to Clark's office has been left ajar, so I peek my head inside, with my (ex)-wife, Danielle. I see many different statues of the Hindu deities on an altar; there are many Eastern relics, Indian figures, strewn throughout the room. There is a shaft, moreover, which extends from the ground floor of the office right up to the sky, like a chute, or an air hole. Clark is busy taking an interest in the other students while teaching his class, so I go my own way with Danielle, toward the Cathedral. I enter the Cathedral door and meet eyes with a beautiful woman bishop who greets the two of us (the Jewess dream-anima and I) from her pew at the tabernacle. She looks heavenward from her seat, and I see the glorious paintings of the Saints and transfigured Jesus, outstretched through an opening at the top of the Cathedral dome, which reaches out to a view of vistas across the sky. I am filled with the holiness of the place, and when I look back at the bishop, I see that she is peering with a deep compassionate look into the very core of my soul. Her look is so intense that I am magnetically drawn to her out of my own love for Christ. The sun begins to filter in through the stained-glass windows, high above us, and a ray of Golden sunlight suddenly*

shines through the painted glass and reflects clearly into her clay-brown eyes. As she is looking directly into my soul, I feel spellbound, separate from her, but mysteriously united. When the ray of light strikes her eye, it casts a sudden mirror reflection in my eye, so that we are both illuminated by the same incredible Light. My body remains firmly grounded, kneeling down upon my pew; however, when the Light penetrates my soul's body, my spirit suddenly takes a vertical ascent, toward the highest rafters of the Church, which opens up to the Cosmos. I can feel the connectedness of my earthly dream-body to the solid Ground, but my spiritual body is soaring above it, while still connected corporeally to the prayer bench at the same time. The Rapture that enters me is truly divine, and I am wholly indebted to the woman bishop, for having chosen me for this spiritual experience. I look across, as my spirit-body exits the dome, and I see with my eyes the Resurrected Christ, with His eyes of peace and tranquility looking directly across at me with his sight and knowledge and love at my spiritualized body [this image of the transfigured Christ reminds me upon awakening of a painting of the risen Christ in Rome, painted majestically against the blue expanse of the sky, I believe, by Rubens].

The basic idea in the dream is that of a ground, or a sense of grounding, as I kneel in the Church pew, from which my physical Body Self is able to experience the ascension of my Spiritual Self to a place of equivalent sight with the Resurrected Christ in the sky. The earthly and celestial spheres are united, in other words, in one grounded experience. The connection between ground or bench, the bishop's clay-brown eyes, and blue sky above the dome parallels the office of the English teacher who has a host of replicas of Hindu divinities and a shaft or air hole connecting above and below in his office. The Eastern and Western parallels are suggestive of upper and lower dimensions of the collective unconscious. In order to gain a vista from above, the light of the sun had to be reflected in my eye first by means of a mediator, or *mediatrix*. This reflective function is supplied by the Catholic anima, the female bishop, who receives a reflection of the Divine light into her eye through the stained-glass window. Only when she has perceived this ray of spiritual sunlight and mirrored it through the window refraction, as a reflection in her eye, can she then refract it back into my dream body's eye, a phenomenon that suddenly uplifts my spiritual body into an inexpressible ecstasy. When I meet eyes above with the Resurrected Christ, I'm in a transfigured state, while my soul's body is kneeling in a grounded way on my pew.

When individuals are not sufficiently grounded in their physical body, an *exstasis* such as this one can lead to a psychological dissociation, which may be dangerous to the ego and its stability in reality. Four things kept me grounded at this time, however: 1) I was a teaching assistant in the poet William Everson's course "Birth of a Poet"; 2) I was practicing Hatha Yoga every day; 3) I was running several times a week; and 4) my wife, Danielle, was close to giving birth to our son, Immanuel; his due date was on Christmas Eve, but he was actually born on December 28, the last day of the Festival of Lights, or Chanukah.

I was also thinking, at this time, about the possible correlations between Eckhart's notion of the Godhead and Jung's hypothesis of the *psychoid continuum,* where the parallelism of psyche and matter are viewed as one indistinguishable unitary reality or *unus mundus*. Although my thoughts on this complementarity of the two parallel concepts was not yet discursively worked out in any specific detail, when I had this dream my intuitions were, nevertheless, in advance of my cognitive abilities (introverted thinking) and seemed to be outside of time. The meeting with the eyes of the Resurrected Christ took place in a *synchronistic* continuum that Jung said added a fourth dimension to the triad of modern science—space, time, and causality.

This dream conveyed to my conscious mind the idea in physics known as *refraction,* when a light wave passes across a boundary between two media and is accompanied by a change in the speed and wavelengths of the wave. The wave of sunlight changes at the boundary between the stained glass and the bishop; the wave of sunlight slows down and transforms into a smaller wave, with a shorter wavelength by the time it enters me. But the intensity of the light is such that when it is transmitted across the boundary, through the painted glass, and hits the bishop's eye, it is nevertheless potent and packed enough with intensity; it is not so charged as to obliterate either the consciousness of the bishop or my dream ego, however. Instead the refraction of light leads to an emotional illumination, an ecstasy, that leads my spiritual body to rise up through the dome, to observe the risen Christ, against the blue vastness of the sky. The Christian anima is, therefore, a medium of *re-flexio* (reflection) in my psyche that makes the transition to a higher plane of perceiving and knowing and loving possible. This kind of inner experience, where my dream ego is enabled to momentarily glimpse its essential equality with the ascended Christ, was facilitated at this time by my reading of Eckhart, my studies in Hinduism and Buddhism, and through my relationship with my spiritual teacher, Bill Everson. Looking back at this dream today, its significance becomes even clearer. The focus on the eyes (both the bishop's and my eyes) and the eyes of the resurrected Christ reminds me of what is perhaps the most famous of all Eckhart's sayings, in a translation by a Theravada Buddhist: "The eye with which I see God is the same eye with which God sees me: my eye and God's eye are one eye, one seeing, one knowing, one love."[28]

The interesting thing about this dream is that I had only stepped foot in a Catholic Church once in my life, in 1967, when I visited the Cathedral of Notre-Dame in Paris with my mother and three siblings. My association to the stained-glass window is to that Mother Church, even though my dream-Cathedral was located at the center of a university in California. Thus, the East-West parallels I worked out thirty-five years later were all there in image-form in my dream.

At the time of the dream, I'd just written a paper on "Analytical Psychology and Kundalini Yoga" for a class in Indic Religious Traditions in the Fall quarter of 1981. The shaft would seem to represent the *Sushumna*: the passageway through the spinal cord through which the kundalini energies pass through seven chakras to the crown of the head, the place of illumination, compassion, and bliss. This is the place of Absolute Knowledge in Vedanta.

Thus, it does not matter whether the doorway is through a Buddhist or Shinto Temple, an Indian Pagoda, the Belur Math, a Jewish Temple, Christian Cathedral, or a Mosque. The doorway to the Universe's deeper recesses, as James and Jung both hypothesized, may be found within each of us. We may see a host of religious figures up there. But all doorways and all religious figures are merely passageways and mediums to the Cosmos, to a deeper and infinitely unknowable experience of the Self.

Notes

1. Jung, *C. G. Jung Speaking*, 392–394.
2. Jung, *MDR*, 276.
3. Vivekananda, *TCWSV*, vol. 1, 213.
4. Vivekananda, *TCWSV*, vol. 1, 272.
5. Vivekananda, *TCWSV*, vol. 7, 43.
6. Sen, *Further Studies in Integral Psychology*, 158–161; referenced in Sengupta, *Jung in India*, 226, 227.
7. Sen, "Personality, Its Development and the 'Inner Voice'"; cited in Sengupta, 229.
8. Jung, *Aion*, CW 9ii, ¶369.
9. Jung, "Psychology and Religion (The Terry Lectures)," CW 11, ¶4.
10. Jung, "On the Nature of the Psyche," CW 8, ¶178.
11. Jung, CW 8, ¶185.
12. James, *Writings 1902–1910*, 700.
13. Jung, *C. G. Jung Speaking*, 428.
14. Jung, 437.
15. Jung, "Answer to Job," CW 11, ¶735.
16. Jung, CW 11, ¶735.
17. Jung, *Letters*, vol. 1, 263, 264.
18. Jung, *C. G. Jung Speaking*, 449.
19. Jung, 463.
20. Jung, CW 8, ¶178.
21. Jung, CW 8, ¶178.
22. Vivekananda, *TCWSV*, vol. 1, 150.
23. Jung, *Letters*, 1, 261–262.
24. Jung, CW 8, ¶178.
25. Jung, CW 8, ¶185.
26. James, *Writings 1902–1910*, 764.
27. Stein, *Minding the Self*, 17.
28. Walsche, *The Complete Mystical Works of Meister Eckhart*, 298.

Chapter 43

JAMES'S HYPOTHESIS OF THE TRANSMISSION OF CONSCIOUSNESS

In the previous chapter, I presented a dream that lends support to the possible reality of the Higher Self, which may be experienced in a non-ordinary state of mind. I did not find corroborating evidence in my reading of William James to support the idea of *refraction as a psychological fact of my own personal experience* until by chance I came upon an essay I had previously overlooked, James's 1896 "On Human Immortality." This was the first time he referred to the German physicist Fechner in a positive way after his earlier dismissal of him. In Leipzig, Fechner's "psychophysics" had launched an entirely new field of research, namely the correlation between sensory experiences, mental states, and brain activity. Building on Darwinian evolutionary theories in biology, James followed Fechner in this essay by postulating a psychological paradigm to account for *evolutionary transformations within individuals and in complex systems that strive for unity within multiplicity, both in humans and in the immeasurable diversity of Nature.*

James viewed consciousness as an ever-flowing "stream" in which thoughts, habits, feelings, will, intuitions, intentionality, and sensations might all be *unified* by flowing successively into the Spiritual Self at its third level of experiential attainment. For James, consciousness was a unique element of human subjectivity, which he termed the tripartite *Empirical Self* in 1890. Beyond the three domains of the Body, Social, and Spiritual Self was the metaphysical *knower*, which he believed was outside the purview of science.[1] James had been quite familiar with ecstatic religious experience through his father, a Swedenborgian, and his meaningful relationship to Emerson. He carefully examined ecstatic religious experiences as a variety of *intuitive knowing*. This led to his theoretical ideas concerning the American Soul and its "waves" of "healthy minded" dispensations, which James felt were sweeping through the country. By

1902, when *Varieties of Religious Experience* was published, his view had broadened to include the Infinite. This transcendental element later entered into the mainstream of American psychology through James's radical empiricism in 1907.

Researchers today are turning increasingly to dynamic systems theory, complexity theory, and Jung's psychology in an effort to explain the scientific notion of synchronicity. At the same time, researchers in the field of neurobiology and neuropsychology are turning to James in an effort to articulate a better understanding of consciousness itself.[2] *The consciousness that is aware of itself through its empirical experiences is what James defined as the Self.* This Self in all of its aspects is encompassed by a "halo," "fringes," or "fields," where the consciousness of many individuals may touch other related fields, which, in turn, may unify through subjective experiences of complexity from some indefinite infinite *thought* outside the margins. How evolutionary thoughts enter our awareness from a metaphysical or cosmic source beyond the margins is through a *transmissive potential* in the human brain, which can act as a carrier of information through the subliminal doorway to the receptive mind.

The subject of immortality needed to be explored not only by philosophers and metaphysicians, but, first and foremost, by an *empirical psychologist* who could lend scientific credence to what the ancients sensed to be true about the existence of life after death. James asserted positively: "Immortality is one of the great spiritual needs of man."[3] For too long the subject of immortality had been reserved for prophets, ministers, and theologians of the world's creeds. For James, because of its central importance to human psychology, *immortality* needed to be explored through a psychological lens that included not only theologians of every kind but also metaphysicians, anthropologists, biologists, physicists, psychical researchers, and even mathematicians.

To get at the kernel of the question, James began by presenting two grains of truth, two points of thought, which he believed fit well enough together to address the difficulty of answering such a complex problem as human immortality:

> The first of these difficulties is relative to the absolute dependence of our spiritual life, as we know it here, upon the brain... How can we believe in

life hereafter when Science has once for all attained to proving, beyond possibility of escape, that our inner life is a function of that famous material, the so-called "gray matter" of our cerebral convolutions? How can the function possibly persist after its organ has undergone decay?[4]

James then proceeded to give his credentials as a "physiological psychologist" and asked his audience to look at the question with him a little more closely:

> Everyone knows that arrests of brain development occasion imbecility, that blows on the head abolish memory or consciousness, and that brain-stimulants and poisons change the quality of our ideas ... What the laboratories and hospitals have lately been teaching us is not only that thought in general is one of the brain's functions, but that the various special forms of thinking are functions of special portions of the brain.[5]

Following this brilliant use of rhetoric, James proceeded for purposes of his argument to ask his listeners to adopt a general doctrine, as if it were established absolutely and without the possibility of any restriction. He asked his listeners to accept the *brain dependency* idea as a postulate: "the great psycho-physiological formula: *thought is a function of the brain*."[6] This postulate, he said, was the objection to immortality, but while the function of the brain might perish, he added, "it is not at all impossible, but on the contrary quite possible, that the life may still continue when the brain itself is dead."[7] James then went on to present his theory of *refraction* to support the transmission hypothesis: "In the case of a colored glass, a prism, or a refracting lens, we have transmissive function. The energy of light, no matter how produced, is by the glass sifted and limited in color, and by the lens or prism determined to a certain path in shape."[8]

Having said all this, James proceeded with this thesis: "when we think of the law that thought is a function of the brain, *we are not required to think of productive function only; we are entitled also to consider permissive or transmissive function*."[9] Outside the margins, beyond the mere surface-veil of phenomena, there is a world of genuine realities behind the door. This is the fourth or metaphysical dimension of the Self that James asked his listeners to take into careful consideration. He asked them to suppose, now, that:

> ... the dome, opaque enough at all times to the full super-solar blaze, could at certain times and places grow less so, and let certain beams pierce through into this sublunary world. These beams would be so many finite rays, so to speak, of consciousness, and they would vary in quantity and quality as the opacity varied in degree. Only at particular times and places would it seem that, as a matter of fact, the veil of nature can grow thin and rupturable enough for such effects to occur. But in those places gleams, however finite and unsatisfying, of the absolute life of the universe, are from time to time vouchsafed. Glows of feeling, glimpses of insight, and streams of knowledge and perception float into our finite world.[10]

When I first read this essay, I did not see any connection to my dream and its possible interpretation because I did not understand what James was attempting to say. After a second reading, I began to see the parallels. At times, when our brains form a transparency in the veil, or margin, or a crack in the doorway, "comparative floods of spiritual energy" may thence pour in. The transformations of consciousness may not end with the decay of the body. For when a brain finally stops acting altogether, or decays, James asserted, the "special stream of consciousness which it subserved" may yet survive death. Vanishing entirely from the natural world, the body perishes, yet "the sphere of being that supplied the consciousness" may "still be intact in that more real world with which, even whilst here, it was continuous, the consciousness might, in ways unknown to us, continue still."[11] Several pages later he went on to quote Emerson and especially Fechner at length.

What interests me here are the metaphors of the dome, colored glass, and the prism, or *refracting lens,* in James's descriptions of the transmissive function. The transmissive hypothesis of the brain asserts as a postulate that the spiritual life of evolving humanity is not dependent on the "gray matter" for consciousness to become Self-aware. Rather, the mind as an independent agency operates beyond the fringes to illuminate itself in humanity's soul. In other words, the brain is a transmissive organ for the transmission of consciousness from a superior intelligence in Nature and the Cosmos. For James, consciousness was already present in Nature and the Universal Mind. To *transmute human consciousness within the margins utterly* and lift itself up into God-consciousness or Divine-awareness, it needed a refractive organ in which to reflect itself. The transmissive agent for this metamorphosis lay in the interactions between the archetype of the soul-image and the subjective ego-consciousness in which the refraction process takes place.

Jung described a "zero point" that is transcendent of all polarities during moments of pure experiencing, being, and seeing. When the "light" of Nature is refracted in ego and anima, the Spiritual Self may experience a quality of consciousness, where the empirical and metaphysical dimensions touch and do not touch.

In this *transpsychic* domain, above the dome of our individualized awareness, is a co-consciousness of higher relations with a metaphysical *Knower*. During such an experience the Knower and Known are one; they are nondual. This is the common ground of psychophysical reality that James and Jung both arrived at in their late works. They were inspired by the findings of modern physics to extend their ideas into the territory of a trans-psychic field and to postulate a *visionary function of the mind*, by which the "I" consciousness sees into the Divine and the Divine sees the subjective "you" or "me."

Notes

1. James, *Writings 1878–1899*, 208.
2. For a discussion of contemporary research on dynamic systems theory, complexity theory, and Jung's scientific notion of synchronicity, see Cambray and Swain, *Research in Analytical Psychology*. For a discussion of contemporary research on James, neurobiology, and neuroscience, see Pribram, "Self-Consciousness and Intentionality."
3. James, 1100.
4. James, 1102.
5. James, 1102–1103.
6. James, 1104.
7. James, 1107–1108.
8. James, 1109–1110.
9. James, 1110.
10. James, 1110.
11. James, 1111.

Chapter 44

Reflections on Non-ordinary Experience, the Spiritualization of Matter, and Synchronicity

In James's 1890 model of the mind, the streams of consciousness in the Empirical Self were said to flow through the 1) Material, 2) Social, 3) Spiritual, and 4) Metaphysical Selves. All four of these plural Selves were included in James's model of the Empirical Self, shown in Diagram 1 on the next page.

In this chapter, I will explore the subject of trans-psychic states of consciousness and provide an example from my own personal experience to ground my hypothesis about vocational dreams and synchronicity (discussed in-depth in Chapter 37). Trans-psychic experiences are outside the psychic sphere because they can also manifest themselves in the world of matter, not only in the mind, brain, or human body, but also in Nature. When the trans-psyche is experienced, everything becomes filled with Self-consciousness: trees, ocean, rivers, birds, animals, bees, butterflies, everything becomes seen as filled with Self-awareness. I will ask in what follows: *What is consciousness? Do trees have a consciousness? What is the hidden organizer behind synchronistic events*? The organizing principle of synchronicity might best be said to correspond in James's model of the Self to the Transcendental Thinker. By Transcendental, James meant that there is a Thinker that is transcendent to ego-consciousness that can sometimes incarnate to think our thoughts. It is probably from this transcendental level of consciousness that meaningful coincidences are organized. I postulate that all four dimensions of the Self James hypothesized can be observed to be united by a complementarity of ordinary consciousness with "supraconsciousness" (in Sanskrit *Asamprajnata*) in a zero-point.

At certain times, a transcendent and meaningful patterning of experience emerges, accompanied by a state of mind in which one feels an equality with everything else present in one's consciousness. I refer to this non-ordinary phenomenon as a Moment of Spiritual Democracy, a *transpsychic* state of mind. Spiritual democracy is the realization of the oneness of humanity with the universe and all its forces. In the transpsychic streams of consciousness, synchronistic events may occur, as there is an experience of connection, complementarity, and unity between the Empirical Self and the whole of Nature.

Diagram 1 (Copyright ©Steven Herrmann)

Wolfgang Pauli and C. G. Jung corresponded for more than a quarter-century, and they explored ways of conceptualizing phenomena that do not appear to be governed by the laws of causality. Pauli was clearly in the role of the physicist by vocation, whereas Jung was operating in the role of a healer of emotional and mental disorders, the medical doctor and administrator of the meaning cure. Jung decided to pursue his vocation toward the natural sciences after his dream about a giant radiolarian. Jung was also someone who had contemplated the conceptual split between spirit and matter, including the study of alchemy and philosophical and religious ideas across cultures and back to ancient times. Their thoughts complemented one another, while they each held differing points of view. Their exchange prompted Jung to develop and clarify his views on synchronicity.

In a letter to Wolfgang Pauli in March, 1953, Jung wrote that in his essay on synchronicity, "I attempted to open up a new path to the 'state of spiritualization' [*Beseeltheit*] of Matter by making the assumption that 'being is endowed with meaning' (i.e., extension of the archetype in the object)."[1] Pauli discussed spiritualization as a process of "going right to the archetypal source of the natural sciences and thus to a new form of religion."[2] Interestingly, Pauli was reading James before he met Jung.

What might Pauli, as a physicist, have meant by *religion*? Wolfgang Pauli and Jung did not hold a dualistic view on this question. Instead, like James, they held a unitary view of the union of science and religion.[3] This is what Jung referred to as living a religious life: *Careful observation of the data of our dreams as our only source of guidance.*

The union of matter and soul in the writings of Fechner, James, Pauli, and Jung is sometimes remarkably complimentary. No writer captured the meaning of what, in a letter to Jung, Pauli called "a symbol of the *monistic union of matter and soul*" as elegantly as Fechner did in *Nanna, or the Soul-Life of Plants*.[4] The creation of a living symbol of the Earth-Soul, for instance, subsumes both aspects of what Pauli believed could be "the possibility of the simultaneous religious and scientific function of the appearance of archetypal symbols" in a living portrait,[5] one that supports the hypothesis that "a *clear sign*" existed, even in 1861, that "the *psychophysical problem* is also now constellated anew in the scientific sphere."[6] Such a nondual symbol was represented by the great bilateral vision of the Earth as a conscious organism, a Soul that perceives within herself two sides of an apparent split between psyche and matter; psychophysics gave Fechner power to unite them in a metaphor that spoke directly to James.

Transpsychic states of mind in children's dreams
In the search for a language that expresses the quintessence of the "presence of a non-psychic essence" or psychoid nature of archetypes, we might turn to child psychotherapy for some clues.[7] Children are sometimes in touch with this expanded level of consciousness as seen in play, fantasy, and dreams. Jung gave four seminars on children's dreams as a professor

of psychology at the Eidgenössische Technische Hochsculue (ETH) in Zürich in 1936, 1938, 1939, and 1940. These four lectures focused on individuation, dreams, and analytical psychology in general. Jung stressed in his opening remarks that "*early* dreams in particular are of the utmost importance because they are dreamed out of the depths of the personality and, therefore, frequently represent an anticipation of the later destiny."[8] In 1950, Jung went further while taking up the arduous task of editing *Symbols of Transformation*. In the book's final chapter, "The Sacrifice," Jung wrote:

> The problem of the child at this period [three to four] is the discovery of the world and of the great transsubjective reality. . . . It would, therefore, be conceivable that through regression in children archaic products would naturally be unearthed; that is to say, old ways of functioning of the thought system, which is inborn with the brain differentiation, would be awakened.[9]

Jung had seen this fact early on in his readings of William James, who led him to an understanding of the psyche's unlimited extent, which encompassed the most objective regions of the Cosmos. In "Symbols and the Interpretation of Dreams," Jung said, moreover, that "the best examples of the spontaneous production of archetypal images are presented by individuals, particularly children, who live in a milieu where one can be sufficiently certain that any direct knowledge of tradition is out of the question."[10] We *were* the natural mind, in other words, but did not *know* it because our ego consciousness was completely submerged within it. "We got rid of it before understanding it."[11] According to Jung's final thoughts, therefore, children's dreams hold an answer to the enigma of how a process of spiritualization can be initiated in children, adolescents, or adults through a movement of the libido into *trans-subjective reality*.

I've italicized Jung's term *trans-subjective* to highlight the fact that there are thoughts in the psyche that are *transcendent* of ego-consciousness and are, therefore, "above" or outside of the personal self; their source may never be fully known empirically but may be hypostasized to exist as an impersonal spiritual reality.

The supraconscious and psychic objectivity

The significance of Fechner's and James' influence on Jung's development of the notion of the supraconscious has not been generally recognized. The experience of objectivity is often accompanied by openings of the mind to expanded states of non-ordinary awareness. The significance of William James in Jung's development of the notion of psychic objectivity may be inferred by a further examination of Jung's literary tropes. Consider Jung's description of the inner figure he called Philemon:

> In my fantasies I held conversations with him, and he said things which I had not consciously thought. For I observed clearly that it was he who spoke, not I. He said I treated thoughts as if I generated them myself, but in his view thoughts were like animals in the forest, or people in a room, or birds in the air, and added, "If you should see people in a room you would not think that you had made those people, or that you were responsible for them." It was he who taught me psychic objectivity, the reality of the psyche. Through him the distinction was clarified between myself and the object of my thought. He confronted me in an objective manner...[12]

The idea here is that there are personalities in the psyche that simply appear at times when we are open to the nonordinary. Earlier, James had expressed this idea of the existence of a capacity for objective thinking. He pointed out that we should not say "I think," but "it thinks," or that "our thoughts think" in us and for us.[13] He used the term *Transcendental Self* to describe this impersonal dimension of the personality as a working hypothesis for an empirical physiological-psychology, a "uniform correlation of brain-states with mind-states" as a general law of nature.[14]

Jung acknowledged the crucial influence of James's ideas:

> I saw that he confronted questions raised by the psychology of religion with real objectivity and did his best to let whatever happened stand as such and not, as I have said, squeeze it into a theory. He approached these phenomena with an unbiased pragmatic attitude, and thus showed me a path which subsequently led me to gratifying results.

James united the full circle of the sciences with the knowledge of a simultaneous empirical and religious function, which Pauli was in quest of in his letters to Jung. James said religious visioning was a person's most important function. As we've seen, the religious function was, in James's view, the very backbone of the world's religious as a whole, and humanity's most important function was seen as a spiritual purpose present in everyone, a determination to give voice to one's personal destiny. The "zero-point" in Jung's 1948 model, moreover, in "On the Nature of the Psyche," where two points of the "cones" meet at a point of extension and both "touch and do *not* touch" may be found in the psychophysical metaphors of their thoughts about plants.[15]

The link between science, religion, and Nature
Fechner and James both held a psychophysical view that there is a superior consciousness in Nature that Fechner had referred to as an Earth-Soul. In James overview of Fechner's work, he referred to it as a great "complexity in unity." The archetype of the Earth-Soul forms one and the same unitary reality, *unus mundus,* or Self-field, in an ecological and cosmological dimension and psychophysical world—the psychoid. What such correlations suggest is that significance or meaning, in Jung's words, "exist outside the psyche" as well as inside[16]; and it is, in fact, "self-subsistent,"[17] "transcendental,"[18] and "*a priori* in relation to human consciousness."[19] Such meaning of a pre-established harmony, psychophysical reality, or Tao, operating in Nature and the spiritual domain presupposes the existence of an objective bilateral place of vision through which Jung was led to "frame a view of the world which adequately explains the meaning of human existence in the cosmos"[20] and of "archetypal equivalences."[21]

Jung's view for most of his career was that consciousness was the prerogative of humanity; *only in humans was the meaning of consciousness in the Cosmos consecrated through the discovery of a myth to live by.* This was not the view of Fechner, who was a pivotal influence on James. Fechner's psychophysical view was, in James's words, one of great "complexity in unity," which was "another sign of superiority" in Nature; for according to Fechner, the "earth's complexity far exceeds that of any organism, for she includes all organisms in herself."[22] "For him [Fechner] the abstract lived in the concrete, and the hidden motive of all he did was to bring what he called the daylight view of the world into ever greater evidence, that daylight view being this, that the whole universe in its different spans and wave-lengths, exclusions and envelopments, is everywhere alive and conscious."[23]

Fechner, in his thesis on the brain, emphasized a psychophysical view that anticipated contemporary neuroscience. James, who followed him, spent fifty pages in *Psychology: A Briefer Course* on "The Structure of the Brain," "The Functions of the Brain," and "Conditions of Neural Activity." But in his chapter "Concerning Fechner" in *A Pluralistic Universe,* James queried: "Can there be consciousness, we ask, where there is no brain?"[24] "Must every higher means of unification between things be a literal *brain*-fibre, and go by that name? Cannot the earth-mind know otherwise the contents of our minds together?"[25] James continued this query by asserting that Fechner, in his book *Nanna,* was led to infer: "Plants develop centrifugally, spread their organs abroad. For that reason people suppose they have no consciousness, for they lack the unity which the central nervous system provides. But the plant's consciousness may be of another type, being connected with other structures."[26]

My personal story: A Moment of Spiritual Democracy
All of these questions lead me to share a personal story I had about synchronicity as an *organizing* principle. *Is the consciousness that organizes synchronicity conscious of Itself? Is the monistic principle involved in mind-matter correlations—the organizer—dual or nondual? What is the Earth-Mind that envelopes our bodies and brains? Do trees have a soul?* Interestingly, before I read Fechner closely in James's works, I had the following experience.

When I was working on my manuscript *Spiritual Democracy,* I was also tending some small seedling redwood trees out in the park behind our home during one of California's worst droughts. In the spring of 2013, I had a *dream that there was an enormous redwood tree towering up right outside my window. It was enormous, and the tree spoke to me; it thanked me for doing this work.* The tree felt compassion toward me and expressed its gratitude. I considered when I awoke: "Was this towering tree the soul of the redwood tree speaking to me?" After this dream, I began to feel that my consciousness, my perception of myself, was being altered. We think of our acts, the little things we do in life, as small deeds of compassion. But that dream felt like a big act of compassion from the tree, for the several small seedlings I'd recently planted seemed like a miracle, a blessing. *I began to think that these trees might have a consciousness of their own.* I find what we did to the old growth redwood trees in the Oakland hills, the butchering of coastal Sequoias in these hills and many other parts of Northern California, heartbreaking. That scar on the Earth's Soul is still healing in these hills. As with the tragedy of what we did to Indigenous Americans, the grief of all Nature and grief of the spirits still here in the land are with us today. My dream woke me to the possibility that consciousness might be something far more complex and ever-present than we realize. Later, I was led to write this book on James and Jung.

Shortly after the dream, I drove to San Francisco with my wife to attend a wedding engagement party. The young man who was throwing a party for our nephew Brandon took us on a tour around his house. The doorway was hand-crafted from beautiful redwood. He was talking as we walked through the door, when I suddenly noticed that all the wall panels were also constructed from redwood. I then asked him what had happened to the house during the 1906 earthquake.

He said, "Well, the house survived the earthquake."

"Then this redwood was cut from the original old growth grove from across the bay?"

"It was," he replied.

"This is the original redwood from the first growth from the Oakland hills then?" I asked again, astonished. "Well, that's very interesting."

We sat down to a five-course meal, and Brandon, who had just gotten engaged to his sweetheart, now our niece Erin, was being toasted. They were engaged at the very spot where, in 1855, the two ancient Navigation Trees were butchered. The "Navigation Trees" were named by Captain Frederick Beechey of the British Royal Navy. The tremendous conifers were so tall that mariners used them to steer by—from approximately 16 miles out—as they navigated safely through the treacherous Golden Gate. At the site of the Navigation Trees a state historical marker reads: "Until at least 1851, redwood trees on this site were used as landmarks to avoid striking the treacherous submerged Blossom Rock in San Francisco Bay, west of Yerba Buena Island. Although by 1855 the original stems had been logged, today's trees are sprouts from their stumps." The Navigation Trees had measured 32 feet in diameter, not including the bark. This makes these two trees more massive than any other *sequoia sempervirins* that exist in the world today, taller than those found in the majestic groves of Northern

California. The trees "must have been among the most remarkable and gigantic individuals of its species," Gibbons wrote in 1893. Gibbons brought conservationist John Muir to see the "sea of stumps" before the turn of the twentieth century. Muir was reportedly so awed by the girth of the two trees that it brought him to his knees.

The host brought out a bottle of red wine from Northern California. He said it was called "Humbaba" wine. I said, "This is Humbaba wine!?" "Yes, what's so special about that?"
"Well," I said, "you should know who Humbaba was: He was the guardian of the forest that Gilgamesh and Enkidu cut down, the cedar forest. Humbaba was the guardian of the forest!" The *spirit of the forest*, the Earth-soul, was speaking to me!

I hadn't planned to drink any alcohol that night, but when I heard that the wine was called "Humbaba," I said, "Pour me a glass of that!" It was like taking in the spirits of plants, the fruit of the vine, in a new way. It was marvelous, a medicine. I thought, *Well, this is a miracle!* My nephew Brandon got engaged in the forest where the two largest redwoods, the Navigation Trees, were cut down in the East Bay. The host at his party then led us through the door of his house and showed us some first-cut redwood paneling, all along his walls, and then we sat down and imbibed some good "Humbaba" wine!

Now, that's a synchronicity, I thought quietly to myself while savoring each sip.

I wondered, What was the consciousness of the organizing principle that constellated these events? The whole house, the door, the wall paneling, and the wine *seemed to be transmitting some kind of consciousness to me, or at least I felt so.* It changed my perceptions about meaning and my small place in the Cosmos. There are things that happen in our lives that simply can't be explained through causal thinking. There's no cause and effect in any of these events. But something organized them, some acausal principle of order in the Universe. What the organizer is can never be known. It's a mystery, baffling really.

Further Reflections

In a lecture delivered in Cologne and Essen, in February 1933, "The Meaning of Psychology for Modern Man," Jung said, "When man became conscious, the germ of the sickness of dissociation was planted in his soul, for consciousness is at once the highest good and the greatest evil."[27] To counter this sickness in the souls of modern individuals, Jung focused on dreams and their interpretations to get at the root causes of neuroses, which he defined as a disseverance of ego-awareness from the *inner voice of our vocation*. "To concern ourselves with dreams is a way of reflecting on ourselves—the way of self-reflection," he continued.

> It is not our ego consciousness reflecting on itself; rather, it turns its attention to the objective actuality of the dream as a communication or message from the unconscious, unitary soul of humanity. It reflects not on the ego but on the self; it recollects the strange self, alien to the ego, which was ours from the beginning, the trunk from which the ego grew. It is alien to us because we have estranged ourselves from it through the aberrations of the conscious mind.[28]

How strange, I thought, after my dream, that the redwood tree would speak to me personally in such a direct manner. And yet from another standpoint, what I would call the perspective of a *spiritual consciousness in the unconscious*, the tree was communicating to me through its own unique knowledge in psyche and Nature. In "The Spirit Mercurius," Jung spoke, moreover, of the tree as an archetype of the Self, which, in its roots possesses a great concealed secret: *the secret of the personality*. This is the hidden secret of our calling. But this calling, surprisingly, is to be found in the rhizomatic roots, the tree's embeddedness in the living earth.

> The secret is hidden not in the top but in the roots of the tree; and since it is, or has, a personality it also possesses the most striking marks of personality—voice, speech, and conscious purpose, and it demands to be set free by the hero. It [the spirit] is caught and imprisoned against its will, down there in the earth among the roots of the tree. The roots extend into the inorganic realm, into the mineral kingdom. In psychological terms, this would mean that the self has its roots in the body, indeed in the body's chemical elements … it is in no way stranger than the miracle of the living plant rooted in the inanimate earth.[29]

In Jamesian terms, the Spiritual Self is hidden, therefore, in the Body Self. The Body Self and Social Self have their own hidden-away consciousness that needs to be freed from its imprisonment in matter.

In a letter to Fritz Künkel, a German psychotherapist who emigrated to Los Angeles, California, Jung said he once discussed the surprising phenomenon of the personification of spirits with an American psychologist, philosopher, and professor at Harvard:

> I once discussed the proof of identity for a long time with a friend of William James, Professor Hyslop in New York. He admitted that, all things considered, all these metapsychic phenomenon could be explained better by the hypothesis of spirits than by the qualities and peculiarities of the unconscious. And here, on the basis of my own experience, I am bound to concede he is right. In each individual case I must of necessity be skeptical, but in the long run I have to admit that the spirit hypothesis yields better results in practice than any other.[30]

The *spirit hypothesis* is what I began to consider as a possible fact following my dream of the redwood tree, which suggests something subjective about my own tendency toward introverted-irrational-intuition and extroverted-rational-feeling. In his essay "Absolutism of Empiricism," James came right out with his own temperamental preference and prejudice by admitting that he had a strong bias toward "Irrationalism," a penchant toward emotions, feelings, and intuitive thoughts, and if Rationalists might "leave the door for a moment off its hinges," he asked, can any power on earth keep the empirical "Fact" from revealing its presence?[31] "But again," he admitted, echoing the words of Martin Luther,

> Ich kann nicht anders. I show my feelings; why will they not show theirs? I know they have a personal feeling about the through-and-through universe... Their persistence in telling me that feeling has nothing to do with the question, that it is a pure matter of absolute reason, keeps me forever out of the pale... What can kindle feeling but the example of feeling?...That they [feelings] may be as prophetic and anticipatory of truth as anything else we have, and some of them more so than others, cannot possibly be denied. But what hope is there

of squaring and settling opinions unless Absolutism will hold parlay on this common ground; and will admit that all philosophies are hypotheses, to which all our faculties, emotional as well as logical, help us, and the truest of which will at the final integration of things be found in possession of the men whose faculties on the whole had the best divining power?[32]

Whether the spirit of the redwood tree spoke to me from a consciousness in Nature or from an unconsciousness in my unconscious does not really matter, for from an irrational standpoint the spirit was present in my intuitions, sensations, thoughts, and feelings. Like Fechner looking at the beauty of plants for the first time after three years of seclusion in the darkness of his room in Leipzig, or like James speaking to a mainly rationalist audience that could, probably for the most part, not comprehend him, it is my personal view that trees and Nature have a complexity of consciousness and there is, in fact, a consciousness of the Spiritual Self hidden away in the unconscious and matter.

Thus, I end where I began, opening the door to let the spirit come in and shutting it again. As Jung said, "if you marry the ordered to the chaos you produce the divine child, the supreme meaning beyond meaning and meaninglessness."[33]

Notes

1. Meier, *Atom and Archetype*, 98. Check the reference: Jung and Pauli are the authors. Meier is the Editor.
2. Meier, 150.
3. The unity of science and religion with regard to Pauli's dreams was discussed on page 298.
4. Meier, *Atom and Archetype*, 87; Fechner, *Nana, or the Soul-Life of Plants.*
5. Meier, 87.
6. Meier, 87.
7. Jung; cited in Meier, 111.
8. Jung, *Children's Dreams*, 1.
9. Jung, *Psychology of the Unconscious*, 396.
10. Jung, "Symbols and the Interpretation of Dreams," CW 18, ¶531.

11. Jung, CW 18, ¶590.
12. Jung, *MDR*, 183.
13. James, *Principles of Psychology*, 224–230; quoted in Progoff, *Jung's Psychology and Its Social Meaning*, 173.
14. James, *Writings 1878–1899*, 15.
15. Jung, "On the Nature of the Psyche," CW 8, ¶418.
16. Jung, "Synchronicity," CW 8, ¶915.
17. Jung, CW 8, ¶944.
18. Jung, CW 8, ¶915.
19. Jung, CW 8, ¶942.
20. Jung, *MDR*, 373.
21. Jung, CW 8, ¶964.
22. James, *Writings 1902–1910*, 701.
23. James, 697.
24. James, 702.
25. James, 703.
26. Fechner, *Über die Seelenfrage*, 170; paraphrased from James, 705.
27. Jung, "The Meaning of Psychology for Modern Man," CW 10, ¶291.
28. Jung, CW 10, ¶318.
29. Jung, "The Spirit Mercurius," CW 13, ¶242.
30. Jung, *Letters*, vol. 1, 431.
31. James, *Writings* 1878–1899, 1016.
32. James, 1019–1020.
33. Jung, *RB,* 370, fn. 164.

Permissions

Permission to paraphrase portions of Collection # H MS C29, or brief quotes from the section "Théodore Flournoy and William James" was granted by Public Services Librarian, Frances A. Countway Library of Medicine, Harvard University, Rare Books (hereafter, CLM). Collection # H MS C29, on November 1, 2019. The James-Jung portion begins on CLM, p. 197 and is approximately two pages long.

Acknowledgments

I am very grateful to those who assisted me during the writing of this book. My "History of Transpersonal Psychology" students at Sofia University in Palo Alto, California, were a source of encouragement and inspiration. I'm grateful for their questions and interest in the lectures I gave on William James and C. G. Jung in the fall of 2015 and spring of 2016. Thanks to Liz Li, PhD, president of Sofia University for inviting me to speak on James and Jung; the phenomenologist Olga Louchakova, PhD, for her interest in my research; Robert Frager, PhD, the founder of the Institute of Transpersonal Psychology (ITP), for his interest in my work; and Pier Luigi Lattuada, PhD, the founder of the Integral Transpersonal Institute in Milan, Italy, for publishing my paper "William James and C. G. Jung: The Emergence of the Field of Transpersonal Psychology." The Anglican priest and author Matthew Fox, who has been a friend and an inspiration for many years, expressed much interest in my manuscript. Jungian analyst Richard Stein was a source of insight into the works of Sri Aurobindo and Jung's psychology of the East. Thanks to William James scholar David Bryce Yaden, for writing to me about the Countway Library Manuscript (CLM) at Harvard University. Many thanks to Jungian analyst Murray Stein, for his spirited exchange of letters about the works of Karl Kerényi and interest in my thoughts about James; to Thomas Kirsch for his reading of my chapter "The Influence of William James" and encouraging me to embrace the calling of this challenging project; to Jean Kirsch for spurring me on to read James and to write about Jung in America; to Sam Kimbles and Thomas Singer for our discussions about the American cultural complex. I want to express my deep gratitude to Dyane Sherwood, founder and publisher of Analytical Psychology Press, for her remarkable integrity, insight, and eye for aesthetics; to Elijah Wood for his typesetting and design work, and to LeeAnn Pickrell for her outstanding copyediting. Special thanks to John Beebe for his insights on Jung's and James's typology. Finally, I'd like to thank my wife, Jungian analyst Lori Goldrich, PhD, who read my manuscript and offered some invaluable editorial suggestions, criticism, and love.

Appendix: Journaling Method

Preamble

Do emotions make us ill? Can the journaling method outlined here help heal emotional ailments? How can a journaling technique be therapeutic?

By *journaling method,* I mean the discovery, through mythopoetic language, of one's personal myth. This discovery may happen through writing as meditation. Walt Whitman called this method *Vocalism:* "the divine power to speak words."

Here are some further questions to consider: What part does the imagination play in healing emotional disorders? One solution to emotional suffering is to give voice to one's personal myth—following one's own individual way—aided by the technique of mythopoetic journaling.

The Method

Now, let's try this simple exercise:
1. First sit down somewhere comfortable, breathe deeply, and then pick up your journal and pen. See during your inward meditations if an emotional-image comes to mind. Now try to let your words breathe fluidly onto your journal's pages, taking careful note with each exhale and inhale, watching your breath as it ebbs and flows. A panacea for disquiet is quiet, silence, and mindfulness to what is present in the moment. So first be quiet, be still, and listen to the stream of words within. Notice if you are sweating or if your heart is racing; let your thoughts, feelings, intuitions, and sense impressions run free and leap onto the page.
2. As you pen your thoughts, notice whether any psychological or somatic changes occur, or not, and try not to hesitate during your writing. Let it be spontaneous, automatic; let it flow. Do not force your language to conform to some preconceived plan in any way; be open to the moment; let go, let be. If you notice that words are not flowing, be with that and bring it forth onto the page.

3. Now try this simple experiment: Take another deep breath and do not censor or criticize your writing in any manner; observe the moments of stillness and silence between your words; pay attention. If an emotion arises in your body, let it speak its own thoughts; let your imagination be your guiding mythopoetic principle.
4. Now, begin to see whether there's a shift in your consciousness and notice whether you can observe your thoughts objectively; try and get outside your subjective lens of normative awareness to a place of psychic objectivity. If you can, objectify what you have just written by seeing more democratically the oneness and unity of all things; expand your consciousness to include the entire Cosmos; then find your place in it while writing. For instance, I like to plant redwood trees in the park and have used journaling as a way to connect with the life of trees and have even allowed trees to have their own voice. Walt Whitman modeled this for us in his poem "Song of the Redwood Tree."

Mythopoetic writing can be therapeutic, just as psychotherapy can. And it is valuable to use this method to engage with the full range of emotions—dark and light—and to reflect on and embody your experience. The aim of mythopoetic journaling is to become more deeply *embodied* and free from the grip of any positive or negative emotions, so that you can consciously create transformative images and new insights out of them.

Remember also that the pen is an instrument that must be kept finely tuned, so practice is necessary, like any other discipline.

As a psychotherapist and a poet and writer, I encourage all of my adult patients and some adolescents, and even a few children, to keep two journals: 1) a dream journal and 2) a journal for processing their thoughts, sensations, feelings, and experiences. Mythopoetic journaling can relieve emotional and somatic suffering and allow you to experience more inner and outer peace. Journal and write as often as you can. Enjoy!

Bibliography

Atmanspacher, Harold, and Christopher A. Fuchs. *The Pauli-Jung Conjecture and Its Impact Today.* Exeter, UK: Imprint Academic, 2014.

Bair, Deirdre. *Jung: A Biography.* New York: Little Brown and Company, 2003.

Basham, Arthur L. *The Wonder That Was India.* New York: Grove Press Inc., 1954.

Beebe, John. *Energies and Patterns in Psychological Type: The Reservoir of Consciousness.* London: Routledge, 2017.

———. "*The Red Book* as a Work of Conscience: Notes from a Seminar Given for the 35th Annual Jungian Conference, C. G. Jung Club of Orange County," April 10, 2010. *Quadrant* XXXX, no. 2 (Summer 2010): 41–58.

Bercovitch, Sacvan. *The Puritan Origins of the American Self.* New Haven: Yale University Press, 1975.

Bergson, Henri. *L'évolution créatrice.* Paris: Alcan, 1907.

Bucke, Richard. M. *Cosmic Consciousness: A Study of the Evolution of the Human Mind.* Philadelphia: E. P. Dutton and Company, Inc., 1901.

Buttimer, Anne. "Beyond Humboldtian Science and Goethe's Way of Science: Challenges of Alexander von Humboldt's Geography." *Erdkune* 55, no. 2 (2001): 105-120.

Campbell, Joseph. *The Mythic Image.* Princeton: Princeton University Press, 1974.

Cambray, Joseph. *Synchronicity: Nature and Psyche in an Interconnected Universe.* College Station: Texas A & M University Press, 2009.

Cambray, Joseph, and Leslie Sawin. *Research in Analytical Psychology: Applications from Scientific, Historical, and Cross-Cultural Research.* London: Routledge, 2018.

Davis, Derek H. *Religion and the Continental Congress 1774–1776.* New York: Oxford University Press, 2000.

Edinger, Edward. *Ego and Archetype.* New York: Penguin Books, 1972.

Ellenberger, Henri, F. *The Discovery of the Unconscious: The History and Evolution of Dynamic Psychiatry.* New York: Basic Books, 1970.

Erickson, Erik. *Identity, Youth, and Crisis.* New York: W. W. Norton & Co., 1968.

Fechner, Gustav. *Über die Seelenfrage.* Leipzig: C. F. Amelang, 1861.

Fox, George. *The Journal of George Fox.* London: James M. Dent, 1924.

Fox, Matthew. *Breakthrough: Meister Eckhart's Creation Spirituality in New Translation.* New York: Image, 1980.

Fredrick, Norris. "William James and Swami Vivekananda: Religious Experience and Vedanta/Yoga in America." *William James Studies* 9 (2012): 37–55

Griswold, Hervey de Witt. *The Religion of the Rigveda.* Oxford, UK: Oxford University Press, 1971.

Grof, Stanislav, and Christina Grof. *Spiritual Emergency: When Personal Transformation Becomes a Crisis.* Los Angeles: Tarcher, 1989.

Hanegraaff, Wouter J. *New Age Religion and Western Culture: Esotericism in the Mirror of Secular Thought.* New York: State University of New York Press, 1998.

Henderson, Joseph. "Ancient Myths and Modern Man." In *Man and His Symbols,* edited by C. G. Jung. Garden City, NY: Doubleday & Co. Inc., 1964.

———. *Cultural Attitudes in Psychological Perspectives.* Toronto: Inner City Books, 1984.

———. "The Inner Vision in Social Organization." In *The Vision Thing: Myth, Politics, and Psyche in the World,* edited by Thomas Singer, 29–33. New York: Routledge, 2000.

Henderson, Joseph, and Maud Oakes. *The Wisdom of the Serpent: The Myths of Death, Rebirth, and Resurrection.* Princeton, NJ: Princeton University Press, 1990.

Herrmann, Steven. "The Case of Clare: The Emergence of the Self in a Six-Year-Old Girl." *Journal of Sandplay Therapy* 18, no. 2 (2009): 111–132.

———. "C. G. Jung and Teilhard de Chardin: Peacemakers in an Age of Spiritual Democracy." In *Pierre Teilhard de Chardin and Carl Gustav Jung Side by Side,* edited by Fred Gustafson. Cheyenne: Fisher King Press, 2015.

———. "Colloquy with the Inner Friend: Jung's Religious Feeling for Islam," *Jung Journal: Culture & Psyche* 3, no. 4 (2009): 123–132.

———. "The Cultural Complex in Walt Whitman." In *The San Francisco Jung Institute Library Journal* 23, no. 4 (2004): 34–61.

———. *Emily Dickinson: A Medicine Woman for Our Times.* Cheyenne, WY: Fisher King Press, 2018.

———. "Meister Eckhart and Carl Jung: On the Recollection of the Self." Senior thesis, University of Santa Cruz, 1982.

———. "Melville's Vision of Evil." *The San Francisco Jung Institute Library Journal* 22, no. 3 (2003): 15–56.

———. "Murray Stein: The Transformative Image." *The San Francisco Jung Institute Library Journal* 17, no. 1 (1998): 17–39.

———. "Teilhard de Chardin: Cosmic Christ." In *Encyclopedia of Psychology and Religion,* edited by David A. Leeming and Stanton Marlan. Berlin: Springer Publications, 2014.

———. "Transpersonal Psychology and the Self-Field: An Overview of the Works of Jungian Analyst Erich Neumann." *Integral Transpersonal Journal of Arts, Sciences and Technologies,* no. 11 (September 2018): 57–77.

———. *Walt Whitman: Shamanism, Spiritual Democracy, and the World Soul.* Durham: Eloquent Books, 2010.

———. *William Everson: The Shaman's Call. Expanded Edition.* New York: Eloquent Books, 2016.

———. "William James & C. G. Jung: The Emergence of the Field of Transpersonal Psychology." *Integral Transpersonal Journal of Arts, Sciences and Technologies,* no. 8 (June 2016): 22–57.

Jaffé, Aniela. *From the Life and Work of C. G. Jung. New Expanded Edition.* Translated by R. F. C. Hull and Murray Stein. Einsiedeln, Switzerland: Daimon Verlag, 1989.

James, William. *The Principles of Psychology,* Vols. 1 and 2. New York: Henry Holt and Co., 1918.

———. *Pragmatism.* Cambridge, MA: Harvard University Press, 1907.

———. *Pragmatism: A New Name for Some Old Ways of Thinking.* London and Longmans, Green, & Co., 1911.

———. "Robert Gould Shaw: Oration by Professor William James." In *The Works of William James: Essays in Religion and Morality,* edited by Frederick H. Burkhardt, Cambridge, MA: Harvard University Press, 1982.

———. *The Varieties of Religious Experience.* New York: Image Books, 1978.

———. *William James: Writings 1902–1910.* New York: The Library of America, 1987.

———. *William James: Writings 1878–1899.* New York: The Library of America, 1992.

Jung, Carl Gustav. "Adaptation, Individuation, Collectivity" (1916). *The Symbolic Life. The Collected Works of C. G. Jung,* vol. 18. Princeton: Princeton University Press, 1976. Hereafter references to Jung's *Collected Works* will be referred to by title, CW, volume number, and date of publication.

———. "The Aims of Psychotherapy" (1931). *The Practice of Psychotherapy.*

CW 16. 1966.

———. *Analytical Psychology: Notes of the Seminars Given in 1925 by C. G. Jung.* Princeton: Princeton University Press, 1989.

———. "Answer to Job" (1952). *Psychology and Religion: East and West.* CW 11. 1969.

———. "Appendix: On Synchronicity" (1951). *The Structure and Dynamics of the Psyche.* CW 8. 1969.

———. "Archetypes of the Collective Unconscious" (1934/1954). *The Archetypes and the Collective Unconscious.* CW 9i. 1968.

———. *C. G. Jung Letters.* Two volumes. Edited by Gerhard Adler. Princeton: Princeton University Press, 1973.

———. *C. G. Jung Speaking: Interviews and Encounters.* Princeton: Princeton University Press, 1977.

———. *C. G. Jung: The Visions Seminars.* From the Complete Notes of Mary Foote. *Postscript by Henry A. Murray.* Zürich: Spring Publications, 1976.

———. *Children's Dreams: Notes from the Seminar Given in 1936–1940 by C. G. Jung.* Princeton: Princeton University Press, 2008.

———. "Commentaries on 'The Tibetan Book of the Great Liberation'" (1935/1954). *Psychology and Religion: West and East.* CW 11. 1969.

———. "Commentary on the 'Secret of the Golden Flower'" (1929). *Alchemical Studies.* CW 13. 1968.

———. "Concerning the Archetypes, with Special Reference to the Anima Concept" (1936/1954). *The Archetypes and the Collective Unconscious.* CW 9i. 1968.

———. "Concerning Rebirth" (1939). *The Archetypes and the Collective Unconscious.* CW 9i. 1968.

———. "Conscious, Unconscious, and Individuation" (1939). *The Archetypes and the Collective Unconscious.* CW 9i. 1968.

———. "Depth Psychology" (1948). *The Symbolic Life.* CW 18. 1976.

———. "The Development of Personality" (1934). *The Development of Personality.* CW 17. 1954.

———. *Dream Analysis: Notes of the Seminar Given in 1928–1930 by C. G. Jung.* Edited by William McGuire. Princeton: Princeton University Press, 1984.

———. "Faust and Alchemy" (1949). *The Symbolic Life.* CW 18. 1976.

———. "The Fight with the Shadow" (1946). *Civilization in Transition.* CW 10. 1968.

———. "Foreword to Suzuki's *Introduction to Zen Buddhism*" (1939). *Psychology and Religion: East and West*. CW 11. 1969.

———. "General Aspects of Dream Psychology" (1916/1948). *The Structure and Dynamics of the Psyche*. CW 8. 1969.

———. "Good and Evil in Analytical Psychology" (1959). *Civilization in Transition*. CW 10. 1968.

———. "Individual Dream Symbolism in Relation to Alchemy" (1936). *Psychology and Alchemy*. CW 12. 1968.

———. "Instinct and the Unconscious" (1919). *The Structure and Dynamics of the Psyche*. CW 8. 1969.

———. Interview. *Good Housekeeping*. December 1961.

———. "Introduction to the Religious and Psychological Problems of Alchemy" (1935/43). *Psychology and Alchemy*. CW 12. 1968.

———. "Jung and Religious Belief" (1956/1957). *The Symbolic Life*. CW 18. 1976.

———. "The Meaning of Psychology for Modern Man" (1933/1934). *Civilization in Transition*. CW 10. 1968.

———. *Memories, Dreams, Reflections*. Edited by Aniela Jaffé. New York: Random House, 1989.

———. "Mind and Earth" (1927/1931). *Civilization in Transition*. CW 10. 1968.

———. *Mysterium Coniunctionis* (1955–56). CW 14. 1970.

———. "New Paths in Psychology" (1912). *Two Essays on Analytic Psychology*. CW 7. 1969.

———. *Nietzsche's Zarathustra. Notes of the Seminar Given in 1934–1939 by C. G. Jung*, Vol. 1. Princeton: Princeton University Press, 1988.

———. "On the Nature of Dreams" (1948). *The Structure and Dynamics of the Psyche*. CW 8. 1969.

———. "On the Nature of the Psyche" (1947/1954). *The Structure and Dynamics of the Psyche*. CW 8. 1969.

———. "Prefaces to 'Collected Papers on Analytical Psychology'" (1916, 1917). Freud and Psychoanalysis. CW 4. 1961.

———. "Psychic Conflicts in a Child" (1910/1946). *The Development of Personality*. CW 17. 1954.

———. "On Psychic Energy" (1928). *The Structure and Dynamics of the Psyche*. CW 8. 1969.

———. "Psychological Aspects of the Mother Archetype" (1938/1954).

Archetypes and the Collective Unconscious. CW 9i. 1969.

———. *Psychological Commentary on Kundalini Yoga. Lectures One and Two—1932.* New York: Spring Publications, 1975.

———. *Psychological Commentary on Kundalini Yoga. Lectures Three and Four—1932.* New York: Spring Publications, 1976.

———. "Psychological Commentary on the 'Tibetan Book of the Great Liberation'" (1939/1954). *Psychology and Religion: East and West.* CW 11. 1969.

———. "Psychological Factors Determining Human Behavior" (1937). *The Structure and Dynamics of the Psyche.* CW 8. 1969.

———. "Psychological Foundations of a Belief in Spirits" (1920/1948). *The Structure and Dynamics of the Psyche.* CW 8. 1969.

———. *Psychological Types* (1921). CW 6. 1971.

———. "Psychological Factors Determining Human Behavior" (1937). *The Structure and Dynamics of the Psyche.* CW 8. 1969.

———. "The Psychology of the Child Archetype" (1940). *The Archetypes and the Collective Unconscious.* CW 9i. 1968.

———. "The Psychology of Dementia Praecox" (1907). *The Psychogenesis of Mental Disease.* CW 3. 1960.

———. "The Psychology of Eastern Meditation" (1943). *Psychology and Religion: West and East.* CW 11. 1969.

———. "Psychology and Literature" (1930/1950). *The Spirit in Man, Art, and Literature.* CW 15. 1966.

———. "On the Psychology and Pathology of So-Called Occult Phenomena" (1902). *Psychiatric Studies.* CW 1. 1970.

———. "Psychology and Religion (The Terry Lectures)" 1938/1940. *Psychology and Religion: East and West.* CW 11.

———. "The Psychology of the Transference" (1946). *The Practice of Psychotherapy.* CW 16. 1966.

———. "On the Psychology of the Unconscious" (1917/1926/1943). *Two Essays on Analytic Psychology.* CW 7. 1969.

———. *Psychology of the Unconscious: A Study of the Transformations and Symbolisms of the Libido.* Princeton: Princeton University Press, 1916/1991.

———. *Psychology of the Unconscious: A Study of the Transformations and Symbols of the Libido, The Collected Works of C. G. Jung, Supplementary Volume B.* With a new Foreword by Eugene Taylor.

Princeton: Princeton University Press, 1991.

———. "Psychotherapists or the Clergy" (1932). *Psychology and Religion: East and West.* CW 11. 1969.

———. "The Realities of Practical Psychotherapy" (1939). *The Practice of Psychotherapy.* CW 16. 1966.

———. *The Red Book.* Edited with an Introduction by Sonu Shamdasani. Translated by Sonu Shamdasani, Mark Kyburz, and John Peck. New York: W. W. Norton & Co, 2009.

———. "The Relations between the Ego and the Unconscious" (1928). *Two Essays on Analytic Psychology.* CW 7. 1969.

———. "Religious Ideas in Alchemy" (1937). *Psychology and Alchemy.* CW 12. 1968.

———. "Reviews of Keyserling's *America Set Free*" (1930). *Civilization in Transition.* CW 10. 1968.

———. "Richard Wilhelm: In Memoriam" (1930). *The Spirit in Man, Art, and Literature.* CW 15. 1966.

———. "The Significance of the Father in the Development of the Personality" (1909/1949). *Freud and Psychoanalysis.* CW 4. 1961.

———. "The Structure of the Psyche" (1927/1931). *The Structure and Dynamics of the Psyche.* CW 8. 1969.

———. "The Structure of the Unconscious" (1916/1966). *Two Essays on Analytic Psychology.* CW 7. 1969.

———. "The Symbolic Life" (1939). *The Symbolic Life.* CW 18. 1976.

———. "Symbols and the Interpretation of Dreams" (1961). *The Symbolic Life.* CW 18. 1976.

———. *Symbols of Transformation* (1911–12/1952). CW 5. 1967.

———. "Synchronicity: An Acausal Connecting Principle" (1952). *The Structure and Dynamics of the Psyche.* CW 8. 1969.

———. "The Tavistock Lectures" (1935). *The Symbolic Life.* CW 18. 1976.

———. "The Theory of Psychoanalysis" (1913). *Freud and Psychoanalysis.* CW 4. 1961.

———. "Transformation Symbolism in the Mass" (1942/1954). *Psychology and Religion: East and West.* CW 11. 1969.

———. "Yoga and the West" (1936). *Psychology and Religion: East and West.* CW 11. 1969.

Kerényi, Karl. *Dionysos: Archetypal Image of Indestructible Life.* Princeton: Princeton University Press, 1976.

———. "The Primordial Child in Primordial Times." In *Essays on a Science of Mythology,* by C. G. Jung and Karl Kerényi, translated by R. F. C. Hull. Princeton: Princeton University Press, 1963.

Kerr, John. *A Most Dangerous Method: The Story of Jung, Freud, and Sabrina Spielrein.* New York: Vintage Books, 1993.

Kumar, Sehdev. *The Vision of Kabir.* Concord, Ontario, Canada: Alpha & Omega, 1984.

Lammers, Ann, and Adrian Cunningham, eds. *The Jung-White Letters.* London: Routledge, 2007.

Meier, C. A. *Atom and Archetype: The Pauli/Jung Letters, 1932–1958.* Princeton: Princeton University Press, 2001.

Molchanov, Elaine, and Al Collins, eds. "Jung and India." *Spring: A Journal of Archetype and Culture* 90 (2013).

Nikhilananda, Swami. *The Upanishads: A New Translation.* New York: Ramakrishna-Vivekananda Center, 1952.

Peirce, Charles S. "How to Make Our Ideas Clear," *Popular Science Monthly,* January 12, 1878, 286–302.

Pfeiffer, F. (1875/1931). *Meister Eckhart.* Translated by C. de. B. Evans, Leipzig 1875 & London 1924-31. 2 volumes. 1: 74-75.

Pribram, Karl. "Self-Consciousness and Intentionality: A Model Based on an Experimental Analysis of the Brain Mechanisms Involved in the Jamesian Theory of Motivation and Emotion," in *Consciousness and Self-Regulation: Advances in Research,* edited by Richard Davidson, Gary Schwartz, and David Shapiro, 51–100. New York: Plenum, 1976.

Progoff, Ira. *Jung's Psychology and Its Social Meaning.* New York: Grove Press, 1953.

Richardson, Robert. *William James: In the Maelstrom of American Modernism.* New York: Houghton Mifflin Company, 2006.

Rosenzweig, Saul. *Freud, Jung, and Hall the King-Maker: The Historic Expedition to America (1909) with Stanley Hall as Host and William James as Guest.* St. Louis: Rana House, 1992.

Sen, Indra. "Personality, Its Development and the 'Inner Voice': A Study in Jung. What Integral Psychology Can Contribute." *Further Studies in Integral Psychology* 39, no. 3 (March 1986): 158–161.

Sengupta, Sulagna. *Jung in India.* New Orleans: Spring Journal Books, 2013.

Shamdasani, Sonu. *Jung and the Making of Modern Psychology: The*

Dream of a Science. Cambridge: Cambridge University Press, 2003.

———. *Jung Stripped Bare by His Biographers, Even.* London: Karnac Books Ltd., 2005.

Shamdasani, Sonu, and John Beebe, "Jung Becomes Jung: A Dialogue on *Liber Novus (The Red Book)*." *Psychological Perspectives* 53 (2010): 410–433.

Singer, June K. *The Unholy Bible: A Psychological Interpretation of William Blake.* New York: G. P. Putnam's Sons, 1970.

Stein. Murray. "Divinity Expresses the self'… An Investigation." *Journal of Analytical Psychology* 53, no. 3 (2008): 305–327.

———. *Minding the Self: Jungian Meditations on Contemporary Spirituality.* London: Routledge, 2014.

———. *Transformation: Emergence of the Self.* Texas A & M: College Station, 1998.

Taylor, Eugene. "William James and C. G. Jung." *Spring: An Annual of Archetypal Psychology and Jungian Thought.* Irving, Texas: Spring Publications, Inc., 1980.

———. *William James on Consciousness Beyond the Margin.* Princeton: Princeton University Press, 1996.

———. *William James on Exceptional Mental States: The 1896 Lowell Lectures.* Portsmouth: Jetty House, 2010.

Vivekananda, Swami. *The Complete Works of Swami Vivekananda.* Nine volumes. Kolkata: Advaita Ashrama, 2007.

von Franz, Marie-Louise. *Projection and Re-Collection in Jungian Psychology.* La Salle: Open Court, 1980.

———. *C. G. Jung: His Myth in Our Time.* Boston: Little, Brown and Company, 1975.

von Franz, Marie-Louise, and James Hillman. *Lectures on Jung's Typology.* Dallas, TX: Spring Publications Inc., 1971.

von Humboldt, Alexander. *Cosmos: A Sketch of the Physical Description of the Universe.* Volume 2. Baltimore: Johns Hopkins University Press, 1997.

von Krafft-Ebing, Richard Freiherr. *Lehrbuch der Psychiatrie,* 4th ed. Stuttgart: Verlag von Ferdinand Enke, 1890.

Walls, Laura Dassow. *The Passage to Cosmos: Alexander von Humboldt and the Shaping of America.* Chicago: The University of Chicago Press, 2009.

Walshe, Maurice O'C. *The Complete Mystical Works of Meister Eckhart.* New York: The Crossroads Publishing Company, 2009.

Wayley, Arthur, trans. *The Way and Its Power.* London: George Allen &

Urwin Ltd., 1934.

Whitman, Walt. *Notebooks and Unpublished Prose Manuscripts.* Edited by Edward F. Grier. New York: New York University Press, 1984.

———. *Walt Whitman: Complete Poetry and Collected Prose.* New York: Library of America, 1983.

Wilder, Thornton. *American Characteristics and Other Essays.* New York: Harper & Row Publishers, 1979.

Zabriskie, Beverly. "The Spectrums of Emotions: in Mythologies, Philosophies, Analytical Psychology, and the Neurosciences." In *Research in Analytical Psychology: Applications from Scientific, Historical, and Cross-Cultural Research,* edited by Joseph Cambray and Leslie Sawin. London: Routledge, 2018.

Zeller, Max. *The Dream: The Vision of the Night.* Edited by Janet Dallett. Los Angeles: The Analytical Psychology Club of Los Angeles and the C. G. Jung Institute of Los Angeles, 1975.

Index

A

above xi, 6, 16, 17, 21, 42, 45, 52, 58, 62, 76, 114, 115, 129, 168, 173, 193, 194, 197, 210, 242, 284, 287, 294, 308, 313, 324, 331, 332, 351, 378, 382, 391, 396
Absolute xv, 50, 53, 66, 68, 84, 86, 87, 90, 91, 94, 169, 178, 221, 222, 223, 225, 226, 230, 237, 239, 240, 245, 248, 252, 253, 255, 256, 261, 262, 270, 285, 287, 331, 332, 362, 365, 376, 378, 380, 384
absolutism 121
acting Self 20, 130, 261, 298, 300, 344
active imagination xvii, 32, 36, 51, 66, 80, 94, 130, 135, 138, 155, 167, 179, 209, 210, 211, 214, 275, 287, 294, 298, 340, 344, 345, 347, 369
Adam Kadmon 300
adaptation 16, 17, 31, 135, 136, 137, 170, 193, 268, 269, 297
Adler, Alfred 86, 267, 431
adolescence 8, 12, 20, 34, 35, 46, 57, 58, 59, 60, 61, 64, 114, 153, 156, 172, 333
Advaita Vedanta 209
affect 44, 45, 54, 91, 113, 168, 187, 271, 272, 280, 314, 340, 371
affect-complexes 44, 45
affective turbulence 44
Agassiz, Louis 163, 234, 240
Agnosticism 378
Aion xxi, 146, 173, 184, 185, 188, 246, 275, 335, 371, 376, 385

ajna 285, 286
alchemy 34, 300, 347, 394
Alcoholics Anonymous 124
America xv, xvi, xix, xx, xxi, xxiii, xxiv, 8, 11, 15, 19, 23, 25, 26, 30, 37, 51, 53, 55, 57, 72, 73, 85, 88, 90, 106, 107, 108, 110, 126, 130, 145, 152, 156, 163, 187, 206, 224, 261, 266, 272, 276, 280, 320, 429, 430, 434, 435, 436, 437
American Democracy xxiii
American mind xv, xx, 203, 309
American Psychological Association (APA) 12
American Self xvii, xviii, xix, xx, xxi, xxii, xxiii, 97, 428
amplification 52, 80, 129, 287, 346
anahata 285, 286, 288, 294
Analytical Psychology iii, iv, 267, 269, 279, 304, 359, 384, 391, 428, 431, 432, 436, 437
Answer to Job xviii, 65, 276, 327, 328, 372, 373, 385, 431
Anthropos xxi, 164, 184, 376
Antichrist 308
anti-Semitism 119
A Pluralistic Universe 37, 76, 79, 81, 84, 85, 221, 223, 230, 236, 261, 330, 399
Aquarian Age xxi, 50, 119
archaic remnants 27
archetypal cores 377
archetypal equivalences 353, 398
archetype xx, xxi, 17, 19, 20, 21, 24, 27, 42, 53, 56, 62, 71, 72, 73, 74, 89, 91, 103, 120, 123, 129, 140, 150, 151, 152,

154, 155, 156, 157, 168, 190, 200, 232, 288, 307, 308, 309, 320, 333, 334, 337, 338, 339, 340, 341, 342, 345, 348, 349, 351, 352, 353, 372, 377, 391, 395, 398, 402
Asamprajnata 375, 376, 377, 379, 380, 393
Atman 173, 184, 197, 212
Atmavictu 51, 56, 65, 169, 177, 178, 179, 341
Aurobindo 349, 376
auseinandersetzung 48, 51
authentic Self 134, 210, 265
automatic writing xvi, xxii, 129, 206, 229, 239, 242, 345

B

backbone 80, 109, 110, 163, 398
Beebe, John ii, xxiv, 29, 30, 31, 33, 34, 35, 36, 38, 39, 74, 79, 80, 81, 90, 97, 110, 145, 428, 436
belief xvii, xxiv, 65, 66, 85, 231, 253, 254, 263, 314, 321, 362, 375, 378
below 6, 17, 43, 44, 52, 168, 169, 173, 193, 194, 228, 284, 287, 331, 332, 351, 370, 373, 382
Belur 215, 223, 348, 349, 384
Bercovitch, Sacvan xviii, xx, 428
Bergson, Henri 367, 368, 428
better cognition 154
Blake, William 90, 120, 125, 436
Bleuler, Eugen 23, 30, 341
bliss xi, xxi, 59, 60, 62, 63, 64, 68, 369, 370, 371, 372, 374, 384
'blissful' feeling 372
Blissfulness 90

Body Self xxiii, 11, 20, 76, 96, 104, 153, 169, 170, 171, 206, 229, 272, 310, 340, 376, 382, 403
Bollingen 62, 142, 145, 291, 330, 345, 347
Brahman 124, 167, 168, 169, 263, 379
brain xx, xxi, xxii, 229, 279, 387, 388, 389, 390, 393, 396, 397, 399
Brazil 163, 234
breath 25, 56, 65, 70, 128, 169, 172, 174, 178, 179, 211, 229, 249, 266, 268, 286, 317, 426, 427
breathing exercises 198, 287
Buber, Martin 65
Bucke, Richard Maurice 253, 262, 428
Buddha 122, 147, 199, 213, 214, 263, 333, 334, 367, 379
Buddhism 57, 100, 108, 157, 159, 204, 223, 246, 324, 334, 367, 384, 432
Buddhist meditation xxii
Burghölzli hospital 23
Bush, George W. 185

C

callings 93, 133, 134, 232, 251, 329, 347, 348, 352, 378
Cambray, Joseph 74, 391, 428, 437
Campbell, Joseph 122, 131, 132, 428
cash value 229
Cathedral xxiv, 381, 384
Catholic anima 382
Chaco Canyon, New Mexico 139
chakras 285, 286, 287, 294, 384
Charcot, Jean 30, 238
child xv, xx, xxi, 12, 13, 15, 16, 17, 18, 23, 24, 25, 26, 28, 41, 44, 45, 50, 52, 53, 54, 55, 56, 57, 149, 150, 151, 152,

153, 154, 155, 156, 157, 300, 307, 330, 364, 372, 395, 396, 404
child archetype xx, 151, 154, 157
Childlikeness 372
children's dreams xx, 152, 395, 396
Christ 30, 32, 52, 58, 59, 61, 62, 64, 66, 67, 122, 124, 146, 147, 173, 184, 185, 199, 201, 213, 214, 261, 263, 300, 301, 308, 376, 379, 381, 382, 383, 384, 430
Christian xix, 32, 34, 39, 41, 54, 55, 56, 57, 58, 59, 60, 64, 94, 107, 114, 145, 157, 184, 190, 212, 215, 224, 225, 261, 301, 319, 327, 332, 333, 347, 349, 381, 383, 384
Christ within 300, 301
church 38, 46, 56, 58, 65, 66, 67, 224, 249, 348
clairvoyance xvi, 115, 341
Clark Conference 11, 12, 26
Clark University xv, 5, 11, 12, 13, 14, 23, 25, 26, 27, 230, 259, 266, 268, 275, 292, 297, 338, 341, 343
CLM 104, 105, 277, 278, 285, 293, 294, 295, 296, 304, 349
coincidences 96, 97, 255, 310, 340, 349, 356, 393
collective unconscious xv, 6, 7, 19, 24, 26, 27, 36, 51, 54, 71, 93, 108, 125, 140, 152, 155, 172, 173, 185, 193, 207, 223, 278, 307, 327, 329, 330, 331, 339, 355, 382
compassion xxi, 93, 119, 172, 190, 262, 320, 326, 384, 399
complementarity xv, xvii, 36, 74, 96, 171, 361, 383, 393, 394
complexes 15, 16, 17, 19, 30, 34, 44, 45, 54, 55, 72, 187, 191, 226, 231, 242, 307, 309, 314, 331, 339, 377
complexity 79, 103, 108, 362, 365, 388, 391, 398, 404
Complexity in unity 79
consciousness xi, xvi, xvii, xviii, xx, xxi, xxii, xxiii, 7, 19, 27, 30, 41, 44, 45, 46, 48, 49, 51, 52, 53, 54, 66, 68, 71, 73, 74, 75, 76, 78, 79, 80, 83, 84, 85, 90, 91, 92, 93, 94, 96, 98, 99, 104, 114, 119, 121, 122, 124, 129, 131, 133, 134, 135, 141, 142, 146, 149, 151, 163, 164, 167, 171, 178, 183, 185, 189, 193, 194, 197, 198, 200, 204, 205, 206, 207, 221, 222, 223, 225, 227, 228, 229, 230, 231, 233, 236, 238, 239, 240, 241, 245, 246, 247, 248, 249, 251, 252, 253, 255, 257, 258, 261, 262, 263, 265, 266, 273, 274, 275, 278, 279, 284, 286, 288, 291, 294, 297, 299, 307, 309, 310, 312, 314, 315, 316, 317, 318, 319, 330, 331, 332, 333, 334, 337, 339, 344, 346, 349, 351, 352, 353, 361, 362, 363, 367, 371, 373, 375, 377, 378, 379, 380, 383, 387, 388, 389, 390, 391, 393, 394, 395, 396, 398, 399, 400, 401, 402, 403, 404, 427
Consciousness Beyond the Margin xxiv, 259, 279, 304, 368, 436
conversion 76, 124, 247, 248, 269, 271
correspondences 141, 142, 339, 343, 346
cosmic xvi, xx, 47, 63, 65, 122, 133, 135, 140, 151, 163, 167, 168, 169, 189, 194, 211, 224, 230, 245, 246, 249, 253, 258, 261, 262, 307, 310, 311,

312, 313, 314, 316, 317, 329, 332, 333, 353, 355, 388
cosmic consciousness xvi, 230, 262, 316, 333
Cosmic emotion 245
cosmic function 163
Cosmic Man 167, 168, 169, 212
Cosmos xvii, xx, 41, 48, 79, 84, 85, 89, 117, 124, 135, 136, 137, 140, 151, 155, 165, 172, 182, 183, 224, 255, 257, 261, 262, 310, 311, 314, 315, 317, 318, 319, 322, 324, 325, 326, 329, 330, 331, 332, 342, 353, 379, 380, 381, 382, 384, 390, 396, 398, 401, 427, 436
Countway Library of Medicine 104, 304
creeds 49, 66, 109, 121, 163, 190, 204, 207, 214, 261, 273, 313, 324, 327, 378, 388
cross xvi, xvii, 32, 35, 41, 68, 96, 136, 145, 146, 147, 168, 222, 255, 257, 265, 302, 377
crucifixion 32, 47, 136, 147
crystal-gazing xvi, 115
cultural attitudes 38, 48
cultural identity 85

D

"Damn the Absolute!" 223
death-wish 25, 26
delight xi, 89, 90
democracy xv, xix, xxiii, 71, 72, 73, 108, 109, 119, 124, 128, 130, 163, 164, 165, 181, 182, 183, 184, 185, 186, 187, 189, 191, 203, 204, 205, 207, 208, 209, 210, 214, 215, 221, 277, 297, 307, 308, 309, 311, 314, 315, 317, 318, 320, 321, 324, 325, 326, 327, 333, 334, 349, 352, 353, 354, 394
democratic spirituality 223, 324, 325, 333
destinations 96, 135, 137
destiny xvii, xix, xxi, 8, 15, 16, 17, 18, 19, 20, 21, 31, 48, 49, 53, 54, 59, 62, 87, 94, 95, 96, 97, 99, 105, 108, 109, 119, 121, 123, 124, 125, 136, 137, 141, 147, 148, 150, 151, 152, 153, 156, 186, 190, 191, 200, 207, 210, 234, 237, 238, 240, 247, 254, 255, 271, 297, 303, 308, 315, 316, 337, 338, 339, 340, 346, 347, 348, 363, 371, 372, 396, 398
destiny dreams 87, 96, 97, 303
detachment 36, 295, 343
devil 47, 64, 120, 185, 231
devotion 49, 60, 66, 85, 269, 274, 302
devout 77, 87, 106, 269, 273
Dharmapala, Angarika 367
Dickinson, Emily ii, x, xix, 85, 87, 97, 98, 99, 101, 107, 178, 323, 362, 429
directed thinking 268, 292, 298
dissociation xxii, 47, 50, 54, 60, 228, 383, 402
divine drama 298, 299, 300, 303, 318
Divinization 83
Dominican 35, 38, 65, 92, 125, 172, 173, 345
door xxi, 6, 13, 16, 65, 91, 92, 93, 94, 97, 100, 109, 119, 120, 121, 122, 123, 124, 128, 133, 135, 139, 141, 152, 153, 154, 155, 156, 157, 165, 211, 213, 222, 223, 242, 247, 248, 249, 254, 263, 291, 292, 293, 305, 333,

Index 425

373, 381, 389, 400, 401, 403, 404
doorway xx, 6, 7, 12, 23, 32, 50, 59, 65, 76, 80, 92, 93, 94, 97, 98, 99, 108, 119, 120, 121, 123, 124, 133, 134, 135, 138, 139, 142, 165, 170, 200, 204, 207, 229, 245, 247, 248, 249, 250, 261, 291, 292, 297, 305, 344, 348, 373, 381, 384, 388, 390, 400
doorways xi, 7, 26, 52, 93, 95, 96, 115, 116, 122, 124, 125, 126, 134, 135, 138, 139, 140, 141, 304, 330, 384
doorways to the Self 122, 125, 139, 141
double vision 353
Dourley, John 35
dream is a little hidden door 133, 291
dream research 279
dreams xxi, 5, 6, 8, 17, 25, 27, 31, 33, 43, 51, 52, 65, 84, 87, 92, 94, 96, 97, 98, 113, 125, 127, 130, 133, 134, 135, 138, 139, 140, 141, 142, 147, 150, 151, 152, 157, 165, 181, 267, 283, 286, 288, 289, 291, 294, 298, 299, 300, 301, 302, 303, 305, 316, 319, 321, 330, 331, 337, 338, 339, 340, 342, 343, 344, 345, 346, 347, 348, 352, 355, 356, 361, 364, 378, 379, 381, 393, 395, 396, 402, 404
Dream Seminars xxi, 76, 98, 154, 157, 158, 159, 287

E

Earth-Soul xx, 85, 252, 253, 395, 398
Eckhart, Meister 32, 34, 35, 36, 37, 38, 39, 64, 65, 70, 90, 92, 93, 94, 100, 132, 155, 156, 157, 159, 168, 169, 172, 173, 174, 178, 194, 214, 285, 293, 300, 317, 341, 371, 372, 374, 381, 383, 384, 385, 429, 435, 436
ecstasy 58, 59, 62, 68, 215, 229, 369, 370, 371, 372, 375, 379, 382, 383
ego xvii, 6, 7, 27, 43, 45, 47, 49, 51, 53, 55, 57, 62, 76, 79, 84, 91, 92, 95, 96, 98, 114, 133, 134, 135, 136, 146, 147, 190, 193, 194, 226, 227, 231, 283, 284, 285, 286, 287, 288, 298, 312, 314, 315, 317, 327, 329, 331, 343, 346, 347, 348, 349, 351, 375, 377, 379, 380, 383, 384, 391, 393, 396, 402
ego complex 146
Ellenberger, Henri 74, 81, 89
Emergence 83, 265, 429, 430, 436
Emerson, Ralph Waldo xix, xx, xxi, 21, 37, 88, 130, 153, 156, 172, 178, 206, 229, 233, 234, 235, 236, 237, 238, 253, 314, 362, 363, 387, 390
emotion xv, xxi, xxii, 24, 41, 58, 59, 68, 74, 75, 90, 113, 114, 177, 235, 245, 271, 272, 315, 365, 369, 370, 371, 372, 374, 377, 427
empirical method 221, 239, 253, 314
empirical psychology 55, 87, 94, 95, 114, 130, 138, 213, 370
Empirical Self xxiii, 127, 135, 169, 170, 246, 247, 387, 393, 394
empirical verification 79, 107
empiricism xv, xvii, 19, 51, 85, 221, 227, 235, 248, 251, 256, 263, 361, 388
energies of men xvi
energy xv, xx, 16, 41, 48, 72, 80, 85, 91, 96, 157, 227, 228, 229, 232, 236, 247, 248, 258, 275, 307, 312, 331, 340, 355, 369, 389, 390

equality 72, 73, 119, 121, 164, 165, 189, 210, 254, 308, 316, 320, 323, 325, 330, 334, 349, 355, 384, 394
Erfurt 38
Erikson, Erik 83, 84, 86, 428
Everson, William ii, 34, 38, 100, 133, 345, 383, 384, 430
Exceptional Mental States 90, 100, 112, 206, 208, 243, 436
experience 7, 13, 14, 24, 26, 31, 41, 43, 45, 47, 48, 55, 58, 59, 63, 64, 65, 66, 67, 68, 73, 74, 79, 80, 87, 90, 106, 108, 109, 113, 115, 116, 117, 120, 121, 124, 127, 129, 135, 138, 139, 163, 164, 165, 173, 189, 190, 194, 199, 203, 205, 206, 221, 222, 223, 224, 225, 227, 228, 229, 230, 235, 238, 240, 242, 245, 248, 250, 251, 252, 256, 257, 258, 262, 263, 266, 267, 272, 273, 283, 284, 285, 286, 294, 295, 305, 307, 308, 309, 314, 316, 317, 320, 321, 325, 332, 340, 341, 342, 343, 352, 361, 362, 366, 369, 370, 371, 373, 376, 377, 379, 382, 384, 387, 391, 393, 394, 397, 399, 403, 427
extra-marginal fields 229

F

facts 11, 28, 29, 66, 85, 87, 90, 97, 105, 106, 147, 181, 203, 213, 252, 255, 256, 257, 262, 263, 269, 274, 276, 284, 286, 294, 330, 364, 375, 377, 379, 381
faith 36, 55, 60, 61, 65, 67, 96, 104, 261, 267, 302, 311, 316, 318, 319, 321, 327, 334, 352, 361
fascinosum 46
fate 15, 32, 42, 49, 55, 58, 62, 63, 83, 94, 96, 119, 137, 147, 149, 150, 151, 152, 153, 303, 315, 347
father archetype 19, 21
Faust 231, 234, 235, 291, 292, 293, 345, 431
Fechner, Gustav Theodore 37, 76, 77, 78, 79, 80, 81, 84, 91, 94, 130, 223, 252, 253, 255, 258, 262, 263, 377, 380, 387, 390, 395, 397, 398, 399, 404, 428
feeling xvi, xix, xxi, xxii, 18, 47, 55, 84, 90, 91, 93, 106, 107, 109, 110, 111, 114, 116, 117, 119, 120, 121, 125, 126, 153, 163, 171, 187, 197, 205, 213, 225, 226, 229, 235, 237, 240, 242, 245, 257, 273, 278, 279, 297, 329, 334, 340, 343, 362, 365, 369, 370, 371, 372, 373, 390, 403
Feeling Function 110
Ferenczi, Sandor 5, 14, 230
Fichte, Johann 94, 234
'field' formula 76, 332
field notion xv, 74, 247, 274, 362
fields of consciousness 74, 75, 279, 352
fight with the shadow 125, 205
fixed ideas 13, 16, 241, 254
floodgates 115, 307
Flournoy, Théodore xvi, 8, 35, 36, 104, 105, 126, 127, 142, 226, 234, 240, 253, 272, 278, 292, 293, 294, 295, 296, 297, 304, 338, 341, 343
foreknowledge 97, 340, 344
fourth wind 179, 229, 232
Fox, George 38, 174, 224, 231, 428, 429

Franz, Marie-Louise von xxiii, 74, 81, 91, 92, 100, 110, 120, 131, 436
Freedom of religion 73
free-will 114
Freud, Sigmund xvii, 5, 6, 8, 11, 12, 13, 14, 16, 17, 18, 23, 25, 26, 27, 30, 78, 86, 94, 103, 104, 105, 106, 127, 147, 227, 228, 230, 236, 241, 255, 258, 265, 266, 267, 292, 295, 296, 303, 341, 343, 347, 361, 432, 434, 435
fringe of consciousness 221, 274, 278

G

Gandhi, Mahatma 209, 301
gate 32, 92, 94, 165, 373
genius xvii, xviii, xx, 37, 90, 186, 207, 242, 285, 364
Gifford Lectures 108, 197, 223, 225
Gnosticism 300
God-complex 146
God-Consciousness 52
God-function 66, 115, 326, 372, 373
godhead 32
God-image xxiii, 54, 57, 146, 147, 182, 209, 210, 253, 261, 308, 315, 316, 319, 320, 372, 378
godlikeness 94
Goethe, Johann Wolfgang von 19, 103, 153, 234, 235, 236, 238, 291, 292, 293, 314, 322, 428
Goodness 58
grace 24, 58, 59, 60, 62, 63, 64, 68, 150, 172
ground 6, 7, 14, 26, 45, 55, 58, 62, 84, 87, 122, 142, 149, 152, 153, 172, 200, 203, 238, 269, 298, 299, 326, 345, 347, 362, 366, 381, 382, 391, 393, 404

H

habits 154, 228, 238, 344, 352, 387
Hall, G. Stanley 11, 12, 13, 14, 23, 26, 236, 266, 279, 435
happiness xvi, xxii, 58, 62, 63, 68, 107, 245, 369, 372
Harvard Medical School xxii, 104, 234
Harvard University 106, 221, 234, 304, 430
Hatha Yoga xv, xxii, 198, 229, 287, 383
Henderson, Joseph L. 38, 103, 127, 128, 129, 132, 134, 163, 164, 429
Herrmann, Steven iv, 86, 101, 111, 112, 143, 188, 279, 429
Hiawatha 87, 148, 307
higher Self xxi, 94, 299
Highest Good 178
Hindu xviii, 52, 147, 169, 184, 194, 197, 209, 212, 226, 284, 327, 328, 332, 333, 364, 367, 373, 375, 381, 382
Hinduism 51, 100, 172, 204, 209, 287, 367, 384
Hiranyagarbha 168, 169, 178
hubris 128
Humbaba wine 401
Hummingbird x, xi
Huxley, Aldus 125
hypnosis xvi
hypotheses 51, 83, 148, 151, 221, 248, 283, 301, 303, 365, 378, 404

I

IAAP 323, 328, 334
identity 18, 27, 34, 83, 84, 85, 86, 190, 209, 224, 265, 284, 403
indeterminable 76, 332
India xv, 49, 51, 53, 55, 56, 57, 61, 67, 132, 142, 167, 169, 174, 181, 199, 203, 209, 210, 213, 214, 223, 233, 272, 273, 289, 317, 318, 323, 326, 332, 335, 348, 349, 352, 367, 376, 378, 385, 428, 435
individuation xv, xvi, xxii, 18, 20, 31, 41, 47, 50, 51, 53, 54, 65, 68, 93, 95, 99, 115, 127, 133, 135, 136, 137, 140, 145, 146, 163, 190, 194, 209, 214, 253, 265, 271, 283, 285, 299, 301, 302, 308, 316, 318, 319, 332, 370, 396
inferior function xxii, 80, 90, 91, 92, 93, 110, 120, 121
infinite xx, 25, 53, 65, 79, 106, 107, 117, 120, 122, 140, 172, 194, 211, 245, 249, 255, 256, 276, 287, 294, 308, 326, 329, 331, 332, 333, 363, 388
inflation 191, 261
instinct xv, xxi, xxii, 7, 41, 47, 52, 53, 72, 84, 113, 114, 154, 155, 181, 185, 212, 257, 269, 270, 283, 285, 297, 348, 351, 379
integrity 29, 55, 65, 83, 86, 129, 187, 222, 255
intellect 100, 110, 111, 117, 237, 333, 352, 363
introversion 182, 226, 325, 371
introversion of war 182
intuition xxii, 30, 36, 80, 91, 92, 94, 95, 100, 108, 117, 126, 172, 297, 332, 338, 403
Islam 62, 72, 73, 100, 204, 209, 214, 324, 429

J

Jaffé, Aniela 42, 71, 277, 293, 430, 432
James, Henry Jr. 233
James, Henry Sr. xxi, 233, 239
James-Lange theory 271
James, William i, iii, xiii, xxi, xxiii, xxiv, 5, 8, 11, 13, 14, 21, 23, 26, 31, 35, 36, 37, 39, 43, 65, 74, 77, 81, 83, 86, 87, 88, 99, 100, 101, 103, 104, 105, 108, 111, 112, 119, 126, 129, 130, 131, 133, 145, 153, 156, 157, 158, 163, 166, 168, 169, 187, 188, 190, 197, 199, 201, 205, 206, 208, 215, 221, 222, 231, 233, 234, 243, 251, 258, 259, 265, 267, 268, 269, 270, 271, 272, 273, 274, 276, 277, 278, 292, 293, 298, 301, 304, 308, 324, 329, 330, 337, 338, 341, 343, 349, 351, 361, 366, 367, 387, 396, 397, 403, 429, 430, 435, 436
Janet, Pierre xvii, 30, 206, 241, 253, 437
Jesuit 45
Jesus 30, 35, 43, 44, 45, 47, 51, 52, 55, 64, 65, 66, 155, 156, 157, 381
John F. Kennedy University 342
Jones, Ernest 5, 23, 230, 297
Jung, Agatha 13
Jung, Carl Gustav xii, 105, 429
Jung, Emma 25, 26
Jung in America xv, 23, 37, 130

K

Kali 67
Keene Valley, Mount Marcy 14, 224
Kerényi, Karl 150, 151, 152, 157, 158, 434, 435
key 11, 16, 80, 91, 93, 94, 138, 146, 150, 154, 167, 168, 214, 232, 255, 291, 292, 293, 304, 333, 334, 376
Kingdom of Heaven 156, 157
kingfisher 142, 330, 341, 342, 345, 348, 353
King, Martin Luther Jr. 301
Kingsnake 342
Knower and Known 391
Kundalini Seminars 291, 312, 327
Kundalini serpent 288, 289
Kundalini Yoga 232, 283, 288, 289, 290, 311, 384, 433
Küsnacht 62, 123, 139, 177, 275

L

Leipzig University 77, 78
letting go xvii, 93, 95
Liber Novus 29, 30, 31, 32, 34, 35, 36, 39, 127, 145, 169, 183, 296, 436
liberty 117, 210, 320, 325
Libido 6, 15, 145, 229, 367, 433
light x, 8, 26, 42, 49, 51, 78, 79, 92, 93, 105, 108, 116, 125, 130, 141, 146, 151, 194, 213, 214, 224, 286, 297, 301, 308, 313, 314, 318, 325, 340, 371, 373, 376, 382, 383, 389, 391, 427
Lincoln, Abraham 333, 334
linga 52, 284, 285, 286, 288
Lingam 51, 52, 308

Longfellow, Henry David 87, 148, 307
longissima via 95
Love 11, 54, 55, 56, 123, 136, 137, 154
Lowell Lectures 206, 234, 238, 242, 260, 436
Luther, Martin 108, 119, 120, 301, 403

M

Maharishi, Ramana 349
Malleus Maleficarum, "Witches' Hammer" 110
mandala 130, 169, 213, 229, 330, 333
man-eater 42, 43, 51, 52, 54
manipura 285, 288
margins 71, 76, 138, 222, 248, 258, 302, 351, 352, 377, 388, 389, 390
Material Self 14, 127, 170, 210, 229
matter xx, 14, 29, 49, 63, 65, 75, 79, 85, 94, 97, 121, 133, 155, 163, 164, 172, 178, 184, 193, 211, 229, 246, 269, 272, 277, 288, 311, 315, 318, 342, 343, 352, 355, 370, 373, 379, 383, 384, 389, 390, 393, 394, 395, 399, 403, 404
maya 299, 318
McCormick, Fowler 348
meaning xvi, xvii, xxii, 28, 30, 32, 50, 51, 53, 56, 61, 62, 66, 77, 80, 89, 91, 94, 97, 98, 115, 116, 141, 142, 145, 146, 147, 148, 149, 150, 156, 157, 163, 171, 178, 179, 182, 183, 190, 210, 230, 238, 242, 251, 253, 254, 255, 256, 258, 271, 299, 300, 301, 303, 308, 309, 310, 311, 312, 313, 314, 315, 316, 318, 319, 324, 326, 327, 329, 330, 337, 340, 342, 343,

344, 345, 346, 348, 349, 352, 353, 362, 366, 372, 376, 394, 395, 398, 401, 404
meaningful chance 39, 142, 298, 304, 337, 339, 340, 345
meaningful coincidence 90, 356
meaninglessness 115, 301, 314, 316, 330, 339, 404
meaning of truth xvi, xxii, 254
mediatrix 382
medicine of spiritual democracy 327
Melville, Herman xix, 85, 107, 188, 225, 352, 362, 429
metamorphosis xviii, 23, 31, 83, 84, 128, 146, 265, 295, 337, 391
metanoia 146
Metaphysical Self xxiii, 171
metaphysics xxii, 52, 184
mindfulness meditation 200
Miracles 318, 348
Miss Miller 19, 147, 148, 307
Moby-Dick xix, 352
monism xv, 198, 221, 222, 237, 256, 257, 263, 361
monotheism 168, 224, 263
moral equivalent of war xv, 179
mother-sea 200, 230, 249, 253, 255, 257
Mrs. Piper 115, 273, 274
Muir, John 85, 401
muladhara 283, 284, 285, 286, 287, 288, 289
multiple personality xvi, xxii
Myers, F. W. H. xvii, 206, 207, 226, 240, 241, 242, 246, 253, 258, 274
Mystical truth 246
mythopoetic fantasies 146
mythopoetic function 333

N

National Cathedral, Washington D.C. xxiv
national complexes 191, 307, 309
national identity 86, 209
Native American spirituality 204
natural religion 107, 108
Nature xvii, 72, 85, 88, 89, 97, 109, 124, 136, 193, 195, 216, 223, 274, 280, 321, 323, 340, 347, 350, 351, 352, 353, 354, 377, 379, 385, 387, 390, 391, 393, 394, 398, 400, 402, 404, 405, 428, 432
Nature's God 124, 323
Navigation Trees 400, 401
Neumann, Erich 142, 430
Neuropsychology xxii
neurosis 16, 19, 20, 59, 60, 136, 153, 226, 231, 301, 339
neurotic 8, 16, 19, 59, 62, 66, 136, 232, 298, 313, 314, 316, 317, 339
New Age Religion 108, 112, 429
New Testament 47, 64, 73, 261
Nietzsche, Friedrich 17, 19, 32, 39, 68, 69, 94, 100, 103, 129, 159, 215, 216, 251, 253, 272, 280, 283, 288, 290, 432
nirvandva 168
non-dual Self 52, 178
nothing but 270, 286, 298, 361
numinosum 255, 309
numinous xx, xxii, 42, 54, 67, 68, 97, 138, 229, 245, 249, 255, 258, 296, 309, 311, 339, 341, 343, 377
numinous experiences 67, 229, 258

O

Oakland, California x, 88, 400
Obama, Barak 72, 73, 80
objective psyche 71, 76, 94, 99, 181, 285, 311, 312, 351
objective reality 83, 105, 109
objectivity 26, 30, 51, 75, 76, 121, 177, 209, 273, 294, 344, 370, 397, 427
Old Testament 59, 261
openings 52, 121, 222, 224, 247, 397
Orbis Pictus 55, 56, 308, 367
organizer 71, 296, 393, 399, 401
organizing principle 138, 309, 393, 399, 401
original mind 27
original revelation 55, 58

P

panpsychicism xv, 78
pantheism 168
Paraclete 56
paranoia 235
parapsychology xvi, xviii, xx, xxii, 26, 34, 71, 72, 138, 221, 295, 332, 341, 365
Parliament of World Religions 67, 204, 325
pathology 13, 67, 68
Pauli, Wolfgang 101, 164, 302, 305, 352, 353, 361, 394, 395, 397, 404, 428, 435
peacekeeping 324
Peacemaker 307
personal destiny 108, 109, 237, 316, 398
personal equation 12, 190, 300, 301
personality xvi, xvii, xxii, 5, 6, 7, 8, 15, 16, 18, 19, 21, 29, 34, 36, 42, 43, 44, 50, 53, 55, 57, 60, 61, 62, 63, 65, 80, 83, 84, 92, 115, 128, 129, 136, 137, 142, 149, 152, 184, 185, 200, 212, 225, 226, 227, 231, 232, 236, 255, 257, 265, 268, 272, 277, 283, 286, 288, 295, 307, 314, 316, 338, 340, 342, 365, 371, 376, 377, 379, 396, 397, 402
personality no. 1 50, 53, 55, 61
personality no. 2 43, 50, 55, 62, 65
personal myth xx, 29, 30, 50, 86, 146, 147, 299, 303, 307, 308, 311, 314, 316, 332, 426
personal secret 55, 284, 307
phallus 42, 46, 51, 52, 53, 54, 56, 58, 284, 303, 308, 319
phenomenological 203, 245, 377
Philemon 35, 36, 104, 127, 141, 142, 177, 209, 219, 232, 285, 286, 288, 291, 293, 294, 295, 330, 341, 342, 343, 344, 345, 347, 353, 397
philosophy xx, xxii, 34, 37, 50, 52, 70, 78, 85, 86, 88, 93, 108, 109, 113, 122, 126, 151, 157, 170, 212, 214, 221, 222, 224, 225, 235, 237, 239, 252, 254, 255, 257, 263, 264, 267, 274, 284, 294, 295, 308, 309, 332, 334, 343, 351, 363
Pluralism 121, 256, 270
plurality of instincts 269
polytheism 224, 263
pragmatic method 253, 254
pragmatism xv, xxi, 37, 51, 79, 108, 163, 170, 187, 198, 205, 251, 254, 255, 257, 261, 263, 271, 295, 297, 298, 303, 343, 361, 366

Prajāpati 167, 168, 169
prana 169, 173, 174, 211, 229, 379
pranayama xxii, 70, 129, 179, 210
prima materia 51
Princeton Theological Seminary 233
Principles of Psychology xx, xxi, xxiii, 20, 104, 117, 169, 174, 239, 240, 266, 279, 280, 298, 305, 405, 430
prospective function 142, 344
psi phenomena 341
psyche xvii, xviii, xxii, 6, 7, 14, 15, 16, 19, 20, 23, 24, 25, 27, 30, 31, 35, 39, 41, 42, 43, 47, 48, 50, 59, 60, 65, 71, 72, 76, 79, 80, 84, 85, 94, 96, 97, 99, 106, 114, 122, 126, 127, 129, 130, 133, 135, 138, 141, 148, 149, 151, 155, 156, 157, 163, 164, 165, 172, 177, 179, 181, 182, 183, 189, 190, 193, 194, 199, 200, 209, 212, 223, 226, 227, 232, 253, 257, 258, 266, 268, 269, 272, 273, 274, 285, 286, 292, 294, 295, 296, 298, 304, 307, 308, 311, 312, 314, 317, 318, 323, 325, 326, 327, 329, 331, 332, 334, 337, 338, 339, 340, 341, 342, 343, 344, 345, 346, 349, 351, 352, 353, 355, 356, 361, 363, 365, 370, 371, 373, 376, 378, 379, 383, 393, 395, 396, 397, 398, 402
psychic energy xv, 41, 80, 85, 331, 355, 369
psychic objectivity 30, 76, 177, 209, 294, 397, 427
psychic phenomena xvi, 77, 206, 272
psychic trauma 241
psychoanalysis 5, 12, 13, 30, 36, 62, 86, 105, 247, 267, 274, 280, 361, 363
psychoid 72, 73, 140, 172, 193, 194, 207, 285, 339, 342, 346, 351, 353, 373, 377, 379, 380, 383, 395, 398
psychological age 189, 191, 230
psychological attitude 30, 37, 103, 105, 263, 334, 364
psychological types xv, 36, 91, 221, 267, 268, 296
psychology as a natural science 95, 198, 366
psychology as the science of all sciences 203
psychoneurosis 312
psychopathology xxii, 12, 55, 207
psychophysics 37, 77, 84, 252, 387, 395
psychosocial relativity 83
Purusa-Sūkta 167

Q

quest 18, 30, 31, 51, 133, 138, 296, 329, 363, 397
Quran 73, 214

R

radical empiricism xv, xvii, 19, 50, 221, 227, 235, 248, 251, 256, 388
radiolarian, Jung's dream of 8, 338, 344, 394
Raja Yoga 197, 200, 203, 246
Ramakrishna 197, 215, 223, 348, 349, 367, 375, 435
reality xi, xx, 30, 54, 65, 71, 72, 76, 77, 78, 79, 83, 84, 96, 97, 105, 107, 109, 122, 139, 152, 156, 163, 164, 165, 172, 177, 182, 184, 185, 198, 199, 206, 207, 209, 238, 240, 254, 257,

258, 261, 262, 268, 273, 284, 286, 288, 291, 294, 332, 337, 340, 342, 343, 345, 351, 362, 370, 373, 379, 383, 387, 391, 396, 397, 398
Red Book xix, 29, 31, 34, 35, 38, 39, 131, 142, 167, 169, 174, 177, 178, 179, 181, 182, 184, 212, 213, 214, 232, 254, 259, 311, 321, 324, 329, 343, 345, 373, 428, 434, 436
redwood trees 80, 366, 399, 400, 427
re-flexio 383
Reformation 119, 164
refraction 382, 383, 387, 389, 391
rehabilitation of religion 121
relative 79, 91, 182, 223, 231, 237, 326, 331, 332, 346, 365, 388
relativity 30, 35, 37, 56, 66, 83, 129, 155, 156, 157, 190, 240, 262, 309, 310, 311, 314, 332, 371
religion xix, xx, 8, 12, 14, 31, 39, 47, 49, 50, 55, 56, 60, 61, 62, 64, 65, 66, 73, 85, 87, 105, 106, 107, 108, 109, 110, 121, 122, 124, 126, 141, 151, 185, 186, 187, 191, 194, 199, 200, 203, 205, 210, 212, 215, 222, 224, 225, 230, 238, 239, 240, 245, 246, 247, 249, 254, 255, 261, 263, 264, 273, 276, 296, 298, 300, 301, 302, 309, 311, 313, 314, 315, 317, 320, 323, 324, 325, 334, 352, 353, 362, 395, 397, 398, 404
Religion of Healthy-Mindedness 107, 372
Religious xx, 12, 21, 33, 75, 95, 100, 101, 107, 108, 112, 114, 117, 129, 138, 148, 163, 187, 197, 223, 225, 235, 245, 269, 270, 271, 272, 274, 277, 280, 292, 294, 298, 301, 324, 331, 335, 351, 366, 372, 384, 388, 429, 430, 432, 434
religious awareness xxii
religious experiences 11, 14, 59, 62, 64, 79, 109, 121, 163, 187, 190, 255, 296, 297, 387
religious function 14, 109, 119, 121, 163, 194, 199, 317, 323, 324, 326, 327, 338, 378, 397, 398
religious insight 117
religiousness 85, 106, 269
religious outlook 313, 314
religious vocation 151
research 26, 27, 36, 71, 79, 87, 103, 104, 108, 130, 135, 138, 152, 213, 227, 241, 248, 252, 259, 264, 266, 267, 279, 305, 307, 342, 347, 353, 376, 379, 381, 387, 391
Rhine 43, 44, 45, 78
Richardson xxiv, 225, 236, 243, 293, 435
Rig Veda 167, 169, 212, 367
Rishis 233
Rosenzweig, Saul 11, 435
Royce, Josiah 86, 87, 88, 99, 100, 122, 224, 225, 226, 230, 237, 238, 239, 287
ruminations 43, 44, 45

S

Samadhi xv, 195, 197, 198, 199, 204, 205, 246, 296, 348, 375, 376, 379
Sandner, Donald 34, 342
San Francisco earthquake 74, 84, 87
Saṅkarāchārya 178
Satan 43, 44, 59, 62, 64
Schopenhauer, Arthur 16, 17, 19, 103, 173, 194, 234, 237, 242

science xx, xxi, 8, 27, 34, 39, 87, 90, 95,
    104, 108, 113, 116, 121, 138, 139,
    145, 148, 150, 151, 153, 163, 172,
    174, 184, 189, 194, 198, 203, 206,
    210, 212, 226, 227, 234, 236, 238,
    239, 240, 241, 246, 247, 248, 249,
    252, 253, 254, 258, 261, 273, 274,
    276, 279, 286, 294, 301, 308, 311,
    312, 313, 317, 324, 325, 327, 338,
    343, 352, 353, 356, 363, 364, 365,
    366, 373, 377, 383, 387, 395, 398,
    404
science of religion 39, 121, 240, 247, 254,
    261, 301, 353
science of the soul 148
scientific research 36, 79, 130, 252, 347
scientific temper 87, 106, 269
secret of the personality 15, 65, 402
Self i, iii, iv, xv, xvi, xvii, xviii, xix, xx, xxi,
    xxii, xxiii, 11, 12, 13, 14, 15, 17, 20,
    21, 24, 31, 32, 34, 41, 43, 45, 47, 48,
    49, 50, 51, 52, 53, 54, 55, 56, 57, 58,
    59, 60, 61, 62, 63, 64, 65, 66, 68, 76,
    79, 80, 83, 84, 86, 87, 90, 91, 92, 93,
    94, 95, 96, 97, 99, 100, 104, 108,
    114, 115, 116, 117, 119, 121, 122,
    123, 124, 125, 127, 128, 129, 130,
    131, 133, 134, 135, 136, 137, 138,
    139, 140, 141, 143, 147, 148, 152,
    153, 154, 155, 156, 157, 169, 164,
    167, 168, 169, 170, 171, 172, 173,
    177, 178, 183, 184, 186, 187, 189,
    190, 191, 194, 195, 198, 199, 200,
    203, 205, 206, 207, 226, 209, 210,
    212, 214, 229, 221, 222, 223, 224,
    225, 226, 227, 229, 230, 232, 236,
    238, 240, 242, 245, 246, 247, 249,
    253, 254, 258, 261, 262, 265, 271,
    272, 275, 276, 280, 283, 284, 285,
    286, 287, 288, 308, 292, 294, 295,
    296, 297, 298, 299, 300, 301, 302,
    303, 307, 309, 310, 313, 315, 316,
    319, 320, 321, 323, 324, 326, 327,
    329, 330, 331, 332, 333, 337, 338,
    339, 340, 341, 342, 343, 344, 345,
    346, 347, 348, 349, 351, 352, 353,
    355, 356, 361, 365, 371, 373, 374,
    376, 377, 378, 379, 380, 382, 384,
    385, 387, 388, 389, 390, 391, 393,
    394, 397, 398, 402, 403, 404, 428,
    429, 430, 435, 436
Self-concept xvii, xx, 48
Self of Selves 171, 297
Self-path 66, 68, 96, 123, 133, 137, 141,
    189, 209, 210, 227, 292, 303
self-sacrifice 30, 31, 128
Sen, Boshi 348, 367
Sengupta 333, 376, 385, 435
Sen, Indra 376
Serrano, Miguel 375, 378
sex 11, 12, 14, 104, 111, 226, 258
Shadow xviii, 54, 127, 129, 131, 161, 181,
    182, 184, 188, 210, 211, 212, 214,
    227, 229, 246, 315, 318, 325, 326,
    327, 376, 431
Shadow Quaternio 184
shaman 62, 103, 345
shamanic archetype 24
shamanism 52, 168
Shamdasani, Sonu xix, xxiv, 29, 30, 31, 32,
    35, 38, 39, 94, 104, 105, 111, 145,
    169, 177, 226, 296, 434, 435, 436
Sherwood, Dyane 127
Shiva 51, 52, 53, 55, 165, 285, 288, 308

Shrine to Philemon 142, 345
significance of life 113
snake xviii, xxi, 184, 185, 246, 289, 308, 342, 376
Social Self xxiii, 20, 76, 104, 127, 153, 169, 170, 206, 310, 403
spaciousness 25, 30, 35, 106, 127, 128, 173, 268, 277, 311, 329
spine 80, 90, 110, 283, 284
spirit hypothesis 403
Spirits 72, 80, 433
spiritual activism 116
Spiritual Democracy ii, xxiii, 71, 73, 80, 111, 112, 161, 189, 214, 216, 296, 323, 334, 374, 394, 399, 429, 430
Spiritual democrats 189
spiritual equality 334
spiritual grandfather 255, 296, 338
spiritualization 13, 104, 340, 395, 396
Spiritual Self xxiii, 13, 14, 15, 20, 24, 76, 79, 104, 127, 129, 136, 169, 170, 171, 172, 206, 207, 224, 225, 229, 236, 238, 245, 271, 276, 283, 286, 295, 297, 307, 310, 341, 342, 343, 348, 353, 382, 387, 391, 403, 404
Stanford University 84, 88
Stein, Murray 83, 84, 86, 127, 265, 279, 380, 430, 436
streams of consciousness xvii, 79, 80, 135, 167, 239, 247, 299, 393, 394
subconscious xvi, xvii, xviii, xxi, xxii, 44, 91, 94, 108, 109, 170, 200, 206, 207, 228, 237, 241, 253, 255, 258, 259, 262, 293, 361
subconsciousness 351, 379
subjective factor 30, 50, 226, 316, 362
subjective story 146, 300

subliminal door 93, 222, 242, 247, 249, 254
Sufi 120, 123, 246, 327
Sufism 122, 204, 246
superconscious xxi, xxii, 27, 52, 94, 97, 98, 99, 135, 197, 198, 207, 296, 351, 374, 375, 376, 377, 379, 397
superconsciousness 94, 99, 193, 246, 351, 375, 379, 393
superhuman intelligence 263, 330, 380
superior function 80, 92
superior intelligence 53, 57, 65, 390
supraconscious xxi, 27, 52, 94, 97, 98, 99, 135, 296, 351, 374, 375, 376, 377, 379, 397
suprapersonal 55, 63, 212
Supreme Meaning 66, 254, 307, 329
Sushumna 384
Swedenborg, Emanuel 233, 235, 238, 239
Switzerland xv, xvi, 92, 124, 151, 153, 154, 157, 158, 182, 211, 215, 234, 288, 338, 430
symbol 20, 41, 42, 47, 51, 52, 53, 70, 92, 128, 129, 133, 141, 146, 151, 152, 155, 156, 169, 179, 213, 221, 229, 232, 275, 284, 285, 286, 288, 289, 291, 301, 302, 341, 342, 343, 362, 371, 372, 376, 395
Symbolic Life 298, 305, 317, 318, 322, 354, 430, 431, 432, 434
sympathy 117, 242
synchronicity xv, 23, 36, 90, 138, 140, 193, 211, 272, 298, 304, 305, 310, 312, 314, 318, 337, 338, 339, 343, 345, 346, 348, 349, 355, 388, 391, 393, 395, 399, 401
synchronism 310

T

Talmud 73
Tantric Yoga 283, 284
Tavistock Lectures 271, 280, 321, 322, 434
Taylor, Eugene xxiv, 104, 105, 111, 112, 201, 206, 208, 226, 243, 252, 266, 366, 367, 368, 433, 436
teleological function 346
temperamental optimism 114
terror 42, 45, 54, 68, 120, 235
Terry Lectures xv, 126, 131, 204, 273, 280, 321, 334, 377, 385, 433
theology xix, 32, 50, 52, 58, 61, 66, 100, 108, 109, 120, 121, 129, 138, 145, 172, 221, 233, 252, 257, 261, 276, 295, 309, 327, 332
Thirty Years' War 119
tough-mindedness 199
trance states xvi, xxii
transcendentalism 57, 365
transcendental Knower 95
Transcendental Self 294, 397
Transcendent Function 216
transcultural mentor 296
transfigured Christ 382
transformation xxiii, 18, 30, 68, 146, 149, 150, 177, 212, 228, 265, 286, 326, 327, 347, 372
Transformative Image 86, 265, 279, 430
transgressive 141, 343, 346
trans-marginal 121
transmission hypothesis 389
transmutation 31, 227
Transnationality 194
transnational unity 74, 189
transpersonal psychology 79, 88, 259, 341, 364
transpersonal unconscious 7, 30, 142, 147, 221, 249, 258
transpsyche 71, 355, 377, 380
transpsychic reality 71, 72, 152, 351
trauma xxii, 16, 43, 44, 45, 47, 54, 55, 149, 241, 280
typology xxii, 106, 251

U

UC Berkeley 33, 88, 225, 251, 252, 254
UC Santa Cruz 133, 342, 366, 379, 381
unconscious xv, xvi, xvii, xviii, xxii, xxiv, 6, 7, 15, 18, 19, 24, 25, 26, 27, 30, 34, 35, 36, 42, 43, 44, 45, 48, 49, 50, 51, 53, 54, 56, 57, 58, 66, 71, 72, 74, 77, 79, 89, 91, 92, 93, 94, 95, 97, 108, 125, 135, 140, 142, 146, 147, 149, 152, 153, 155, 172, 173, 178, 181, 182, 185, 193, 197, 198, 203, 207, 212, 213, 214, 221, 223, 249, 255, 258, 273, 274, 278, 283, 284, 286, 292, 296, 299, 300, 301, 302, 304, 307, 314, 319, 320, 327, 329, 330, 331, 332, 333, 339, 343, 344, 346, 351, 352, 355, 361, 371, 375, 376, 377, 378, 379, 382, 402, 403, 404
United Nations 73, 204, 325
United States of America 187
uniting symbol 52, 169
universal consciousness 262, 331, 334, 377
University of Calcutta 375
University of Geneva 234
Unus Mundus 79, 172, 194
Upanishads xviii, 70, 124, 169, 173, 178, 179, 194, 212, 367, 435

US Constitution 191, 320, 321

V

Varieties of Religious Experience xx, 21, 33, 75, 100, 107, 108, 112, 114, 117, 129, 138, 163, 187, 197, 223, 225, 245, 269, 270, 271, 272, 274, 277, 280, 292, 294, 298, 301, 324, 331, 351, 366, 372, 388, 430
variety xxiii, 91, 124, 154, 187, 198, 203, 209, 245, 252, 256, 277, 296, 387
Vedanta xxii, 20, 70, 100, 165, 178, 190, 197, 199, 200, 205, 209, 221, 223, 229, 256, 260, 324, 367, 384, 429
violence 41, 42, 45, 46, 47, 48, 49, 53, 59, 62, 64, 67, 68, 72, 73, 88, 119, 149, 150, 151, 181, 182, 183, 184, 186, 204, 326, 346, 376
visions xvii, 51, 58, 74, 92, 129, 138, 141, 267, 271, 283, 288, 319, 321, 331, 342, 369, 370, 371, 372, 373, 374
vista xvi, xx, xxiii, 76, 83, 127, 311, 325, 326, 382
visuddha 285, 286, 288, 289, 294
Vivekananda, Swami 37, 65, 67, 70, 86, 122, 130, 131, 173, 197, 198, 199, 200, 201, 203, 204, 205, 208, 210, 221, 222, 223, 224, 226, 230, 237, 246, 248, 256, 257, 260, 270, 287, 348, 349, 363, 364, 367, 375, 379, 385, 429, 435, 436
vocation xv, xvi, xvii, xix, 8, 18, 19, 20, 33, 47, 50, 55, 57, 60, 63, 66, 90, 96, 115, 117, 123, 125, 130, 131, 133, 136, 138, 151, 154, 165, 194, 222, 224, 225, 227, 229, 232, 234, 235, 238, 251, 259, 265, 274, 295, 296, 299, 310, 312, 314, 315, 316, 323, 338, 339, 344, 346, 363, 365, 376, 394, 402
vocational archetype 91, 337, 341, 345
vocational correspondences 141, 343
Vocational dreams 135, 140, 337, 344, 348
vocational Self 346
vocation of the Self 130, 131
von Humboldt, Alexander 163, 240, 313, 428, 436

W

Walt Whitman Bicentennial xxiii
Washington, George xiii, xxiv, 5, 23, 26, 30, 185, 188
waves 25, 71, 74, 75, 96, 152, 279, 355, 387
white crow 115
White, Victor 65, 125, 345
Whitman, Walt ii, xix, xxiii, xxiv, 37, 73, 85, 86, 107, 111, 114, 115, 116, 117, 122, 130, 148, 178, 188, 207, 215, 224, 230, 231, 233, 234, 237, 238, 242, 246, 253, 257, 270, 308, 309, 310, 311, 313, 314, 323, 352, 362, 374, 426, 427, 429, 430, 437
wider Self 253, 262
Wilder, Thornton 127, 134, 437
wisdom 30, 50, 57, 63, 99, 126, 185, 189, 209, 295, 312, 319, 334, 340, 341, 344, 376
Wolff, Kurt 277, 293, 296
World Soul ii, 71, 112, 121, 323, 334, 352, 363, 374, 430
Wundt, Wilhelm 78, 81, 91, 104, 238, 265, 266, 272, 362

Y

Yale Divinity School 139
Yale University xv, 14, 126, 255, 273, 289, 323, 329, 334, 377, 428
Yoga xv, xxii, 51, 57, 65, 70, 129, 130, 173, 174, 197, 198, 199, 200, 203, 205, 207, 209, 210, 211, 212, 213, 215, 221, 229, 232, 246, 283, 284, 287, 288, 289, 290, 291, 296, 311, 324, 347, 364, 367, 376, 381, 383, 384, 429, 433, 434
yogi 213, 214, 348, 349

Z

Zabriskie, Beverly 74, 81, 437
Zarathustra 32, 39, 68, 69, 94, 100, 159, 215, 216, 272, 280, 283, 288, 290, 432
Zen Buddhism 157, 159, 432
zero-point 352, 393, 398
Zürich xvi, 26, 135, 142, 145, 149, 153, 158, 177, 267, 269, 303, 328, 330, 341, 396, 431

About the Author

Steven Herrmann was born in Carmel-by-the-Sea, California. His parents, Friedrich and Madeleine Herrmann, and his brother and two sisters lived in Pacific Grove, California for the first four years of his life, and the children played on the beach every day. The family moved to the San Francisco Bay Area and settled in East Bay communities that were not densely populated at that time. Steven attended elementary school in Pleasant Hill, and while in high school at Las Lomas High in Walnut Creek he competed in the California State Track and Field championships. At Diablo Valley College, where both his parents had taught foreign languages, he took a life-changing English class taught by Clark McKowen, with whom he developed a deep literary friendship.

At 19, Steven was introduced to Carl Jung's popular book *Man and his Symbols*, which he devoured. After a numinous dream, he entered his first Jungian therapy with Katherine Whiteside Taylor, a Jungian psychologist who was 80 years old when they first met. She mentored Steven until her death at 92. Through these initial exposures to the field of analytical psychotherapy, Steven pursued his BA Degree at the University of California, Santa Cruz (UCSC). It was there that he met the Jungian poet, William Everson, a former Dominican lay brother who had been initiated into the art of dream interpretation by Father Victor White in 1956, the same year Steven was born. After numerous spiritual experiences, while practicing yoga, recording his dreams daily, and attending Everson's course on the UCSC campus, Steven worked as a teaching assistant for Everson from 1980 to 1981. Steven taught Jung's theories of dream interpretation and led dream groups with a special research focus on vocational dreams.

As an undergraduate, Steven created his own individual major in "Depth Psychology and Religion" after an experience of synchronicity that confirmed his decision to write his senior thesis on the thirteenth century theologian and preacher, Meister Eckhart. Steven received his Master's degree in clinical psychology at John F. Kennedy University in Orinda, CA, and his PhD from Rosebridge Graduate School of Integrative Psychology. During his graduate studies, Steven was in analysis with Jungian analyst Donald F. Sandner for 13 years, followed by work with two more San

A photograph of the author taken by his son Immanuel Herrmann, in front of the doors to the National Cathedral, Washington, DC, on the occasion of the Walt Whitman Bicentennial, at which he was a main speaker, June 1, 2019 (Photograph courtesy of Immanuel Herrmann)

Francisco analysts. In 1995, Steven met Jungian analyst John Beebe, who became his consultant and mentor for two decades. Steven has also been an active member of several shamanic journeying groups.

Steven has published numerous journal articles, several book chapters, and six books. His works cover the subjects of analytical psychology, sandplay, Jungian child psychotherapy and analysis, shamanism and American poetry, religion, transpersonal psychology, and William James.

Steven is an analyst member of the C. G. Jung Institute of San Francisco and has a private practice in Oakland California. He lives with his wife, Jungian analyst Lori Goldrich Ph.D., in the Oakland Hills and he is the proud father of a son. Steven enjoys gardening, hiking, cooking, meditating, and writing poetry.

ANALYTICAL PSYCHOLOGY PRESS

Please support our mission to publish books of quality by purchasing your book directly from our website. Thank you for your support!

https://analyticalpsychologypress.com